CORRECTIONAL MANAGEMENT

Nelson-Hall Series in Law, Crime, and Justice

Consulting Editor: Howard Abadinsky
St. Xavier University, Chicago

CORRECTIONAL MANAGEMENT
Functions, Skills, and Systems

James Houston
St. Ambrose University

Nelson-Hall Publishers/Chicago

Project Editor: Rachel Schick
Production/Design: Tamra Phelps
Cover Painting: *Reflections of Corporate Society* by Bruce Cegur
Typesetter: Precision Typographers
Illustrator: Nicholas Communications
Printer: R.R. Donnelley & Sons

Library of Congress Cataloging-in-Publication Data

Houston, James, 1943–
    Correctional management : functions, skills and systems / James
  Houston.
      p.   cm.
    Includes bibliographical references and index.
    ISBN 0-8304-1309-X
    1. Prison administration—United States—Case studies.   I. Title.
  HV9469.H68 1995
365′.068—dc20   94-11995
                                                      CIP

Manufactured in the United States of America

10 9 8 7 6 5 4 3 2

 The paper used in this book meets the
minimum requirements of American
National Standard for Information
Sciences—Permanence of Paper for
Printed Library Materials, ANSI
Z39.48-1984.

To my wife, Peggy,
and our children, Melinda, Andrew, and Meredith

CONTENTS
IN BRIEF

CONTENTS

ix

PART III
The Organizational Process 81

CHAPTER 6
Policy and the Correctional
Organization 83

CHAPTER 7
The Budget Process 107

CHAPTER 8
Organization Development 121

PART IV
Working Through and
with Others   137

CHAPTER 9
Motivation   139

CHAPTER 10
Managing the Informal
Organization   157

CHAPTER 11
Leadership   175

PART V
The Manager and
the Organization   191

CHAPTER 12
Planning and Organizing   193

CHAPTER 13
Organizational Control   215

CHAPTER 14
Decision Making   233

PART VI
Topics of Special Interest 251

CHAPTER 15
Unit Management in a Correctional Institution 253

CHAPTER 16
Privatization 271

CHAPTER 17
Ethics and Social Influence 291

PREFACE

This book has been in progress for nearly twenty years. When I was promoted to drug abuse program manager at the U.S. Penitentiary, Terre Haute, Indiana, in 1973, I learned that there were holes in my education. I knew a lot about criminal behavior, criminal justice systems, and prison in particular. What I came to realize very quickly was that I lacked knowledge of how to manage the organization, or in my case a unit. With the help of competent colleagues and several training sessions courtesy of the U.S. Civil Service training center, I began to catch up. The subject of organizational management within the correctional setting has continued to intrigue me and is the focus of my teaching and some research.

The goal of this text is to provide students and practitioners with information they need to become the managers and leaders of correctional organizations. I hope the book is interesting, enjoyable, and readable. The text is rooted in personal experiences and the experiences of friends and colleagues over my nearly twenty years' work in prisons, jails, and community programs. The book is intended to be friendly. The photos, tables, and figures enrich the material and drive home important points.

Part I brings the reader up to date on what we know about correctional management. The truth is that there is a real paucity of informa-

tion on how to manage the correctional organization. As a consequence, I was forced to draw heavily upon business and public administration literature for this book. Most writers on correctional management confuse inmate or client management with management of the organization. This is unfortunate because correctional organizations face unique challenges. Managers need to know that there is a difference between developing programs that meet the needs of inmates or clients and leading, preparing a budget, or implementing policy. Part II discusses the relationship of the correctional organization to its environment and looks at the impact of law, the media, and the community on the organization as it attempts to fulfill its mission. Part III investigates the processes at play inside the organization vis-à-vis making the organization work. Part IV probes the joys and problems of working with and through others. A critical question it addresses is "How do we motivate and lead others to excellence?" Part V searches for ways the executive can assure himself or herself that the organization is doing what it says it will do and find out whether or not it is doing it effectively. Part VI explores special topics. Unit management, privatization of corrections, and ethics are discussed because of their importance to the executive as he or she searches for excellence.

xvii

I started to seriously think about this book during a conversation with Mark Hamm when I was a juvenile court administrator. Mark and I originally discussed coauthoring the book, but the pressure of another project kept him from getting involved. However, he encouraged me to pursue the idea, and I am grateful for his support.

A project this size is not possible without the support and encouragement of many people. I am fortunate to have had a great deal of help in writing the manuscript, particularly from Judy Noel, whose patience in typing the manuscript was most gratifying. I am especially grateful to John Klofas and William Osterhoff, Jr., who read the entire manuscript and whose critical comments and suggestions were most helpful. Any shortcomings found in this book are certainly not to be laid at their feet. Several colleagues also read specific chapters, and I found their suggestions invaluable. The joys of teaching in a small college are many, but the following anecdote illustrates the generosity and sharing typical of such a setting. One day I was working in my office with the door open, struggling with a particularly difficult passage. A colleague joined me and looked over my shoulder, offering suggestions. Another was soon offering advice, and then another. After a while, two political scientists, one sociologist, and one philosopher were helping me in my search for clarity of expression.

For their insight and patience I owe special thanks to Bill Parsons, Jack Moore, Mike Halstead, Paul Koch, Al Sivell, and Carl Herzig. There are others whose contributions are greatly appreciated: Babe Crockett, Charley Faulkner, Nic Howell, Judy Simon, and Cathy Thompson, as well as the contributors of the introductory essays. A special thank you goes to Andy Swift for his encouragement and for coauthoring the chapter "Ethics and Social Influence." My wife, Peggy, also deserves a thank you for her support and for understanding when I was at the library instead of at home. Finally, the people at Nelson-Hall have proven themselves to be among the best in the field. Richard Meade is to be commended for his willingness to take a risk, and Rachel Schick for her skill and pleasantness while she guided me through the intricacies of bringing a book to market. Rachel has been a real joy to work with.

Writing *Correctional Management* has been an educational and challenging experience. I hope that those who read it will be similarly challenged. We are in the midst of a critical time in corrections, and we must prepare capable leaders and managers to lead us into the next century.

CORRECTIONAL ADMINISTRATION AND THE EVOLUTION OF CORRECTIONAL MANAGEMENT

PART I

The effective management of correctional organizations requires a thorough knowledge of many areas. In addition to being familiar with the criminal justice system and the etiology of criminal behavior, the effective manager must know the areas of policy, budget preparation, organizational development, motivation of individuals, use of groups, leadership, planning, and decision making. In short, a unidimensional individual will do poorly as a correctional manager.

Understanding management theory is essential to guiding an organization along the path to excellence. Management principles are universal; be it a church, a university, a factory, or a prison, the same principles apply to working with and through people to attain organizational objectives. Chapter 1 reviews what we know about correctional management today and points out that too many correctional managers and scholars have confused inmate/client management with the management of the organization. In truth, there are two organizations in every correctional institution—the informal inmate organization and an organization designed to serve the community and the taxpayer. It is important that the reader understand the difference between them. Chapter 2 reviews the evolution of management theory. Together these two chapters serve as a framework for the rest of the book.

A Review of Correctional Administration

Case Study: Problems

The scenes are from Oregon, but they have become all too common in jails and prisons around the country.[1] In the early evening hours at the Multnomah County jail in downtown Portland, two dozen men loll in front of a television set just inside the jail's booking area. Other prisoners sleep on blankets strewn on the floor. In the housing units men sleep on mattresses in the Day Room area.

Forty-five miles south, at the Oregon State Correctional Institution in Salem, men are jammed into what used to be a television room. Vocational training rooms have been closed and other areas turned into makeshift dormitories. The prison was designed for 476 inmates; it now holds 1,000.

Jail and prison overcrowding in Oregon, as in nearly every state, had become a major public policy issue by 1987. Correction systems in forty-one states are operating under some form of court decree or under the threat of litigation dealing with overcrowding. California's inmate population is expected to top 100,000.[2] Texas is building new penal institutions to relieve its swollen prisons, and some Louisiana prisoners live in tents. An Arkansas sheriff, driven to frustration, chained his surplus jail inmates to a state penitentiary fence.

Oregon is a microcosm of the national problem. By 1987

nineteen of its thirty-six counties had jails, prisons, and reform schools under judicial review. The state's crime rate is the fifth highest in the country, and judges have no hesitation in sending convicted felons to prison or jail. First-term governor Neil Goldschmidt made reform of the correctional system one of his top priorities.

Even before his inauguration, Mr. Goldschmidt proposed an ambitious criminal justice reform package. The $54.2 million program would add 1,661 minimum-security and medium-security beds, and law enforcement areas would be upgraded. Oregonians, like citizens in other states, have been reluctant to pay for new prison beds, but they may be softening a bit. One reason for the change of heart: to comply with court orders dealing with prison overcrowding, officials in several Oregon counties have been releasing inmates before their sentences are completely served. The court rulings resulted from suits brought by inmates who said that their constitutional rights were violated by existing prison and jail conditions.

As in other states, Oregon's prison crowding has worsened steadily. The increase is the result of a social and political consensus that, in the words of Governor Goldschmidt, criminals should do "hard time for hard crime." In 1977, for example, the average length of prison stay for those convicted of the most serious felony counts was eighteen months. By 1983, it was up to twenty-eight months.

The average inmate has also changed from a property offender to one who has committed a crime against a person. Judges are upset with early release of prisoners and have been handing out more jail sentences. Finally, overcrowding has halted most efforts at prisoner rehabilitation behind the walls. According to Jerome LaBarre, a Portland attorney, "We're paying $20,000 a year (per inmate) to have inmates watch TV sixteen hours a day."

Oregon's reform efforts have received national attention and some praise. The state is one of seven receiving money and consultant help from the Philadelphia-based Center for Effective Public Policy. "Oregon is on the verge of some really exciting possibilities," says Becki Ney, a state coordinator for the private research firm. In a study on Oregon's correctional problems, the National Council on Crime and Delinquency points out that Oregon still has time to correct its problems.

Introduction

On any given day, approximately 1.2 million people are locked away in our prisons and jails. Another 3,201,641 are under the supervision of probation and parole officers.[3] This represents a substantial investment on the part of our government. Yet, in many instances, we entrust that investment and responsibility to managers who are by and large untrained in the art and craft of management. Most corrections agencies promote workers to supervisory or management positions because they do well in their specialties. The assumption is that workers who are effective sergeants, case managers, cooks, or probation officers will also be effective managers of a department, or ultimately of a complex organization. Without formal training, managers often make decisions without benefit of staff input, implement policy through the writing of memoranda, and motivate employees through the threat of disciplinary action. To an extent, however, we have been lucky. The men and women who have been promoted to management levels in their organizations have most often earned the trust placed in them.

Corrections Management Today

Our colleges and universities can do more. Departments of criminology and criminal justice churn out graduates who have a reasonably good grasp of criminological theory and have completed a host of courses in case work methods, correctional institutions, counseling, and probation and parole. Often, however, instruction in management is limited to only one course. Still, faculty members, department chairpersons, and deans proudly proclaim that their graduates have the training and potential to one day head large, complex agencies.

In 1980 Duffee[4] pointed out that most correction managers have been promoted from within the system and have no formal training in management. Nearly ten years later, Shannon[5] surveyed correctional administrators and found that on the average they have eight and a half years of experience in their institutions, that around 70 percent have less than six years of experience as chief executive officers (CEOs), and that few have corrections-related college training. While most CEOs have backgrounds in management, the majority of college degrees held by correctional administrators are in the social sciences, with ten out of sixty-five holding law degrees and doctorates. Shannon politely points out that there are several career paths leading to the office of chief executive of a department of corrections.

In his review of Wolford's[6] study of corrections executives, Champion[7] points out that many of the respondents to Wolford's survey possess bachelor's and master's degrees. Additionally, several hold doctorates. Champion continues:

> If these samples of administrators are typical, they suggest strongly that corrections today is managed largely by an administrative aggregate drawn from noncorrectional backgrounds. These officials are inclined to base their managerial philosophies on organizational strategies that work well in business or service organizations rather than in penal institutions. These strategies may or may not be applicable to corrections.[8]

Champion raises a valid point; that is, management philosophies learned in business, or elsewhere, may or may not work in corrections. In today's overheated atmosphere in corrections, there simply is not time to learn by trial and error. Therefore, managers need to learn what will work *before* they assume supervisory responsibilities, not through workshops or seminars *after* they become supervisors.

The purpose of this textbook is to introduce

the student to the many aspects of corrections management. While the author uses prisons to illustrate many points because of his familiarity with these institutions, this textbook is aimed at all areas of corrections. Thus, community corrections are not ignored, and many examples are also drawn from the probation and parole systems. Before continuing, however, it may be useful to briefly review the history of corrections management and the corrections enterprise.

Corrections Management as a Skill

Until 1975 there were no texts on corrections management,[9] and in the years since then, only a handful have been published. Most of them are specialized, and all have to do with governing prisons and inmates as a group rather than managing an organization. Only one management text addresses important areas such as policy, leadership, and decision making within a correctional environment. One reason for this scarcity could be that sociologists have been the main contributors to what we know about corrections. Other scholars, such as Richard McCleery[10] and Jameson Doig[11], have looked at corrections from a different perspective, but by and large, corrections falls under the purview of sociological criminologists.

Representative of many books on correctional management is DiIulio's *Governing Prisons*.[12] DiIulio compares prisons in Texas, California, and Michigan and concludes that authoritarian regimes maintain order and that less authoritarian regimes such as those in California and Michigan do not maintain good order.

As DiIulio points out,

A paramilitary prison bureaucracy, led by able institutional managers and steered by a talented executive, may be the best administrative re-

sponse to the problem of establishing and maintaining higher-custody prisons in which inmates and staff lead a calm, peaceful, and productive round of daily life. Prison workers can simultaneously share a sense of mission, identify with each other, care about the inmates, and perform a vital service to the people of the law-abiding and tax-paying community.[13]

The author hits the nail on the head, but *Governing Prisons* sheds little light on how the "talented executive" should go about delivering this vital service to the community. Duffee's[14] earlier work does a much better job of guiding the student on how to manage an organization, as do Archambeault and Archambeault.[15] A recent and welcome addition to the literature is *Criminal Justice Organizations: Administration and Management*.[16] Its highly readable style introduces the student to a variety of issues that up until now have been ignored in textbooks on criminal justice management. In order to put corrections management into perspective, a review of the history of corrections growth is helpful.

The Growth of the Corrections Enterprise

Early Contributions

The Anglo-American custom of imprisonment as a means of dealing with lawbreakers can be traced to the invasion of England by William the Conqueror. Undoubtedly William found a number of manors that were used to confine undesirables, and he added to their number. Still, execution, mutilation, exile, and branding were the most popular means of punishment at that time. Jails were for holding prisoners until they were punished.

In the sixteenth and seventeenth centuries, significant reforms were made, spurred on by colonialist England's insatiable appetite for workers. In 1552 King Edward VI established Bridewell as a workhouse for vagabonds, idlers, and rogues.[17] Soon every county had a Bridewell where employment under a contract system was offered. However, by the end of the seventeenth century, England had abandoned its reformative impulses, and the Bridewells soon were characterized by idleness. Little difference between a Bridewell and the county jail could be discovered.

The eighteenth century saw the contributions of men such as Bentham, Beccaria, and Howard. Their efforts were slow to bear fruit, but in 1779[18] a penitentiary act was passed that allowed the establishment of a prison system based on solitary confinement, hard labor, and religious instruction. Around 1784 the Norfolk Prison at Wymondham was opened. This was followed by the opening of the national penitentiary at Millbank in 1821 and the infamous prison at Pentonville in 1842. In 1877 control of the county jails in England was transferred to a board of prison commissioners. In 1895 the Gladstone Committee found the entire system to be a failure and recommended for the "future that deterrence and reformation should be made equal, compatible objectives through a more humanized regime of training in the prisons."[19]

Prisons in the United States

Not surprisingly, English immigrants brought their most familiar institutions with them when they settled in the American colonies. In addition, England's transportation of convicts to the colonies (about 200,000 by 1776) added to the population a number of persons with first-hand knowledge of the English method of dealing with criminals.

The Walnut Street Jail, which opened in 1776 in Philadelphia, is generally credited as being the first prison in the United States. Although by 1800 it was abandoned because of deterioration and overcrowding, it was the prototype for other prisons opened in New York City; Charleston, Massachusetts; Baltimore; and Windsor, Vermont.[20] The new prisons, however, were different in one way: they had congregate rather than solitary cells.

The Pennsylvania System

By 1826 population pressures forced the state of Pennsylvania to build the Eastern State Penitentiary. This facility featured a system based on solitary confinement and labor. Each cell had a small exercise yard, including an area for a hand loom at which the prisoner was expected to work several hours each day. The term *penitentiary* derives from the term *penitent*. Through solitude and reading the Bible, the prisoner was supposed to undergo a spiritual and emotional transformation and to eventually leave the penitentiary a reformed person. Interestingly, reformers considered the penitentiary to be a step forward. It was a reaction to the filthy, overcrowded Walnut Street Jail, where dignity and privacy were nonexistent. In 1829 the state completed a second facility, the Western State Penitentiary. Here, too, the inmate's remorse and penitence were to be reinforced by solitude, biblical study, and labor.

Apparently inmates frequently were driven mad by the isolation. Nevertheless, as an export, Pennsylvania's Eastern Penitentiary did well; several European countries adopted versions of it as models for their prisons.

The Auburn System

Solitary confinement as an approach to managing a prison was doomed in the United States by the opening in 1816 in New York of the Auburn Prison with its congregate confinement. Even though silence, lock step, and flogging for violating rules were the norm, Auburn represented a step in a positive direction in that it allowed some social intercourse. In addition, the institution was cheaper to construct, and a contract factory inside the prison allowed for congregate work.

The state contracted with private industry for the manufacture of such items as barrels, boots, and clothing. Thus, the United States entered the era of the large industrial prison (big house), and prisoners were believed to be a part of the industrial expansion that was beginning to push the young nation into modern

times. Their labor was believed to benefit themselves and the country.

At Auburn cells were constructed back to back, a style of prison architecture that endures to this day. As the United States entered the

TABLE 1.1
Federal and State Institutions 1880–1990*

	Federal	State
1880	1	61
1890	1	Not available
1904	4	67
1910	3	58
1923	3	61
1933	16	101
1940	31	114
1950	31	127
1960	Not available	Not available
1974	33	559*
1980	38	521
1985	38	530
1990	47	702

*For the period 1880–1970, the figures must be viewed with caution. The census counts budget units rather than actual institutions, thus the numbers are presumably inflated.

Sources:
U.S. Department of Commerce, Bureau of the Census: Washington, D.C., 1880, 1890, 1904, 1910, 1923 Children Under Institutional Care, 1923; 1927; pp. 262–63. Prisoners 1923; 1926; p. 3.
1933 Juvenile Delinquents in Public Institutions 1933; 1936; p. 1. Prisoners in State and Federal Prisons and Reformatories 1933; 1935; p. 1
1960 U.S. Census of Population 1970: Inmates of Institutions; 1963; p. 13.
1970 U.S. Census of Population 1970: Persons in Institutions and Other Group Quarters; 1973; p. 23.
1980 Census of Population 1980: Persons in Institutions and Other Group Quarters; 1984; p. 5.

U.S. Department of Justice, Federal Bureau of Prisons; Washington, D.C. 1972–1983 Statistical Report of the Fiscal Years 1981–1983; pp. 255–61.

U.S. Department of Justice, Law Enforcement Assistance Administration; National Criminal Justice Information and Statistics Service; Washington, D.C. 1972–1974 Census of State Correctional Facilities 1974; Advance Report; National Prisoner Statistics Special Report Number SD-NPS-SR-1; 1975; Table 1.
U.S. Department of Justice, LEAA; *Census of Correctional Facilities;* 1974; Advanced Report: Number SD-NPS-SR-1; July 1979. It is difficult to explain the drop in institutions between 1974 and 1990; therefore, the figures must be viewed with caution.

U.S. Department of Justice, Bureau of Justice Statistics; Washington D.C. 1979 Bureau of Justice Statistics Bulletin: Prisons and Prisoners; 1982; p. 3.

American Correctional Association, Information Specialist.

FIGURE 1.1
Sentenced State and Federal Prisoners

Number of sentenced State and Federal prisoners, yearend 1925–87

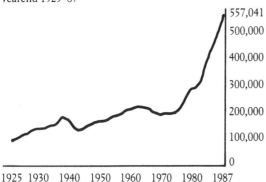

Number of sentenced State and Federal prisoners, per 100,000 U.S. population, yearend 1925–87

Source: Bureau of Justice Statistics Annual Report Fiscal 1988 (Washington, D.C.: Bureau of Justice Statistics, 1989), p. 60.
Note: Prior to 1977 prisoner reports were based on the custody populations. Beginning in 1977 focus is on the jurisdictional population.

nineteenth century, it also entered the era of the "Big House"—a prison designed to house from 1,000 to 6,000 inmates. "Big Houses" still in operation include Michigan State Prison at Jackson, San Quentin, and the U.S. Penitentiary at Leavenworth, Kansas.

Today, in spite of population pressures, corrections planners no longer build "Big Houses." The trend is to construct institutions that house 400 to 600 inmates. However, this means that there are presently more correctional institutions in operation than ever before, and others are on the drawing board. Figure 1.1 shows the increase in prison population from 1925 to 1987.

Table 1.1 shows the numbers of federal and state prisons in the United States from 1880 to 1990. While one should interpret these numbers cautiously, it is clear that since 1933 the number of prisons has increased nearly sevenfold.

The Social Organization of the Prison

What is a prison? Who makes up the population that must be locked up, often for many years or for a lifetime? We need to understand the culture that exists inside a prison if we are going to effectively manage the care, custody, and control of hundreds of inmates and at the same time accommodate the needs of staff.

For the purposes of this textbook, inmate management is comprised of counts, discipline, programs, prison industry, medical care, food, and so on. Organizational management consists of planning, organizing resources, influencing staff to achieve organizational goals, and controlling staff activities.

A prison is a unique organization. If judged by the standards of the private sector, it has no real purpose. Its function is to be of service to the community. In order for a prison to function, it must have an administrative staff, with a chief

executive and a body of workers. Irwin points out that the duties of the official administrators, including the warden and his or her assistants; the business manager; the head cook; the captain; and the other department heads, are to:

1. maintain order (that is, keep down internal disruption and violence and prevent escapes);
2. supply the prisoners with their life necessities (usually on a very skimpy budget) and
3. manage the prison industries, which are restricted to the production of commodities consumed within state institutions—furniture, clothing, and food—and items sold by the states, such as license plates.[21]

Those duties have not changed in 100 years, and one must keep in mind that they are carried out under conditions that are often unbusinesslike.

Donald R. Cressey[22] sums up the nature of prison social organization when he states that any prison is made up of the synchronized actions of hundreds of people. All of them hate a number of staff and other inmates; respect and love others; fight physically and psychologically; and vie with each other for favors, prestige, power, and money. The amazing thing, Cressey concludes, is that prisons "work." Somehow, the personnel—including prisoners—are bound together in such a way that most misunderstandings are not critical. According to Cressey, prison "social organization" is a complex phenomenon with subtle and almost invisible aspects. Organizational charts show the official lines of authority and communication, but they often do not hint at the real institutional organization: who has real power, or who influences whom?

The Prison as a Total Institution

Even though the social organization of the prison is extraordinarily complex, social scientists have produced an extensive literature on this topic. Goffman[23] asserts that the central feature of "total institutions," a major version of which is the prison, is the breakdown of the barriers that ordinarily separate sleep, play, and work. He points out that in prisons, all aspects of life are conducted in the same place, under the same authority, and in the company of the same people—all of whom are treated alike. Under tight scheduling, and with all the various forced activities aimed at fulfilling the official aims of the institution, an institution can be brought together in a single rational plan. The total institution is also characterized by barriers to social intercourse with the outside world. Those barriers are often built into the physical plant and include locked doors, barbed wire, and/or isolation.

The "Pains of Imprisonment"

On the matter of the social organization of the prison, Sykes[24] observes that the uniqueness of the frustrations imposed on the inmates, or what he calls "the pains of imprisonment," as well as prisoners' previous training in deviance, results in a social group characterized by a high degree of internal exploitation, where "fellow sufferers are scorned as powerless victims even more than the custodians are despised as symbols of oppression."[25] Rather than being a community, Sykes points out, prison inmates tend to react as lone individuals and refuse to suspend intramural conflicts even when they confront prison officials.

Goffman[26] contends that while the inmates bring their own cultures into the institution with them, once they submit to the processes aimed at managing their daily lives, they are stripped of this support through mortification and dispossession. Sykes and Messinger[27] speculate that the prison is characterized by a single-value system that dominates the social fabric of the inmates' lives. The inmate code advises other inmates: "don't interfere with inmate interests" and "don't exploit inmates." Sykes and Messinger's primary argument is that the inmate code is situational; that is, it is a response to the "pains of imprisonment."[28]

Those pains are identified as:

The Deprivation of Liberty. Not only is the inmate confined to a few small acres of land, he or she is also confined within that area. The resulting boredom and loneliness are a problem, but more importantly, confinement represents a deliberate rejection of the prisoner by the free community.

The Deprivation of Goods and Services. Prisoners are kept in a painfully spartan environment. They are made poor by virtue of being confined. And in a culture that equates material goods with personal worth, prisoners have the additional burden of being poor for no edifying reasons such as religious principles, deferred gratification, or the good of the community they live in. They are poor by their own misdeeds, which they perceive as a bitter attack on their self-image.

The Deprivation of Heterosexual Relationships. The psychological problems caused by being confined with only members of the same sex are far more damaging to the self-concept than mere deprivation of physical relationships. The absence of half of the audience to whom one normally relates and from whom one draws a good portion of one's self-concept causes the self-image to become cracked and distorted from the lack of contrast.

The Deprivation of Autonomy. The prisoner's inability to make choices, along with the administration's refusal to explain decisions and commands, threatens the inmate's self-image by reducing her or him to the weak, helpless, and dependent status of early childhood.

The Deprivation of Security. The prisoner's being locked up with others whom he views as "dangerous" or "unstable" arouses great anxiety, not so much because of violence and exploitation but because he knows that sooner or later he will be "tested." The waiting and stress call into question his ability to cope—"Can he take it?"

While the social organization of the prison is governed by an inmate code, Stanton Wheeler[29] and George Grosser[30] both suggest that much of the inmate subculture may be brought into the prison by newly arrived inmates rather than being solely a product of the prison experience.

Cressey and Irwin[31] identify three inmate subcultures: a prison subculture, a criminal subculture, and a legitimate subculture. The legitimate subculture and the criminal subculture influence persons whose in-prison orientation is to life on the outside of prison, while the prison subculture focuses on prison social values. For example, inmates oriented to the convict or prison subculture seek positions of power and influence. A job as captain's clerk carries great power and influence, which can be used to the inmate's advantage through the assignment of prison jobs and cells, for example. That influence, in turn, can be used to purchase symbols of status among persons oriented to the convict subculture, including information and material possessions such as "bonaroos," which are specially tailored and starched prison clothing; unique belts and belt buckles; and unusual shoes or any other possession that will set the inmate apart from the general population. Thus, these three subcultures reflect the different orientations of different groups of prisoners. More importantly, they lend credence to the importational or diffusionist perspective on the makeup of inmate culture and the social organization of the prison.

The Prison Staff Culture

Other aspects of the social organization of the prison have also been the subject of inquiry.

For example, some investigators have studied guards. Lombardo[32] found that corrections officers at Auburn Correctional Facility in New York learned their jobs on their own, or even from inmates. That pattern of training contrasts with the training given police rookies, who enter into a strong apprentice relationship with their fellow officers. Lombardo also found that the prison guard attempts to find assignments that accommodate his or her own needs. "Whether he seeks to make the time pass, to control his work environment or help or get away from inmates, the guard's work, as he performs it, is often a reflection of his personal preferences."[33] McCleery discovered that "custodial control of communications imposed custodial attitudes, values, and behavior throughout the industrial program of a large maximum-security prison, thus negating its formal institutional position and purposes."[34] Cressey[35] reports that there is no counterpart in the private sector to the prison guard and that most guards have nothing to do except "guard"; that is, they concentrate their efforts on watching others and are not employed productively any more than inmates are employed productively. Jacobs,[36] in his study of a major correctional institution, found a highly rational, professional, detached, and problem-oriented corporate model of prison management. Most recently Kauffman[37] studied correctional officers and the officer code that governs their behavior. She found a work force that is alienated and often misunderstood.

Probation

David Dressler defines probation as "a treatment program in which final action in an adjudicated offender's case is suspended so that he remains at liberty, subject to conditions imposed by or for a court, under the supervision and guidance of a probation worker."[38] Probation began in Boston in 1841 when John Augustus convinced the judge to release a man to his custody. The man was returned to court three weeks later, and the judge was pleased with the change that had occurred.[39]

The idea of probation spread and by 1956 all state and federal courts in the United States had a system of probation for both juveniles and adults. Today there are over 2.5 million people on probation in the United States.[40] Diversity is the key word in describing how probation agencies are organized in different states. Bureaucratic expediency has also caused a change in how probation is viewed.[41] Today probation officers are more service brokers than social workers and more peace officers than confidants, not because the rehabilitative ideal has been rejected but because the number of clients is so large.

Parole

The earliest historical event directly related to parole was the "ticket of leave" system devised by Alexander Maconochie. Maconochie was the governor of Norfolk Island off the coast of Australia, to which prisoners were transported from England. Maconochie had assumed his new post in 1840 and found the prisoners' living conditions so arduous that he was determined to do something to prevent the depravity and demoralization that resulted.[42] He instituted a system whereby a prisoner could receive "marks" for good conduct. By accruing enough marks, the prisoner could earn his way out of confinement. Maconochie devised a graded system that included (1) strict custody, (2) labor in government gangs, (3) freedom within a prescribed area, (4) tickets of leave (which allowed prisoners to live where they chose, but under certain conditions), and (5) restoration of liberty.[43]

In 1884 the state of Massachusetts passed legislation that implemented parole as part of its prison system. By 1900 twenty states had statutes allowing parole, and by 1944 all states had approved parole legislation. Along the way, the U.S. Board of Parole was established, which allowed parole for federal prisoners.[44] Today many states have moved to abolish parole, and others use it only on a limited basis. Gone are the days when parole was used as an adjunct to rehabilitation and as a means of controlling population pressures. At present there are over 520,000 prisoners on parole in the United States.[45]

Summary

On any given day in the United States, over 4.4 million persons are under the control of corrections managers. This represents a substantial investment of tax dollars, for which taxpayers are interested in getting the best services possible. Traditionally, corrections agencies have not attempted to recruit professionally trained managers. Rather, they have looked inward and promoted those individuals who performed best in their specialty. Today, managers trained specifically for corrections management are rare because our universities have largely ignored correctional administration as a separate course of study. The result is a bifurcated subsystem—that is, a system biased toward either the custodial function because only the custodial division or department affords its workers the opportunity to learn (on the job) such skills as decision making, leadership, and policy implementation, or toward executives trained in fields other than corrections and seldom in management skills at the university level.

The correctional enterprise has grown steadily since the early 1800s, and today there seems to be an almost insatiable need for capable corrections workers and managers. Prisons are difficult places in which to work, because one must deal not only with an organization that is attempting to complete its mission (care, custody, and control of prisoners) but also with people who are being held against their will, who have a separate subculture, and who would like nothing more than to see the prison fail in the execution of its mission.

Nevertheless, management principles are universal, whether the organization is a factory, a church, a nonprofit organization, a probation or parole agency, or a prison. Of course, the manager's job is somewhat different in each of these organizations because each has unique political and working environments. But certain basic activities must be carried out in all of them: planning, organization, controlling, budgeting, coordinating, influencing, and supervising staff and staff development. In short,

> if our correctional agencies can attract and hold onto able executives, talented managers, and conscientious workers, if they can operate according to a realistic management philosophy and are given sufficient (though not necessarily ample) resources, and if they can develop a sense of mission, an espirit de corps, and learn to manage their power over convicted criminals with common sense and compassion, then our correctional institutions will probably be safer, cleaner, less idle, more productive, and maybe even cost less to operate.[46]

Reviewing the Case

The entire nation faces a problem similar to Oregon's. Two factors have come together to create serious overcrowding in our prisons. The first factor is the post–World War II baby boom, which has caused correctional facilities to overflow in the same way that it caused our schools

to overflow. The second factor is related to a public demand for longer prison sentences and more conservative guidelines for paroling inmates as well as for the abolishment of the indeterminate sentence. Both these factors make it unlikely that prison populations will drop in the near future.

Consequently, not only is the universe from which the prison population comes larger than in the past, but also there is a greater likelihood that lawbreakers will be sentenced to longer prison terms and that they will complete more of their sentences before being released. Clearly, today's policy and public attitudes play a larger role in the overcrowding of correctional facilities than does the crime rate. As a consequence, many states and local jurisdictions are forced to build new facilities and devise new programs to accommodate the growing population of offenders. The result is a demand for a greater number of competent managers to take charge of these institutions and programs.

For Further Study

John Irwin, *Prisons in Turmoil* (Boston: Little, Brown, 1980).
Lucien X. Lombardo, *Guards Imprisoned* (New York: Elsevier North Holland, 1981).
Bruce Wolford, "Wardens and Superintendents: A Diverse Group," *Corrections Compendium*, 1983, 13:1–7.

Key Terms

Bridewell
Pennsylvania Model
Big House
Inmate Code

Transportation
Auburn Model
Total Institution

The Evolution of Management Theory

CHAPTER 2

Case Study: Partnerships

In March 1987, Bishop L. Robinson was appointed as the Secretary for the Maryland Department of Public Safety and Correctional Services.[1] The DOC is responsible for the confinement of over 13,000 adult offenders. Managing a large organization is never easy, and Secretary Robinson needed all the tools he could muster in order to effectively serve the citizens of the state of Maryland.

One way of improving service was to establish partnerships between the DOC and various other state and local governments and citizens. Education is one partnership, in which the Maryland State Department of Education (MSDE) provides direct educational programs to inmates during the day and evening. During fiscal year 1988 over 2,000 inmates earned an eighth-grade certificate, a high school diploma, vocational certificate, or a college degree.

The DOC offers social services to inmates via social workers for both addiction needs and other social welfare needs. The DOC, in partnership with a large number of registered volunteers, supplement those efforts by donating at least 25,000 hours of service to the DOC each year, resulting in an estimated savings to the taxpayer of nearly $200,000. Services include religious services, assistance with inmate service and self-help groups such as Jaycees, AA,

Seventh Step and Veterans groups, and assistance in music and the arts.

Partnerships are also at work to directly serve the community. Work release and work crews maintain highways, improve state parks, and in general, assist in a variety of state and county projects. Finally, Prison Industries has greatly expanded its work force and profits by increasing sales to government agencies through an improved marketing approach.

In 1987 the Secretary, with the Governor's blessing, created the Joint Legislature/Executive Committee on Corrections Capital Planning. The Committee created the Action Agenda Plan, which features a long-range, integrated, systematic approach for improving the Department of Corrections. Those improvements focus on physical plant, inmate programs, and employee development. The Governor and the Secretary are pinning the future on the Action Agenda Plan.

The Beginnings of Public Administration

The first public administrator of note was probably Moses, although he did not accomplish much during the days that followed his disorganized trek through the Red Sea. Communication was poor, and the children of Israel were generally unhappy. Moses' father-in-law, Jethro, told Moses that he was trying to do too much himself and advised him to appoint leaders over groups of thousands, hundreds, fifties, and tens. Moses did so and thus created manageable units, improved communication, and developed an organization that helped his people attain their mission.

Management as a science developed no further for approximately 4,000 years. Primitive organizations such as clans, tribes, villages, churches, and even armies were governed by the charismatic model, and little thought was given to planning and organization, leadership skills, and motivation.

Long before public administration and management science emerged as fields of study, Alexander Hamilton and Thomas Jefferson strenuously argued their points of view in *The Federalist* papers. Leonard White[2] points out that Hamilton believed in a strong national government, with a great deal of power placed in the hands of the chief executive. This was, according to White, based upon elitist tendencies among the Federalists in general. That elitism reflected a distrust of the people and the belief that managing the nation was best left to well-educated men with trained minds and broad experience. Hamilton also believed that the single executive offered the best leadership not only because of the unified command that resulted but also because the single executive could be held directly accountable for his actions.

Jefferson, on the other hand, believed in a decentralized government because it allowed the personal participation of each citizen. In contrast to Hamilton, Jefferson argued for strict legal and constitutional limits on the power of the executive branch. The Hamiltonian and Jeffersonian views underlie many of the current conflicts in public administration theory.[3]

During the century that followed Hamilton and Jefferson, the various branches of government functioned as nearly separate units. As Robert Denhardt points out, "Too often, autonomy became arrogance, insulation became isolation, and independence became caprice. Lubricated by the remaining influence of the spoils system, government was not only dispersed but disorganized and sometimes even downright dishonest."[4] Public outcry for accountability of elected officials gave birth to the science of public administration. Early scholars, however, found it difficult to separate politics from public administration.

Public administration as a separate field of study can trace its beginnings to Woodrow Wilson. In his 1887 essay "The Study of Administration,"[5] Wilson points out that writers and scholars did not study public administration systematically but rather repeatedly asked the same questions: "Who shall make the law, and what shall that law be?"[6]

According to Wilson, the field of administration is a field of business, and he called for the infusion of business practices into the running of government. He notes that "the democratic state has yet to be equipped for carrying those enormous burdens of administration which the needs of this industrial and trading age are so fast accumulating."[7]

Scientific Management

According to Samuel Certo[8] the Classical School of Management is the result of a concerted effort to develop a science of management. The history of management can be divided roughly into five schools of thought. While they overlap at the edges, they clearly result from an evolutionary process. The reader will recognize that the concepts introduced by these various schools have been incorporated into the way we do things today. For example, many agencies, prisons, and probation agencies hire consultants to do time and motion studies. This is an instance of scientific management in our work force today.

The contributions of several pioneers in management science are presented below.

Fredrick W. Taylor

Fredrick W. Taylor is considered the father of Scientific Management. Taylor's goal was to increase worker efficiency by scientifically examining how each worker performed his or her job. His approach was basically at the "shop level." In the spring of 1899 Taylor was retained by the Bethlehem Steel Company in Pennsylvania to improve management of the laborers responsible for unloading coal and ore from railroad cars and then shoveling the raw materials into the large open-hearth furnaces. Taylor placed the men on a piecework basis and was successful in improving production. He did this by using a stopwatch and studying the mechanics of motion as the men shoveled coal or ore.

For example, in the case of a man loading pig iron onto a car, Taylor decided that the elements of motion should be: picking up the pig iron from the ground or pile (time in hundredths of a minute); walking with it on a level (time per foot walked); walking up an incline to a car (time per foot walked); throwing the pig iron down (time in hundredths of a minute); walking back empty-handed to get another load (time per foot walked).[9]

However lasting Taylor's contribution to Bethlehem Steel was, and there has been some debate on this issue, it is unarguable that Taylor introduced new ideas and a new and controversial approach to management.

Henry L. Gantt

Henry L. Gantt was an associate and disciple of Fredrick Taylor. However, where Taylor was austere in his study of the mechanics of work, Gantt was interested in the people who performed the work. He believed that the willingness to use the correct methods was at least as important as having the skills in the first place. As a consequence, he was interested in motivation and the human element in productivity. Gantt believed in "paying a liberal compensation for improved methods of work. . . . The compensation should be sufficiently liberal not only to induce him to part with what information he may have, but to use his ingenuity to devise better methods."[10] He is best known for the Gantt chart, a device to aid in the allocation of time and personnel necessary to complete a task. This will be discussed more fully in chapter 12.

Frank and Lillian Gilbreath

Frank Gilbreath, trained as a bricklayer, was interested primarily in motion study. His wife, Lillian, was trained as a psychologist and pioneered the new field of industrial psychology. Their work emphasized the importance of the relationship between management and the social sciences. Frank authored two books of note: *Motion Study* (published in 1911) and *Applied Motion Study* (published in 1917). Lillian's book, *The Psychology of Management*, is a significant contribution to the field of industrial management.

Scientific management began as an attempt to gain control of the workplace and to replace arbitrariness and personal charisma with methods of science. The results were increased production and less autonomy for the worker. But whereas scientific management was basically a shop-level approach, there soon arose a stream of thought that viewed the workplace comprehensively.

The Classical School

Conventional wisdom states that nothing can stop an idea whose time has come. For example, the concept of probation arose at about the same time in both the United States and England. During the histories of engineering and science there have been many such instances of the simultaneous birth of similar ideas, such as the development of the automobile and the airplane. The field of management is no different. Various pioneers in the study of management were experimenting, writing, and putting new ideas to work in various parts of the United States and Europe. Following is a brief look at the contributions of a few of these pioneers.

Henri Fayol

About the time Taylor was examining piecework for Bethlehem Steel Company, Henry Fayol was contemplating top management in France. Fayol, like Taylor, believed that there are certain principles of management and that they can be learned.

Fayol spent his entire business career with a French industrial and mining company, whose operations he successfully reorganized and expanded. His writings on the elements of management and the general principles of management[11] have led many to consider him the father of administrative theory.

Fayol's Principles of Management[12]
The general principles of management as outlined by Fayol are still considered important to

the success of any organization. However, Fayol's *Administration industrielle et generale* was not translated into English until 1930 and did not receive wide attention in the United States until 1949. Fayol's principles are summarized below.

1. *Division of Work.* The object of division of work is to produce more and better work with the same effort. Work specialization promotes skill, confidence, and accuracy, which increase output.
2. *Authority and Responsibility.* According to Fayol, authority is the right to give orders and the power to exact obedience. Authority and responsibility are two sides of the same coin; responsibility means accountability. Authority is sought after as much as responsibility is feared.
3. *Discipline.* Fayol was convinced that discipline is essential for the smooth running of an enterprise. It requires common effort and agreement as well as sanctions judiciously applied.
4. *Unity of Command.* Dual command is a perpetual source of conflict. Thus, workers should receive orders from only one person.
5. *Unity of Direction.* A group of activities having the same objective and plan. The same department head or supervisor gives unity of direction.
6. *Subordination of Individual Interests to the General Interests.* The interests of one employee or group of employees should not take priority over the interests of the organization as a whole.
7. *Remuneration of Personnel.* In determining fair compensation for services employees render, several things need to be considered, such as cost of living, abundance of personnel, and general business conditions.
8. *Centralization.* Centralization as a system is neither good nor bad. The issue of centralization or decentralization is one of propor-

tion and the extent of one or the other that will yield the highest productivity.

9. *Scalar Chain.* The scalar chain, according to Fayol, is the chain of supervision from the top to the bottom. Each level possesses more authority than the position below it. The scalar chain is necessary if organizations are to be successful, and adherence to it is necessary if superiors are to be kept informed of each person's work activity.
10. *Order.* There is both a social order and a material order. There must be an appointed place for every person and item in the organization.
11. *Equity.* Employees should be treated fairly and equally.
12. *Stability of Tenure for Personnel.* It costs money to train personnel, and less successful firms have a high turnover of personnel. Therefore, the retention of good personnel should be a high priority for a manager.
13. *Initiative.* Management should give personnel the freedom to initiate, propose, and execute ideas.
14. *Espirit de Corps.* Management should promote harmony and prevent dissension among subordinates.

Max Weber

While Henri Fayol was studying top management, Max Weber, the German sociologist, was looking at the organization of human effort.[13] "Bureaucracy," according to Weber, "provides a way of consciously organizing people and activities in order to achieve specific purposes."[14] Bureaucracy emphasizes the conscious and formal structural aspects of organizations over their natural, more traditional forms.

According to Weber there are four major characteristics of an organization:[15]

- *Specialization and division of labor.* Bureaucracy involves obligations to perform certain tasks, and the worker has the necessary authority to complete those tasks.

- *Positions arranged in a hierarchy.* Like Fayol, Weber saw each level of the organization as being under the control of a person in authority who reports to someone higher in authority.
- *A system of abstract rules.* Weber believed that in organizations rules and procedures should persist even though personnel change, thus permitting continuity of function.
- *Impersonal relationships.* Weber felt that if bureaucrats are to be effective, they must make decisions free of emotional considerations of subordinates.

Mary Parker Follett

While the work of Fayol and Weber are considered highly significant today, the contributions of Mary Parker Follett stand out as being years ahead of her time. The various streams of thought seem to have come together through her. In 1868, Follett was born in Boston to a wealthy family. She seemed in her early life to be an unlikely candidate for the position in history she now holds. She attended an elite prep school and later went on to Radcliff, which because of its close affiliation with Harvard University was known as "the Annex." She graduated summa cum laude in 1898 and later pursued graduate studies in Paris.[16]

While she is best known as the author of many articles and books in the field of business, as a young woman she was interested in social work. Follett was the first to conceive the idea of opening up schoolhouses in the evenings for children who worked all day in factories. She was also the founder of the Roxbury Debating Club, which later expanded into the Highland Union and the Roxbury League. These centers provided social, recreational, and educational facilities for children of poor families.[17]

Follett's book *The Creative Experience*[18] deals primarily with human relationships. The author illustrated many of her points with examples drawn from the business world and thus elicited a large response from businesspeople, who began to ask Follett for help with their business problems. During 1924 and 1925 Follett made her first real contributions to the science of business management by teaching a course entitled "Scientific Foundations of Business Administration" for the Bureau of Personnel Administration in New York. Over the years her lectures and papers covered such topics as conflict, giving orders, power, and the psychology of control. Her efforts earned her a place in the pantheon of pioneers in the field of management.

James D. Mooney

James D. Mooney and Alan C. Reiley wrote *Onward Industry* in 1931. It was revised by Mooney in 1947 and retitled *The Principles of Organization.*[19] These works complemented Fayol's work very nicely. In Moody's view, management is the technique or art of inspiring others. Organization, he believed, is the technique of relating specific duties or functions as a coordinated unit.

The framework of Moody's text is a system of logic that proclaims that every principle has a process and effect that in turn has a principle, process, and effect. For example, the primary principle of organization is coordination, which is "the orderly arrangement of group effort to provide unity of action in the pursuit of a common purpose."[20] All the other principles subordinate to the primary one of coordination become effective.

Mooney's analysis, though somewhat cumbersome, was a valuable contribution to management theory. While his views were compatible with Fayol's, it was up to Lyndall Urwick to integrate the views of these two men.

Lyndall Urwick

Urwick's *The Elements of Administration*[21] combined the thoughts of Fayol, Mooney, and Taylor into one framework. Based on Mooney's approach, Urwick's analysis moved through three abstract levels.

1. *Planning.* The primary principle of management is scientific investigation for the purpose of forecasting. The result of forecasting is a plan that directs the scope, nature, and interrelationship of each operation.
2. *Coordination.* The purpose of coordination is to provide a structure of tasks and authority that assures that the functions Mooney identifies are provided. Those functions are determinative, applicative, and interpretative.
3. *Control.* According to Urwick, control is produced by centralization, selection, and placement and equity. Urwick recognized that the entire range of human motives accounts for human behavior; he thus provided for more than financial rewards in controlling an organization.

Chester I. Barnard

Chester I. Barnard[22] introduced the idea of using communication as a means of acquiring co-operation. It was his contention that an effective system of cooperation within an organization is the means by which employees are induced to cooperate. He further challenged the idea of relying only upon the authority structure to achieve compliance. His acceptance theory of authority states that the subordinate will determine the legitimacy of an order and will also determine whether to accept or reject the order. Further, he will accept the order only if the required behavior is consistent with his view of the purpose for the existence of the organization *and* his own personal interests.

These days it is universally accepted that the manager must know something about human behavior. As we shall see, Barnard was the forerunner of the Human Relations School in the field of management.

The Human Relations School

The Hawthorne Studies

At the end of the 1920s a stream of thought developed that was in opposition to the Classical School. It began with research conducted by Elton Mayo and his associates at the Hawthorne Plant of the Western Electric Company in Chicago.[23] The purpose of the project was to discover the best way to improve work productivity. It was, in other words, an extension of the scientific management tradition.

The Relay Assembly Room

The research began with an attempt to determine the relationship between lighting and productivity. The conditions for a successful experiment were fulfilled, and a control group and an experimental group were established. With all conditions held steady, the lighting was improved in the experimental room. Production went up. Lighting was turned down in the experimental room, and production still went up. In addition, production in the control room also went up. Thus, what had begun as a fairly easy experiment yielded inconclusive results.

These results, needless to say, were a surprise to the researchers. After an extensive interview program, the following factors were noted:

1. The subjects enjoyed working in the test room.
2. The women knew they were taking part in new and interesting research.
3. Their different relationship with supervisors allowed the women to work without fear.
4. The group became a team, and all participants gave of themselves wholeheartedly.

The conclusion of the researchers was irrefutable: the human factors within an organization can significantly influence production. This is called the **Hawthorne effect**. Further, they concluded that informal work groups—the social environment of employees—influence their productivity.

The Bank Wiring Observation Room

The purpose of the Bank Wiring Observation Room experiment was to confirm the observations made in the Relay Assembly Test Room. Specifically, researchers looked at the effect of group piecework incentives. Those conducting the research believed that the group would influence individuals to work harder and faster in order to increase the pay for the group.

Again, to the surprise of everyone, just the opposite occurred. The informal work group established production norms that were not in accordance with the goals of management. In short, a worker who was perceived as working too fast would be pressured by fellow workers to slow her or his output.

The Bank Wiring Room experiment clearly shows the strength of the group in setting norms, status roles, and social interactions that are removed from organizational policies and procedures.

Contributions of the Human Relations School

There are two primary orientations to the Human Relations School of management. The first

is a basic concern for people in the organization. Mayo,[24] for example, called for modifications in the industrial system to give greater recognition to human values. The second orientation was the utilization of scientific research methods to study organizational behavior.

Other concepts were developed and promoted by the Human Relations theorists:[25]

1. The organization is a social system as well as a technical-economic system.
2. The individual is motivated not only by economic incentives but also by diverse social and psychological factors. Behavior is affected by feelings, sentiments, and attitudes.
3. The informal work group becomes a dominant unit of consideration.
4. Leadership patterns should be modified substantially to consider psychological factors. The Human Relations theorists emphasize "democratic" rather than "authoritarian" leadership patterns.
5. Worker satisfaction is generally associated with productivity, and increased satisfaction leads to increased effectiveness.
6. Channels of effective communication between levels in the hierarchy are important to organizational efficiency.
7. Workers' participation in the decision-making process is important for worker satisfaction and organizational effectiveness.
8. Management requires effective social skills as well as technical abilities.
9. Workers in the organization can be motivated when certain social-psychological needs are fulfilled.

The Classical-Human Relations Synthesis

Just as the Classical School overemphasized the technical and structural aspects of the organization, the Human Relations theorists overemphasized the psychological and the sociological. The result was, however, a synthesis or an amalgamation that gave rise to what Denhardt[26] calls the generic approach to administration. He points out that there are often greater differences between large and small organizations than there are between public and private organizations. The emergent generic study of management or administration is an amalgam of findings from the social sciences, including business, that has taken on its own identity. As a consequence, according to Denhardt, public administrators within departments of political science in various universities have come to discover that they have more in common with their colleagues in schools of business than with those in their own departments.

Herbert A. Simon

In 1946 Herbert A. Simon published an article entitled "The Proverbs of Administration" in which he outlined his rational model for administration. The article later appeared in his *Administrative Behavior: A Study of Decision Making Processes in Administrative Organization*. Denhardt states Simon's position well: "Simon's critique was by far the most biting [as opposed to Robert Dahl's critique of earlier writers], describing the principles of administration of Gulick, Urwick, and others as 'proverbs' . . . [who] were often in contradiction to one another."[27] Simon's attack was based on four general principles of administration: specialization; unity of command; span of control; and organization by purpose, process, clientele, and place.

Simon equates rationality with efficiency and says that to behave rationally is to further the aims of the organization. Problems occur because people have feelings, interests, and concerns.

Simon summed up his position by stating:

Administrative description suffers currently from superficiality, oversimplification, and lack of realism. It has confined itself too closely to the mechanism of authority and has failed to bring within its orbit the other, equally important modes of influence on organizational behavior. It has refused to undertake the tiresome task of studying the actual allocation of decision-making functions. It has been satisfied to speak of "authority," "centralization," "span of control," "function" without seeking operational definitions of these items.[28]

Lindblom's "Muddling Through"

Simon's work in decision making focused the attention of scholars on the tension between rational behavior and real life. Charles E. Lindblom,[29] points out that the rational model of administration calls for the manager to prioritize alternatives and values and then choose an objective. Next, the decision maker would develop a list of alternative policies, examine how well they would achieve the goal, and select an alternative that would maximize the value chosen. On the other hand, using the incremental approach, the decision maker would choose a limited objective and then move to solidify that step before moving on to another incremental step. In real life, the public administrator chooses the incremental method over the rational method.

In Lindblom's view, two aspects of the incremental method stand out:

1. In real life it is never possible to sort out and rank all the values of objectives related to a particular problem.
2. The incremental approach helps the decision maker/policy maker pursue a pluralist objective of reaching some kind of agreement between competing interests.

During the 1960s the various streams of management theory began to come together. The quantitative approach that was an outcome of World War II began to be employed by a number of social scientists who conducted research into many areas.

McGregor's Theory X and Theory Y

Inspired by Abraham Maslow's hierarchy of needs, Douglas McGregor postulates two theories of human behavior. One, Theory X, is responsible for materially influencing managerial behavior in a wide sector of U.S. industry. Further, McGregor states that the principles expressed in most of the literature of management could have been derived only from assumptions of the Theory X type.

Theory Y, on the other hand, points out "that the limits on human collaboration in the organization setting are not limits of human nature, but of management's ingenuity in discovering how to realize the potential represented by its human resources."[30] McGregor indicates that Theory X provides management a ready explanation for its poor performance.

Herzberg's Motivation-Hygiene Theory

In 1959 Fredrick Herzberg, in *Work and the Nature of Man*, reported the results of a study of 200 engineers and accountants. The primary question they were asked regarded events experienced at work that had resulted in improvement in their work or had led to significant job dissatisfaction.[31] Five factors stood out as strong determinants of job satisfaction (satisfiers): achievement, recognition, the work itself, responsibility, and advancement. The primary sources of job dissatisfaction (dissatisfiers) were company policy and administration, supervision, salary, interpersonal relations, and working conditions. It appeared to Herzberg that the satisfiers stemmed from the relationship between workers and what they do, while the dis-

TABLE 2.1
McGregor's Theory X and Theory Y

Theory X Assumptions	*Theory Y Assumptions*
1. The average human being has an inherent dislike of work and will avoid it if possible.	1. The expenditure of physical and mental effort in work is as natural as play or rest.
2. Because of this human characteristic of dislike of work, most people must be coerced, controlled, directed, or threatened with punishment to get them to put forth adequate effort toward the achievement of organizational objectives.	2. External control and the threat of punishment are not the only means of bringing about effort toward organizational objectives. People will exercise self-direction and self-control in the service of objectives to which they are committed.
3. The average human being prefers to be directed, wishes to avoid responsibility, has relatively little ambition, and wants security above all.	3. Commitment to objectives is a function of the rewards associated with their achievement.
	4. The average human being learns, under proper conditions, not only to accept but also to seek responsibility.
	5. The capacity to exercise a relatively high degree of imagination, ingenuity, and creativity in the solution of organizational problems is widely, not narrowly, distributed in the population.
	6. Under the conditions of modern industrial life, the intellectual potentialities of the average human being are only partially utilized.

Source: D. S. Pugh, ed., *Organization Theory*, 2d ed. (New York: Penguin Books, 1984), pp. 317–27.

TABLE 2.2
Characteristics of Hygiene and Motivation Seekers

Hygiene Seeker	*Motivation Seeker*
1. Motivated by the nature of the environment.	1. Motivated by the nature of the task.
2. Chronic and heightened dissatisfaction with various aspects of the job; e.g., salary, supervision, working conditions, status, job security, company policy, administration, fellow employees.	2. Higher tolerance for poor hygiene factors.
3. Overreaction with satisfaction to improvement in hygiene factors.	3. Less reaction to improvement in hygiene factors.
4. Short duration of satisfaction when the hygiene factors are improved.	4. Similar.
5. Overreaction with dissatisfaction when hygiene factors are not improved.	5. Milder discontent when hygiene factors need improvement.
6. Realizes little satisfaction from accomplishments.	6. Realizes great satisfaction from accomplishments.
7. Shows little interest in the kind and quality of the work he or she does.	7. Shows capacity to enjoy the kind of work he or she does.
8. Cynicism regarding positive virtues of work and life in general.	8. Has positive feeling toward work and life in general.
9. Does not profit professionally from experience.	9. Profits professionally from experience.
10. Prone to cultural noises (a) ultraliberal, ultraconservative; (b) parrots management philosophy; (c) acts more like top management than top management does.	10. Belief systems sincere and considered.
11. May be successful on the job because of talent.	11. May be an overachiever.

Source: D. S. Pugh, *Organization Theory*, 2d ed. (New York: Penguin Books, 1984), p. 350.

satisfiers were all related to external variables.

Herzberg called the dissatisfiers "hygiene factors." He believed that hygiene factors led to job dissatisfaction because of a worker's need to avoid unpleasantness. He further believed that the satisfiers, which he called "motivator factors," led to job satisfaction because of a worker's need for growth or self-actualization. Herzberg concluded that the hygiene seeker, as opposed to the motivation seeker, is motivated by the environment of the job rather than by the job itself. The hygiene seeker suffers from an overreaction to improvement in hygiene factors, and a "shot in the arm" has only short-term consequences. Herzberg also concluded that hygiene seekers will let the company down when their talents are most needed. They are motivated only for short periods and only when there is also an external reward. The Motivation-Hygiene Theory is covered more completely in chapter 9.

Corrections management seems to have undergone the same development as management theory. Scientific management and the Classical School are evidenced by job descriptions and post orders. The Human Relations School is reflected in executives' attempts to solicit input from their staffs and by the implementation of functional unit management.

It cannot be said that corrections management theory adheres to one school of thought over another. There are Theory X managers and there are Theory Y managers. And while we are aware that employees need more than adequate compensation and benefits, we sometimes fail to provide them. They also need recognition and the opportunity to advance and to be creative.

Every day the contributions of the people thus far discussed affect the lives of correctional workers. But our survey is not yet complete. There remains one more view to examine: the systems approach, which allows us to look more critically at the corrections enterprise and to understand how the parts fit together.

The Systems Approach

The term *system* has broad applications in the human, plant, and animal kingdoms. According to Ludwig von Bertalanffy[32] there are two types of systems: closed and open. Closed systems do not interact with their environment; open systems interact with and are influenced by their environment. An example of a closed system is a clock. Assuming an existing power source, the gears and other parts of the mechanism do not interact with the outside environment in order to work properly. A plant is an example of an open system. It needs CO_2 and sunlight from the environment in order to exist.

Over the past thirty years, management theory in general and systems theory in particular have provided a sound basis for the study of organizations. Kast and Rosenzweig[33] have defined a system as "an organized, unitary whole composed of two or more interdependent parts, components, or subsystems and delineated by identifiable boundaries from its environmental suprasystem."

The writing of Herbert Simon and others heralded a new age in public administration and management, one that acknowledged the structure of organizations as well as the human factor. However, these authors failed to note that the organization survived and conducted its business as part of a larger environment that is connected in some way to government, education, and the public. In addition, workers bring their own values, attitudes, and problems into the organization every day. Therefore, the organization is an open system, not a closed system; a prison is an example of an open system. Employees bring their values and attitudes to work with them, the inmate culture is constantly revitalized and sustained by the arrival of new inmates; the courts and legislatures affect its daily operation; and finally, food, water, and other necessities are brought into the institution on a daily basis.

The system must be viewed as a whole; changes in one part of the system affect the other parts. The administrator or warden must have sound knowledge of the various parts and their interrelationships in order to be most effective. Hopkins[34] calls our attention to six guidelines that emphasize system wholeness.

1. The main focus of analysis should be the whole, with the parts being secondary.
2. The key variable in the analysis is integration. Integration is defined as the interrelatedness of many parts.
3. Any modification in any part should be considered in terms of the impact it would have on the whole.
4. Each part has a role to perform in order for the whole to function.
5. The nature of the part and its function are determined by its position in the whole.
6. Any analysis must begin with the assumption of the existence of the whole. The parts and their interrelatedness should then evolve to best suit the purpose of the whole.

The Corrections Management System

Kast and Rosenzweig[35] view the organization as an open system composed of several subsystems. It receives input from the environment, transforms the input, and returns something to the environment. A correctional institution receives input of inmates, materials, electricity, water, and so on. It transforms those elements into a service—protection of the community. An additional output is, one hopes, a reformed human being who will abide by the rules of society.

FIGURE 2.1
The Corrections Management System

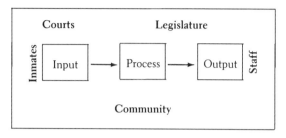

The organization can be thought of as containing several subsystems. *Organizational goals and values* are an important aspect of the organization. A prison takes its values and goals from the broader society; not only is there a staff value system, but there is also an inmate value system. The two systems coexist, but rarely do they interpenetrate. Both inmate and staff values are imported from the larger society.

The *technical subsystem* refers to the knowledge required to accomplish the institutional objective—protecting the community. The technology required to run a contemporary prison is broad and includes input from the social sciences, business, law, industry, and such areas as computer science. The technology affects not only the organizational structure but its attitudes and personal relationships as well.

The *psychological subsystem* is made up of individuals and groups, both formal and informal. There are certain dynamics, attitudes, and relationships that affect the organization as a whole. In addition, there is a certain organizational climate[36] that sets the "tone" of the organization. Organizational climate comprises a composite of social, psychological, and architectural features that produce a distinct "personality." Human beings work and interact in an environment that is influenced by this personality.

The *structural subsystem* comprises organizational procedures and the way tasks are divided up and completed. Other parts of the structural subsystem are policies, chain of command, channels of communication, and aspects of the built environment. There is thus a formal and an informal structure; these will be discussed in a later chapter.

The *managerial subsystem* spans the entire organization by planning, establishing policies and procedures relating to the larger environment, setting goals, coordinating activities, and influencing employees.

Summary

Early human beings probably needed little in the way of managerial skills. A club or a sword, along with loyal subordinates, may have been all that were necessary to motivate others to get the job done. With the advent of the Industrial Revolution, many tasks became more difficult and complicated. Finally, efficiency demanded that workers become specialized in the jobs they were expected to perform. At the same time that workers' jobs were becoming more complicated, so too were the jobs of those who oversaw the workers.

Beginning in the late 1800s serious thought was given to both public and private sector management. Woodrow Wilson, Fredrick Taylor, and Henri Fayol are partially responsible for the revolution in management. The *Scientific Management* approach, which was a shop-level approach to management, gave way to the *Classical School*, which concentrated on structure and the organization as an entity. The *Human Relationists*, however, thought that not enough attention was given to the workers. Their movement, which began with the Hawthorne Experiments, grew into a school of thought that believed conflict could be resolved. Today a new train of thought is emerging, one that holds that the inherent strains in an organization can be reduced but never eliminated.

One must view the correctional organization as an open system because it depends on the outside environment. It is a unique organization, to be sure, for it has no identifiable product, and its line employees are supervisors who do nothing productive in terms of private sector criteria.

In the chapters that follow, we will relate

FIGURE 2.2
The Organization System

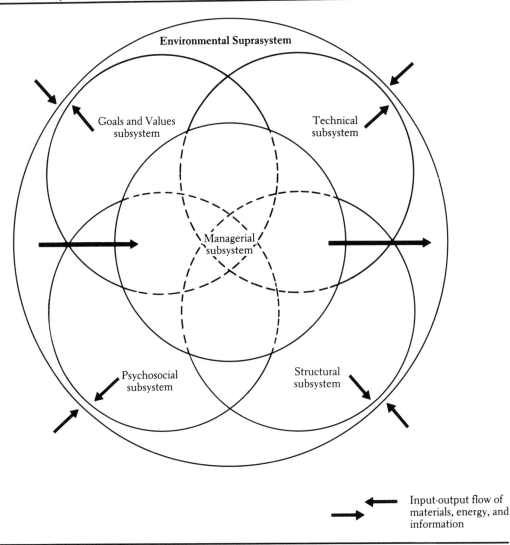

Source: Fremont Kast and James Rosenzweig, *Organization and Management, A Systems and Contingency Approach*, 3rd ed. (New York: McGraw-Hill, 1979). p. 19.

principles of management to all of corrections, not just to prisons or jails. For example, community programs, which are unique entities with their own problems and issues, are very much a part of the larger environment.

Reviewing the Case

Secretary Robinson doesn't have an easy job. He is responsible for protecting the community and for offering programs that occupy prisoners' time and that have rehabilitative value. Partnerships appear to be one way of effectively meeting both goals.

Secretary Robinson needs to be familiar with sound management principles and to know how to communicate effectively. He needs to know how the structure of the organization affects performance and the importance of satisfying the needs of employees and volunteers. Finally, he must view the organization as an open system that depends upon the input of the community.

For Further Study

A. Cary, "The Hawthorne Studies: A Radical Criticism" *American Sociological Review* (1967), 32: 403–16.

William F. Franklin, Jr., "What Japanese Managers Know That American Managers Don't," *Administrative Management* (Sept. 1981), 42:36–39, 51–54, 56.

John Klofas, Stan Stojkovic, and David Kalinich, *Criminal Justice Organizations: Administration and Management* (Pacific Grove, Calif.: Brooks/Cole Publishing Company, 1990).

Mary Parker Follett, *The Creative Experience* (New York: Longmans, Green and Company, 1924).

D. S. Pugh, *Organization Theory*, 2d ed. (New York: Penguin Books, 1984).

Woodrow Wilson, "The Study of Administration," *Political Science Quarterly* (June 1887), pp. 197–222.

Key Terms

Scientific Management
Bureaucracy
Satisfier
System

Scalar Chain
Incremental approach
    to decision making
Dissatisfier

THE ENVIRONMENT

PART II

Having established that management principles are universal, we now turn to the impact of the environment on the organization. It is indisputable that the correctional organization is an open system sensitive to changes in its environment. In the close of chapter 2, the interdependency between the organization, its components, and its environment was emphasized. Clearly, the correctional organization does not exist in a vacuum.

We now turn to specific influences on the correctional organization from the community, the courts, and individuals and groups. Chapter 3 explores how the various influences from the community determine, for example, the siting of correctional facilities and makes a number of suggestions to help the manager deal sensitively and effectively with the community. Chapter 4 reviews several court decisions and how they have affected management of correctional organizations. In chapter 5 the goals and values of individuals and the organization are explored in terms of how they can shape an organization and its purpose.

The Community

Case Study: Circling the Wagons in Waukegan

Halfway House of Northern Illinois (HHNI) is facing one of its biggest challenges in its twenty-six-year history—that of the NIMBY (Not-in-My-Backyard) Syndrome.[1] In 1966 the agency was founded to provide a halfway house setting in order to provide independent-living skills to young people in trouble with the law. Located in Waukegan, Illinois, "Halfway House" currently serves young men ages seventeen to twenty-five. With the growing need in the local criminal justice system for a program of this nature and the need to update the agency's current physical structure, the board of directors and administration decided four years ago to expand the current eighteen-resident program and seek a new facility that would be more conducive to meeting the supervision and programming needs of its residents.

HHNI is a community program in which all residents are required to be employed, participate in self-improvement classes, and complete public service work if ordered to do so by the court. It is important for the facility to be in a centralized location with accessibility to jobs and schools in order for the residents to learn behaviors that will enable them to become contributing members of the community. After an extensive two-year search for vacant land to build on, or for an existing building that could be renovated, an ideal location was found. It meets all stated criteria for accessibility to transportation and other community resources. Another very important consideration was that there be very little residential housing located nearby and that all other nearby land be zoned commercial, with the property in question zoned R-2 (residential/duplexes).

A purchase contract was entered into with the landowner, and HHNI completed environmental testing at considerable cost. A land-use planner/architect was retained who would also assist with the zoning particulars.

Following an aldermanic election, and the loss of the incumbent alderman for that ward, the executive director of Halfway House, Janet Mason, met with the new alderman, who is also a full-time employee for the County Work-Release Program. A three-hour meeting resulted in the alderman voicing his strong support for the program and his belief that this is the best location for it in Waukegan and that it would affect the least number of community residents as opposed to other possibilities. A plan was decided upon to present the proposal to the neighborhood at a community meeting hosted by Halfway House. Notices were mailed stating that the alderman would be present at the meeting with the agency to hear concerns and discuss the issues.

Prior to mailing the notices, a Halfway House board member spoke to a friend who lives in the neighborhood in order to set up a meeting to informally discuss the project. The friend stated that she didn't think it important to meet and didn't believe that there would be much objection from the neighborhood. In fact, she said that she probably wouldn't even attend the community meeting. With those encouraging words, the agency did not follow through with its original plan to walk the neighborhood and speak individually with the homeowners, believing instead that the community meeting would suffice. In retrospect, this was a mistake. Approximately fifty people came to the meeting, and a petition against the agency was available at the door for people to sign as they entered the meeting room.

Although there were several people who changed their minds and admitted that they regretted having signed the petition, the great majority had already positioned themselves and were not about to be swayed. The major objections naturally revolved around a fear of increasing crime rates and decreasing property values. The fact that a nearby landfill/superfund site would have a more negative impact on their property values had no effect on their opinion. Neither did the testimony of the Waukegan chief of police who stated that a computer check revealed that Halfway House residents do not cause problems in the neighborhood, that the program polices itself well, and that in his opinion, they are very good neighbors.

Following the meeting, Ms. Mason had many telephone conversations with the alderman, who completely reversed his earlier support of the program's relocation efforts. He reported that he should never have voiced his support as he must vote the way the people want. In addition, he voiced fears of not being re-elected and spoke of further political aspirations. Some of his political advisors and friends spoke with him on behalf of Halfway House, but to no avail. One of his final statements to Ms. Mason was, "Even if the people are as wrong as two left feet, that's the way I have to vote." After spending three months on this futile task, the agency filed for rezoning (application fees were $2,000). Newspaper articles, local cable television shows, and public speaking engagements gave good publicity to the agency's mission, and a zoning attorney was secured who embraced the cause and agreed to donate time.

The review from the city, which makes a recommendation to the development commission (zoning board), pointed out that the project should be approved based upon the program and the comprehensive city plan, which calls for that property to be rezoned multifamily (apartments). At the public hearing before the development commission (which makes a recommendation to the judiciary committee of the city council), expert witnesses presented facts and testified to the excellent program over a twenty-five-year period. The objectors, however, repeatedly voiced their fears based on misconceptions and prejudices. Following a three and one-half hour meeting, the commissioners, caught in a wave of emotional fervor, voted five to three against HHNI's proposal. One commissioner stated, "None of the objectors produced a shred of evidence that Halfway would be detrimental to the neighborhood." He added that the proposal provides a better land use for the property than an apartment complex. The final decision, however, rests with the city council, who will decide how best to meet the needs of the whole community when a vocal minority is in opposition. The chances of winning are slim. The time and money already invested is substantial, and if the proposal loses, the agency must decide whether or not to pursue the expensive option of litigation where its chances in a court of law may be much better than in the political arena.

Introduction

Fear of crime permeates our existence. Everyone, it seems has been victimized or knows someone who has been victimized. But the fear of crime is disproportionate to the probability of being victimized.[2] Nevertheless, the consequences of fear on the activities of some of our citizens, such as the elderly, are significant. The increasing urbanization of our society and the public's belief that public institutions are unable to do anything about crime are a source of frustration and anger to the average citizen. The media constantly remind us that urbanization has destroyed our community and with it security and a sense of belonging. Small-town life has traditionally been upheld as the ideal, and in our lifetimes we have witnessed the erosion or decline of that ideal.

In our minds crime is associated with urbanization. This association is not based on reality,[3] but it is nevertheless difficult to shake. For example, Gibbons[4] calls our attention to the facts of rural crime and points out that the function of a sheriff's department in rural areas is more to keep the peace than to enforce the law. A glance at the statistics[5] reveals that the same kinds of crime exist in both rural and urban areas, but that there is more of it in urban areas. It is important for the corrections manager to understand the dynamics of urban life because it shapes the way we view ourselves, others, and the institutions that govern our very existence. Taking the city or community into account is important when a site for an institution or work release center is being chosen, because announcements of these decisions unleash a host of fears that need to be dealt with in a sensitive and caring way. Finally, no agency or organization stands apart from the community in which it is based.

It is worthwhile to briefly review the history of urbanization in order to put the correctional organization into perspective and to gain an idea of how it fits into the community. By doing so, we may better understand the expectations and fears of community members. Duffee and McGarrell point out that "corrections is not something that happens in the community or something that is done for the community, and it certainly is not meant as something the community should do. Corrections is like business or education: it simply exists as one aspect or function of the community."[6] Thus, the community serves as a foundation upon which rest the efforts of corrections officials. Without a solid foundation to support those efforts there can be only partial successes.

The Growth of the City

Gideon Sjoberg[7] estimates that the world population remained relatively stable from about 500 B.C. to A.D. 1800. However, with the beginning of the Industrial Revolution, cities began to grow and expand at an unprecedented rate. Today much of the world population is concentrated in urban areas. Government struggles to keep pace with the demand for services but often fights a losing battle.

The First Urban Revolution

What we call the first urban revolution occurred around 3500 B.C. in Mesopotamia and later in the Nile River Valley, the Indus River Valley (in the area we know as Pakistan), the Yellow River Valley, and in Meso-America around 300 B.C. In order for cities to emerge, technology needed to advance to the point that people had a surplus of time. Spare time allowed: (1) increased production of food that supported an elite; (2) the emergence of a warrior or priest class that could extract "surplus" goods from the population; and (3) a trading capability. Janet abu-Lughod[8] points out that many cities collapsed because of the decay of the class system. Clearly, surplus could not be mobilized without conquest, slavery, and extortion.

Urban development in what we know as Europe lagged far behind that in Asia, Africa, and Meso-America. However, people's insatiable curiosity and migratory urges caused developments in technology and art to spread throughout the various regions. The Greek city-state or "polis"[9] represented a different path to urbanization because it relied on associations and trading rather than on an extortionist elite. Greek innovations were carried to even greater heights by Rome. By the second and third centuries A.D., Rome, with its population of one million,[10] had become the largest city the world had ever known. Rome eventually stood astride a vast system of urban settlements tied together by sea and land routes. On a grand scale, Rome plundered its colonies to profit the ruling class. But in return, Rome exported its technology, architecture, language, art, and culture. When Rome declined, so did other cities, except those European cities tied to the sea, such as Venice and Genoa.

The Second Urban Revolution

The Middle Ages were a time of intellectual hibernation, when the great manors controlled the life of the average person. However, beginning around A.D. 950, the population of Europe began to grow. Trade routes were established, political organization (or reorganization) occurred, and core areas began to amass a surplus of agricultural products.[11] An agricultural revolution occurred in which a crop economy changed to a pastoral economy, forcing serfs to migrate to the towns.

The onset of the Industrial Revolution heralded the second urban revolution. By 1750 fewer than three out of every 100 persons in the world lived in urban settlements. However, the shift had begun, and by 1850 London, Manchester, and Liverpool, for example, had large concentrations of people living in squalor and poverty. At the time London's population probably exceeded one million people. Today two out of every five people in the world live in cities.[12]

The Industrial Revolution occurred because the harnessing of water and steam power gave rise to huge factories and to the transportation necessary to carry goods over great distances. Early accounts from England describe cities not as jewels in the crown of civilization but as "the barracks of an industry."[13] People were pushed off the manor and lured to the city. There they provided the labor industry needed and thus aided the growth of a new elite—the capitalist class.

The migration had begun. People were moving from the countryside to the city, from country to country, and from continent to continent. Some migrated in hope of a new start and others to flee oppression; still others were forcibly transported under the yoke of slavery. Throughout this period the new United States was the destination of many.

The Urbanization of the United States

The urbanization of the United States can be divided into roughly three periods: the Colonial Period (1609–1820), the Expansionist Period (1821–1920), and the Urban Transformation Period (1921–present). During the **Colonial Period,** the American wilderness was viewed as an area to be exploited for its wealth, and the first colonists were sent to establish outposts for the various empires that had claims on the continent. The first cities resulted from charters granted by the English king for purposes of mercantilism. As the population grew, so did the

TABLE 3.1
U.S. Population 1860–1920

Census Year	Total Population (in thousands)	Urban Population (percent) (in thousands)		Immigrants Arriving Preceding Decade	Immigrants as Percent Net Gain Previous Decade
1860	31,443	6,217	19.8		
1870	39,818	9,902	25.7	2,081,261	25
1880	50,156	14,130	28.2	2,742,137	27
1890	62,948	22,100	35.1	5,248,568	41
1900	75,995	30,215	39.6	3,644,294	28
1910	91,972	42,064	45.6	8,202,388	51
1920	105,711	54,253	51.2	6,347,380	46

Source: Janet L. abu-Lughod, *Changing Cities* (New York: HarperCollins, 1991), p. 98.

influence of the few settlements that had larger populations. By 1790 New York had a population of 33,131, and the population of Boston was 18,320.[14]

During the Expansionist Period the United States began to fill the vast spaces between its borders. It was a time dominated by men and women of strength, vision, and courage. It was a time of cruelty and often senseless violence, but above all it was a time of hope as people searched for a better life for themselves and their families. During this period, the population of the United States grew from 3.9 million in 1790 to 105.7 million in 1920. In the period between 1860 and 1920, the urban population shifted from 20 percent urban to 51 percent urban.[15] This transformation came about because of the tremendous numbers of people immigrating to the United States—over 32 million during these years.

As pioneers and settlers pushed back the frontier of the new nation, the idea persisted that cities were unhealthy places full of temptations. The general opinion was that "deviancy was primarily the result of the corruptions pervading the community and that organizations like the family and church were not counterbalancing them. . . ."[16] The conviction that the only way to save the unfortunate and wayward was to separate them from temptation led to

the development of the asylum, which is how the penitentiary was viewed at that time. Rothman puts it very well:

Since the convict was not inherently depraved but the victim of an upbringing that had failed to provide protection against the vices at loose in society, a well-ordered institution could successfully reeducate and rehabilitate him. The penitentiary, free of corruptions and dedicated to the proper training of the inmate, would inculcate the discipline negligent parents, evil companions, taverns, houses of prostitution, theaters, and gambling halls had destroyed. Just as the criminal's environment had led him into crime, the institutional environment would lead him out of it.[17]

Thus, the reformers believed that just as individuals had succumbed to temptation while in the city, their separation from the city would allow them to contemplate their circumstances and enable them to return to society reformed and penitent. The result was the Pennsylvania system of solitary confinement and the Auburn system of congregate work and solitary confinement at night, all under a system of silence. The culmination was the reformatory for youthful offenders, where they received education and skill training and read the Bible.

The Urban Transformation Period began around 1921, when the rural-urban shift occurred. The city had developed as a way of meeting the manufacturing, finance, and trading needs of the region. It had been transformed by the huge numbers of immigrants who streamed in both from abroad and from the countryside. While it was still marked by contrasts of wealth and poverty, a new middle class was emerging that would soon fuel the engine of social progress. The city was also marked by its heterogeneity. In his description of the U.S. city with its different ways of life, Louis Wirth[18] called it a "mosaic of social worlds."

The urban transformation of the United States seemed nearly complete when the U.S. Congress passed legislation that would have a profound affect on the city. This event can be considered the start of the **third urban revolution** in the United States. Beginning around this time changes were occurring in cities all around the world—changes that were brought about by increased population, increased poverty, and increased demand for services.

In the United States the event that was to transform the cities was the passage in 1956 of the Federal Aid Highway Transportation Act. This act, passed ostensibly to facilitate the transport of military equipment and supplies in time of national emergency, enabled the middle class to divide its time between city and suburb. This trend began shortly after World War II, when suburbs such as Levittown, on Long Island, New York, were constructed to meet the pent-up housing needs of returning veterans and their families. Between 1950 and 1960 there was an 18 percent shift in population from central cities to suburban rings.[19] The passage of the 1956 Federal Aid Highway Transportation Act solidified the trend.

The flight of middle-class whites from the central cities meant that housing was available for the African Americans and farm laborers who were at the same time migrating to the cities.

The loss of the middle class and its tax base, coupled with an influx of mostly poor immigrants from the farm, created a financial crisis for the cities and rendered them incapable of keeping up with the demand for services. Further complicating the situation was the increased loss of jobs as employers began to follow the middle class to the suburban ring. At the same time there began a subtle shift in population and jobs to the Sunbelt. By 1980 the shift had crippled many cities, particularly in the heavily industrialized Northeast and Great Lakes areas. As a further blow, the federal government has been unable or unwilling to establish policies and tax incentives that would stem the loss of manufacturing jobs to foreign countries.

By 1990 the third urban revolution in the United States was in full swing. Table 3.2 illustrates the shift in population from the heavily industrialized Northeast and Great Lakes areas to the Sunbelt. For example, California gained 25.7 percent in population and Florida gained 32.7 percent. Nevada gained 50.1 percent and Iowa lost 4.7 percent. The results of this shift are obvious: poverty, despair, a permanent (mostly black) underclass, and few meaningful jobs for a sizable number of people. Many city neighborhoods have become battlegrounds, and the law-abiding inhabitants cry out for help while they attempt to hold on to a shred of dignity and security.

The Human Costs of Urbanization

For over 100 years scholars have attempted to explain the impact of urbanization. Sir Henry Maine[20] believed that urbanization contributed to the breakdown of the family through a decline in predetermined bonds between people, the growth of the individual as a legal entity, and increased dependence on contracts. Ferdinand Tönnies[21] views the urbanizing society as moving from a gemeinschaft society to a gesellschaft society. The former is characterized by face-to-

TABLE 3.2
The Sunbelt Shift in the United States (Total Resident Population by State: 1990 and 1980)

1990 Total Population Rank	State	1990 Total Population	1980 Total Population	Number Change 1980 to 1990	Percent Change 1980 to 1990
1	California	29,760,021	23,667,902	6,092,119	25.7
2	New York	17,990,455	17,558,072	432,383	2.5
3	Texas	16,986,510	14,229,191	2,757,319	19.4
4	Florida	12,937,926	9,746,324	3,191,602	32.7
5	Pennsylvania	11,881,643	11,863,895	17,748	0.1
6	Illinois	11,430,602	11,426,518	4,084	0.0
7	Ohio	10,847,115	10,797,630	49,485	0.5
8	Michigan	9,295,297	9,262,078	33,219	0.4
9	New Jersey	7,730,188	7,364,823	365,365	5.0
10	North Carolina	6,628,637	5,881,766	746,871	12.7
11	Georgia	6,478,216	5,463,105	1,015,111	18.6
12	Virginia	6,187,358	5,346,818	840,540	15.7
13	Massachusetts	6,016,425	5,737,037	279,388	4.9
14	Indiana	5,544,159	5,490,224	53,935	1.0
15	Missouri	5,117,073	4,916,686	200,387	4.1
16	Wisconsin	4,891,769	4,705,767	186,002	4.0
17	Tennessee	4,877,185	4,591,120	286,065	6.2
18	Washington	4,866,692	4,132,156	734,536	17.8
19	Maryland	4,781,468	4,216,975	564,493	13.4
20	Minnesota	4,375,099	4,075,970	299,129	7.3
21	Louisiana	4,219,973	4,205,900	14,073	0.3
22	Alabama	4,040,587	3,893,888	146,699	3.8
23	Kentucky	3,685,296	3,660,777	24,519	0.7
24	Arizona	3,665,228	2,718,215	947,013	34.8
25	South Carolina	3,486,703	3,121,820	364,883	11.7
26	Colorado	3,294,394	2,889,964	404,430	14.0
27	Connecticut	3,287,116	3,107,576	179,540	5.8
28	Oklahoma	3,145,585	3,025,290	120,295	4.0
29	Oregon	2,842,321	2,633,105	209,216	7.9
30	Iowa	2,776,755	2,913,808	− 137,053	− 4.7
31	Mississippi	2,573,216	2,520,638	52,578	2.1
32	Kansas	2,477,574	2,363,679	113,895	4.8
33	Arkansas	2,350,725	2,286,435	64,290	2.8
34	West Virginia	1,793,477	1,949,644	− 156,167	− 8.0
35	Utah	1,722,850	1,461,037	261,813	17.9
36	Nebraska	1,578,385	1,569,825	8,560	0.5
37	New Mexico	1,515,069	1,302,894	212,175	16.3
38	Maine	1,227,928	1,124,660	103,268	9.2
39	Nevada	1,201,833	800,493	401,340	50.1
40	New Hampshire	1,109,252	920,610	188,642	20.5
41	Hawaii	1,108,229	964,691	143,538	14.9
42	Idaho	1,006,749	943,935	62,814	6.7
43	Rhode Island	1,003,464	947,154	56,310	5.9
44	Montana	799,065	786,690	12,375	1.6
45	South Dakota	696,004	690,768	5,236	0.8
46	Delaware	666,168	594,338	71,830	12.1
47	North Dakota	638,800	652,717	− 13,917	− 2.1
48	District of Columbia	606,900	638,333	− 31,433	− 4.9
49	Vermont	562,758	511,456	51,302	10.0
50	Alaska	550,043	401,851	148,192	36.9
51	Wyoming	453,588	469,557	− 15,969	− 3.4

Source: U.S. Bureau of the Census, 1990. The population counts set forth herein are subject to possible correction for undercount or overcount. The United States Department of Commerce is considering whether to correct these counts and will publish corrected counts, if any, not later than July 15, 1991.

face encounters; the latter by impersonal relationships. Emile Durkheim[22] saw society as moving from primary to secondary relationships and believed that the increasing specialization of labor in an industrialized society was responsible for that change. Georg Simmel[23] distinguishes between simple and complex groups and shows how group ties are progressively loosened by urbanization, thus permitting greater development of the individual. He also distinguishes between traditional behavior based upon contracts and secondary relationships in which one's group is immersed in the whole rather than the individual being immersed in the group.

Max Weber[24] may have summed up scholars' thinking by noting increased bureaucratization. In Weber's view, bureaucratization is a positive rather than a negative trend, as we tend to think today. He attempts to describe an ideal organization; that is, one that is rational and efficient. According to Weber, the characteristics of a bureaucracy are:

- It attempts to eliminate irrelevant criteria for the selection of employees.
- It uses tenure to protect employees against arbitrary authority, changes in job demands, and declining ability.
- It uses rules and regulations to assure that employees are treated fairly and to create stability over time.
- It has a vertical hierarchy with clear lines of authority to facilitate decision making and to ensure accountability of decisions.[25]

In short, in Weber's view bureaucracy fosters predictability of behavior, promotes employee loyalty and commitment to the organization, and calls for a reduction in nepotism and arbitrariness in the selection of employees.

Sumner[26] views society as moving from folk ways to state ways. Redfield[27] reaches a similar conclusion in his earlier study of a Mexican village, declaring that society is moving from a folk society to an urban society. Oscar Lewis[28] criticized Redfield's findings; Redfield subsequently reexamined his conclusions and declared that both he and Lewis were right. Redfield later stated that folk ways and urban ways coexist side by side.

Mosaics, Scenes, and Networks

Early writers believed that society was moving along a continuum; that is, that society began as rural and was gradually and continually becoming completely urban. Bender[29] and Fisher[30] point out that this is a totally false assumption, stating that folk and urban ways coexist in time and space.

The concept of community has proved to be elusive. Bender[31] asserts that we have subscribed to a concept that has not existed for hundreds of years, if it ever did. The detrimental effects of this mistake are that city dwellers have had to bear an unnecessary sense of loss that has pushed them in search of something that does not and cannot exist in today's society because with modern communications and transportation, what occurs in one region of the country is felt and known in all other regions.[32] Thus, we cannot return to the isolation of a truly gemeinschaft society.

On the other hand, the contemporary urban community is a patchwork of scenes, networks, and social worlds that have broad implications for government and business. Louis Wirth[33] defines the city as "a relatively large, dense, and permanent settlement of socially heterogeneous individuals." After discussing the city on both a psychological and a sociological level he concludes that the city causes the family to be less significant in a variety of ways and that the city resembles a "mosaic of social worlds" in which people deliberately settle among those who are similar to themselves.

John Irwin[34] avers that people seek out others

with similar views and attitudes for companionship and social fulfillment. He calls these groupings "scenes" and points to certain characteristics of them: (1) the availability of potential sex partners; (2) voluntary recruitment; and (3) an element of risk, either physical or reputational. To make the "scene" is to step on stage and participate in an activity that has direct rewards.

Urban dwellers are also members of networks that cross geographical boundaries.[35] While the family is usually considered nuclear, the extended family still exists—it simply no longer shares the same household. Fisher and Bender both point out that kinship ties are still strong and that when distance is controlled visitation remains the same and family ties stay as strong as ever.

Networks also include occupational groups. Pilcher,[36] in a study of longshoremen in Portland, Oregon, found that they have a distinct lifestyle. They marry each other's sisters and bring friends and family into the union. Other occupational groups tend to develop in the city, including those working in corrections and law enforcement. People also tend to join special interest groups as a means to an end.[37] That is, they supplement friendship and kinship ties by associating with people from other groups while trying not to undermine intimacy with primary groups.

From a nation with roots in farms and small towns the United States has grown to an urban society where over 70 percent of the population lives in urban areas. With urbanization and industrialization have come a host of problems requiring government attention, and among those problems is crime. Meeting the needs of offenders is not easy, especially because old ideas about how to deal with criminals and about the causes of crime do not die easily.

Our attitude toward criminals has evolved from the belief that the offender needs to be separated from the evil influences of the city to the belief that the offender needs to be separated from "good," law-abiding people. The corrections manager needs to understand this change in attitude if he or she is to effectively deal with the community.

Not in My Back Yard (NIMBY)

With the increasing numbers of correctional facilities to accommodate the increasing inmate population, correctional administrators need to be aware of the host of problems they may face in choosing a site for a new facility.

Many administrators have experienced community resistance to correctional institutions being placed in certain areas. For example, citizens of Putney, Vermont, protested because they did not want the tone and reputation of their town altered;[38] residents of Carbondale, Illinois, were apprehensive of how a minimum custody facility would affect their city;[39] and inhabitants of Torrence, California, and North Las Vegas, Nevada, had similar fears about the presence of work-release facilities in their cities.[40]

The objections to correctional facilities can be boiled down to a few:

- fear of increased assaults, rapes, and property crime
- fear that the presence of the facility will keep other businesses away
- fear that property values will decline
- fear that the presence of a prison in the community will place unreasonable demands on local institutions and infrastructure
- fear that the economic strains will outweigh the benefits

Fear of Increased Assaults, Rapes, and Property Crimes

People living near prisons affirm that there is nothing to fear from having such an institution nearby. Yet the fear of increased crime is one of the greatest emotional barriers administrators must overcome. In fact, if a single issue can sink a project, it will be fear of increased crime in the area.

In their investigation of a neighborhood near a Florida prison, Abrams, et al.,[41] found that the respondents reported no direct impact from the prison. Nearly half of the respondents were concerned about personal safety, but they did not attribute their concern to the prison. Jacobs[42] reports that the Vienna Correctional Facility in southern Illinois is well accepted by the community and that while there are criticisms of the "country club" image of the facility, no one voiced a concern for personal safety. Tully, et al., note in their study that "the concern for personal and public security was largely ill-founded."[43] Krause[44] views the site selection process as the initial social interaction out of which the ongoing relationship between facility and community emerges. The key to alleviating community fears is to begin an education program that works through the community elite as well as through community groups and institutions.

Fear that Other Industries Will Stay Away

It isn't fear of the facility that keeps other industries away but rather the fear that the infrastructure cannot accommodate both a large institution and large industry. Considering the proven impact[45] of an institution on the local economy, it is possible that the prison could act as a magnet and attract some industries to the area, particularly those that can support the institution.

Fear that Property Values Will Decline

Other than fear for personal safety, the most frequently cited argument against the location of a facility, be it a large institution or a work-release center, is that it will cause property values to decline. One can easily understand property owners' fear. Certainly the purchase of a home represents a family's largest single investment, and loss of a home's value has repercussions far into the future. Yet evidence suggests that a decline in property values does not necessarily follow the location of a correctional facility in a community. Abrams, et al.,[46] found that property values went up in areas near the Florida prison they studied. Using regression analysis they examined property values in areas near prison facilities and in control areas. When they controlled for differences, they found that prison location did affect property values—positively. Assessed property values in the neighborhood increased from $27 to $35 per 100 feet of frontage.

Fear of Unreasonable Demands on Local Infrastructure

In this day of declining revenue and the inability of some small communities and counties to maintain roads, bridges, and public transportation, citizens are fearful that government will be unable to adequately provide for law-abiding citizens. This is not a problem in an urban community with a diversified economy and population, but in smaller, rural communities with limited resources, any impact can be of consequence. Abrams[47] notes this and states that it is wise to work out arrangements with local institutions before the new institution opens. Presumably, increased revenue to the area in the form of new jobs and purchasing by the institution will generate more taxes to aid in the repair and upgrading of other parts of the infrastructure such as transportation and streets.

The Vienna Correctional Center (VCC) in southern Illinois is very much a part of the local community.[48] The community college teaches courses at the center for both inmates and non-

PART II—The Environment

inmates. The assets of the three banks in the county increased after the center opened. Inmate programs, such as the emergency medical technician training program and ambulance service, are often tied to the needs of the community.

Fear of Economic Strain on Infrastructure

Recently we have witnessed the phenomenon of towns and cities lobbying hard to get correctional facilities located in their areas. Community leaders recognize that the addition of an $8 million annual payroll will provide a significant boost to the local economy. Tully, et al.,[49] found that the Warkworth Institution in Ontario had a significant impact on the local economy and that it could have been greater were it not for federal regulations.

In their study of the Federal Correctional Institution at Loretto, Pennsylvania, Rogers and Haimes[50] completed the most comprehensive study of the impact of a correctional institution on a local economy. They found that the institution's 1985 budget of $19.8 million was quite a stimulus indeed. More than $7.6 million went to firms and individuals within twenty-five miles of Loretto. Included in this sum are 55.8 percent of all nonsalary expenditures, with $5.6 million going to small businesses within twenty-five miles. When one adds an economic multiplier to these figures, it becomes clear that correctional institutions have a strong positive impact on the community.

The Institution as Part of the Community

No organization that purports to serve the community can remain apart from it. Too often correctional institutions make little effort to be part of organized community life.

Jacobs[51] calls our attention to the Vienna Correctional Center and its successful integration into the community. The new warden (who grew up in the area) began by implementing an education campaign and by encouraging townspeople to tour the facility. Purchases for the institution are made locally, and inmates are taken on shopping trips to the town. Those trips resulted in significant spending (according to one store owner purchases by inmates amount to 20 percent[52] of his business). The warden has a personal relationship with the local elite, and there is a strong relationship between the institution and the local junior college. Outsiders volunteer to work at the center in a variety of capacities: they participate in church services, service organizations such as AA/NA, and sports.

Community volunteers play an important role in other institutions as well. Rose[53] points out that a local group called Volunteers in Prison visit inmates and lead workshops at the State Correctional Institution (SCI) in Rockview, Pennsylvania. Wilkinson[54] asserts that failure to maintain good community relations may result in a lack of community support and a concommitant decrease in volunteers. And according to Callison,

> Volunteers are a valuable source of community education, informing other citizens about corrections. They also operate as mediators bringing together correctional personnel and offenders to resolve a common problem. Finally, volunteers serve as sources of information for correctional officials regarding community opinion.[55]

Community-Based Corrections

The value of community-based corrections has long been recognized: we intuitively think of the rehabilitation of inmates and service by citizens when we think of probation or halfway houses. Community-based corrections is defined as a correctional program aimed at meeting the needs of the offender while he or she remains in the community under some form of supervision. Further, such programs take into account the community's need for safety and security. Those programs include probation, parole, work-release centers, halfway houses, and diversion programs. Some authorities even list jails among these programs, but for the purposes of this text, jails will constitute a separate category.

Probation and Parole

Probation and parole originated in the 1800s in both the United States and England. John Augustus of Boston is generally regarded as the father of probation, but Matthew Davenport Hill was performing the same service in Birmingham, England, at about the same time. Alexandre Maconochie is regarded as the father of parole because of his experiment on Norfolk Island with the ticket-of-leave system.

Elements of early diversion and community programs are to be found in the use of recognizance, judicial reprieve, and bail. These types of releases allowed defendants to remain in the community if they promised to appear in court at a future date when ordered to do so. It wasn't until the 1960s that diversion programs increased as critics of the criminal justice system pointed out shortcomings in the system's inability to cope with increasing numbers of defendants, many of whom did not need to be held in jail.

Residential Programs

Halfway houses first arrived on the American scene during the 1800s. It wasn't until Wisconsin passed the Huber Act in 1913 that their possibilities as a tool for criminal rehabilitation began to be recognized. When the U.S. Congress passed the Federal Prisoners Rehabilitation Act in 1965, halfway houses became more wide-spread. The National Institute of Corrections estimates that nearly 700 halfway houses, work-release centers, and restitution centers are presently in operation in the United States.

Elmer Johnson's[56] early and continuing interest in community residential programs is well documented, and others have also investigated their purpose and function. Waldo, Chiricos, and Dobrin[57] investigated the type and extent of inmates' attitudinal change while in work-release programs. They conclude "that there is no discernable improvement in the levels of perceived opportunity, achievement motivation, legal self-concept, and self-esteem expressed by work-release participants."[58] In addition, they point out that work release appears to have a harmful effect upon self-esteem. Waldo and Chiricos[59] have also looked at recidivism and work release in Florida and determined that it does not have any real rehabilitative impact.

Lattessa and Allen[60] investigated halfway houses, their goals, and their objectives on a national level. They conclude that halfway houses may be as effective as any other parole program and strategy and that they may be more cost effective. Mrad, Kabacoff, and Duckro[61] validated Magargee's classification system using the population of a halfway house. They suggest that such a profile would be valuable to community program managers in their efforts to manage inmate populations.

Dowell, Klein, and Krichmar[62] reviewed a group of female residents of a halfway house and compared them with a matched group of parolees who did not receive the benefit of halfway house services. They conclude that release through a halfway house reduced both the number and severity of offenses once the women were released. Latessa and Travis[63] looked at a matched sample of probationers and halfway house residents and found no difference in post-release behavior. They conclude that halfway house placement may be better for some offenders, but that such a placement might best be based on the offender's need rather than on a desire to increase the penalty.

This rather brief summary of halfway houses and their effectiveness illustrates that research on the rehabilitative effectiveness of halfway houses is inconclusive. However, as the populations of correctional institutions climb, halfway houses are used more and more as an alternative to institutionalization. Thus, their visibility in the community will increase,[64] placing a greater burden on staff, and in particular the director or manager, to be part of community life and to vigorously educate the public about the goals and procedures of the organization.

Prisons as a Growth Industry

Much has been said about communities not wanting jails or other correctional facilities in their areas, but the reality is that these institutions create jobs. As a consequence, many communities compete to get a prison located nearby. The local economy was stagnating in Kinross Township, Michigan, which lost Kencheloe Air Force Base in 1977 along with its 15,210 military personnel and 572 civilian workers. The area was revitalized when the Michigan Department of Corrections established a prison on the former air base and then followed up by creating three more facilities in 1987 and 1988.[65] Together the prisons' operating budgets total $55 million per year. The Department of Corrections estimates that for each job in the prisons, three additional jobs are created in the private sector.

After intense competition with other communities in the state, Sparta, Georgia, got a medium-security prison located there.[66] The 750-bed prison provides 350 jobs in an economically depressed county. Florence, Colorado, the site of the largest prison complex ever constructed,[67] had had its ups and downs beginning with the oil and gold booms in 1862, but prisons

(nine at present, not counting the new U.S. Bureau of Prisons complex) have introduced economic stability to the area.

Some communities are deliberately building facilities in order to create income. Sherman County, Oregon,[68] has attempted to construct a regional jail with the intention of renting space in it to other Oregon counties, other states, the U.S. Marshal Service, and the U.S. Bureau of Prisons. Political problems have held up construction, but the sheriff is still trying to sell the idea. Coalinga, California,[69] has opened a 500-bed facility. It was constructed in order to lease beds to the California Department of Corrections and has resulted in considerable income for the city's general fund.

The above examples illustrate many communities' attitude toward jails and prisons. Many people view prisons as nonpolluting industries that contribute to the local economy. With the continuing upward spiral in incarceration rates, more and more communities will most likely view prisons as a good source of income.

Maintaining Community Support

The successful corrections manager is one who is able to help the organization fit into the community. How this is accomplished seems to vary from organization to organization and from manager to manager. By and large, however, institutions that succeed appear to have some traits in common:

- The manager develops mutually beneficial relationships with the media.
- The manager belongs to at least one service organization, such as the Optimists' Club or Kiwanis, allowing her or him to forge relationships with the business community.
- The organization has a speakers' bureau that sends employees into the community

to speak to schools, clubs, and other organizations.

- The organization performs community service. Residents of a work-release center, for example, can clear trails or collect the trash in a local park. A major institution can allow minimum-custody inmates to do volunteer work in the community, or the institution can host appropriate community events on vacant land or in unused buildings.
- The manager encourages members of the community to tour the facility.

Summary

Urbanization is a relatively recent phenomenon. Improved technology enabled early humans to grow surplus food, which in turn encouraged them to live together in relatively permanent settlements. In time as the population increased, the settlements became cities, and various populations began to migrate.

The United States has grown from a few settlements along the Atlantic Ocean to a nation of over 250 million. Our cities are overburdened and in many instances unable to meet the needs of their inhabitants. Crime is viewed as an urban phenomenon, and people often use that fear to justify blocking the opening of a correctional facility. They fear that the status quo will be disturbed and feel threatened by the presence of "criminals" in their neighborhoods.

The corrections manager must often work very hard to win and maintain the community's acceptance of a facility. The manager must be part of the community, encourage tours of the facility, and cultivate relationships that will benefit the organization.

Reviewing the Case

It is often difficult to establish a community corrections program. Usually everyone agrees that such programs are a necessary part of community life, but few want them in their neighborhoods. Executive Director Janet Mason knows that she may have lost the fight. She knows that she made a mistake in not personally speaking to each one of the facility's future neighbors. However, she can still pursue litigation, but to do that she needs to arm herself with pertinent data on how the facility affects its neighbors. Now that preliminary measures have failed, she and her board need to decide whether to invest additional money in the project and to pursue litigation. They need to ask themselves and each other the following questions:

- What is the probability that the court will reach a favorable decision?
- Are there other suitable sites that may be acquired for less cost and effort?
- Can officials educate the neighborhood residents and ask for a rehearing?

For Further Study

Thomas Bender, *Community and Social Change in America* (Baltimore: Johns Hopkins University Press, 1978).

George O. Rogers and Marshall Haimes, "Local Impact of a Low Security Federal Correctional Institution," *Federal Probation* (September 1987), pp. 28–34.

Louis Wirth, "Urbanization as a Way of Life," *American Journal of Sociology*, Vol. 44 (July 1938).

Key Terms

Urban Transformation	**Probation**
Gesellschaft	**Gemeinschaft**
NIMBY	**City Defined**

The Impact of the Courts and the Media on the Correctional Organization

Case Study: The Public Information Officer and the Media

I once overheard two reporters making bets on which of the state's prisons would first erupt in violence during the upcoming summer.[1] What made it worse was that the betting occurred during a speech by the secretary of the Department of Public Safety on what was being done to improve the prison system.

Police and emergency room personnel have a mystical belief in the power of a full moon to cause problems. Newsroom assignment editors also seem to have such beliefs, but for them it is a hot sun that begins to scorch the deteriorating, overcrowded prisons. Lookouts who scan the horizon for smoke rising from within the walls are posted everywhere. I was headed home on a hot July night when I was notified that inmates in the maximum-security penitentiary had taken control of a housing unit. They had keys, radios, guns, and hostages.

Planning my strategy on the way, I knew I would need to use the advice given me during my first prison riot. I was a state trooper, sitting quietly at headquarters, when I was dispatched to handle the role of spokesman at the penitentiary, where a full-scale riot had just occurred. The only thing I knew about prison was that it was the place I hoped most of the people I arrested would be sent.

The secretary of the Department of Public Safety met me there and said simply, "Speak in general terms. Details will be changing. Be general." Later, the governor arrived for a briefing. After learning that the situation was under control he said, "Our priority must be to assure the public they are safe." The advice worked then and I believed it would work now.

The key is to respond. Good reporters have a multitude of sources. Whether it's an inmate on the phone, a disgruntled employee, or a prison neighbor who just saw fifty state troopers drive by, the media will have at least one version of the story.

Your response will set the record straight. It will also have a calming effect on reporters frantically searching for someone to talk to before their next live shot. More importantly, your response will affect the public's view of both the situation and your department.

Either way, the media will convey a message to their audience. You, of course, will not have ultimate control of the way the message is presented, but you can have an effect on it. If you do not aggressively respond to reporters, or if you give incorrect information about details that shouldn't be discussed anyway, the public will sense your insecurity and likely give more credence to some other source, such as the inmate on the phone. However, if you respond in a calm, articulate, reassuring manner with general information underscored with the theme of public safety as your number one priority, your message will get through. Although the media coverage of the hostage situation was intense, the message was the same: "The situation is confined to one building. An inner and outer perimeter is established to guarantee it stays that way. The rest of the prison is locked down and secure. There have been no escapes and the public is in no danger. There are enough correctional officers and state troopers ready to handle whatever situation may arise, although we certainly want this to be resolved peacefully."

Remember, not only are the media conveying your message to the public, they are beaming your report live to the inmates involved in the incident. It's important that both audiences recognize that your side is in control. An unusual example of this concept occurred during the hostage situation. Eighteen hours after the incident began, one officer was still being held, and the inmate negotiators were demanding access to the media. Prison officials had no desire to give them access while they had a hostage.

A state police negotiator recalled a policy established by some of the local television stations several years ago. They agreed that they would not interview hostage takers while hostages were still being held. Officials believed this could work to their advantage.

The inmate negotiators were told the media would be brought in to talk with them, but only if they came out with the hostage. The inmates agreed to this and returned to the building to inform the others of the proposal.

This is certainly a moment to savor as a spokesman. You face more than thirty reporters, who have been desperately trying to see over the prison walls, and tell them you'll take them inside—if they want to go. To say that a deafening silence fell upon the crowd would be an understatement.

Surrounded by armed correctional officers, the group was moved into the prison yard, in full view of the inmates. The prison administration had kept its word. The largest group of reporters to ever tour the penitentiary stood ready to listen to the inmates. All they had to do was release the hostage.

It didn't work. At least, it didn't work immediately. The inmate negotiators were unable to sell it to the rest of the inmates. Some of them, appearing at the windows in ghoulish hoods, called for specific reporters to be sent inside the building for interviews. Officials wouldn't have let that happen, but the reporters themselves made it clear to the inmates that there would be no interviews without the release of the hostage.

Without warning, the reporters were escorted out of the prison. The inmates had missed their chance. They called the bluff of prison officials and lost. Less than two hours later, the inmates gave up. The hostage, who was released unharmed, credits the surrender to the effective use of the media.

Of course, no matter how prepared you are, you'll never be able to answer all the questions. Following the hostage situation, the inmates involved were housed in tents in the prison yard while their building was searched. One afternoon, they decided to loosen the poles and collapse the tents.

The media arrived en masse, convinced that another

reign of terror was underway. Trying to emphasize the less-than-serious nature of this action, I remarked that inmates had been seen singing and dancing in the middle of the yard. "What song were they singing?" asked one earnest reporter.

Introduction

Two institutions in the United States have been instrumental in shaping the course of corrections and the way corrections is viewed by the public—the courts and the media. They may seem like strange bedfellows at first glance, but their importance cannot be overestimated, and the effective manager must understand both. Indeed, as Crouch and Marquart[2] observe, when outside observers such as courts, media, legislators, or ordinary citizens fail to attend to what is going on in a correctional organization, administrative concerns for expediency and control create unacceptable conditions.

The courts are an important part of the correctional process. Not only do they sentence offenders to institutions or place them on probation, they also have been pivotal to many important innovations in corrections. For example, it's doubtful that the institutional disciplinary process would have evolved as it did without prodding from the courts. Of critical importance to bringing about change in corrections has been Section 1983 of Title 42 of the U.S. Code, which states:

§ 1983. Civil action for deprivation of rights
Every person who, under color of any statute, ordinance, regulation, custom, or usage, of any State or Territory or the District of Columbia, subjects, or causes to be subjected, any citizen of the United States or other person within the jurisdiction thereof to the deprivation of any rights, privileges, or immunities secured by the Constitution and laws, shall be liable to the party injured in an action at law, suit in equity, or other proper proceeding for redress. For the pur-

poses of this section, any Act of Congress applicable exclusively to the District of Columbia shall be considered to be a statute of the District of Columbia.

Prisoners seeking redress for many grievances have successfully invoked Section 1983 and brought about needed change. (The ruling's profound effects are described throughout the first part of this chapter.) Many other such changes have been brought about over the past thirty years because of the influence of the courts.

The media are another important aspect of the correctional agency's external environment. The media have chronicled the influence of the courts and thus provided a service to the taxpayer. They have also thoroughly documented the reluctance of many corrections executives to comply with the edicts of the courts. Today the media are under attack by critics who have charged them with either one-sided reporting or attempting to sway public opinion. However, when it comes to criminal justice issues, the media only report what they are told. We therefore need to ask ourselves: "Are we telling the whole truth to the media?"

This chapter explores the influence of the courts and the media on the corrections agency.

The Courts

Ronald Goldfarb[3] presents an excellent discussion of the courts and their impact on jails and prisons. He points out that "as recently as ... [1965] courts generally denied any responsibility for supervising the treatment of jail inmates."[4] The noninterventionist attitude of the courts slowly changed, and during the 1960s Supreme Court cases began to show a growing inclination to become involved with the grievances of prisoners.

During the 1960s a number of legal questions were addressed in cases such as *Mapp v. Ohio*,[5] *Escobedo v. Illinois*,[6] and *Miranda v. Arizona*[7] that ultimately changed law enforcement for the better. Several cases reviewed by the U.S. Supreme Court in the early 1960s also affected corrections. The first, *Monroe v. Pape*,[8] ruled that the Court has a right to hear claims of interference with federally protected rights by state authorities regardless of whether the individual had exhausted state remedies. Three cases heard in 1963 (*Fay v. Noia*,[9] *Townsend v. Sain*,[10] and *Sanders v. the United States*[11]) all expanded prisoners' right to relief despite their not having exhausted state remedies. The Court further held that state prisoners are entitled to redress in federal court when aggrieved by unconstitutional detentions. Perhaps most important, the Court held that "conventional notions of finality of litigation have no place where life or liberty is at stake and infringement of constitutional rights is alleged."[12] *Cooper v. Pate*[13] was similar in focus but specifically held that state prisoners are entitled to the protection of the Fourteenth Amendment.

The Legal Process

Archambeault and Archambeault[14] point out that the processes of passing correctional law differ significantly from the processes associated with normal legislation. Normally, (1) bills are introduced via lobbying or through the efforts of some special interest group; (2) the proposed legislation is debated; (3) the legislation is vetoed or signed into law by the governor or president; (4) the law is enforced or applied; (5)

the law's constitutionality is challenged; and (6) if the law is upheld, step four is repeated; if it is declared unconstitutional, it must return to step two for modification. Figure 4.1 illustrates the process.

According to Archambeault and Archambeault, the processes of passing correctional law are not quite so democratic. In normal processes, public opposition or interference by special interest groups can kill the bill at several points. This is not the case with correctional law, where lobbying and special interest groups play a very small part and laws are changed largely as an administrative matter. Figure 4.2 illustrates this process. Archambeault and Archambeault state that it is a unique "feature of correctional law that, as they attempt to make rulings more specific, courts tend to generate new issues and new litigation, for each specific ruling poses the possibility that the same principle might apply in another specific set of circumstances."[15]

FIGURE 4.1
Normal Law Making Process

Lobbying
Passed by the legislature
Signed by the Chief Executive
Enforced
Tested in court
Upheld or return to step 2

FIGURE 4.2
Offender Litigation and Court Order

Appeals process
Signed by the Chief Executive
Signed into law
Put into effect
New litigation

There is a six-step process to correctional law making:

1. An offender (or employee) or a class action lawsuit gains access to a court and alleges some grievance that is upheld by the court. The court issues an order or opinion. (The point should also be made that much correctional law is initiated via the normal legislative process.)
2. The lower court decision is challenged in a higher court, with only a very few of the cases reaching the Supreme Court. The original decision is upheld, modified, or reversed.
3. In response to court orders or expected court litigation, legislative bodies write laws that will minimize future court involvement. State and local rules and regulations are modified.
4. Where new legislation is concerned, the executive usually signs the bill without delay.
5. The new legislation is then put into effect.
6. The new ruling or the new law or the new change in rules becomes the basis for new litigation, and the whole process may be repeated.[16]

Thus, corrections law often evolves along a different dimension than normal law. Prisons, inmates, and prison staff have few champions outside the system, and as a consequence, courts, agencies, and inmates are often the initiators of law.

There are many court decisions that affect the management of correctional agencies, but this chapter is not the place to review all of them. However some aspects of case law highlight the progression from the charismatic approach to correctional management to the due process approach. Of particular importance are decisions in the areas of cruel and unusual punishment, religion, freedom of expression, and inmate discipline.

Cruel and Unusual Punishment

Until the 1960s the courts refused to review punishments inflicted upon prisoners.[17] The Eighth Amendment points out that excessive bail or fines shall not be imposed and that cruel and unusual punishment shall not be inflicted on any person. Generally speaking, the courts had taken the position that institutions should be left to themselves without interference from the courts. On the surface it seems peculiar that even though the Eighth Amendment is directly applicable to prisoners, it took the Supreme Court more than 150 years to get around to reviewing the punishment of criminals. In reality it is not peculiar at all. The amendments to the U.S. Constitution were written to guide, or hold in check, the behavior of the federal government. Only when the Supreme Court's approach to jails and prisons evolved from nonactivist to activist did prisoners become full beneficiaries of the equal protection clauses of the Fourteenth Amendment.

It is obvious that changes in the management of prisons and jails followed the courts' review of claims of cruel and unusual punishment. In *Sweeny v. Woodall* (1952)[18] and *Dye v. Johnson* (1949)[19] the defendants argued that their being remanded to prison after escaping confinement in Alabama and Georgia respectively constituted cruel and unusual punishment. While both were returned to custody, Justice Douglas in his dissent stated:

> [Assuming] the allegations of the petition are true, this Negro must suffer torture and mutilization, or risk death itself to get relief in Alabama. . . . I rebel at the thought that any human being, Negro or white, should be forced to run a gamut of blood and terror in order to get his Constitutional rights. . . . The enlightened view is indeed the other way.[20]

Indeed Justice Douglas was pointing the way. In 1966 in *Jordan v. Fitzharris*[21] a federal district judge held a hearing at the Soledad Correctional Training Facility in California to determine the truth of a prisoner's charges that he had been held in a strip cell as punishment for twelve days without "adequate heat, light or ventilation, without bedding, clothing, adequate medical care or any means of keeping himself clean."[22] The court was convinced and issued a permanent injunction against the imposition of cruel and unusual punishment as a part of solitary confinement.

One year later the Court of Appeals for the Second Circuit held that if inmates could prove that they had been subjected to "debasing conditions," they would have established that their rights under the Eighth Amendment had been violated.[23] In *Sostre v. Rockefeller*[24] a prisoner spent thirteen months in solitary confinement. He was forbidden to use the library, read newspapers, see movies, or attend classes. The court found that the New York Department of Corrections had gone beyond the limits of tolerance in this instance and stated that subjecting a prisoner to the potential loss of sanity constituted cruel and unusual punishment. However, upon appeal the decision was reversed because the prisoner was allowed to practice rudimentary hygiene and was given a reasonable diet and daily outdoor exercise and allowed to communicate with other prisoners. Thus, we begin to see the parameters for the use of segregation beginning to take shape. In this case, however, the court refused to put a limit on how long a prisoner could be confined.

One issue that concerns corrections administrators is overcrowding. *Holt v. Sarver* was the first case on this subject to be considered. In this case, the majority ruled that:

> [T]he prolonged confinement of numbers of men in the same cell under the conditions that have been described is mentally and emotionally traumatic as well as physically uncomfortable. It is hazardous to health; it is degrading and de-

basing; it offends modern sensibilities, and in the court's estimation, amounts to cruel and unusual punishment.[25]

The practice of "double bunking" has also come under attack, but litigation has failed to bring a halt to the practice. In fact, in *Bell v. Wolfish*[26] the Court held that certain individual constitutional freedoms must be reduced to accommodate the prison's duty to protect all, and in *Rhodes v. Chapman* it held that other unwholesome conditions besides double bunking must be present to argue cruel and unusual punishment.

Religion

Most Americans are willing to go to extreme lengths to protect their right to practice their faith. However, prisons and jails have in many instances flagrantly denied inmates the opportunity to worship as they choose.

Courts distinguish between an inmate's right to religious beliefs and his or her right to engage in religious practices. In *Long v. Parker* the court stated: "Within the prison society as well as without, the practice of religious beliefs is subject to reasonable regulations, necessary for the protection and welfare of the community involved."[27]

Many cases involving freedom of religion have revolved around the Nation of Islam. During the late 1960s and early 1970s this group wrested a measure of freedom of worship from prisons and jails, whose unwillingness to grant such freedom must be seen in the context of the times. The late 1960s and early 1970s were a period of great social upheaval. Student demonstrations, riots in the cities, and the assassinations of beloved political figures all combined to create an exceedingly threatening situation to many criminal justice workers. Thus, when a group professing hatred for whites demanded the right to practice a religion that legitimized hostility against whites, few corrections workers (black or white) were willing to go along with them. Attitudes today have moderated, and nearly every correctional institution has a Muslim minister on call.

While *Cooper v. Pate*[28] (1964) decided that inmates retain their right to worship, it wasn't until 1972 that the matter was brought sharply into focus. The ruling in *Cruz v. Beto* (1972) states:

> A special chapel or place of worship need not be provided for every faith regardless of size, nor must a chaplain, priest or minister be provided without regard for the extent of the demand, but reasonable opportunities must be afforded to all prisoners to exercise the religious freedom guaranteed by the First and Fourteenth Amendments without fear of penalty.[29]

Following *Cruz v. Beto*, correctional administrators began looking at policies and procedures regarding the observance of religious beliefs. As a result, most, if not all, systems have developed procedures that allow inmates access to ministers of their choice.

Freedom of Expression

Prison authorities were once largely free to censor inmates' communication and speech if they could prove that such communications were detrimental to the tranquility of the institution. However, since 1970 nearly every corrections system has developed policies and procedures that allow inmates unrestricted access to courts, attornies of record, and federal- and state-elected officials. A certain degree of contact with the media is also allowed. Since 1970 the court has intervened to protect these rights.

Sostre v. Otis[30] determined that prison authorities cannot screen literature without notice to a prisoner that literature addressed to him has been censored or withheld; an opportunity to present arguments, either oral or written, in favor of a finding that the literature is acceptable; and a decision by a body that can be expected to act fairly.

The court has also forbidden prison and jail officials to open or read incoming mail other than to inspect it for contraband.[31]

Figure 4.3 shows the U.S. Bureau of Prisons' policy statement on contact with the media. Contact between inmates and the media is authorized, but only under certain conditions. The policy statement and procedures (not shown) assure institutional tranquility and privacy of inmates and staff.

Inmate Discipline

No area of correctional management has undergone such revolutionary change as inmate discipline. Prior to 1970 few institutions (jails or prisons) published a handbook for inmates specifying rules and their sanctions. Today nearly all prisons and jails have such a publication; some even have videotaped such messages, which are viewed via closed-circuit television.

This has been a necessary change. As Goldfarb points out, "Even where written rules exist, they may be so vague as to be meaningless. One pervasive regulation outlaws any manifestation of 'disrespect' toward correctional officers."[32] Similar vagueness in the rules existed in all areas of inmate conduct and in all corrections systems around the nation.

During the 1970s things began to change. In *Sostre v. Rockefeller*[33] the court held that even though a person is incarcerated, he or she continues to retain the right to procedural due process. More important, in *Morris v. Travisono*[34] prison officials agreed to a number of procedures to govern disciplinary hearings. Among them were required

1. a written charge by the employee or officer,
2. a hearing before a disciplinary board, and

3. an automatic review of the record by the warden.

This important decision became the linchpin of prison discipline. No longer could officers

---

FIGURE 4.3
Bureau of Prisons P/S on Contact with the Media

---

1. *Purpose and Scope §540.60.* The Bureau of Prisons recognizes the desirability of establishing a policy that affords the public information about its operations via the news media. Representatives of the news media (see §540.2) may visit institutions for the purpose of preparing reports about the institution, programs, and activities. It is not the intent of this rule to provide publicity for an inmate or special privileges for the news media, but rather to insure a better-informed public. The Bureau of Prisons also has a responsibility to protect the privacy and other rights of inmates and members of the staff. Therefore, an interview in an institution must be regulated to insure the orderly and safe operation of the institution.
2. Directives Affected.
   a. P.S. 1480.1 (N.S.) News Media, Contacts with, is superseded.
   b. Rules cited in this statement are contained in 28 CFR 540.2 and 450.60–65.
3. *Definitions §540.2(b).* "Representatives of the news media" means persons whose principal employment is to gather or report news for:
   a. A newspaper which qualifies as a general circulation newspaper in the community in which it is published. A newspaper is one of "general circulation" if it circulates among the general public and if it publishes news of a general character of general interest. A key test to determine whether a newspaper qualifies as a "general circulation" newspaper is to determine whether the paper qualifies for the purpose of publishing legal notices in the community in which it is located or the area to which it distributes. It is generally held that for a newspaper to be considered, by law, a newspaper of general circulation, and so be qualified to publish legal notices, it must contain items of general interest to the public such as news of political, religious, commercial or social affairs;
   b. A news magazine which has a national circulation and is sold by newstands and by mail subscription to the general public;
   c. A national or international news service; or
   d. A radio or television news program of a station holding a Federal Communications Commission license.

   These rules apply to inmates in federal institutions. When a federal prisoner is confined in any nonfederal facility the local or state facility rules and regulations will govern.

4. *Authorization §540.61.*
   a. A news media representative who desires to make a visit or conduct an interview at an institution must make application in writing to the Warden indicating that he or she is familiar with the rules and regulations of the institution and agrees to comply with them.

   This will be accomplished by the use of an agreement similar to Attachment 1.
   b. As a condition of authorizing interviews and making facilities available to conduct an interview, the news media representative shall recognize a professional responsibility to make reasonable attempts to verify any allegations regarding inmate, staff member or institution.
   c. A representative of the news media is requested to provide the Bureau of Prisons an opportunity to respond to any allegation, which might be published or broadcast prior to distribution.
   d. A representative of the news media shall collect information only from a primary source. A representative of the news media may not obtain and use personal information from one inmate about another inmate who refuses to be interviewed.
   e. The Warden may be contacted concerning discussions or comments regarding applicability of any rule or order.
   f. Failure to adhere to the standards of conduct set forth in this policy by the news media representative constitutes grounds for denying that news media representative, or the news organization which he or she represents, permission to conduct an interview.
   g. Any questions as to the meaning or application of this subpart are resolved by the Director of the Bureau of Prisons.

and managers arbitrarily and capriciously enforce an often ill-defined set of rules. Instead, officials began to be required to adhere to due process requirements that allow the inmate to present the facts as he or she determines those facts to be.

In 1974 *Wolff v. McDonnell*[35] found that some adjustment in due process requirements for infractions of a less serious nature may be necessary to institutional security. *Wolff v. McDonnell* also established the due process procedure that is followed by institutional disciplinary boards or committees if an inmate is likely to lose earned good time or be punished with segregation.

Largely because of *Wolff v. McDonnell*, most systems today have a disciplinary process that includes:

1. a written statement of the charges by an employee who has witnessed the incident or who has knowledge of a violation of the rules (a copy is given to the inmate);
2. an investigation by a senior officer or supervisor;
3. a formal hearing according to due process requirements:
   a. determination that the inmate understands the charges
   b. plea of guilty or not guilty
   c. the right to representation by a staff person
   d. the right to call witnesses;
4. notice of action taken;
5. an appeal process; and
6. a time element for all steps.

The U.S. Bureau of Prisons has a well-defined policy on inmate discipline. The policy statement, which is summarized in figure 4.4, is quite detailed and stretches to eleven chapters, including procedures, prohibited acts, sanctions, appeal procedures, and appropriate forms.

Many changes in corrections were mandated by the courts. For nearly 200 years the courts had remained uninvolved with prisons, jails, and probation and parole. In the early 1950s and especially during the civil rights movement of the 1960s, prisons in particular began to feel the force of due process. Through court decisions in a number of areas, but particularly those affecting religious freedom; freedom of expression; inmate discipline; and issues involving allegations of cruel and unusual punishment, jails and prisons began to institute policies and procedures that incorporated due process requirements. These requirements also extended to probationers and parolees.

Change is never easy, and in a large bureaucracy it is often painful. The transformation of the Texas Department of Correction (TDC) is an example of how an organization can be dragged, kicking and screaming, into compliance with court-ordered change. By the end of a class action trial begun on October 2, 1978, and ending September 20, 1979, relations between Judge William W. Justice and the TDC had become so strained that Judge Justice appointed a special master to oversee mandated reform.[36] There were many legal fights and a good deal of resistance, but according to Crouch and Marquart, Texas prisons were brought into compliance. One important sidelight of the Texas litigation is that it served to "homogenize" institutional corrections. Evidence suggests that changes occurred in other parts of the country because executives recognized the potential applicability of the same case law to their own situations.[37]

Regardless of grumbling from both administrators and the rank and file, the courts have ensured the livability of institutions; they have assured inmates, probationers, and parolees that they will be treated with dignity; and perhaps most important, in instances where managers have made an effort to comply with due process requirements, they have shielded these

FIGURE 4.4
Bureau of Prisons P/S on Inmate Discipline

1. Purpose and Scope §541.10.
   a. So that inmates may live in a safe and orderly environment, it is necessary for institution authorities to impose discipline on those inmates whose behavior is not in compliance with Bureau of Prisons rules. The provisions of these rules apply to all persons committed to the care, custody, and control (direct or constructive) of the Bureau of Prisons.

Examples of persons to whom this policy applies include, but are not limited to, an inmate who is on pretrial status, or on writ, or on escorted trip or furlough, or who is escorted by U.S. Marshals or other federal law enforcement, or who is in a camp, contract facility (other than contract CTCs) or hospital, or who is returned to Bureau custody from a contract facility (includes contract CTCs). These provisions do not apply to a federal inmate designated to a nonfederal facility (e.g., inmates serving federal sentences in state facilities or contract CTCs).

   b. The following general principles apply in every disciplinary action taken:
      (1) Only institution staff may take disciplinary action.

   The term institution staff ordinarily refers to Bureau of Prisons employees. Any exception to this provision may be made only with the prior written approval of the Regional Director.
   In contract CTCs, Community Programs Managers have the authority to take disciplinary action as specified in the Community Programs Manual.

      (2) Staff shall take disciplinary action at such times and to the degree necessary to regulate an inmate's behavior within Bureau rules and institution guidelines and to promote a safe and orderly institution environment.
      (3) Staff shall control inmate behavior in a completely impartial and consistent manner.
      (4) Disciplinary action may not be capricious or retaliatory.
      (5) Staff may not impose or allow imposition of corporal punishment of any kind.
      (6) If it appears at any stage of the disciplinary process that an inmate is mentally ill, staff shall refer the inmate to a mental health professional for determination of whether the inmate is responsible for his conduct or is incompetent. Staff may take no disciplinary action against an inmate whom mental health staff determines to be incompetent or not responsible for his conduct.
         (a) A person is not responsible for his conduct if, at the time of the conduct, the person, as a result of a severe mental disease or defect, was unable to appreciate the nature and quality or the wrongfulness of his acts. When a person is determined not responsible for his conduct, the Incident Report is to show as a finding that the person did not commit the prohibited act because that person was found not to be mentally responsible for his conduct.

         The Incident Report is to be retained in the inmate central file. The Discipline Hearing Officer (DHO) or the Unit Discipline Committee (UDC), if it takes final action, shall record the DHO or UDC finding that the person was not responsible for his conduct on the Chronological Disciplinary Record form located in the inmate central file.

         (b) A person is incompetent if that person lacks the ability to understand the nature of the disciplinary proceedings, or to assist in his defense at the proceedings. When a person is determined incompetent, the disciplinary proceedings shall be postponed until such time as the inmate is able to understand the nature of the disciplinary proceedings and to assist in his defense at those proceedings. If competency is not restored within a reasonable period of time, the Incident Report is to show as a finding that the inmate is incompetent to assist in his or her defense at the disciplinary proceedings.

         The Incident Report is to be retained in the inmate central file. The DHO or the UDC chairman shall record the finding that the person was determined incompetent on the Chronological Disciplinary Record form located in the inmate central file.

It is generally the UDC which initiates referral to the appropriate mental health professional. Where this occurs, the completed mental health evaluation is to be returned to the UDC. The UDC will then decide whether the incident may be handled by the UDC (other than greatest severity), or whether it should be referred to the DHO. In Greatest Severity cases, the UDC may refer an inmate for a mental health evaluation concurrently with the required referral to the Discipline Hearing Officer. The completed evaluation is to be returned to the UDC, who will then forward it to the DHO.

      (7) Accurate, detailed reports of disciplinary actions shall be maintained in accordance with the requirements of this Program Statement.

agencies from costly litigation and settlements.

If the courts have shaped the direction of corrections over the past thirty years, the media have helped shaped public opinion about corrections. Reporters and corrections officials often blame each other for their problems, and each often fails to understand the other's job or even the other's value to society. The remainder of this chapter explores the role of the media and how the corrections executive can use the media to educate and inform the public about emergencies and everyday operations.

The Media

If a single institution in American life were chosen as correctional executives' strongest ally and best friend, then the media would have to be it. Unfortunately, most corrections executives view the media as the enemy or at least as a necessary evil to be avoided whenever possible.[38] This is unfortunate, because the media enable the manager to convey the message of the agency. That is, corrections is a public endeavor funded by taxes for the purpose of protecting the public and carrying out punishments administered by the courts. Taxpayers are paying the bills, and they deserve to be told how their money is being spent.

On the other hand, Public Information Officers (PIO's) complain that the media are often ill-informed. In a 1988 survey of fifty prison PIO's[39] it was revealed that most of the respondents believed the media gave short shrift to inmate programs and more coverage to riots and disturbances. While they acknowledged that the latter are more newsworthy, they correctly insist that the former deserve attention as well. In addition, they complained that not enough attention is given to analysis and investigative projects. PIO's are also concerned with how reporters cover stories. That is, reporters often perpetuate the "Hollywood myth" of prisons; they only report the inmate side of the story and, in general, mislead the public. PIO's offered these suggestions for improving news coverage of corrections:

- Reporters should have a broad knowledge of corrections.
- Reporters should make more frequent on-site visits.
- Reporters should work more closely with information officers to avoid misinformation and to strive for accuracy.

What seems to frighten and even anger some corrections managers is that many reporters ask questions that require honest answers and are sometimes obnoxiously persistent. This conflict is understandable, because it is the reporter's job to get answers and the manager's job to refuse to answer if necessary. On the other hand, the media are an excellent vehicle to garner public support and spread good news. The truth is that in the smaller markets at least, the media will publish or broadcast news on just about anything, often without a comment from those directly concerned. This is why it is important that the manager or PIO promptly return calls from the media, especially in regard to a good story such as a disturbance.

The Media as a Management Tool

Many agencies have a well-developed policy that regulates inmate-media contact. However, very few regular contacts are initiated between the media and the CEO of an agency or institution.

Reporters who are given regular access to an institution, for example, become acquainted with programs, staff, and policies. Such contact can prove valuable in the event of inmate claims of unfair or brutal treatment at the hands of staff.[40] Regular contact can be accomplished by

FIGURE 4.5
Important Court Decisions Affecting Corrections—1964–1990*

Cooper v. Pate, 378 U.S. 546 (1964)
  Freedom of Religion is retained by the inmate.
Cruz v. Beto, 405 U.S. 319, 31 L. Ed. 2d 263 (1972).
  Establishment of religion clause review and review of exercise of religious beliefs without impairing security of the
  institution.
Johnson v. Glick, 481 F.2d 1028 (2d Cir. 1973).
  The court held that necessary and reasonable force may be used to prevent disorder or to restore order, discipline, and
  security.
Pell v. Procunier, 417 U.S. 817, 41 L. Ed. 2d 495, 95 S. Ct. 2800 (1974).
  An inmate retains those constitutional rights that are not inconsistent with his or her status as a prisoner.
Procunier v. Martinez, 416 U.S. 396, 94 S. Ct. 1800, 40 L. Ed. 2d 224 (1974).
  Two-pronged censorship test for mail to or from community
  a. does not show interference with right to freedom of expression, and
  b. security must be upheld and institution is not bound to pass on mail that shows knowledge of a crime.
Wolff v. McDonnell, 419 U.S. 539, 94 S. Ct. 2963, 41 L. Ed. 2d 935 (1974).
  Established the due process procedure required for purposes of discipline of an inmate if the sanction imposed loss of
  good time that the inmate earned to reduce his or her period of confinement or placement in segregation as
  punishment. The court also recognized less due process for less serious sanctions and a need for "mutual
  accommodations between institutional needs and protection afforded the individual by the constitution."
Estelle v. Gamble, 429 U.S. 97 S. Ct. 285, 50 L. Ed. 2d 251 (1976).
  A Texas inmate complained that he suffered a back injury performing prison work and that prison authorities were
  indifferent to his complaints. The court found that the authorities were not indifferent in this case but emphatically
  stated that the government has an obligation to provide medical care for those whom it is punishing via incarceration.
Bounds v. Smith, 430 U.S. 817, 97 S. Ct. 1491, 52 L. Ed. 2d 72 (1977).
  The Court held that prisons are bound to provide legal assistance to inmates in the form of:
  1. Adequate legal libraries and/or encouragement to experiment with new ways to promote legal assistance in order to
      assure inmates access to Courts.
  2. Indigent inmates are to be provided with adequate paper, pencils, stamps, and notarial services.
Jones v. North Carolina Prisoners' Labor Union, Inc., 433 U.S. 119, 97 S. Ct. 2532, 53 L. Ed. 2d 629 (1977).
  Established that prisoners could not collectively bargain and could not form a union because of the "reasonable" belief
  of the danger this could cause to security and the orderly operation of an institution.
Bell v. Wolfish, 441 U.S. 559, 99 S. Ct. 1984, 60 L. Ed. 2d 481 (1981).
  The court recognized that certain individual Constitutional freedoms must be reduced to accommodate the need of
  the prison to protect all.
Rhodes v. Chapman, 452 U.S. 337, 101 S. Ct. 2392, 69 L. Ed. 2d 59 (1981).
  No right to a single cell; the prisoner must have other complaints in order to prove cruel and unusual punishment.
Hewitt v. Helms, 459 U.S. 460, 103 S. Ct. 864, 74 L. Ed. 2d 675 (1983).
  Pennsylvania inmate claimed that authorities had no right to confine him to administrative segregation and that such
  segregation violated his right to due process. The court held that the inmate had no right to be housed among the
  general prison population and that prison administrators should have discretion in execution of policies that preserve
  institutional order, discipline, and security.
Block v. Rutherford, 104 S. Ct. 3227 (1984).
  a. County jails' blanket prohibition against contact visits is an entirely reasonable response to security concerns and
      consistent with the Fourteenth Amendment.
  b. The practice of conducting random, irregular shakedown searches of cells in the absence of the prisoner is a
      reasonable response to legitimate security concerns and not a violation of due process.
Hudson v. Palmer, 468 U.S. 517, 104 S. Ct. 3194, 82 L. Ed. 2d 393 (1984).
  There is no legitimate expectation of privacy in the prisoners' individual cells that would entitle them to Fourteenth
  Amendment protections. Staff may search an inmate's cell at any time for any reason.
Thornburgh v. Abbott, et al., 490 U.S. 401, 104 L. Ed. 2d 459, 109 S. Ct. 1874 (1989).
  Upheld prison regulations prohibiting incoming publications or any incoming correspondence sent by prisoners or
  nonprisoners as such regulations do not violate First Amendment rights if such regulations are reasonably related to
  legitimate concerns for institutional tranquility.

*This list was composed by Mr. Charles Faulkner, Regional Counsel, North Central Region, U.S. Bureau of Prisons.

hosting an open house for the media two or three times a year. An alternative is that the CEO or his or her representative hold periodic press conferences.

Law enforcement more than corrections appears to be aware of the need to work with the press. President Robert W. Landon of the International Association of Chiefs of Police agrees that "an adversarial relationship need not exist between the media and law enforcement and, if it should exist . . . it can be overcome."[41] He points out that it is the reporter's job to ferret out information with or without the help of the agency. Furthermore, Chief Landon asserts that we cannot consider media relations as a form of damage control to be put into action only when there is a problem.

Getting Along with the Media

One way of getting along with the media is to appoint a public information officer. This may not be possible in smaller agencies or institutions, so in these cases it will be up to the director, chief probation officer, or warden to deal with reporters. Appointing a PIO has both advantages and disadvantages. One advantage is that the PIO can shield the CEO from the media and thus free her or him to concentrate on the task at hand. Second, the presence of a PIO will protect the CEO from the charge of being uncooperative with the media. Disadvantages include the risk that the PIO will appear uncooperative by withholding information in the event of a disturbance or unusual incident.

Choosing a PIO is relatively simple in theory but difficult in fact. In a nutshell, the PIO must be intelligent, articulate, and attractive and have a sound grasp of both the workings of the media, criminal justice, and the organization. In reality, the midlevel staff often take on the position of PIO as ordered. In some agencies the job may be given to someone who has

worked for the media and has caught the eye of the CEO. At the institutional level, or the chief probation officer level, the executive assistant to the warden or chief will often function as the PIO. The individuals in those positions may or may not do well, and when they fail to do an adequate job, the agency and the public suffer.

According to Arthur F. Nehrbass,[42] the PIO's most effective functions are "set-up and screening." The PIO should be the individual to whom routine requests for statistics and other information are routed. He or she should also handle all arrangements for press conferences and be responsible for all press releases.

Nehrbass gives some valuable tips on how to ensure accurate and effective media coverage.

1. Use the PIO to screen all inquiries. Routine requests can be handled by the PIO, but all inquiries of a policy nature can be routed to the appropriate staff member; answers can be returned to the PIO for release with the CEO's approval. All of this should be done in a timely manner.
2. Provide news releases in a timely manner. Any news release that is intended for the 6:00 P.M. news should be released by 3:00 P.M. Press conferences should be scheduled for 9:00 A.M. in order to accommodate afternoon newspapers and the 6:00 P.M. news. In this electronic age, missing the 6:00 P.M. news may cause your story to slip to filler status because of more urgent stories.
3. Know the local lead reporters in both the print and electronic media. Give assistance wherever possible so that they are knowledgeable about the agency and its functions.
4. During any given event, only one person should talk to the media, which is why it is important to appoint a PIO. Several people talking to the media tend to give conflicting

information. For the sake of the print media, which require more human interest than the electronic media, it may be a good idea to allow someone else close to the incident to supply "color" during press briefings.
5. Avoid playing favorites with reporters. Other reporters may catch on and fail to attend future press conferences or ignore press releases.

The Critical Story

Sooner or later every corrections executive is the subject of a critical story. Before retaliating the official should take stock and determine whether the story is true. If it is, the situation must be treated as a learning experience, no matter how painful, and the official must make sure that the reasons for the story disappear.

Nehrbass[43] points out that if the CEO refuses comment when the reporter calls, there is little room for complaint when a story appears that is critical of the agency or the CEO. Often, however, there is room for rebuttal by the agency chief. In such cases it is wise to make only objective comments. Failure to do so may make the official appear defensive and thus cause the comments to be interpreted as a cover-up. The official should avoid all traces of anger or condescension. Occasionally a persistent reporter will seem obnoxious, but the official should keep in mind that the reporter is only doing his or her job. The PIO and CEO need to memorize one phrase: "I'm not willing to comment on that matter right now" and should use it if there is a need to withhold information that is in violation of the Privacy Act or that will jeopardize security or an ongoing investigation.

Public Relations Specials

As pointed out earlier, it is possible to educate the media and to build good will. This reservoir of good will may pay great dividends in the future. Radio and television are voracious consumers of information.[44] The organization can use this appetite to its own advantage by putting the PIO to work creating specials; for example, human interest stories on various departments in the agency, recruiting efforts, charity activities, and other stories pointing out employees' activities in the community. At the institutional level, including juvenile detention centers, an open house for representatives of the media, retirees, and other interested members of the community will build good will and spread the message that the organization considers itself a full member of the community. The PIO needs to have a feel for a "good" story and should be on speaking terms with assignment editors (TV) and city editors (newspapers) and solicit friendly advice as to what is considered a good story. Thus, by walking a fine line between being a pest and remaining aloof, the PIO will get his or her story out and keep the public informed.

The Media Reporter

The corrections manager who expects to use the media to get his or her point across to the public must know how reporters work. Similarly, reporters should know how corrections works. Melvin Mencher[45] offers five suggestions to prospective news reporters for effectively covering the news beat:

1. *Know how things work.* Know the laws that guide those in charge, the regulations and rules, and the processes that underlie the daily activities of the agency, department, or unit.
2. *Cultivate sources.* The best sources are not always those in charge. Secretaries, elevator operators, clerks, deputies, and telephone operators can provide valuable information.

3. *Keep abreast.* Know what is happening in the field you are covering by reading good newspapers and specialized journals.
4. *Be persistent.* Dig beneath the handout and the press release. Do not take "no comment" for an answer from public officials.
5. *Anticipate developments.* Follow developments on the beat closely so that you have a sense of what logically must follow the present situation.

These five points can help the corrections manager anticipate a reporter's moves. For example, at the above-mentioned open house the reporter is informed of the processes and rules that are at work in the organization. The manager can tell the staff that reporters may attempt to cultivate sources and that employees should refer any inquiries to the PIO.

Do not be afraid to copy informational articles and mail them to competent reporters in the area. In the event that a "big" story arises at the facility, anticipate the reporter's persistence. If you cannot answer a question, do not just say "no comment." Tell the reporter why you cannot answer his or her question.

News Conferences

The corrections manager can use the news conference to inform the public about a serious incident such as a riot or a murder or a sex crime committed by a probationer or parolee. While in the event of such crimes the manager must be mindful of the Privacy Act, he or she can nevertheless use the news conference as a forum to counter the bad news and inform the public about programs that are having a positive effect, including the personal efforts of parole or probation officers.

The news conference can be tricky. Stein asserts that the "press conference is a game and almost any number can play."[46] Most press

conferences are geared to television, so it is helpful if they are held in a room large enough to accommodate reporters and their gear and that has adequate lights and electrical outlets. This setup displeases many print reporters, but it helps the manager and may encourage the electronic media to treat the organization well.

The news conference is an excellent opportunity to present the agency's position. Guarding against overkill is important, though; therefore, press conferences should last only thirty to forty-five minutes. (Most reporters are sophisticated enough to ask the important questions in that time.) The PIO or executive needs to keep the following points in mind when approaching the news conference:

- Figure out what you have to say and say it, and then ask for questions. Remember that television favors short, crisp answers or statements. These are called *soundbites*. Novice TV reporters often take their soundbites from the opening remarks. The more experienced reporters will also use soundbites from the question and answer session; ideally *their* question.
- Personal interviews—many reporters will request a personal interview after the news conference. A personal interview often appears to be an "exclusive" interview for a TV station. The "exclusive" should be determined before the news conference. The PIO will be unaware of the pressure the reporter's supervisor has put on him or her to play the story. It may be a slow news day and so the story will be played up, or the supervisor may think he or she smells a rat. Never, however, refuse the interview without reason. Keep in mind that if an "exclusive" is given to one reporter, it must be available to all.
- Have no more than one or two speakers at the news conference. Too many speakers

present editing problems, and usually the third and subsequent speakers do not have anything important to add.

- If possible, try to help the TV reporter get video for "cover" on the story. This is the video one watches while a speaker (the reporter or PIO) is telling the story.

Summary

The correctional organization does not exist in a vacuum. Its processes are shaped and guided, to an extent, by actors beyond the control of the manager. The courts and the media are primary examples of those actors. Since the 1960s the courts have taken an active role in reviewing correctional organizations. The courts have taken a real and active interest in the management of prisons and jails under the rubric of Section 1983 of Title 42 of the U.S. Code. Of particular interest to the courts has been due process, religion, freedom of expression, and inmate discipline. The courts' intervention has improved many areas of corrections and resulted in institutions that are governed by law and not by people.

The electronic age enables the manager to "sell" his or her organization to the public. This is a point largely ignored by corrections executives. News organizations are hungry for news, and the skillful manager can enhance the image of the organization and educate the public about the needs and special mission of corrections. Open houses and news conferences are two ways to educate reporters and the public.

Reviewing the Case

Greg Shipley is an experienced PIO. He knows that in order to gain the confidence of media reporters, he must know what to say and how to say it. He also knows that the reporter will get the story one way or another. Before meeting with the media, Mr. Shipley will confer with the secretary of corrections and/or the warden, compose his remarks, and then meet with the press. In his job, he knows that it is important to assure the public that they are safe and that the situation (or organization) is under control.

Another important reason for good relations with the media is that Mr. Shipley knows that the courts may have cause in the future to review the actions of institutional and departmental personnel. The unbiased comments of reporters lend credence to the professionalism of employees and preclude many unwarranted and supercilious lawsuits.

For Further Study

Ronald Goldfarb, *Jails: The Ultimate Ghetto* (New York: Anchor Press/Doubleday, 1973).

Arthur F. Nehrbass, "Promoting Effective Media Relations," *The Police Chief*, Vol. 56:1, January 1989.

M. L. Stein, *Getting and Reporting the News: A Guide to Reporting* (New York: Longman, 1985).

Key Terms

Monroe v. Pape	Six Steps to Correctional
Holt v. Sarver	Law Making
Open House	*Morris v. Travisono*
Soundbites	**Public Relations Specials**

Goals and Values of System Actors

Case Study: Hidden Agenda

Ray Thompson didn't care if he was caught. "I've had it up to here," he thought to himself as he raised a hand and brought it across his throat in a cutting motion. The anger and disappointment burned deep inside, and he felt an almost unbearable sense of frustration that gave little comfort to the course his life had taken.

Ray gripped the steering wheel tightly as the institution came into view. He thought back to his first months on the job and how enthusiastic he had been. He hadn't graduated from college planning to be a corrections officer, but he needed a job and when a friend suggested he apply at the nearby U.S. Penitentiary, he thought, "Why not?"

He remembered how well he seemed to fit in with the staff. Everyone worked together, and even though as officers, case managers, teachers, and so on, each had their specialty, it was pulling together that appealed to him. When an officer called for help you were just as apt to be run over by a case manager as by another officer. He never made another staff person look bad in front of an inmate, and he had always been the first one to volunteer for overtime if the need arose. As far as he was concerned, he had been paying his dues for seven years.

"Then what happened?" he wondered silently as he walked up to the gate with over $700 worth of cocaine in his lunch bucket. He had always been for the organization. Why didn't they pay him back?

"Ka-thunk" went the gate as it closed behind him.

He was just as qualified as that ignorant fool who had been given that case manager's job two years ago. And why did that "wet-behind-the-ears" woman get the community programs job in St. Louis that he had applied for around Christmas? Hell, he had five years seniority on her, and there was no way she knew how to deal with those thugs anyway.

"Go figure," he thought. "If the Bureau wouldn't give me a promotion, then I'll just manage one for myself. So I don't get to wear a suit, but the pay is great," he chuckled to himself as he began to regain his confidence. The money had been a big boost in paying off his car and other bills. He had been smart though: no flash; no big bank accounts; just a real big comfort zone. Still, this kind of thing wasn't really him. He'd quit selling in a few weeks, and at least he would be comfortable, even if he never got a promotion.

As he entered the lobby, the desk officer told him that the associate warden of operations wanted to see him for a moment before he went in to roll call. In an instant, the sense of panic passed.

As he entered the associate warden's office, he recognized the two other men in the room. "Mr. Thompson, I'm Special Agent Morrison, and this is Special Agent Jolly."

Introduction

Correctional organizations are human inventions whose purpose is to supervise and care for people placed in their custody. As human organizations, they can be influenced by the values brought in by very diverse groups. What is unique about correctional organizations is that the set of values of those incarcerated influences the organization, even though those values are often directly opposed to the values of the staff and administration.

Each correctional organization has a set of goals. There are two kinds of goals, formal and informal, and they may work in opposition to each other, or at least the interaction of the two sets of goals may cause internal conflict among some staff.

Formal goals are those established by the organization and its managers as desirable results of concerted action. They are usually clearly stated in the organization's charter, mission statement, or public statements by key executives. Formal goals are also often stated in the Management by Objectives (MBO) annual statement. Informal goals are unwritten but commonly accepted objectives. For example, an organization's formal goal could be to decrease the amount of monthly overtime by 30 percent. An informal goal might be that line employees use their accrued sick day each month.

Values are the element that set human beings apart from other forms of animal life. According to Milton Rokeach, a value system is "an enduring organization of beliefs concerning preferable modes of conduct or end-states of existence along a continuum of relative importance."[1] While values shape one's behavior, they do not do so individually. Rather, behavior is affected by "clusters of values and beliefs described . . . as value systems that act in concert with each other."[2] These values help the individual establish goals and make decisions. This chapter will explore goals and values within the context of the correctional organization.

The Organizational Mission Statement

One of the most important documents in an organization is the **mission statement**. The mission statement has been defined as "an enduring statement of purpose that distinguishes an organization from other similar enterprises"[3] or as the purpose society expects of the organization and its responsibilities as an organization.[4] A mission statement provides direction in formulating goals. Broadly speaking, a mission statement should at least address the following:[5]

- the purpose of the organization;
- the organization's responsibilities to its inmate population and other major constituencies, including the citizenry, local government, social agencies, and other elements of the criminal justice system; and
- the direction in which the organization is headed.

A mission statement is important because it reveals the vision of the organization's managers and employees and is the foundation upon which policies, procedures, and objectives rest. It identifies what it wants to do in the long term

and whom it wants to serve. A mission statement should motivate employees; it should establish a general organizational attitude, explain how resources are allocated, and impart a vision.

The Illinois Department of Corrections expresses its mission thus:

> To protect the public from criminal offenders through a system of incarceration and supervision which securely segregates offenders from society, assures offenders of their Constitutional rights, and maintains programs to enhance the success of the offender's reentry into society.

The adult institutions and community correctional centers within the Illinois Department of Corrections express their mission as:

> To incarcerate in a safe and humane manner all adult offenders sentenced to the department of corrections, to provide for the basic needs of these inmates, and to assist in their reintegration to the community by providing an opportunity to participate in programs and leisure-time activities.

These mission statements are reasonably clear in articulating the organization's mission, responsibilities, and direction. From a management standpoint it makes sense to develop organizational goals that flow from the mission statement. For example, the DOC mission is, in part, to create a system that "securely segregates offenders from society. . . ." Thus, a goal for the DOC for the coming fiscal year might be "to decrease escapes and walk-aways by 50 percent." This goal clearly flows from the mission statement and is specific, objective, and measurable. However, establishing goals and objectives is not quite as simple as the above paragraph indicates.

What Are Goals?

Generally speaking, goals express the desired future state of the organization. Goals include targets, quotas, and objectives that the administration has determined to be desirable. Management by Objectives (MBO) is a program some organizations have adopted to plan for the future. Management by Objectives is covered in more detail in chapter 12, but briefly it is a philosophy of management that compels managers to establish objectives and then to strive to meet those objectives over a period of time, usually one to five years. It is a process that allows all members of an organization to participate in decisions that affect the future of the organization. Goals can also be personal. One can have a goal to advance to supervisor in five years or to complete a graduate degree in two years.

Organizational and Individual Goals

Organizations are established to achieve certain goals, and there are many individuals whose personal goals and activities affect organizational goals. Cyert and March[6] point out that people have goals but that collectivities of people do not have goals. They assert that in order to define a theory of organizational decision making we need to develop goals at the organizational level that account for individual goals.

Kast and Rosenzweig[7] offer a framework that organizes any discussion of organizational goal setting. They point out that we need to consider goals from three different perspectives: the environmental level, the organizational level, and the individual level.

Environmental Level

Following the lead of Thompson and McErven,[8] we can view organizational goals as being influenced by (a) competition, (b) bargaining, (c) co-optation, and (d) coalition.

Competition between organizations is often intense as resources become more scarce. The various divisions in a department of corrections compete for tax dollars, positions, and favorable attention from the legislature and the media.

Bargaining between organizations and within organizations is inevitable. A good example of bargaining is that which takes place between the organization and the labor union. Each must modify its own goals to an extent in order to continue to meet the needs of the public. For example, the organization may want to abolish the practice of bidding for positions based on seniority, and the union may want higher wages and greater benefits. Both will need to modify their stands through bargaining if progress is to be made.

Co-optation is defined by Thompson and McErven as "the process of absorbing new elements into the leadership or policy-determining structure of an organization as a means of averting threats to its stability or existence."[9] In other words, the organization must satisfy the demands of constituencies in its environment whose support is important for its continued survival. Co-optation is not "selling out" but rather an approach that considers the interdependencies of individuals and organizations.

For example, a prison administrator must consider both the needs of the institution and the influence of the union in making policy or program changes that might be controversial. As a consequence, the warden would be well advised to place a union representative on any committee or task force established to study an issue and make recommendations. This policy can also be carried over to inmate programs with often successful results. In 1970 Warden James D. Henderson at the Federal Correctional Institution in Milan, Michigan, was considering changes in the Honor Unit. The Honor Unit was a housing unit reserved for inmates who had exhibited exemplary behavior and completed assigned programs. Warden Henderson was aware of the need to co-opt potential inmate and staff opposition, and so he named two inmates to the committee established for the purpose of upgrading the unit. The effort proved successful in that there were few complaints from staff or inmates, and there was a high degree of satisfac-tion among the general population because their views had been solicited.

Coalition refers to two or more organiza-tions combining their resources and personnel for the purpose of achieving a certain objective.

FIGURE 5.1
Types of Organizational Goals

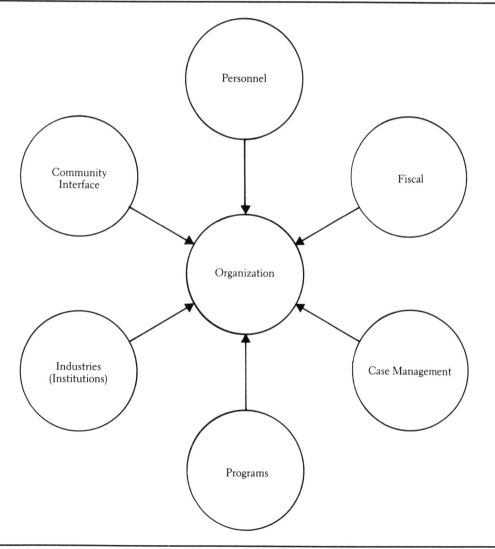

This approach is primarily political and can be used as a form of co-optation. Public organizations often form a coalition to overcome a particular problem. For example, in many states the Department of Public Health helps Department of Corrections personnel develop AIDS-related policies and trains personnel in the proper procedures for handling blood, blood products, syringes, and HIV-positive inmates.

Organizational Level

The organization is a contrived unit whose purpose is to achieve certain goals. For example, a prison pursues official goals of protecting the community while caring for, programming, and controlling inmates. Perrow[10] calls our attention to the difference between official and operative goals. Official goals, he explains, are those put forth for public consumption. They are intentionally vague and general. Operative goals specify what the organization is actually trying to do, regardless of the official goals. Prisons, jails, and community programs and agencies such as probation or parole organizations serve an integrative function[11] and usually specify congruant official and operative goals. For example, protection of the community is an inherent function and a specific task of a prison. Operative goals are expressed as official goals for public consumption, and they also tell us what goes on inside the organization. While the goals of protecting the community and caring for, programming, and controlling inmates are not exclusive of each other, they do require effort that seems to run in different directions. These seemingly competing goals are influenced by both external and internal influences, and there are alternative ways of achieving each of them.

Internal Influences
Type of Client. The type of client the agency is dealing with influences the type of goals it establishes and the time frames for accomplishing them. For example, a probation agency may establish a goal of completing all pre-sentence investigations within ten working days. On the other hand, a prison may establish a goal to increase the percentage of non-high school graduates completing the GED program. A probation agency is interested in the clients' positive involvement in community affairs, but the prison's job is to keep the inmate out of the community. These simple examples illustrate how the type of clientele affects the goals of the agency and why the goals may appear to be at odds with each other.

Education and Commitment of Staff. Many probation agencies typically hire only college graduates as probation officers. In the larger agencies it is not unusual to find probation officers who have earned law degrees and doctorates while working with the agency. On the other hand, prisons are not likely to have personnel with more than bachelor's degrees, and most often line staff will be high school graduates with some college. This is changing as correctional officers and others come to see themselves as professionals and as officers come to value the benefits of a university education. As a consequence, the formulation and implementation of goals are likely to take on a much different character in one agency as opposed to another. In addition, probation officers may all see themselves as professionals, and correctional officers may see themselves as craftsmen. Each view may influence the employee's willingness to work extra hours as well as her or his strength of commitment to the organization.

Unity of Purpose. Corrections is a diverse field, and employees of the same agency and of different agencies will often support conflicting goals. A prison, for example, is a complex organization, and within it there are a number of groups competing for scarce resources. On the one hand, the department that includes the counselors or case managers may have an entirely different view of what goals should be pursued, such as software, computers, and facilities for counseling. Members of the custodial department may see a need, on the other hand, for radios, riot equipment, and weapons. Competition between the two departments, if improperly handled, could lead to hard feelings and reinforcement of the programs-custody dichotomy.

External Influences

Klofas et al.,[12] point out that the organization is able to influence input from the political system. This is accomplished by the administration controlling the type, amount, and flow of information to the legislative committees. The organization also manages input by providing rationale for budget increases or for new programs and testimony in regard to new legislation. Additionally, the successful administrator is able to solicit support from special interest groups that are outside the system but have influence with the legislative or executive bodies. Atchison and Hill[13] note several external influences on goal setting. Among them are:

Political. The political sector continuously puts forth laws, regulations, and rules that affect the organization's day-to-day operations. They affect the care, custody, and control of inmates, probationers, and parolees in a variety of ways, which in turn affect staff hiring, internal procedures, and programs.

Social. The attitudes and customs of society change over time. Social attitudes are reflected in the legal code, and informally they affect how the correctional organization, its employees, and its clients are perceived and treated.

Technological. Technology greatly affects how the correctional organization is managed. Radios, copy machines, computers, word processing, and home detention are just a few of the innovations that require specialized skills previously not central to corrections management.

Individual Level

The individual level in Kast and Rosenzweig's framework is made up of the goals of the individual and their relationship to the organization. The important issue here is whether organizational goals and personal goals can be compatible. Many practices developed to increase organizational effectiveness may create dissatisfaction in the workplace.[14] For example, the U.S. Bureau of Prisons has developed an outstanding ability to track the case management of inmates. The case manager's daily life is managed by SENTRY (an automated information system). The case management manual dictates the frequency of reviews and demands periodic updates in many categories on the system. The result is a manager's dream: quality control is excellent, the director and regional directors are assured that functions are performed the same on the West Coast as they are on the East Coast, and no inmate is forgotten. But what with high caseloads, slavish attention to paperwork, and auditors from the regional or central office who are insensitive to the demands of the job, the result is job dissatisfaction and burnout.

Still, a strong bond sometimes develops between the individual and the organization. This is most satisfying to both the individual and the organization for it means that the needs of both are being met. Two studies note the extent of reciprocity between the individual and the organization. Lorsch and Morse[15] and Porter and Lawler[16] found that managers experience a sense of competency, are motivated to achieve organizational goals, and have a high degree of satisfaction when the organization is designed to meet both organizational goals and personal goals. Further, when the organization rewards performance, the employee has a heightened sense of personal satisfaction.

The internalization of goals occurs when the "individual develops a personal commitment to meeting organizational goals."[17] Once internalization occurs, it removes the possibility of conflict between individual motivation and organizational goals. Commitment involves three separate but related attitudes:

1. a sense of identification with the organizational mission;
2. a feeling of involvement or psychological immersion in organizational duties; and
3. a feeling of loyalty and affection for the organization as a place to live and work—quite apart from the merits of its mission or its purely instrumental value to the individual.[18]

Even in the best organization, an ideal match between organizational and personal goals is not likely. Corrections employees must be alert to the effects of stress and burnout and their impact on commitment to organizational goals. Whitehead[19] argues that burnout and job dissatisfaction are not two sides of the same coin. Broadly speaking, burnout is a depletion of psychological energy caused by stress. It is not too much of a stretch to assume that chronic burnout will reduce the individual's commitment to organizational goals. Therefore, the prudent manager will take steps to deal with burnout and its effects, even if it is by doing nothing more than preparing an informative booklet on the subject.

Goal Displacement

Robert K. Merton[20] points out that people are affected by bureaucratic organizations and of-

ten seek the security of rigid adherence to rules and regulations for their own sake. The result is goal displacement, in which adherence to rules becomes an end in itself. In other words, rules become ritualized and following them becomes more satisfying than achieving organizational goals. If staff focus on the safety of the job and the adherence to rules and lose sight of the reason behind the rules, there may be cause for concern because creativity and initiative will suffer.

Personal goals and organizational goals are not the same. Personal goals relate to job satisfaction, personal satisfaction, and the fit between job and personal life. Organizational goals relate to the accomplishment of organizational objectives. Goal displacement occurs when an individual places a personal goal ahead of an organizational goal, with resultant conflict. While it may be unrealistic to expect perfect compatibility between personal and organizational goals, individuals must give up a measure of personal autonomy and self-expression in order to gain full benefit from the organization.[21] The optimal situation is one where the personal goals of the individual are the same as, or complement, those of the organization.

Management's Role in Setting Organizational Goals

One role of organizational management is to achieve established goals. Management must drive the organization toward those goals by effectively organizing resources. Certo[22] identifies four management processes that move the organization toward the attainment of established goals.

1. *Planning.* Planning involves assigning tasks and determining how they must be performed and when they must be completed.

2. *Organizing.* Organizing means assigning tasks to various groups and individuals as well as putting plans into action.
3. *Influencing.* Commonly called motivating, leading, and directing, influencing usually means causing people to do things they would not ordinarily do.
4. *Controlling.* Controlling is an ongoing process that includes gathering information; monitoring, that is, comparing the performance of two or more individuals or groups; and modifying, that is, making changes in procedures to achieve organizational goals more efficiently.

Values

Rokeach's definition of values was spelled out earlier in terms of clusters of values. These clusters of values act in concert with each other to produce behaviors that either conform to or are at odds with the organizational culture. In corrections, staff values revolve around staff solidarity, safety of personnel, and perceived dangers.

Values Defined

Values are qualities that are prized or believed to be good or of benefit to the individual or group. Vander Zanden defines a value as an "ethical principle to which people feel a strong emotional commitment and which they employ in judging behavior."[23] We value education, hard work, and fidelity in relationships. As correctional workers we also value community safety, the public's support, staff solidarity, and personal safety on the job. These values reflect a system of beliefs and goals shared by our fellow correctional workers.

Kauffman points out that the inmate subculture has been the subject of a great many studies by criminologists but that the employee

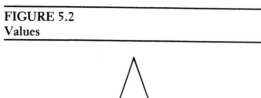

FIGURE 5.2
Values

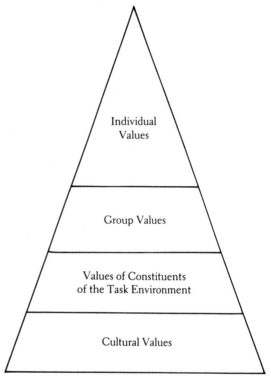

subculture in prisons has been largely ignored. In her view, there is an officer subculture that is the product of a "complex interaction of importation, socialization, deportation, and cultural evolution."[24] She makes the point that regardless of the recruits' attitudes, over time the officers' attitudes toward inmates and the organization fall into line with predominating attitudes of officers at the institution of assignment.

Individual Values

All people hold values that affect their actions. The correctional officer or employee who exhibits fairness in his or her interactions with inmates and who is willing to quickly respond to alarms is a valued member of the organization and is said to be loyal and hard working. Conversely, the officer, counselor, or probation/parole officer who is erratic in his or her interactions with inmates or clients and who is always "too busy" to respond to alarms or concerns of inmates or clients is unpopular and is not an employee or officer one wishes to work with or relieve on post. The warden or assistant warden who remains in his or her office and doesn't freely move about the institution is viewed as disinterested in staff, aloof from the daily grind, or even afraid to appear in the yard. This type of executive may be viewed as not subscribing to the values of solidarity and concern for fellow staff.

Group Values

Informal and formal groups hold values that affect the behavior of individuals and the organization. The group is a demanding master, and its values heavily influence the members. In fact, individual group members' assessment of peers may be too harsh. Klofas and Toch[25] found that officers underestimated the professional orientation of fellow officers and overestimated their cynicism. In discussing values, solidarity, and the like in prisons in Massachusetts, Kauffman describes how members of the guard force stick together and become a tightly knit group with its own rules and code of conduct. Violation of the rules is likely to cause the group to invoke sanctions to one degree or another. She calls our attention to the officers' subculture and states that their "beliefs and code of conduct set them apart from administrators, social workers, and of course, inmates."[26] Kauffman identifies nine norms that reflect the values of the officer subculture.[27]

1. *Always go to the aid of an officer in distress.* This is the norm upon which officer solidar-

ity is based. It reflects the perceived danger of an institution and the need to look out for each other if one is to survive.

2. *Don't "lug" drugs.* According to Kauffman, the reason for this norm is not a revulsion to the use of drugs but rather it points to the dangerousness of the job. An inmate high on drugs is dangerous and may cause injury or even death.

3. *Don't rat.* There are two prongs to this norm: (a) never rat on an officer to an inmate, and (b) never cooperate in an investigation of an officer in regard to mistreatment of an inmate. Violation of either is a betrayal of the group.

4. *Never make a fellow officer look bad in front of inmates.* Violations of this norm violate appearances of solidarity against inmates. Officers believe that inmates will exploit divisions among staff and that one should never hand an inmate the opportunity to drive a wedge between staff members.

5. *Always support an officer in a dispute with an inmate.* This is a positive counterpart to norm 4. Even though one may disagree with an officer's actions, support of him or her is imperative if solidarity is to be preserved.

6. *Always support officer sanctions against inmates.* Correctional officers often have a good deal of discretion in dealing with inmates, and often an officer will view sanctions imposed by another officer as either too lenient or too harsh. Regardless of one's opinion, support of the sanction is necessary. Occasionally the officer is faced with a quandary when violence is involved. This issue will be discussed more thoroughly in chapter 17, but in general a sense of professionalism in the case of violence should be the rule.

7. *Don't be a white hat.* One should never be sympathetic to inmates or identify with them or their needs. According to Kauff-

man this is the most easily violated norm. It's difficult for officers and detail supervisors who work alongside inmates for months or even years at a time not to come to know each other well and even to respect one another. In this instance, staff with seniority and who enjoy the respect of fellow staff can, and do, violate this norm. Examples include bringing in cigarettes for inmates on one's detail at Christmas or a plate of cookies for those in one's shop to share on a special occasion. Most officers know how far one can go in violating this norm, and usually there are no problems.

8. *Maintain officer solidarity versus all outside groups.* Kauffman was able to identify this norm perhaps because the institution had been under fire from media, courts, and the legislature for some time. She points out that this rule even applied to administrators and family. The purpose of the norm was to promote officer solidarity. Officers felt that no one understood what it is like in the institution.

9. *Show concern for fellow officers.* This is an ideal that is rarely lived up to, according to Kauffman. Two aspects of this norm are: (a) never leave another officer a problem and (b) help your fellow officer with problems outside the institution. No sanctions are applied for violation of these norms, but the belief that one can count on fellow officers makes the job more bearable.

Few who have worked in a prison would argue with the nine norms identified by Kauffman. The degree to which they are observed will vary, of course, from individual to individual and from institution to institution. For example, a rural institution such as the Illinois State Penitentiary at Menard or even the U.S. Penitentiary at Terre Haute will boast a relatively tightly knit work force who often see each other off duty. On the other hand, the Federal Correctional Institution at Terminal Island, California, is an urban institution, and the work force is less unified because it is widely dispersed.

Organizational Values

Organizational values are a composite of individual, group, and agency values. Etzioni[28] states that the same organization can serve the dual goals of order and economics; that is, in a corrections context, the goals of detaining convicted criminals and providing employment for the area are compatible and serve the twin values of order and economics.

Values of Constituents of the Task Environment

Persons in direct contact with the organization—inmates, suppliers, and other governmental agencies—hold values that affect the operation of the organization. There is a rich and varied literature on inmates' social system and its impact on the organization and a growing literature on the staff subculture, but no inquiries have yet been made into the influence of the values of other agencies and suppliers on the corrections organization. The executive staff must understand the impact of the inmates' social system on the organization. They must also understand the valuative demands of the public, which interacts with the organization in a variety of ways. Private sector organizations and employees have distinct values, as do their counterparts in government. These value systems need to be considered by the correctional organization management team.

Cultural Values

The correctional organization exists in a society that holds clearly defined values on nearly everything under the sun; crime and criminals are just one area. In fact, the criminal justice agency is an expression of societal values such as segregating "bad" people from "good" people and rehabilitation. Over time, however, societal values change. In the past twenty years we have seen a shift in emphasis from rehabilitative values to "just desserts."[29] Correctional institutions and probation/parole agencies have changed to reflect that shift. The enterprising and competent manager is able to anticipate societal attitudinal change.

The Correctional Value of Rehabilitation

Paul Tappan[30] sums up the goals of punishment and correction. He points out that the purpose of punishment is to exact retribution; to incapacitate the offender through, for example, imprisonment; and to deter would-be offenders both generally and specifically and that rehabilitation is also a legitimate goal of punishment. In earlier times in U.S. history we believed that through punishment and imprisonment the offender would reflect on his or her transgressions and return to society as a rehabilitated and productive member of the community.

According to Gibbons,

[In] the long, complex history of punitive actions against criminals, all manner of reactions have been employed at one time or another. Offenders have been subjected to death or torture, social humiliation such as the pillories and stocks, banishment and transportation, imprisonment, and financial penalties. Responses toward lawbreakers were originally retributive, compelling them to make amends in some way. Later, restraint and punishment became the principal reaction to deviants; this approach is still dominant in Western societies and elsewhere in the world.[31]

Prison reform and progressivism beginning in the 1890s launched the idea that criminals could be rehabilitated,[32] and the notion of rehabilitation caught on so well that by the middle of the 1950s the primary aim of imprisonment was rehabilitation. Probation was established in all states by 1956, and halfway houses, whose principal aim is to reintegrate the prisoners back into the community, began to take hold. Correctional experts and scholars who had been marinated in the pragmatism of John Dewey believed that a bit of pressure in the prison would achieve results once the inmate reentered the community. Subsequent to the release of the report by the President's Commission on the Administration of Justice, policymakers armed themselves with flow charts that vividly described how prisoners and probationers would march through the system, entering as criminals at one end and exiting as productive, happy citizens at the other.

Unfortunately, human nature is not so simple. The suspicion that treatment as a correctional goal might not be valid began to set in during the late 1960s.[33] Beginning with articles by Robert Martinson,[34] Lipton, Martinson, and Wilks,[35] and a number of other scholars, the value of attempting to provide treatment in a correctional setting was questioned. The 1970s and 1980s were characterized by the decline of treatment as a correctional goal and the warehousing of prisoners was substituted as a reasonable and just correctional goal.

In general, the shift from treatment to warehousing has caused a good deal of turmoil in the field of corrections because of the lack of a clear, formal philosophy. That the "nothing works" attitude may have been grabbed and held onto by a coalition of ultraconservatives and by jurisdictions seeking justification for cutting correctional budgets may be evidenced by the minimization of successful rehabilitation efforts.[36] According to Van Voorhis, "The issue is not simply one of effectiveness . . . [but] that research findings are susceptible to selective use in order to support ideological concerns."[37] Those closest to the action, so to speak, have also been uncomfortable with the "nothing works" attitude.[38] In addition, citizens have not lost faith in rehabilitation as a correctional goal.[39]

For the present, the "nothing works" approach appears to remain in vogue. But there is hope that the goal of rehabilitation will return in some form. For as Cullin notes: if nothing else, the value of rehabilitation is "that it provides a vocabulary, a way of talking about crime and its correction, that remains legitimate and understandable to people."[40]

Summary

Aided by a clear and well-written mission statement, correctional organizations pursue certain goals; that is, the care, custody, control, and supervision of inmates and clients placed under their authority. The achievement of organizational goals is influenced internally and externally by forces of which the manager needs to be aware.

Personal goals and organizational goals can be either congruent or incongruent. If the goals are congruent, the functioning of the organization will be much smoother and the employee will be more satisfied. Values greatly affect the individual's goal identification and performance. Values are those principles believed to be good or to benefit the individual, the organization, or society. Each individual brings to the workplace a personal set of values that management needs to recognize. Corrections officers as a group have a distinct subculture and a normative system that promotes officer solidarity. In addition, the organization has certain values, and the inability to reconcile personal values and organizational values leads to conflict that is often destructive to the organization.

Rehabilitation as a correctional goal was replaced in the 1970s by the goal of incapacitation. A sense of drift set in among correctional staff and a belief in purpose has not returned. Rehabilitation may return again as a goal of corrections, but until then we need to recognize the successes of treatment efforts and not minimize them.

Reviewing the Case

Every individual and organization has goals and values. Ray Thompson started his career full of hope and with wholehearted commitment to the goals of the organization and to the values of the officers and staff. All correctional organizations are committed to maintaining the integrity of employees and institutional security.

In this instance, Ray Thompson had been disappointed in his career advancement and substituted personal goals that were in opposition to organizational goals. In addition, his personal value system had undergone a radical change, which resulted in behavior that was in conflict with the organization. Without doubt, Ray Thompson's personal values were affecting the organization and his work.

In a work environment as harsh as a penitentiary, the effective manager would have counseled Ray each time he didn't get a promotion. Effort needs to be spent on ensuring that the devoted employee receives recognition in a variety of ways short of promotions. Being singled out at roll call for special effort, short-term transfers to "cushy" jobs, and the opportunity to go away for specialized training are just a few examples. There is no substitute for Ray's supervisors and executives being cheerleaders, coaches and counselors.

For Further Study

Patrick E. Connors and Boris W. Becker, "Values and the Organization: Suggestions for Research," *Academy of Management Journal* (September 1975), pp. 550–61.

James Jacobs, *Stateville: The Penitentiary in Mass Society* (Chicago: University of Chicago Press, 1977).

Kelsey Kauffman, *Prison Officers and Their World* (Cambridge: Harvard University Press, 1988).

Jeanne M. Liedtka, "Value Congruence: The Interplay of Individual and Organizational Value Systems," *Journal of Business Ethics* (October 1989), pp. 805–15.

Lucien X. Lombardo, *Guards Imprisoned: Correctional Officers at Work* (New York: Elsevier/North Holland, 1981).

James G. Thompson and William J. McErven, "Organizational Goals and Environment: Goal Setting as an Interaction Process," *American Sociological Review* (February 1958), pp. 23–31.

Patricia Van Voorhis, "Correctional Effectiveness: The High Cost of Ignoring Success," *Federal Probation* (March 1987), pp. 56–62.

Key Terms

Goals	Formal Goals
Informal Goals	Values
Group Values	Organizational Values
Cultural Values	

THE ORGANIZATIONAL PROCESS

PART III

We have established that correctional organizations are open systems. We next address how the organization should be directed toward outcomes that are determined by managers and not by external events. To do so, the organization must exert a measure of control.

Three distinct areas addressed in Part III take up the challenge of directing the organization: policy, budgeting, and organizational development. A policy is a general statement that channels thinking toward an issue. Chapter 6 differentiates between policy and procedures and offers a framework for policy formulation. Further, it introduces steps necessary to bring a policy to life. One of the most important documents in determining where an organization places its priorities is the budget. Chapter 7 discusses budgeting and the budget cycle. Chapter 8 covers approaches to overcoming problems in the organization.

Policy and the Correctional Organization

Case Study: "You Are Ruining the Bureau of Prisons!"

The voice belonged to the assistant director for Correctional Services, the highest-ranked security person in the federal prison system.[1] It was directed toward Roy Gerard, assistant director for correctional programs, and myself, Roy's deputy. The subject was Unit Management (UM).

This was the beginning of a loud discussion at the regular Monday morning executive staff meeting in the Washington, D.C., central office of the Federal Bureau of Prisons (BOP). The director was out of town this particular day; therefore, the meeting was somewhat less structured than usual. However, the nature of the exchange following that opening accusation was more than a little out of the ordinary.

Circumstances leading up to this incident as well as subsequent events and their outcomes provide insight into how a major change came about in the operation of a large organization.

The Bureau of Prisons—Then

In the late 1950s several BOP institutions for youthful offenders (ages twenty-one to twenty-three) began to staff inmate living quarters in innovative ways. For example, the position of liaison officer was established to help case workers gather information about individuals on their caseload from work detail supervisors.

Other innovations led to a more fully realized approximation of what has come to be known as Unit Management. Its most complete realization began in 1961 at a federal institution for juvenile delinquents in Washington, D.C.—the National Training School for boys (NTS). Initially funded by a special grant from the Department of Justice, the Demonstration Counseling Project at NTS housed inmates on each case worker's caseload in a single living unit, began to use correctional counselors,[2] and eliminated within-institution transfers between housing units.

In 1968 Roy Gerard became the first warden of an institution designed around the Unit Management concept—the Robert F. Kennedy Youth Center in Morgantown, West Virginia. At KYC everything from its architecture—campus style—to its management approach differed from a typical prison's. That is, the inmates' living quarters consisted of five buildings, each with its own staff: unit manager, case managers, correctional counselors, secretary, and (round-the-clock staffing by correctional officers. The concept that most distinguished KYC, however, was **decentralized management**, which is at the heart of Unit Management.

Unit Management

Unit Management has been called many things—some of which should not be said in polite society. Officially, Unit Management is defined as a small, self-contained, inmate-living and staff-office area, operating semiautonomously within the confines of a larger institution.[3] As the superintendent of a prison in Alaska recently put it: "Unit Management is *not* a program; it is a more effective way to manage programs."

Because Unit Management significantly changes how the business of corrections is carried out, its introduction met considerable resistance.

Change in Corrections

To state the obvious, correctional systems are extremely conservative. If most large organizations are difficult to change (and they are), this is particularly the case in corrections. How then did Unit Management win the day?

Basically, there are two ways change is introduced in corrections: by "outside" forces and by staff "inside" the system.

Externally Induced Change: It is rare that an idea comes along and corrections officials analyze it, decide that it's "good," and put it into practice. Most often external change is not a rational process.[4] Frequently it is a consequence of progress by "catastrophe"—a prison riot or an inmate lawsuit leads to court-mandated changes.

Internally Generated Changes: Less dramatic (but in the long run more integral) internal changes originate within an organization. Someone who understands how things are done gets a bright idea. Because he or she *really* knows how the organization functions, that notion is nurtured and grows. This was the case for Unit Management.

Legitimation of Unit Management

The single most critical factor in the successful introduction of a new idea in corrections is support from the top. Unit Management did not gain acceptance in the BOP until Roy Gerard became an assistant director in 1970. Before then, a few wardens had tried UM because of their own belief that it was a better way to run a prison; but more prevalent was the view that at best Unit Management might be "OK for the kiddie joints." It wasn't until 1976 that Unit Management was introduced into federal penitentiaries.

Central office staff cannot run institutional programs. That is the responsibility of facility personnel. No program can survive unless the people running it believe in it and perform their duties with enthusiasm and integrity. Often such a commitment rests on staff's "what's-in-it-for-me" attitude. While this may not be the most altruistic philosophy, correctional administrators ignore it at their peril.

The answer to staff's question is complex: institutions that adopt UM become safer and easier to manage. Additionally, staff from every discipline gain access to a new career ladder. Unit managers, who function at the level of department head, have been likened to miniwardens; performing well is a career boost toward top management positions.

Organizational change must occur. Unless change happens, it is too easy for the system to slide back to the old and familiar ways, particularly if problems arise or the concept's innovator moves on to some new challenge.

The Bureau of Prisons established a central office position to oversee Unit Management operations across the federal system. One of the first tasks assigned to the office was to develop a national Unit Management policy statement that would establish operating standards for all BOP units. Additionally, a set of audit guidelines was to be prepared so that, as with other departments, regularly scheduled on-site program reviews could be conducted.

The unit manager, a new position, had to be incorporated into the bureau's staffing pattern and table of organization. The first unit managers were trained by the originators of the concept; for the most part, however, these "new kids on the block" learned on the job. Subsequently, staff newly promoted to this position were sent to existing units for a week's training by unit managers, who served as role models. Eventually, a training curriculum was developed and incorporated into the courses provided at the bureau's training academy.

Have You Succeeded?

So you have gone through all the steps. Your bright idea is now policy. You're a success, right? Well, probably, but not necessarily—remember the opening quotation!

Studies comparing the situations before and after the change to Unit Management show substantial postimplementation improvements. This data helped strengthen UM against die-hards still convinced that the old way was better.

Another, but more unobtrusive measure of success was what staff said. When personnel say: "It's the only way to run a prison" or "I'd never want to go back to the old way" or "I don't go home with a headache every night," one knows something positive has happened.

When the assistant secretary for penal institutions in the New Zealand Department of Justice says (during a 1991 visit to the United States) that their Unit Management system follows the Danish model, you know the term has taken on a life of its own.

But perhaps one of the most meaningful indicators of Unit Management's success occurred several years after the date of the opening quotation. That same gentleman, at a national wardens' conference, stood up and said he had been wrong.

Introduction

The term *policy* is used in many different ways. The warden of a prison will declare that the institution has a policy on visiting, the chief probation officer of a court will declare that the agency has a policy on hiring minorities, and a halfway house manager will state that there is a policy on residents finding work. In each case, the manager may or may not be referring to policy. It is just as likely that she or he will be referring to procedure.

The difference between policy and procedure confuses many managers. In chapter 5 the mission statement is described as a statement that defines the organization. The mission statement is exceedingly important because from it flow most of the policies directed toward managing the organization. A policy is a broad philosophical statement that channels thinking toward an issue or a solution. A procedure, on the other hand, is a plan that includes a series of actions that must be completed to achieve an objective. The confusion stems from the fact that action-oriented corrections managers and executives think in terms of activity.

In many instances policy seems to acquire a life of its own. Wildavsky[5] observes that "policy is evermore its own cause; programs depend less on the external environment than on events inside the sectors from which they come." It is the correctional manager's job to scan the internal and external environment and to propose solutions that are effective and not the cause of even greater problems.

Policies, Procedures, and Rules

For the moment, policy may be defined as general philosophical principles that guide development of strategies and programs on behalf of the agency. In order for policies to be effective, they should meet the following criteria:

1. Staff with diverse viewpoints should have access to the committee or executive formulating the policy.
2. If at all possible, in the case of major policy changes, top executives (or in the case of a single agency or institution, all department heads) should be notified that a policy formulation process is under way. The notification should advise all concerned to notify their subordinates and solicit their input.
3. Where relevant, various disciplines such as education and psychological services and the law should be consulted for their input.
4. The policy statement should contain a discussion of the theoretical issues involved.
5. Once a policy has been formulated, a policy statement should contain a reference to past policy related to the issue at hand.
6. The policy statement should contain a brief description of how the policy will be implemented.

A good policy is one that accomplishes one or several of the following:

1. It attempts to correct a past error in policy. We often call this "fine-tuning."
2. It attempts to prevent future errors in policy by articulating policy formulators' thinking and trying to channel future thinking on a subject.
3. It clarifies numerous and different goals, separates competing goals, and/or brings to light previously unidentified goals.
4. It enables the organization to accomplish stated goals.

Policy Defined

Heinz Eulau and Kenneth Prewitt[6] define policy as a "standing decision characterized by behavioral consistency and repetitiveness on the part of both those who make it and those who

---

FIGURE 6.1
A Sample ACA Policy

CLASSIFICATION

Principle: Inmates are classified to the most appropriate level of custody and programming both on admission and on review of their status.

3–ALDF-4B-01 (Ref. 2-5352)	Written policy, procedure, and practice provide for a written inmate classification plan in terms of level of custody required, housing assignment, and participation in correctional programs. They are reviewed at least annually and updated if necessary.

Comment:
None.

3–ADLF-4B-02 (Ref. 2-5353)	The inmate classification plan specifies criteria and procedures for determining and changing the status of an inmate, including custody, transfers, and major changes in programs. The plan includes an appeals process for classification decisions.

Comment:
None.

Source: American Correctional Association, *Standards for Local Adult Detention Facilities.*

abide by it." Accordingly, we should view policy as the end result of the decision-making process; it is characterized by certain behavior on the part of those who conceive it and by those expected to carry it out.

Certo defines policy as "a standing plan that furnishes broad, general guidelines for channeling management thinking toward taking action consistent with reaching organizational objectives."[7] In this instance, policy is seen as being related to the attainment of organizational goals.

Pressman and Wildavsky[8] point out that policies "contain both goals and the means for achieving them." Often intentions are articulated in a policy. For example, a correctional institution will have a policy to provide on-the-job training to new staff with little written down as to how this will be done. Policies also imply theories. Pressman and Wildavsky state, "Policies point to a chain of causation between initial conditions and future consequences."[9] They assert that policies become programs when we attempt to do something about a particular problem. Programs are the result, but there are other parts to the equation. The American Cor-

rectional Association (ACA) has developed standards for important areas and issues in corrections. Figure 6.1 illustrates a policy and procedures for inmate classification in an adult local detention facility. Note that the policy provides broad direction; the procedures specify how the policy is to be implemented.

Procedures

If a policy is a broad philosophical statement that portrays a desired state of affairs, then there must be some statement about how that state of affairs will be reached. Procedures provide a standing plan that spells out certain actions necessary to accomplish a task. The booking procedure in a jail is one example.

The booking policy of a jail might state the following:

The Central County Jail will process all newly arrived prisoners in a timely and humane manner. Their health, proper identification, and proper disposition of money and belongings will be of the utmost importance.

A procedure is now needed to accomplish the above task. The procedure will outline in detail specific tasks to assure that the new prisoner is fingerprinted, properly identified, evaluated for condition of health, and considered for a diversion program or bail. Once these tasks are completed, the prisoner can be moved to a regular cell. Figure 6.2 illustrates the booking procedure at a major urban jail.

Rules

According to Certo,[10] a rule is "a standing plan that designates specific required action." A rule allows no latitude for individual interpretation and specifies what the employee should or should not do. An example of a rule is: "All correctional officers will report for roll call thirty minutes before the beginning of each shift."

The Value of Well-Written Policies and Procedures

It is important to have clearly written policies and procedures in any agency. This is especially true in corrections. The American Correctional Association (ACA) expends a great deal of time and effort promoting the accreditation of cor-

---

FIGURE 6.2
Sample Booking Procedures

Issued: 11/88
Review: 11/89, 11/90
ACA 2–5344
ORS 169.076
CHAPTER 010

MCDC Operational Procedures

010.101.000 *Admission Procedure-Intake*

010.101.010 Policy

Corrections staff shall follow procedures for admitting new inmates to MCDC which address at a minimum the following subjects:

Verification of court commitment papers, or other legal documentation of detention.

Complete search of the individual and his/her possessions.

Disposition of clothing and personal possessions.

Medical screening involving tests for infectious diseases.

Telephone calls by inmates.

Shower and hair care if necessary.

Issue of clean clothing.

Photographing and/or fingerprinting, including notation of identifying marks or unusual characteristics.

Interview for obtaining identifying data.

Screening interview by counselor or other trained interviewer.

Orientation.

Issue of personal hygiene items.

Classification for assignment to a housing unit.

Assignment to a housing unit.

010.101.020 Purpose

To ensure that all inmates are admitted in accordance with the law in a manner designed to protect the safety of all persons and the security of the facility.

Source: Policies and Procedures Manual, Multnomah County Detention Center, Portland, Oregon (rev. 1988).

rectional agencies and institutions, which can only be accomplished by establishing and writing clear policies and procedures. Thus, everyone gains in the process: employees, the public, and the inmate/clients.

The accreditation process, which began in 1978, applies to all local, state, and federal agencies. Gaining accreditation means that the agency or institution meets nationally recognized standards for the management of the organization. The standards developed by the ACA address a host of issues in addition to staff and inmate management, such as physical plant and community concerns. Accreditation benefits the organization because it provides a good defense against lawsuits as well as credibility and a safe, humane environment for inmates and staff.[11]

Policy and Its Development

The policy process is somewhat more complicated than many administrators realize. Obviously, memoranda issued from the CEO's office are insufficient. Each manager needs a clear understanding of the policy process and its elements: formulation, legitimation, appropriation, implementation, and evaluation.[12]

Formulation

Formulation is defined as the systematic development of a plan to meet a need or to act on a problem. Formulation is the first step in the policy process, and the policymaker must realize that policy formulation is very much a political activity. Jones[13] offers six guidelines for policy formulation:

1. Formulation need not be limited to one set of actors. There may be two or more groups producing competing or complementary proposals. Thus, getting one's issue on the agenda is important. Others may not per-

ceive a problem or they may view another problem as more pressing.
2. Formulation may proceed without the problem ever being clearly defined or without formulators ever having much contact with the affected groups.
3. There is no necessary coincidence between formulation and particular institutions, though it is a frequent activity of executive agencies.
4. Formulation and reformulation may occur over a long time without sufficient support for any one proposal ever developing.
5. There are often several appeal points for those who lose in the formulation process at any one level.
6. The process itself is never neutral.

None of these guidelines are terribly profound. They are offered only as a guide to action. As Jones suggests, they can "become advisories for those wishing to influence decision making."[14] Say, for example, that you are in favor of implementing Unit Management as a department-of-corrections-wide approach. You would first organize those in sympathy with your viewpoint and make sure the commissioner and key legislators understand the concept and the problems it would solve. Once key executives and legislators begin to understand the concept, they will begin to formulate proposals, and you may want to formulate a proposal of your own. In addition, you will want to ease all proposals along in the direction you wish. As pointed out earlier, "Formulation . . . is very much a political, though not necessarily a partisan, activity."[15]

Types of Formulation
There may be as many types of policy formulation as there are correctional agencies or even formulators, depending on the criteria for classification. For example, every corrections executive has developed policies relating to personnel

FIGURE 6.3
The Policy Formulation Framework

Stage 1: The Input Stage

Internal Factor Evaluation (IFE) Matrix	External Factor Evaluation (EFE) Matrix	Other Agency Profile Matrix

Stage 2: The Matching Stage

Threats-Opportunities Weaknesses-Strengths (TOWS) Matrix	Strategic Position and Action Evaluation (SPACE) Matrix

Stage 3: The Decision Stage

Quantitative Strategic Planning Matrix (QSPM)

Source: Reprinted with the permission of Macmillan College Publishing Company, from *Fundamentals of Strategic Management* by Fred R. David. Copyright © 1986 by Macmillan College Publishing Company, Inc.

matters, prison industries, and inmate programs. There are three types of formulation:

1. *Routine formulation.* This is a repetitive and mostly changeless process of reformulating similar proposals about an issue. It has a well-established place on the department or institutional agenda.
2. *Analogous formulation.* This refers to treating a new problem by relying on what was done in developing proposals for similar problems in the past.
3. *Creative formulation.* Creative formulation involves developing an essentially unprecedented proposal.[16]

Every type of policy problem will fit one of the above types. However, in order to effectively approach policy formulation, the executive or policy analyst needs a framework to help him or her develop a complete, thorough, and effective policy. The following framework attempts to address that need.

A Framework for Policy Formulation

How can one be assured that all possible variables in policy formulation have been considered? Fred R. David[17] offers a framework that allows the analyst or formulator to consider the variables that influence policy formulation. Figure 6.3 illustrates a three-stage decision-making framework consisting of an input stage, a matching stage, and a decision stage. Not all cases present enough information to enable the use of all the tools represented in this framework. However, in the field of corrections, it is important to gather as much information as possible when considering a new policy or reformulating an old one. One caveat before we proceed: the following tools are offered to aid the policy formulator, and the issue of bias must be considered. The value of the approach suggested here is that it encourages one to uncover and control bias as much as possible. In the end, the amount of bias present is left up to the individual formulator.

Stage 1: The Input Stage. Stage 1 is called the input stage because the three tools illustrated summarize the basic input needed before a policy can be generated.

The Internal Factor Evaluation (IFE)

The IFE summarizes the strengths and weaknesses of the organization's key management, public relations, finances, output of services, and planning and research. All factors should be stated objectively. Note that it is possible for a factor to be both a strength and a weakness. If this should occur, the factor should be included twice in the IFE Matrix.

TABLE 6.1
An IFE Matrix for Muscatine County, Iowa, Sheriff's Department

Key Internal Factor	Weight	Rating	Weighted Score
1. Poor management team	.10	1	.10
2. Very good public relations	.10	4	.40
3. Adequate service image	.12	3	.36
4. No ability to plan or research	.05	1	.05
5. Stable work force	.10	3	.30
6. Good employee relations	.10	3	.30
7. No promotional opportunities for employees	.05	1	.05
8. Stagnant work force	.03	1	.03
9. Rising jail inmate population	.15	3	.45
10. $20,000 per month to board prisoners to other jails	.20	3	.60
	1.00		2.64

Source: Reprinted with the permission of Macmillan Publishing Company from *Fundamentals of Strategic Management* by Fred R. David. Copyright © 1986 by Macmillan College Publishing Company, Inc. Information provided by: Lt. Ronald Dusenberry, Project Manager, Muscatine County, Iowa, Sheriff's Department.

The IFE answers four major questions about the organization.[18]

1. What are the organization's key strengths and weaknesses?
2. What is the relative importance of each strength and weakness to the organization's overall performance?
3. Does each factor represent a major weakness (a rating of 1),
   a minor weakness (a rating of 2),
   a minor strength (a rating of 3), or
   a major strength (a rating of 4)?
4. What is the organization's total weighted score resulting from the analysis of the IFE? Is the score above or below 2.50? A score above 2.50 indicates that the organization is favorably positioned for a major policy change.

In establishing the weight for each variable, the formulator is left to his or her best judgment. At this particular point, bias is apt to creep into the decision and so it is suggested that the decided weight be reached after consultation with a co-worker or subordinate. The weighted score is reached by multiplying across the chart. For example, table 6.1 shows that the first factor is "Poor Management Team" with a weight of .10 and a weighted score of .10 (.10 × 1 = .10). Be careful that the sum of all weights does not exceed 1.00.

The External Factor Evaluation (EFE)

The second tool in the policy formulation framework is the EFE. This tool is similar to the IFE except that its focus is on economic, social, cultural, demographic, political, governmental, legal, and technological opportunities and threats rather than on internal strengths and weaknesses.[19] Determine the weight of each factor and the weighted score the same as for the IFE. Table 6.2 illustrates this task. The EFE answers four questions of interest to the CEO.

1. What are the organization's environmental opportunities and threats?
2. What is the relative importance of each opportunity and threat to the organization's overall performance?
3. Does each factor represent a major threat (a rating of 1),
   a minor threat (a rating of 2),
   a minor opportunity (a rating of 3), or
   a major opportunity (a rating of 4)?

TABLE 6.2
An EFE Matrix for Muscatine County, Iowa, Sheriff's Department

Key External Factor	Weight	Rating	Weighted Score
1. Strong diversified tax base	.05	4	.20
2. Low unemployment	.05	3	.15
3. Broad community support for new jail	.10	4	.40
4. High transient population	.10	1	.10
5. Rising crime rate	.30	1	.30
6. Large age group 15–21	.05	1	.05
7. Various governments supportive of new jail	.05	4	.20
8. State jail inspector has put sheriff on notice that old jail may be closed	.30	4	1.20
	1.00		2.60

Source: Reprinted with the permission of Macmillan Publishing Company from *Fundamentals of Strategic Management* by Fred R. David. Copyright © 1986 by Macmillan College Publishing Company, Inc. Information provided by: Lt. Ronald Dusenberry, Project Manager, Muscatine County, Iowa, Sheriff's Department.

4. What is the organization's total weighted score on the EFE? Is the score above 2.50? A score greater than 2.50 indicates that the organization is well-positioned for a major policy change.

Other Agency Profile Matrix (OAPM)

Identifying and analyzing other agencies' strengths, weaknesses, policies/strategies, and objectives can be a valuable aid to the policy analyst or CEO. It could be particularly helpful in private corrections when other firms are attempting to penetrate a particular market, or if a public agency is attempting to thwart a private corrections firm overtures to the legislature, governor, or elected county officials. Therefore, the other agency profile is valuable as an "input" tool that summarizes information about others in the field, or in the case of private corrections, competitors.

The Other Agency Profile probes the following:[20]

1. Who are the other agencies/competitors?
2. What key factors are most important to their success in the field of corrections?
3. What is the relative importance of each key factor to their success?

4. To what extent is each agency/competitor strong or weak on each of the key factors? a major weakness (a rating of 1), a minor weakness (a rating of 2), a minor strength (a rating of 3), and a major strength (a rating of 4)
5. Overall, how strong or weak are the other agencies? Again, a score of 2.50 indicates a sound position for change.

The value of the OAPM is that it can objectively summarize the general performance of other agencies and their specific performance in certain areas, assuming that there is no need to reinvent the wheel each time a policy problem arises. If for any reason information on a public agency is not readily available from staff members, other sources are available, such as government documents. In the example in table 6.3, the Muscatine County sheriff could have considered contracting with one of two hypothetical private corrections companies. After reviewing the county's performance against what he knew about the private companies, the sheriff may decide that the taxpayer could get a better bargain from a private corrections firm. However, in the issue of private corrections,

TABLE 6.3
Other Agency Profile Matrix

Key Success Factors	Weight	Muscatine County		Corrections Company of the Midwest		Universal Corrections	
		Rating	Weighted Score	Rating	Weighted Score	Rating	Weighted Score
Service delivery							
Custody	.16	4	.64	4	.64	3	.48
Programs	.09	1	.09	2	.18	1	.09
Food	.16	4	.64	3	.48	3	.48
Health	.12	2	.24	2	.24	2	.24
Per diem cost	.22	4	.88	3	.66	2	.44
Technological ability	.05	1	.05	4	.20	1	.05
Relations with government in other contracts	.13	—	0	4	.52	3	.39
Financial strength	.07	4	.28	4	.28	3	.21
Total Weighted Scores	1.00		2.82		3.20		2.38

many other variables come into play that override the possibility of contracting with a private corporation to build and manage a jail. This issue is dealt with further in a later chapter. In the present illustration, given the scores of the three agencies, the sheriff could have seriously considered contracting with the fictitious Corrections Company of the Midwest to build and manage a jail for the county.

Stage 2: The Matching Stage. The Matching stage includes the TOWS Matrix and the SPACE Matrix.[21] These tools depend upon input from Stage 1. Matching means that the analyst or CEO can match internal and external factors to develop strategies for action or policy alternatives. For example, the Illinois Department of Corrections is overcrowded and needs new beds to alleviate the problem. The policy of the DOC is to provide inmates with safe and humane care, custody, and control, and overcrowded conditions do not fit into that policy. After obtaining needed information from Stage 1, the commissioner could take advantage of a projected budget surplus and the good will of certain key legislators to

push for the development of new institutions to alleviate overcrowding. This simplistic example illustrates that objective information is needed to justify many decisions that affect the department budget as well as the security of the community.

Threats—Opportunities—Weaknesses—Strengths (TOWS) Matrix

The TOWS is a matching tool that can help develop four different policy approaches: Strength-Opportunity (SO) strategies, Weakness-Opportunity (WO) strategies, Strength-Threat (ST) strategies, and Weakness-Threat (WT) strategies. Figure 6.4 illustrates how the TOWS Matrix is constructed.

All CEOs would like to exploit opportunities and ward off threats. Action can be based on matching key internal and external factors. Analysis and choice mostly involve making subjective judgments based on objective information.

Matching key internal and external factors requires a good deal of judgment. There is often no best answer; in addition, the purpose is to determine feasible alternatives, not to select the one best way to tackle a problem.

The Strategic Position and Action Evaluation (SPACE) Matrix

The SPACE Matrix (figure 6.5) provides a visual representation of what type of policy development approach is best for an organization. It is a four-quadrant framework that suggests whether an aggressive, conservative, defensive, or competitive type of approach should be used. Again, not all the tools need to be used. But the SPACE Matrix is relatively quick and visually indicates what approach to take.

There are five steps to the SPACE Matrix:[22]

1. For financial strength and agency strength assign a numerical value ranging from +1 (worst) to +6 (best) to each of the variables that comprise these dimensions.

2. Compute an average score for financial strength, competitive advantage, industry strength, and environmental stability by summarizing each dimensional factor rating and dividing by the number of variables included in the respective dimension.

3. Plot the average scores for the four dimen-

FIGURE 6.4
TOWS Matrix

(leave blank)	Strengths—S	Weaknesses—W
	1. 2. 3. 4. (list 5. 6. strengths) 7. 8. 9. 10.	1. 2. 3. 4. (list 5. 6. weaknesses) 7. 8. 9. 10.
Opportunities—O 1. 2. 3. 4. (list 5. 6. opportunities) 7. 8. 9. 10.	SO Strategies 1. 2. 3. 4. (use strengths 5. to take 6. advantage of 7. opportunities) 8. 9. 10.	WO Strategies 1. 2. 3. 4. (overcome 5. weaknesses by 6. taking 7. advantage of 8. opportunities) 9. 10.
Threats—T 1. 2. 3. 4. (list 5. 6. threats) 7. 8. 9. 10.	ST Strategies 1. 2. 3. 4. (use strengths 5. to avoid 6. threats) 7. 8. 9. 10.	WT Strategies 1. 2. 3. 4. (minimize 5. weaknesses and 6. avoid threats) 7. 8. 9. 10.

Source: Reprinted with the permission of Macmillan College Publishing Company from *Fundamentals of Strategic Management* by Fred R. David. Copyright © 1986 by Macmillan College Publishing Company, Inc.

sions (FS, IS, ES, and CA) on the appropriate axis in the SPACE Matrix.
4. Add the two scores on the horizontal axis and plot the resultant point on X. Add the two scores on the vertical axis and plot the resultant point on Y. Plot the intersection of the XY point.
5. Draw a directional vector from the origin (XY

intersection) through the new intersection point. This vector reveals the policy/strategy most effective or appropriate for the agency.

Figure 6.5 illustrates an agency that is stable, benefits from an economically sound community, and has the support of the community. Thus, an aggressive pursuit of a new jail is called for.

The Muscatine County Jail	The Muscatine County Jail was built in 1907 for a capacity of twenty-eight inmates. By 1988 the jail was totally inadequate, and by 1989 the county was spending approximately $250,000 annually to house prisoners in surrounding counties. In 1989 a variance was obtained from the state to operate a temporary thirty-two bed minimum-security facility. This variance was granted only as a temporary solution, with the condition that a major jail renovation or a new jail bond issue would soon be approved in Muscatine County.
	In 1988 the county began a public information campaign to let taxpayers know the projected need for and cost of housing prisoners. County supervisors and sheriff's personnel attended planning sessions on assessing a need for a new county jail through the National Institute of Corrections (NIC) in Boulder, Colorado. After seeking NIC assistance in pressing a needs assessment study on the project, the board hired a jail architect and consultant to prepare a preliminary design and cost proposal. Because of cost considerations, a 10-acre site already owned by the county was picked for the jail and sheriff's office. This 10-acre plot was part of 140 acres of county-owned farmland located at the edge of the city limits of Muscatine and adjacent to the intersection of two major highways. Also located upon this acreage was the county's care facility. Concerns over the possibility of stigmatizing the residents of the care facility with the close proximity of the jail, along with other considerations (both political and public), caused this site to be discarded.
	A major industrial employer in the city of Muscatine, which has its corporate headquarters in the downtown city area and wields considerable influence, campaigned over the years for a downtown revitalization project. By November 1990, the company successfully led a campaign to locate the jail project downtown, "where its location could serve as an anchor for other government agencies and businesses seeking to relocate." Part of the lure of locating downtown was the company's promise to give the project $850,000 that would offset the higher cost of obtaining a downtown site. Also, an additional $100,000 gift from a private donor was added to bring the total gift to $950,000 for obtaining property to create a plaza for the jail and surrounding government buildings. To make it possible to have a design for a plaza as proposed by the company and benefit the city's downtown district, the city of Muscatine offered to vacate streets, alleys, and a parking lot in the

Stage 3: The Decision Stage.
The Quantitative Strategic Planning
Matrix (QSPM)

At some point the CEO must make a decision, and perfect information is never available. Nevertheless, after gathering as much information as possible on the issue, the CEO must put it together. The QSPM is a valuable technique for analyzing policy-strategy alternatives.[23] The QSPM brings together information from Stage 1 and Stage 2 to help the CEO objectively decide what alternative to pursue.[24]

The format of the QSPM is illustrated in table 6.4. The key factors column is made up of key internal factors and key external factors, and the top row is comprised of possible alterna-

proposed three and one-half block plaza area. A never-before-used law in the Iowa code was promoted by the company and the city as an additional enticement. It allowed a government body to pass a bond issue with a simple majority vote of the public. This law requires a county government to enter into an agreement with its county seat's government (Muscatine) to develop a bond project. Under this law the project could only be implemented with the creation of another government entity, called an Authority, consisting of three private citizens appointed to oversee the bond vote, bond issuance, and bond retirement process. Among the citizens appointed to the Authority was its chairman, a vice president in the local company promoting the downtown plan.

The location downtown posed problems not found in a more rural site, and the downtown site did not lend itself easily to an efficient one-level jail design, as requested by the sheriff. A less desirable two-story operational design was proposed for downtown so as to not crowd the site. The site had to accommodate at least a 100-bed facility with a 50-bed expansion capability. The estimated construction costs of locating only the jail downtown was $8.5 million, not counting the gift money to obtain land, and it eliminated the Sheriff's Department road patrol offices and other areas. It was determined later in the schematic design phase that a one-story jail could be made to fit on the site with the possibility for expansion, but the addition of future sheriff's offices would be problematic and parking would always be especially difficult. The sheriff's office having separated from the jail project, political arguments to eventually build it downtown or at the rural site also involved a design issue. A long-term master plan had been formulated for the entire multiblock area, which involved government building additions and landscaping for the plaza grounds, but most of these plans were cost prohibitive. Differing opinions and perspectives concerning design issues and control of the building and plaza area caused the project to move along at a slower pace and the design to change often to accommodate the desires of city, county, and authority officials.

The Muscatine County Jail Project, scheduled for completion by the end of 1994 or early 1995, will present a visually pleasing addition to the downtown area. In the long run, however, will it serve the citizens of the county well into the future? The experience of Muscatine County serves as a lesson in the policy process. It also reminds us that the policymaker can win the formulation war but very easily lose at later stages in the process. (See the photo gallery.)

FIGURE 6.5:
Space Matrix for Muscatine County, Iowa,
Sheriff's Department

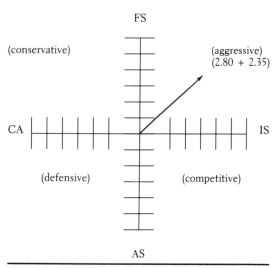

Source: Reprinted with the permission of Macmillan College Publishing Company from *Fundamentals of Strategic Management* by Fred R. David. Copyright © 1986 by Macmillan College Publishing Company, Inc.

tives. (Note that the IFE and EFE contribute to the left column.) The next column (rating) is composed of ratings from the IFE and EFE. The next column is the Attractiveness Score (AS), which is multiplied to provide the Total Attractiveness Score (TAS). The TAS is then summed to provide a score that when compared to another TAS provides a relative assessment of whether to pursue that particular choice.

Identifying the organization's key internal strengths and weaknesses and key external threats and opportunities should be relatively easy when the IFE and EFE Matrices are reviewed. One also assigns ratings to the key factors as listed on the IFE and EFE.

By reviewing the matching matrices (TOWS and SPACE) one can identify possible alternatives. Determining this involves simply attaching a numerical score of 1 to 4 (not acceptable to most acceptable). One then simply com-

putes the TAS and sums the scores for an indication of which direction to pursue.[25]

Application of the QSPM
The question of whether to build a new jail or renovate the old jail was a thorny problem for several years for Muscatine County, Iowa. By using the QSPM, the county sheriff could have objectively plotted a course to guide the county through an issue fraught with emotion.

Limitations of the Policy Formulation Framework. The major limitation of the framework is that the subjective ratings allow bias to creep into the process. Bias can be used by the policymaker or planner to justify (or fail to justify) a major policy decision. Therefore, the administrator, sheriff, or warden must constantly be on guard against personal bias as well as the bias of subordinates. Another issue is time. If the CEO has a planning department that can devote time to gathering information and devising alternative courses of action, the framework is well worth it. On the other hand, in smaller agencies where there is no planning department and the planning function is left up to the sheriff or director, the framework may prove to be cumbersome and time consuming. However, in a small agency, there may not be as many variables that need to be considered, and the CEO may be able to work out a QSPM without going through all of the other stages.

Legitimation and Appropriation

While the formulation process rarely occurs in a vacuum, the legitimation of policy is absolutely necessary if the policy or program is to get off the ground. According to Jones,[26] there are two forms of legitimation. The first refers to the basic political process; that is, those processes that approve specific proposals for solving problems. The second form of legitimation comprises those specific processes through which government pro-

TABLE 6.4
QSPM for Muscatine County, Iowa, Sheriff's Department Policy Alternatives

Key Factors	Rating	Build New Jail		Renovate Old Jail		Private Corrections Company		Rationale for Attractiveness Score
		AS	TAS	AS	TAS	AS	TAS	
Internal Factors								
Poor management team	1	4	4	1	1	4	4	Coming retirements allow for
Very good public relations	4	4	16	3	12	3	12	good people to move up.
Adequate service image	3	3	9	1	3	3	9	Close-knit community.
No planning or research capability	1	2	2	1	1	4	4	
Stable work force	3	3	9	3	3	3	9	
Good employee relations	3	1	3	1	3	3	9	
Stagnant work force	3	2	6	2	6	2	6	Slow vertical movement.
External Factors								
Rising inmate jail population	1	4	4	1	1	1	1	
$20,000 per month to board prisoners out	1	4	4	1	1	4	4	
Sum total attractiveness score			57		31		58	

Source: Lt. Ron Dusenberry, Muscatine County, Iowa Sheriff's Department. Reprinted with the permission of Macmillan College Publishing Company from *Fundamentals of Strategic Management* by Fred R. David. Copyright © 1986 by Macmillan College Publishing Company, Inc.

grams are authorized. Jones refers to the first as legitimacy and the second as legitimation.

For example, the Department of Corrections wants a policy of establishing a minimum level of literacy for inmates who pass through the system. To enforce that policy the DOC needs legislative support for denying parole to eligible inmates who have not achieved the desired minimum literacy level. The legislature's support of such a policy would provide the legitimacy for the proposal. Referring the proposal through committees, lobbying key legislators, and traversing various other legislative obstacles comprise the legitimation process.

The key to the legitimation process is getting the issue on the agenda of the legitimators and building coalitions among those whose approval is needed. It is a process whereby someone always loses and someone always wins. Rarely is anyone totally satisfied.

As many authors have pointed out, one can win in the legitimation phase and lose in the appropriation phase. For example, the 1988 Indiana legislature approved the construction of a new maximum-security institution but failed to appropriate the money for site acquisition and construction until 1989, when $1.5 million was approved for site acquisition and other preliminaries. Finally, in 1990, $5.6 million was approved for construction. This example shows how key figures who were against the project lost the legitimation battle but nevertheless were able to slow the project. In some instances key figures are able to win the battle by stopping appropriation entirely.

Policy Implementation

It is easy to understand implementation, but it is tough to accomplish it. Usually we call implementation "getting the job done." It is important to remember that implementation is highly interactive with policy formulation, legitimation, and formulation. It wasn't until the 1960s and early

1970s that implementation began to be seen as a separate activity, not just the end result of formulation.

Implementation Defined

Pressman and Wildavsky define implementation as "the ability to forge subsequent links in the causal chain so as to obtain the desired results."[27] They point out that simple sequences of events are dependent on complex chains of reciprocal interaction. Simplicity is the key, and these authors assert that simplicity in policies should be the rule of thumb, because the fewer the steps involved in implementing a program the fewer the opportunities for something to go wrong.

Ripley and Franklin define implementation as "what happens after laws are passed authorizing a policy, a benefit, or some kind of tangible output."[28] The policy implementation process involves

> many important actors holding different and competing goals and expectations, who work within a context of an increasingly large and complex mix of government programs that require participation from numerous layers and units of government, and who are affected by powerful factors beyond their control.[29]

Implementation and the CEO

The warden or chief probation officer will rarely be involved in grand, sweeping policy changes that affect the operation of the entire agency. On the other hand, they do formulate and implement policy that affects the day-to-day operation of the agency. These are not to be confused with procedures.

Figure 6.6 illustrates the local process. Imagine the warden of a correctional institution who has noticed a need to revise visiting policy and procedures, or perhaps a staff member has brought the need to his or her attention. The

FIGURE 6.6
The CEO and Policy Implementation

warden should first obtain input from the staff, in particular the officers who work in the visiting area. He or she will then appoint a committee or task force to look at all aspects of inmate visiting. The committee will then report back to the warden. After studying the report, the warden will convene the committee for further discussion. Once all issues and changes are clarified, the warden will then appoint a staff member, often the person responsible for planning and research, to implement the new policy and procedures.

This is a simple and straightforward process. On the surface, it is a process that one intuitively understands. All too often, however, wardens devise policy and order implementation simply through memos. To do this is to invite resentment and opposition.

The Policy Organization

In large organizations and even at the local level rarely is anyone placed in charge of policy implementation. This is largely for two reasons: (1) the decentralized nature of policy formulation in many agencies, and (2) most formulators view the implementation process as an extension of formulation.

Mazmanian and Sabatier[30] have identified a process that is successful in implementing policy on a grand scale. They point out that each public policy carries a need for organization, structure, and procedures to complete tasks mandated by the policy. The necessary organization can be provided by a new entity, by part

The Multnomah County Detention Center: The Policy Organization at Work	Multnomah County, Oregon, had several years' difficulty with the Rocky Butte Jail, which was opened in 1947. The jail was outdated from the beginning and by 1980 proved totally inadequate for the increased population of the county. In the spring of 1982, construction began on a new downtown detention center that was a welcome addition to the central business district. The center included ground-floor space for restaurants and shops and second-floor office space for state criminal justice agencies and the courts. (See the photo gallery.) In the fall of 1982, a transition team was organized to facilitate the move into the new jail. Hundreds, if not thousands, of details needed attention if the facility was to open on time and with a minimal number of problems. Thanks to the organization and planning of J. H. (Jack) Chapman, the Multnomah County Detention Center (MCDC) opened on time and under budget on November 7, 1983. The transition team was composed of a director and five full-time members. These five people were responsible for all the details, such as policies and procedures, furniture, equipment, and coordinating the efforts of the various subcontractors, the project manager, and the county. The efforts of all team members resulted in few details being overlooked. To supplement the efforts of the team, others with particular skills were recruited on a full-time, temporary, or part-time basis from the Corrections Division, courts, and prosecutor's office.

of an existing unit, or by an aggregation of parts of several existing units. The members of the "policy organization" may not realize it, but they have a separate identity.

The policy organization has its own task, and as Mazmanian and Sabatier point out, "It exists, is affected by, and influences its environment. It has structure and resources; it carries out tasks, makes decisions, and communicates."[31]

The members of the policy organization are given full or part-time assignments to carry out the specific tasks of the organization. At the direction of a chief or director, the members pursue various tasks that meet organizational needs and attain organizational objectives. Members can volunteer for the assignment or they can be directly assigned to the task; they can work in the assignment for a specific period of time or until the job is completed. Assignment to the organization is usually considered a plus as it gives the member the opportunity to pursue entrepreneurial urges and to be creative.

On the other side, the organization benefits from the members' talents, skills, and enthusiasm. Finally, the policy organization has a definite life span. Once the task is completed, the organization is abolished and members return to their original assignments.

FIGURE 6.7
The Policy Organization

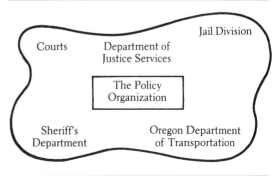

Mazmanian and Sabatier[32] identify several roles in the policy organization.

- *The politician.* This person represents the organization's awareness of and interest in such areas as elected politics and the elected legislative body with which the policy organization must contend. He or she is helpful in creating formal authorizations that aid in getting the job done.
- *The entrepreneur.* Entrepreneurial skills are necessary to plan and organize. A certain amount of charisma is helpful to assure that the needs of the organization and its members are met in order to get the job done.
- *The technicians.* The technicians are those who have command of certain skills. These are the people who can articulate and implement ideas conceived by the politicians and entrepreneurs. To a large extent, everyone is a technician, but here we refer to those who have the necessary operational skills.
- *Full-time/Part-time.* The organization is held together by a group of full-time employees who are supplemented by full- or part-time members contributing their spe-

cial skills for a short period; for example, two to four weeks.

Policy Evaluation

We cannot simply formulate policies, go to the trouble of legitimation and appropriation, and finally implement the policy or program without some attempt to determine whether the policy is working. We need to identify flaws and shortcomings in order to fine-tune the process so that it better meets the needs of those the policy or program is intended to serve. Evaluation research is one of the few available ways for us to methodically and realistically change the direction of a program or policy.

Evaluation usually brings to mind sophisticated schemes and paradigms to which the action-oriented corrections executive is unable to relate. This need not be so. We are basically asking, "How are we doing?" or "How did it go?" or "Can we do it differently or better?"

Figure 6.8 illustrates several levels of evaluation. We have discussed policy implementation and the steps involved. Attention must be given to the evaluation phase during implementation in order to build in the evaluation

---

FIGURE 6.8
The Policy Evaluation Process

Policy Process				
Formulation ⟶	Legitimation ⟶	Appropriation ⟶	Implementation ⟶	Evaluation

Policy Implementation Evaluation Concurrent Activities				
		Level		
1	2	3	4	5
Monitor Daily Tasks	Assess Program/Policy Activities	Evaluate Outcome	Measure Effectiveness	Assess Impact on the Problem

Source: Adapted from Karen Sue Trisco and V. C. League, "Evaluation of Human-Service Programs," *The 1980 Handbook for Group Facilitators* (San Diego: University Associates, 1980), p. 225.

procedures.[33] Since programs usually flow from specific policies, one way to assess the impact or effectiveness of the policy is to review the program, or programs, that have resulted from policies. There are five levels of program evaluation:

Level 1: Monitor Daily Tasks. Level 1 of the evaluation scrutinizes all internal workings, such as: (1) Are staff working where and when they should? (2) Are contracts being honored? and (3) Are daily tasks being carried out?

Level 2: Assess program/Policy Activities. Here we ask who is doing what and how well the activities are planned. In addition, we need to assess, for example, the program's image and whether or not the target group is being served.

Level 3: Measure Effectiveness. At level 3 we need to enumerate the effects of the program. Who? what? and when? are key questions. Of interest are unanticipated outcomes: (1) Have objectives been achieved? and (2) Should we substitute activities for those currently being carried out?

Level 4: Evaluate the Outcome. In level 4 we assess the outcomes of the activities in levels 1 and 2. Not only should we use official records to gather hard data but we should also use survey instruments and personal interviews to determine our success.

Level 5: Assess Impact on the Problem. We are now ready to ask the question "How did we do?" We are interested in whether or not the problem has been reduced and to what extent. Finally, have we generated new knowledge that will help resolve the problem in the future?

Evaluation greatly contributes to our understanding of the policy process. It is defensive in nature in that we can anticipate future needs and yet remain relatively free of criticism for not attempting to look to the future. It is necessary to make one further point before closing this section. The ability to assess impact may be limited unless one is able to measure the social, economic, and political indicators and how they have changed because of programs and policies. This enters the realm of policy analysis, an area that agencies are seldom asked to explore. Program evaluation attempts to discover whether bureaucrats have followed proper procedures and routines and whether inmates or clients have changed as a result of the program. But the evaluation alone is only one factor that will be considered when decisions are made about next year's agenda and budget. Program evaluation does not take into account budget restraints, taxation issues, public opinion changes, and changes in state or national priorities. It only reveals: "How did we do?"

Unanticipated Policy Consequences

In chapter 3 the 1956 Federal Aid Highway Transportation Act was discussed relative to its purpose of aiding travelers as they drove their automobiles around the United States. The unintended consequence was that it made it easy for people to move out of the city and thus created the suburban rings that absorbed the white middle class, leaving the central city to the poor and mostly black inhabitants. Policies sometime appear to take on a life of their own, and planners sometimes fail, or are unable, to effectively account for all possible outcomes. Thus, "because of their complexity, social systems are capable of producing problems neither expected nor results intended."[34]

One illustration may shed light on this area. On September 20, 1979, the Texas Department of Corrections (TDC) lost a civil rights trial when Judge William W. Justice issued an opinion roundly criticizing the TDC. The result was a "substantial reordering of relations between the prison system and the legislature, a redistribution of power within TDC, and a new system of management and control."[35] Judge Justice had earned a reputation as a "kamikaze liberal"[36] and genuinely believed that change in the TDC was necessary within Constitutional limits.

The ordered changes in TDC policy and procedures had consequences unanticipated by Judge Justice or his appointed special master, who was designated to oversee ordered change. There was a dramatic rise in inmate violence, disobedience on the part of inmates, and a fractured and disorganized officer force.[37] The ordered changes were very costly in terms of dollars and staff morale. Had the court undertaken steps such as scenario planning and computer simulation they may have been able to anticipate some of the consequences and perhaps could have ameliorated many of the problems that followed. However, perfect foresight is never possible, and uncertainty will never be totally eradicated. As social complexity increases (and the TDC example was extremely complicated), the more unanticipated externalities will appear.

Summary

All too often policy is conceived and implemented without much thought. Correctional managers need to be aware of the policy process and cognizant that each step has a separate set of activities that are easily identified.

Policy formulation is a process that includes many actors. Often it is dependent on the skill of the formulator in getting the issue on the agenda of those in power. Policy legitimation is the process of approving specific proposals to address certain issues and the processes of getting those programs or policies approved.

Policy appropriation is the process of funding a specific policy initiative. One can win in

the policy legitimation phase and lose the appropriation battle. Policy implementation is the skillful implementation of the policy aimed at addressing a specific problem. The policy process is incomplete without an evaluation phase. We need to ask: "How are we doing?" Finally, the effective manager needs to be aware of the unanticipated consequences of policy formulation and implementation. The more complex the social situation, the more likely it is that unanticipated consequences will appear.

Reviewing the Case

Roy Gerard and Bob Levinson faced a difficult task. The U.S. Bureau of Prisons wanted to improve service delivery and security. Violence plagued many institutions, and programs were suffering. Gerard and Levinson knew there was a better way to manage institutions, but the problem was convincing others.

They decided to attack the problem by establishing Unit Management at the newly opened Kennedy Youth Center and using that success to sell bureau personnel on UM. The project was a success, and when staff were transferred from KYC to other institutions they readily raised their voices in favor of UM. Before long all youthful-offender institutions were converted to Unit Management. In 1972 the Bureau of Prisons regionalized, further reinforcing the aims of decentralization and Unit Management. In the meantime, cooptation, education, and even bureaucratic coercion were used to implement Unit Management.

The final hurdle was cleared with the successful implementation of Unit Management at the U.S. Penitentiary at Lewisberg, Pennsylvania. It was a long, tough battle. It pitted respected old-line wardens against respected visionary wardens. The adoption of UM has saved hundreds of thousands of dollars in overtime costs and facility repairs. It opened a new career ladder to personnel and allowed decisions to be made by line staff. Most important, it was a brilliant demonstration of policy formulation, legitimation, and implementation.

For Further Study

Ben M. Crouch and James W. Marquart. *An Appeal to Justice: Litigated Reform of Texas Prisons* (Austin: University of Texas Press, 1989).

Karen Sue Trisco and V. C. League, "Evaluation of Human-Service Programs," *The 1980 Handbook*

for Group Facilitators (San Diego: University Associates, 1980), pp. 224–32.

Charles O. Jones, *An Introduction to the Study of Public Policy*, 3d ed. (Pacific Grove, Calif.: Brooks/Cole, 1984).

Key Terms

Policy	**Procedures**
Rules	**Policy Formulation**
Routine Formulation	**Policy Legitimation**
Policy Implementation	**Policy Organization**

The Budget Process

7

Case Study: Claremont Custody Center, Coalinga, California

In 1987 the California legislature approved a bill that allows the Department of Corrections to contract with municipal governments for services.[1] Shortly afterward, the officials of Coalinga approved the construction and operation of a 420-bed facility exclusively under contract to the California Department of Corrections. This unique arrangement provides jobs for the area and income to the city treasury.

The uniqueness of this relationship, as well as the responsibilities of operating a correctional facility, required the city to learn and implement sound correctional policies and procedures as well as meet new state regulations. The facility budget was one of the more difficult tasks for the city to put into place. First, the actual costs for workers' compensation and utilities were underestimated. The staffing plan did not provide for enough positions in the Food Service Department, and there was insufficient funding for the Maintenance Department. Therefore, from the beginning, management staff knew it would be necessary to divert funds to these departments in order to meet minimal needs. Finally, the severe economic recession of 1990 and 1991 forced the state to make substantial funding reductions for fiscal year 1992.

Since most department managers in the facility had little or no budgetary experience, it was apparent that a system to ensure the most efficient use of limited funds was necessary.

Cost centers were established for nine departments, and managers were held accountable for line item expenditures. Considerable latitude to cost center managers was provided by delegating responsibility to the department managers for overseeing their own budgets. Two procedures were established for monitoring expenditures. First, departments were required to submit a purchase requisition that identified the specific line item that was to be debited for the purchase of goods or services. This enabled management to monitor expenditures on a day-to-day basis. Secondly, monthly meetings with all department managers were conducted. This permitted all departments to gain a better understanding of the overall budget operation. It also enabled the group to identify previously unknown needs and to make line item adjustments where appropriate. This proved to be an important exercise during the first budget year when several needs could not be anticipated prior to preparing the budget.

These procedures and safeguards for accountability have been effective. At the end of the first fiscal year the facility was successful in balancing its budget. At the end of the first quarter of the second fiscal year the facility was within budget, and all departments had learned to operate within budgetary guidelines.

Introduction

Total criminal justice system expenditures are now over $60 billion and growing. In 1988 over $19 billion of that amount was spent by corrections alone. The U.S. government spent $1,226,395,000, and state and local government spent over $17 billion.[2] This investment represents a respectable percent of the total national product, and it is money spent on services not directly used by all of our citizens. Put another way, if $16,000 is spent in keeping a prisoner for one year in prison, then that figure represents money not spent on parks, education, health care, or other services that are directly consumed by the inhabitants of a state.

Corrections and the Budget

Corrections budgets continue to spiral. Secretaries and commissioners of corrections continue to request funds to build new institutions or to update older facilities. More employees are hired to supervise and otherwise work with offenders. Institutions need more money to cover the increased costs related to food, utilities, and other services at the same time the public demands longer and more definite prison sentences. Yet few are willing to have their taxes increased to pay for the cost of corrections.

The knowledgeable corrections manager knows that in the future he or she will have to do more with less money. In fact, the corrections

TABLE 7.1

Direct Expenditures for Correctional Operations and Capital Outlay—1971–1985 (in thousands)

Level	Actual Costs		Inflation-Adjusted Costs in Constant 1971 Dollars		Level	Actual Costs		Inflation-Adjusted Costs in Constant 1971 Dollars	
	Operations	Capital	Operations	Capital		Operations	Capital	Operations	Capital
1971					**1979**				
Federal	106,024	4,777	—	—	Federal	324,582	29,379	181,582	16,393
State	1,179,821	143,283	—	—	State	3,173,302	358,197	1,770,703	199,874
Local	788,215	68,953	—	—	Local	1,958,984	195,376	1,093,113	109,020
1972					**1980**				
Federal	125,524	7,748	121,507	7,500	Federal	375,000	12,000	184,125	5,892
State	1,270,238	107,538	1,229,590	104,097	State	3,693,931	563,578	1,813,720	276,717
Local	840,037	71,245	813,156	68,965	Local	2,030,232	226,010	996,844	110,971
1973					**1981**				
Federal	149,474	21,380	136,171	19,477	Federal	403,000	10,000	179,335	4,450
State	1,435,259	98,661	1,307,521	89,881	State	4,203,970	639,887	1,870,767	284,750
Local	943,285	92,149	859,333	83,948	Local	2,321,014	290,951	1,032,851	129,473
1974					**1982**				
Federal	170,133	44,396	139,679	36,449	Federal	499,000	14,000	209,580	5,880
State	1,688,071	124,458	1,385,906	102,180	State	4,887,192	672,600	2,052,621	282,492
Local	1,091,427	121,911	896,062	100,089	Local	2,638,840	337,315	1,108,313	141,672
1975					**1983**				
Federal	196,009	20,769	147,399	15,618	Federal	555,000	21,000	225,885	8,547
State	2,015,826	177,174	1,515,901	133,235	State	5,610,585	712,655	2,283,508	290,051
Local	1,283,389	150,147	965,109	112,911	Local	2,990,917	512,206	1,217,303	212,131
1976					**1984**				
Federal	242,886	13,466	172,692	9,574	Federal	632,000	49,000	246,480	19,110
State	2,276,335	198,448	1,618,474	141,097	State	6,313,548	847,262	2,462,284	330,432
Local	1,485,243	169,134	1,056,008	120,254	Local	3,328,554	598,537	1,298,136	233,429
1977					**1985**				
Federal	253,555	45,163	169,375	30,169	Federal	670,000	50,000	251,920	18,800
State	2,561,067	285,953	1,710,793	191,017	State	7,304,000	1,066,000	2,746,304	400,816
Local	1,609,475	178,853	1,075,129	119,474	Local	3,826,000	633,000	1,438,576	238,008
1978									
Federal	305,314	31,860	189,295	19,753					
State	2,855,318	321,645	1,770,297	199,420					
Local	1,813,931	194,642	1,124,637	120,678					

Note: The figures for 1985 differ from those published by the Bureau of Justice Statistics in *Justice Expenditure and Employment, 1985*. BJS figures for 1985 were obtained from a special survey by the Bureau of the Census, using the methodology of the 1971–1979 Expenditure and Employment in the Criminal Justice System series. That series was discontinued in 1979, so expenditure amounts were obtained from the Bureau of the Census' general surveys of government finances. The Bureau modifies these data each year for the BJS to publish in its post-1979 Justice Expenditure and Employment series, but the methods of data collection and analysis differ from those used in the earlier series. For the sake of consistency, I have used the 1984 and 1985 Bureau of the Census figures from the general government finance survey rather than the 1985 figures from the special survey done for the BJS.

Sources: All 1971–1979 data from various annual reports in the *Expenditure and Employment Data for Criminal Justice System* series, Washington, D.C.: U.S. Department of Justice (1971: Tables 4, 5; 1972: Tables 4, 39; 1973 through 1975: Tables 4, 39; 1975: Tables 4, 40; 1976: Tables 4A, 45; 1977: Tables 4, 47; 1978: Tables 4A, 47; 1979: Tables 4, 44). 1980–1984 federal data and 1982–1984 state/local data from unpublished sources provided by U.S. Department of Commerce, Bureau of the Census. 1980–1981 state and local spending from *Justice Expenditure and Employment Extracts: 1980 and 1981*, Washington, D.C.: U.S. Department of Justice, 1985, Tables 2 and 21. 1985 data from U.S. Bureau of the Census, *Government Finances in 1984–1985*, Washington, D.C.: U.S. Government Printing Office, 1986, Table 8. This information was compiled by Douglas C. McDonald, "The Cost of Corrections: In Search of the Bottom Line," in National Institute of Corrections, *Research in Corrections*, (Boulder National Institute of Corrections, 2:1, February 1989), pp. 13–14.

manager has become one of the more skillful managers in the public sector when it comes to getting the most for the dollar. No one is certain when we will see the top of the growth curve. Real costs have exceeded all estimates.[3]

It is extremely difficult to estimate the cost of corrections. The problem lies in part with governmental accounting procedures. Often some of the costs for one agency are paid by another agency; hence, corrections managers are rarely able to give an accurate response to the question "How much per inmate did it cost you to keep all state prisoners confined and under supervision last year?" The response is often calculated by dividing the agency budget for the fiscal year by the number of prisoners. This figure is always low for the reason that the state departments of corrections, for example, rarely include pensions and fringe benefits in their costs. Some jurisdictions do not even include maintenance costs for the physical plant in their budgets because that item is managed by another agency. Thus, we really do not know the cost of corrections.

Indirect Budgetary Expenditures

McDonald[4] provides an excellent discussion of the cost of corrections. He asserts that it is necessary for correctional managers to have a clear and precise understanding of the fiscal consequences of different choices and of how correctional costs are calculated or miscalculated. In addition to the direct costs of corrections, i.e., food, salaries, and utilities, he calls our attention to five areas (capital expenditures) often overlooked by corrections managers.

Amortizing capital expenditures. Most analyses of correctional costs do not amortize capital spending over time. Consequently capital spending is often understated. McDonald points out that the best method is to spread the cost of a facility evenly over the years the facility is in operation and providing a useful service. This is called the "straight-line" method of allocation.

Financing. If financed by borrowing, the costs of acquiring assets should be considered current operating costs. In public accounts this is rarely the case.

Expenditures of other agencies. Direct costs incurred by other agencies that help the corrections agency accomplish its mission should be counted. Teachers' salaries, utility bills, and transportation are examples of costs often paid by other branches of government.

Disentangling costs within an agency. Agencies often perform a variety of functions, and it is often difficult to disentangle the costs. For example, a probation agency performs both a correctional function (supervision and counseling of offenders) and a law-enforcement function (investigations for pre-sentence reports and violations). The Sheriff's Department may include jail costs with many law-enforcement costs.

Expenditures from other accounts. Some costs are paid out of general government accounts. Examples include pension and fringe benefits, which are handled for all state or county employees by one branch of government. Failure to include these items causes the costs of corrections to be vastly understated.

Establishing a budget is a complicated procedure, and the effective manager needs to be familiar with the process and pitfalls in order to efficiently manage his or her agency and provide accurate figures to taxpayers and legislators. Budgets are murky waters indeed, and most corrections managers are content to leave them to the "bean counters," who often wield disproportionate control over the agency.[5] The corrections manager needs to be aware of the history and process of public budgeting in order to have full control over his or her agency.

The Budget Process

Budgeting is the process of determining priorities and how to achieve them. In a correctional organization this can be as simple as writing out estimated expenditures for the coming fiscal year, as the supervisor of a work release center must do each spring or summer. It can also be as complicated as attempting to anticipate population growth, cost of programs, cost of new facilities, and so on, as the commissioner of corrections must do each year. In both cases, the work-release center supervisor and the commissioner must establish priorities and request or allocate certain funds to achieve those priorities.

The History of Budgets and the Budget Process

The literature on budgeting has tended to obscure the fact that we know very little about it.[6] Wildavsky points out that "there is nothing of substance about how or why budgeting decisions are actually made."[7] Before proceeding, we are well advised to review the history of public budgeting, which Nicholas L. Henry[8] has summarized very well.

Figure 7.2 illustrates the evolution of budget-preparation theory. Line-item budgeting, for example, began in 1921. It lives on today as a means of allowing the budget preparer to organize his or her thoughts. Performance budgeting as a separate point of view had a definite life span, and upon its foundation rests PPB. PPB has fallen from favor, but its contributions such as up-front planning, gave rise to zero-based budgeting. One can assume that politics have always played a role in budget preparation, but only since 1980 when ZBB was officially

canceled as the official approach to preparing the U.S. budget has the political approach been recognized through the use of incrementalism. All forms of budgeting are seen in the preparation of village, town, city, county, and state government budgets.

Line-Item Budgeting (1921–Present)

The traditional line-item budget is so-called because of the way it is composed. An item is noted in the left column and the cost of the item in the right column. For example,

Potato chips (2 cases) $25

Henry asserts that all governments have always had line-item budgets and that in the United States the refinement of the line-item budget was due to the pressure of several forces. The first was the need to establish a consolidated executive budget. The second was what Henry calls the "administrative-integration movement." This movement advocated the consolidation of agencies, bureaus, and various boards to enhance the president's appointive power; all such reforms were aimed at ensuring efficiency and coordination in government. The third pressure was the desire to build administrative honesty by restricting the discretionary powers of public administrators.

These forces led to competitive bidding, centralized purchasing, and standardized accounting procedures, to name a few innovations in government, and to the passage of the Budget and Accounting Act of 1921. This act created the Bureau of the Budget (BOB) and established the General Accounting Office (GAO) as a congressional check on federal spending.

The result was that line-item budgeting became associated with governmental honesty and efficiency. The problem with line-item bud-

FIGURE 7.1
Components of Correctional Costs

Agency expenditure for a correctional purpose

Expenditures by other agencies for correctional purposes

Expenditures by other governmental accounts for correctional purposes

Repair and maintenance

} Operating costs

Financing costs (interest portion of debt service)

Cost of constructing/renovating the physical plant, including replacement of equipment

} Capital Costs

} Direct government costs

Cost of services dedicated to correctional purposes by overhead governmental organizations

Cost of public assistance of families of persons jailed or otherwise prevented from supporting them

Cost of not being able to use correctional resources for other purposes ("opportunity costs")

} Indirect government costs

Losses/injuries due to particular correctional practice

Impact on environment

} Indirect social costs

} Total costs

Source: Douglas C. McDonald, "The Cost of Corrections: In Search of the Bottom Line," in National Institute of Corrections, *Research in Corrections* (Boulder: National Institute of Corrections, 2:1, February 1989), p. 7.

geting was that it stressed inputs only and gave no concern to the quality of service given.

Performance Budgeting (1940–1960)

Several influences caused performance budgeting to be implemented. Many people in government raised their voices in favor of an approach that would control government behavior as well as account for objects. During the presidency of Franklin D. Roosevelt, three historical factors merged that brought about a shift in thinking.[9]

First, the line-item budgeteers had long advocated certain control techniques that finally became firmly established. The resulting accounting, purchasing, and personnel practices released many people from traditional "watchdog duties." Second, with the expansion of government, there emerged a need to coordinate and centralize government activities. Third, government became increasingly viewed as a mechanism for delivering benefits, and the budget was seen as an appropriate managerial delivery system. Thus, the budget was more and more seen as a tool to measure effectiveness.

During this time, public administration as a skill rose to prominence, and a managerial orientation toward the budget emerged. While the line-item budget was interested in how much for what item, government began to ask: "How many people are served?" or "How many service units can we derive from this expenditure?"

Planning-Programming-Budgeting (1961–1970)

Performance budgeting represented a significant step forward in terms of governmental accountability, but it still ignored basic questions such as: "What are the most important programs?" and "How can we evaluate the performance of these programs?"

The response was the implementation of Planning-Programming-Budgeting (PPB). PPB concepts began originally with General Motors

in the 1920s. During World War II the War Production Board used PPB concepts to control expenditures and measure performance. In the 1950s the RAND Corporation used systems analysis to evaluate weapons systems and suggested the use of "program packages" as budgeting units in air force planning.

President Kennedy's appointment of Robert McNamara as Secretary of Defense in 1960 changed the way government in general and the military in particular did business. McNamara stepped into a highly contentious arena in which all branches of the military competed with each other. McNamara thought that the Pentagon's competitiveness was a major contributor to inefficiency, and PPB via systems analysis allowed him to take control. President Lyndon Johnson was so impressed that he ordered PPB to be applied throughout the federal government. In

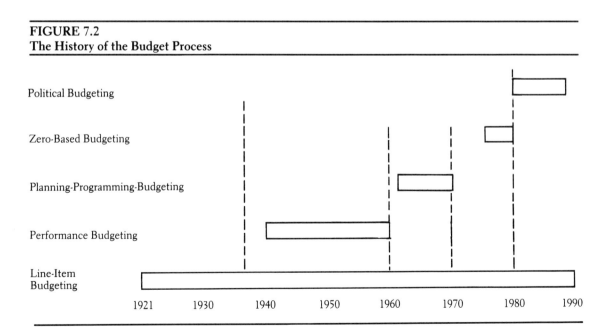

FIGURE 7.2
The History of the Budget Process

1967 the Bureau of the Budget ordered twenty-one federal agencies to use PPB.

PPB Defined

According to Henry,[10] to know what PPB is, one need only look at its three components.

- *Planning*—operational goals of the organization and the methods to be used to achieve those goals over a specified period of time.
- *Programming*—the scheduling and implementation of the particular projects aimed at fulfilling the organization's goals in the most efficient and effective way possible.
- *Budgeting*—the price estimate attached to each goal, plan, program, and project.

Gross[11] asserts that there is great disagreement among proponents of PPB as to what PPB is and is not. He states that the spirit of PPB is more important than the definition—that there is "really no one system" and that without the union of program planning and budgeting, planners may lose touch with the constraints imposed by scarce resources.[12]

The advantage of PPB appears to be that it clarifies options available to policymakers.[13] It forces the user to formulate objectives. Planning may then be keyed to programs, which in turn are keyed to budgeting.

Thus, PPB is useful because it forces the planner and the executive to think about results. Long-term goals, costs of programs, consideration of alternatives, and so on, all contributed to its popularity. However, PPB's strengths were the cause of its demise, because budgeting at the federal level is characterized by unclear goals and often overlapping programs. However, PPB is still used by many states and local jurisdictions, with apparently satisfactory results. Further, it stimulated an interest in other approaches, and zero-based budgeting (ZBB) was one of them.

Zero-Based Budgeting (1977–1980)

In a literal sense, zero-based budgeting implies constructing a budget without considering what has gone on in the past. This interpretation of ZBB is held by most street-level bureaucrats, but Taylor[14] points out that it has been criticized as being naive and simplistic.

Peter A. Pyhrs developed ZBB at Texas Instruments as a method of controlling overhead costs. Subsequently, Governor Jimmy Carter implemented ZBB in Georgia and claims to have made the operation of the state more cost-effective. When Carter assumed the presidency, he again implemented ZBB, but it was officially terminated by the Office of Management and Budget in 1981. However, by that time ZBB had been adopted by many states and local governments.

The most distinctive feature of ZBB is its focus on the total budget request. The previous year's budgeted amount is not considered when the administrator draws up the new budget request. The three basic elements of ZBB are:[15] the identification of "decision units"; the analysis of decision units and the formulation of "decision packages"; and ranking.

The decision units are the lowest level of the organization for which a manager is responsible. The manager must have the authority to establish priorities and prepare a budget for the decision unit. Presumably, the decision unit manager asks questions such as: "Can this program be eliminated?" "Can I cut back in this area?" "Do we need to add more resources to this program?" "How can we be more cost-effective?" The decision unit manager then prepares a series of packages. The first package contains those programs or parts of programs that are deemed to be of the highest priority. The second package contains those of the second-highest priority, and so on.

The packages are then passed on to a higher-level manager, who is responsible for establishing priorities for all decision packages from all subordinate decision units. The entire ranking is then reviewed with an eye to probable funding. This approach is a common sense one and not too different from that taken by many managers as they begin to put a budget together.

Political Budgeting (1980–Present)

When Ronald Reagan became president in 1980, he promised to cut the federal budget and trim the size of government. He was unable to meet those objectives. One reason for his failure is that the budget is no longer driven by congressional or presidential initiative. A quick glance at a budget sheet gives one the impression that the budget process is rational and well thought out. In reality, a large part of the budget is derived from formulas that automatically determine the amount to be budgeted.[16] These formulas are called **entitlements**. Nearly all entitlements are payments to individuals in the form of Social Security, for example. Such payments comprise as much as 75 percent of the federal budget.[17]

Entitlements are an example of the political aspect of budgeting. According to Rosenbloom, the "political approach to public budgeting emphasizes several concerns: representation, consensus and coalition building, and the locus of power in allocating funds."[18] As a consequence, the way most legislators and others approach public budgeting is by way of **incrementalism**. In this way of preparing a budget, last year's appropriation is a base that should be reduced only under the most unusual circumstances.

Incrementalism is politically comfortable for at least three reasons:[19]

- It provides widespread representation to diverse groups and interests and does not demand a comprehensive statement of objectives, nor does it question the base

appropriation. Therefore, it is possible to have governmental programs that conflict with one another yet not have to give serious thought to making fundamental choices. For example, manys states have passed stiff drunk-driving laws while at the same time operating state-owned liquor stores. Special interest groups have agitated for stronger penalties against drivers convicted of driving under the influence. At the same time religious groups agitate for strong control, or abolition, of sales of alcoholic beverages while the brewers and distillers lobby for the opportunity to sell their product. Thus, public policy is made through compromise, and its effects are reflected in the budget.

- It allows for coalition and consensus building through funding to diverse interests. Coalitions make it possible for politicians to be elected, and if conflict is quieted, consensus can develop. If governmental objectives are stated in the abstract, conflict can be avoided. Who would disagree that thugs and thieves should be locked up? But while these objectives are desirable in the abstract, when they are translated into specific programs with specific objectives—to build more prisons, hire more staff, and expand community services such as probation and work release—one gets an entirely different reaction. One of the main problems with PPBS and ZBB is that they increase conflict, break down consensus, and make it difficult for the political system to work.

- It tends to place the locus of power for budgetary decisions in the hands of legislators. PPBS and ZBB placed that power in the executive branch and thus displaced legislative appropriations committees.

One can argue that the political budgeting process, through representation in the legislatures, makes each citizen accountable for budget decisions. Through the checks and balances of the system, public control over the purse is maintained. Wildavsky and Hammond sum up the nature of political budgeting:[20]

> Whatever else they may be, budgets are manifestly political documents. They engage the intense concern of administrators, politicians, leaders of interest groups and citizens interested in the "who gets what and how much" of governmental allocations. Participants in budgeting use its political components as aids to calculation. They drastically simplify their task by concentrating on the relatively small portion of the budget that is politically feasible to change. The previous year's budget, the largest part of which is composed of continuing programs and prior commitments, is usually taken as a base needing little justification beyond that offered in the past. Attention is normally focused on a small number of incremental changes, increases and decreases, calling for significant departures from the established historical base of the agency concerned. Parts of the total budget are given to various administrative agencies, appropriations subcommittees, Budget Bureau divisions, and other interested parties for special attention. This fragmentation is increased because all budgetary items are not evaluated together, but are dealt with in sequence by the various participants, so that only a small number of items need to be considered by any participant at any one time.

The Budget Cycle

Budgeting is a regular cycle that follows predictable timetables. The budget cycle occurs in three stages: formulation, legislative approval, and execution.

Formulation

This phase is the most difficult to describe because it varies from budget unit to budget unit and from agency to agency. The important

thing to remember is that the budget document is the best descriptor of agency values and goals.

There are two approaches to putting a budget together: a top-down approach and a bottom-up approach. A top-down approach looks in two directions at once: external variables that impact tax collections and past spending commitments. Those who use the top-down approach often fail to solicit input from organization members down the ladder. Many corrections supervisors and executives are most familiar with the bottom-up approach. This is a department-level budget (excluding salaries, which are part of the budget prepared for the CEO by the business manager or even someone higher in the organization) that reflects a need for such things as lawnmowers, paper clips, and fifty-pound bags of rice and beans. These department-level (decision units) budgets are then collected by the CEO and his or her business manager, prioritized, and put together in a package for submission to the commissioner or director, who in turn submits all packages from the department of corrections to the governor's office.

This procedure illustrates the process for a large agency such as a department of corrections. The process is basically the same for smaller agencies, such as a probation department or a not-for-profit agency like a halfway house. The chief probation officer or agency head begins by calling all supervisors together (in small agencies everyone should be included). Through a process of negotiation, they work out a budget that meets the agency's goals. The key to successful budget preparation is justification of expenditures. In this age of shrinking dollars, public sector executives have had to do more with less, and in this regard Drucker[21] points out that private sector executives can take a few pointers from the public sector.

The justification of expenditures is zero-based budgeting (discussed earlier in this chapter) in that programs are reviewed, key questions asked, and decisions made on the premise

FIGURE 7.3
The Budget Cycle

	Formulation	*Legislative Approval*	*Execution*
Request ⟶	Review and ⟶ Submission	Authorization, ⟶ Appropriation, and Budget Resolution	Obligation and Expenditure
Institutions and Field Offices	Commissioner Field Office Chief, Chief Probation Officer	Congress (in case of U.S. BOP)/State Legislature: Budget, Authorizing and Appropriation Committees	Various Agencies, i.e., Institutions and Field Offices
Timing	12–18 Months	January to June in case of states and January to September in case of U.S. Bureau of Prisons	July 1 to June 30 for states and local jurisdictions and October 1 to September 30 for U.S. Bureau of Prisons

that perhaps money ought not be spent on a particular program. Management by Objectives (MBO) is another way to key expenditures to requests. MBO, discussed at greater length in chapter 12, goes hand in hand with the budget process and may proceed at the same pace.

Approval

Every budget prepared by every corrections executive is approved by the Congress, a state legislature, a county board of supervisors, a city council, or a board of directors. At the federal level, the budget is approved on a piecemeal basis, with the various committees and subcommittees rarely talking to each other. This process becomes complicated as one works one's way down through the various levels of government.

Execution

Once the budget is approved, each department head or cost center manager is notified of his or her allocation for the coming year. Some agencies allot one-fourth of the approved budget at the beginning of each quarter. Others, particularly small agencies, do not, but department heads usually know how to pace themselves.

Execution of the budget is simply spending the allocated money. While not difficult in theory, it is more difficult in practice. Procedures for spending the money must be followed; for example, many agencies require bids on any capital item over $500 in cost. Other procedures may call for efforts to make purchases locally, and so on. The effective manager will pace him- or herself and not return to the council or legislature for an emergency allocation.

It is a cumbersome process. The budget that is submitted in January or March of each year is usually cut up, distributed, and put back together at the federal or state level. At the county, medium- and smaller-sized city, and not-for-profit levels, the budget is simply reproduced, distributed, and acted upon. At all levels, the agency head is usually asked to appear before the approving body to answer questions or to justify the request. An ill-prepared executive can be made to look extremely inept.

One example of budget formulation, approval and execution, can be illustrated via Functional Unit Management, which is explored in a later chapter. An institutional unit manager is a cost center manager who is responsible for preparing a yearly budget for his or her unit. The budget is then sent to the associate warden of programs, who presents it to the bud-

U.S. Bureau of Prisons— Annual Budget Preparation	The U.S. Bureau of Prisons designates certain management areas as cost centers. For example, cost centers are traditional departments such as food service and the custodial department. The warden's office is a separate cost center, and so is Unit Management. Each cost center is responsible for putting together a budget and forwarding it to the appropriate budget officer.

A completed budget request form must be submitted to the budget officer by each July 20. Any request that exceeds the previous year's request in a particular category must be justified. All institutional and regional office requests must be approved by a standing budget committee before being sent on to the next higher level of management. The budget committee may alter any request after consultation with the cost center manager. Once the budget is approved, funds are allotted on a quarterly basis.

Cost center managers are responsible for:

- preparing estimates of resources required to meet the budget initiatives during the coming fiscal year as specified annually by bureau staff;
- preparing the next fiscal year's Budget and Execution and Management Reports;
- including sufficient information to permit management to determine that every phase of the operation has been considered;
- after the operating plan has been adopted, determining how additional funds will be spent or in what areas reductions in obligations will be required to permit programs to be managed within funds available;
- managing programs within funds allotted unless written approval has been granted by the budget committee to exceed funds available for the cost center (the obligational limitations established for a decision unit may not be exceeded as a result of local authorization furnished to a cost center);
- monitoring the number of obligations and notifying the budget officer and the planning committee of changes from the authorized operating plan;
- advising the planning committee *by memorandum*, prior to each meeting, that a review of current status has been conducted and that funds available in the cost center are known. The cost center manager will also review his or her plans to assure that the funds available for the ensuing quarter are not exceeded.

Source: Information provided courtesy of Frank Bai, Business Manager, U.S. Penitentiary, Terre Haute, Indiana (retired); Bureau of Prisons Policy Statement 2100.1 (Budget Execution Manual), issued January 21, 1987.

TABLE 7.2
Unit Management—Budget for U.S. Bureau of Prisons

	FY 90	*FY 91* *Request*	*Net* *Change*	*FY 91* *Funding*
Alderson	20.9	34.0	−.7	20.2
Ashland	0	0	0	0
Butner	0	12.0	0	0
Lexington	0	30.0	0	0
Milan	3.5	10.0	−.7	2.8
Morgantown	16.4	29.5	−.7	15.7
Petersburg	26.3	26.3	−.7	25.6
Seymour Johnson	4.0	28.8	−.7	3.3
Terre Haute	18.2	21.2	−.7	17.5
Regional Office				
Reserves				
Totals	89.3	191.8		85.1

Source: U.S. Bureau of Prisons Annual Budget, FY 1991.
Note: Amounts in thousands.

get officer. As a member of the local budget committee, the associate warden should be prepared to argue in defense of his or her unit managers and their budget requests. Unit managers are often somewhat skeptical about how strongly the associate warden defends them. (The associate warden's understanding and commitment often depend on which career ladder she or he has ascended.) Table 7.2 illustrates Unit Management funding for FY 1991 for the North Central Region of the U.S. Bureau of Prisons.

Summary

In the United States today corrections budgets are growing at an unprecedented pace. U.S. courts place more people under correctional jurisdiction than courts in any other country in the world. Rules governing convicted felons' eligibility for parole have also grown more stringent, and felons from the post-World War II "baby boom" are now entering prison. The result is a skyrocketing demand for prison services to serve a growing population.

While attempts to make government more re-sponsible in its spending habits can be traced to the beginning of the republic, the history of responsible budgeting goes back only to the 1920s, when line-item budgeting was implemented. During World War II performance budgeting was adopted as an attempt to control spending as well as to account for inventory. During the 1960s Robert McNamara. implemented Planning-Programming-Budgeting (PPB). PPB attempted to tie organizational goals to performance and budget requests. Its advantage was that it helped clarify options and forced planners and budgeters to develop objectives. President Carter implemented zero-based budgeting in the latter 1970s. In ZBB the various "decision units" put together decision packages consisting of programs and parts of programs, rank them in order of priority, and forward the entire package to a higher unit. Since 1980 political budgeting or incrementalism has been the favored approach to budget preparation. Incrementalism begins with last year's appropriation and builds on that amount. The attractiveness of political budgeting is that it does not require a statement of objectives, nor is the base appropriation questioned. Theoretically, the budget decisions are in the hands of citizens and their representatives.

Every executive and head of a corrections department must prepare a budget every year. Some decisions will be easily justified, others will require consensus building, and a few will be controversial. The smaller the agency, the less controversial the budget may be, and the process may be more amenable to the rational approaches of PPB or ZBB. Whichever approach the manager chooses, one thing is certain—corrections budgets are controversial and of great interest to the public. How one approaches the budget and how requests are justified will have a great deal to do with the outcome.

The budget cycle begins early in each fiscal year for the coming fiscal year. Ideally, the budget is formulated through a "top-down" and a "bottom-up" process. It is then forwarded to the appropriate higher echelon for approval. Management by Objectives (MBO) is a part of the budget process. The cost center manager or decision unit manager formulates objectives and determines costs. Those costs are aggregated to make up the total budget. Consequently, a glance at the organizational budget reveals organizational objectives and how they are prioritized.

Reviewing the Case

Claremont Custody Center is a new institution established by the city to provide services to the state of California. Since it is a new service, city employees were unaccustomed to the budgetary expertise of the new warden. Mr. Conte recognized that he had the opportunity to establish front-end accountability in the budget process and so he established cost centers and allowed department heads the autonomy to manage their own budgets. The result has been relative financial stability in a time of economic uncertainty in a new institution.

For Further Study

Peter Drucker, "What Business Can Learn from Non-profits," *Harvard Business Review* (July-August [4], 1989), pp. 88–93.

Albert C. Hyde and Jay M. Shafritz, eds., *Government Budgeting* (Oak Park, Ill.: Moore, 1978).

Douglas C. McDonald, "The Cost of Corrections: In Search of the Bottom Line," National Institute of Corrections, *Research in Corrections*, 2:1 (February 1989).

Key Terms

Budgeting	Decision Units
Performance Budgeting	Line-Item Budgeting
Zero-Based Budgeting	Planning-Programming- Budgeting

Organization Development

Case Study: Director of Jails Resigns

Frank Hall resigned this week as director of the Santa Clara County Department of Correction, ending weeks of speculation about his fate and closing a controversial chapter in the fledging department's three-year history.[1] Jail commanders announced the resignation to most of the department's roughly 700 sworn officers at evening squad meetings. The terse announcement gave no reason for Hall's resignation.

Hall's departure comes after nine months of wide-ranging criticism surrounding the department, including allegations of officer brutality, a grand jury report critical of Hall's hiring practices, and charges of illegal influence on the officer's union. His letter of resignation to the board of supervisors stated that he was proud of creating the first correctional department in a major county in California.

"We have vastly expanded the inmate programs available, hired an almost entirely new sworn staff, come in under budget for the past three years, and greatly exceeded the board's commitment to the public in savings to taxpayers," he wrote.

The supervisors named Assistant Correction Director Robert Conroy, forty-four, as temporary director of the approximately 5,000-inmate system while they conduct a national search for a permanent successor.

"My focus for right now is going to be on our staff," said Conroy. "It's been a difficult time for them and I want them to know how important they are. . . . I'm going to put a lot of energy into the things that make the department run day-in and day-out."

Diane McKenna, chair of the board of supervisors, characterized Hall's departure as voluntary. But, in a closed-door meeting on October 9, the supervisors told Hall that he no longer had their support and asked for his resignation, according to several county officials, who asked not to be named. Since then, Hall and the county's attorneys have been negotiating an amicable departure.

"I think Frank helped us initiate a department at a very difficult time," McKenna said. "He helped us through the opening of several facilities and started several programs that the supervisors wanted. I look upon his service to the county in a positive way."

A Change Needed

Supervisor Ron Gonzales, who publicly declared his lack of confidence in Hall last month, was more blunt. "There were enough big problems to lead me to believe there was a change needed at the top," said Gonzalez. "The biggest concerns for me were budget and management issues. There was a big gap between what the director knew and what was going on."

Under the terms of Hall's agreement with the county, the $98,000-a-year director will receive salary and benefits until January 5, 1992. The county also will pay seven months toward his pension. Hall has seven days to revoke the agreement.

The Department of Correction was created four years ago after a bitter and expensive court fight between the supervisors and then-sheriff Robert E. Winter, whose political independence and budget overruns had alienated the board.

Hired in 1987

The board hired Hall, a veteran of several state prison systems on the East Coast, in July 1987 to help create the new department. Hall, a strong advocate of rehabilitation for inmates, has been praised for instituting a variety of programs, from literacy classes to drug rehabilitation and a military-style boot camp for recidivist women. Plans are in the works for a program that would allow inmates to remove tattoos as a step toward a new life.

But from its first months, the department was hit with two controversies that would not be put to rest—a rising number of inmate suicides and questions about the quality of its officers. This year those controversies were joined by a series of others that led to Thursday's announcement.

In January the *Mercury News* detailed inmates' allegations of brutality by some jail officers, prompting investigations by the U.S. Department of Justice and the district attorney. Both probes remain open. In the wake of the allegations, Hall moved to fire five officers. The district attorney's office charged two others with assault under color of authority. They were subsequently convicted.

Other problems plagued the department. There were allegations that some correction officers use illegal steroids. A lawsuit is pending that will force the jails to obtain state licenses for its medical and psychiatric units, and the controversial suicide of inmate-activist Charles Bush, whose death in the jail psychiatric unit went undiscovered for nearly five hours, are all troublesome matters for the department.

In late June, the county grand jury released a report that said one out of every five officers hired by the department had a recent history of drug abuse, criminal acts, or psychological problems. Hall dismissed the findings as "hogwash and absolute nonsense." The supervisors later agreed with the jury's findings, but added that most of the officers' problems were not sufficient to have barred them from employment at the time. The board also tightened hiring practices.

Mutual Mistrust

Throughout the controversies, Hall defended himself and his department, while sometimes blaming sheriff's deputies— angry about their former boss's loss of jail control—for his problems. But by most accounts, the mistrust was mutual. And during Hall's final months, it was correction officers Hall had hired who came forward to say they no longer had confidence in his leadership.

By late summer, it appeared the department this year might not fulfill the promise supervisors made when they created it: to save money and increase accountability.

During recent budget hearings, Supervisor Gonzales told

Hall, who had overspent his overtime budget by nearly $7 million, that his answers to questions sounded too much like those of his predecessor, Sheriff Winter.

In his letter of resignation, Hall stressed that his department has repeatedly saved money for the taxpayers.

Until recently, the supervisors appeared reluctant to publicly acknowledge problems in a department that had taken great financial and political capital to create.

Introduction

Correctional institutions and many community corrections agencies are paramilitary organizations with rigid lines of communication and authority. Often supervisors and executives wonder why desired results do not follow the issuance of a memo or a directive. Many times correctional organizations experience problems that are correctable; with the proper diagnosis and intervention, productivity increases, or a bottleneck is eliminated.

For example, some years ago a small juvenile court in the Midwest, plagued for many years by ineptness, political intrigue, and underfunding, hired a new administrator. The new administrator was given a mandate by the judges to improve the court's operations. The first thing he did was administer two instruments to help him determine the informal lines of communication and power and find out what employees thought of the organization and what could be done to "fix it." He then developed approaches and programs based on the information he had gathered. The court's operations did improve. Service to children increased; accountability of staff and probation officers improved; and negative, traditional, informal lines of communication and authority were disrupted. Unfortunately, however, the story does not have a happy ending. Political intrigue won out over sound management, the administrator left in disgust, and the court is just where it

started—inept, patronage-ridden, and with few programs for children.

This example clearly illustrates that without top-level support, large-scale efforts to develop an organization will not work. No matter how skilled the practitioner of organization development or how committed to change midlevel management is, large-scale efforts must be initiated and supported by top executive staff.

Organization Development Defined

Organization development (OD) implies change. Argyris,[2] for example, has suggested that an effective organization is one that allows both the individual and the organization to grow and change. Burk points out that we need to be

> concerned with change in the organization's culture—change that will more fully integrate individual needs with organizational goals; change that will lead to greater organizational effectiveness through better utilization of resources, especially human resources; and change that will provide more involvement of organization members in the decisions that directly affect them and their working conditions.[3]

Harvey and Brown[4] define OD as planned, systematic approaches to change. McGill agrees and defines OD as:

a conscious, planned process of developing an organization's capabilities so that it can attain and sustain an optimum level of performance as measured by efficiency, effectiveness, and health. Operationally, OD is a normative process of addressing the questions: "Where are we?" "Where do we want to be?" "How do we get from where we are to where we want to be?" This process is undertaken by members of the organization using a variety of techniques, often in collaboration with a behavioral science consultant.[5]

As McGill points out, while the above definition is lengthy, shorter definitions may tend to be simplistic. McGill's definition emphasizes that OD is action oriented and it includes what OD is, how to do it, and who is involved in it.

Organization Development and Its Roots

Moses' talents in public administration were mentioned in chapter 2. We could even go so far as to say that Moses was the first to improve his organization's productivity and to streamline the organization's structure. Along the same vein, we could say with some certainty that his father-in-law, Jethro, was history's first recorded OD consultant, since the changes were Jethro's ideas. From that time until the mid-twentieth century, attempts to improve organizational performance were usually based on intuition or on instilling fear in subordinates.

It wasn't until the Hawthorne studies that the stage was set for the growth of organization development. The Hawthorne studies clearly demonstrate that the individual and the group are forces to be reckoned with in the workplace. This view is in contrast to the mechanistic approach of the classical thinkers.

Others such as Maslow[6] state that human needs can be arranged in a hierarchical order,

beginning with the basic needs for air, food, and water. At the other end of the continuum is the need for self-actualization. Maslow asserts that an unsatisfied need creates a tension that results in motivation and that a satisfied need creates no tension and thus no motivation or goal-seeking behavior.

Fredrick Herzberg[7] differs somewhat with Maslow in that he declares that there are two continua, one having to do with dissatisfaction and the other with satisfaction. He calls these *hygiene factors* and *motivating factors*. Only motivators such as recognition, opportunity for achievement, and autonomy on the job lead to satisfaction. Hygiene factors, such as belonging and safety, prevent dissatisfaction but do not ensure job satisfaction. Certainly Maslow and Herzberg made a significant contribution to the development of OD, but others, including Sigmund Freud, Lawler,[8] Vroom,[9] B. F. Skinner,[10] and Hackman and Oldham,[11] made significant contributions as well.

It wasn't until the post–World War II period that OD began to emerge. With an employee shortage plaguing many organizations, managers began to search for ways to stretch their resources. Out of this climate grew the "basic-skill-training group," which was to have a profound impact on OD. (It became more popularly known as a "T-group" and "sensitivity training.") Not long after World War II, the laboratory group, which grew out of the T-group, became an important impetus for the development of OD. The laboratory method provided a means for group participants to receive feedback about their behavior and performance, which they used as a learning experience. The group was viewed as a laboratory that promoted the learning and relearning of ways of behaving that improve organizational performance. The change in name from skill-training groups to T-groups and sensitivity groups illustrates the shift in emphasis from group skills to interpersonal learning.

FIGURE 8.1
Maslow's Needs Hierarchy

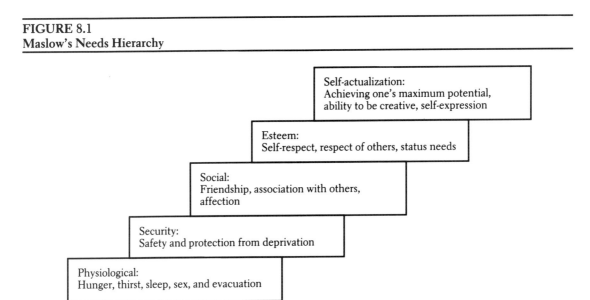

Roles, Norms, and Values

As pointed out in chapter 5, roles, norms, and values are essential to an organization's culture. If we fail to understand them, OD is impossible to accomplish. Norms are specific standards of behavior and are spelled out in the organization's policies and procedures. Roles are the organization's and individuals' expectations for behavior; failure to fulfill a role results in difficulty for the individual. For example, a corrections officer is expected to favor fellow corrections officers over inmates. A corrections officer's violation of this norm will bring him or her a good deal of grief in the form of ridicule and ostracism, if not termination of employment.

Values are principles or qualities that are believed to be valuable or desirable. In the above example, officer solidarity is a value. If an officer ignores this value, he or she does so at the risk of suffering a good deal of discomfort.

Organization development is a "process of cultural change and . . . the value system of an organization is a significant component of its culture."[12] Thus, if an organization is going to change, its culture must change—not an insignificant task for most corrections organizations.

OD and the Diagnostic Process

There are many diagnostic tools that the OD consultant or corrections manager can choose from. Three are discussed in this chapter: the Organizational Diagnosis Questionnaire (ODQ), the Motivational Analysis of Organizations—Climate (MAO-C), and the Organizational Norms Opinionnaire.

Organizational Diagnosis Questionnaire

One effective diagnostic instrument is the Organizational Diagnosis Questionnaire (ODQ). The ODQ is based on Weisbord's Six-Box Model[13] and generates data in each of Weisbord's six areas as well as a seventh, attitude toward change. Preziosi[14] added the seventh area to help the OD agent determine how amenable the organization is to change and thus direct efforts more effectively.

The ODQ is useful when the manager or consultant needs a picture of an existing work unit or of an organization or part of it. It can be used to assess the thinking of line staff, supervisors, and executives. Weisbord depicts his model as a radar screen upon which appear "blips" that tell us something of an organization's functioning. Just as the air traffic controller must consider the entire screen when directing traffic, so must the manager consider the entire organization when attempting a diagnosis.

Data are gathered via a questionnaire consisting of 35 items, five in each of the seven areas. The respondents are asked to give their views on a scale of 1 to 7, with 4 representing a neutral stance. Aggregate scores are computed, with 1 representing "strongly agree" and 7 representing "strongly disagree."

The value of the ODQ lies in its ability to tell the manager what the primary problem areas are; that is, leadership, how the work is divided among workers, relationships, and so

forth. It also sheds light on the organization's strengths in these same areas.

Burke[15] asserts that Weisbord's model is most useful

- when the manager or consultant does not have much time for diagnosis,
- when a relatively uncomplicated organizational map is needed for quick service, or
- when subordinates, or clients, are unaccustomed to thinking in terms of systems.

Motivational Analysis of Organizations-Climate (MAO-C)

A second instrument that is useful in the diagnosing of organizational climate regarding motivation is the MAO-C. This instrument can focus on the overall organization or its various branches or departments. The MAO-C assumes that since most organizations have structure, systems, and norms, these three elements make up an organizational culture.

The organizational climate, in turn, can be

TABLE 8.1
Weisbord's Matrix for Survey Design or Data Analysis

	Formal System (work to be done)	Informal System (process of working)
1. Purposes	Goal clarity	Goal agreement
2. Structure	Functional, program, or matrix?	How is work actually done or not done?
3. Relationships	Who should deal with whom on what? Which technologies should be used?	How well do they do it? Quality of relations? Modes of conflict management?
4. Rewards (incentives)	Explicit system What is it?	Implicit, psychic rewards What do people feel about payoffs?
5. Leadership	What do top people manage? What systems are in use?	How? Normative "style" of administration?
6. Helpful mechanisms	Budget system Management information (measures?) Planning control	What are they actually used for? How do they function in practice? How are systems subverted?

Source: M. R. Weisbord, "Organizational Diagnosis: Six Places to Look for Trouble with or Without a Theory," *Group and Organizational Studies*, 1 (1976), pp. 430–47.

FIGURE 8.2
Organizational Diagnosis Questionnaire

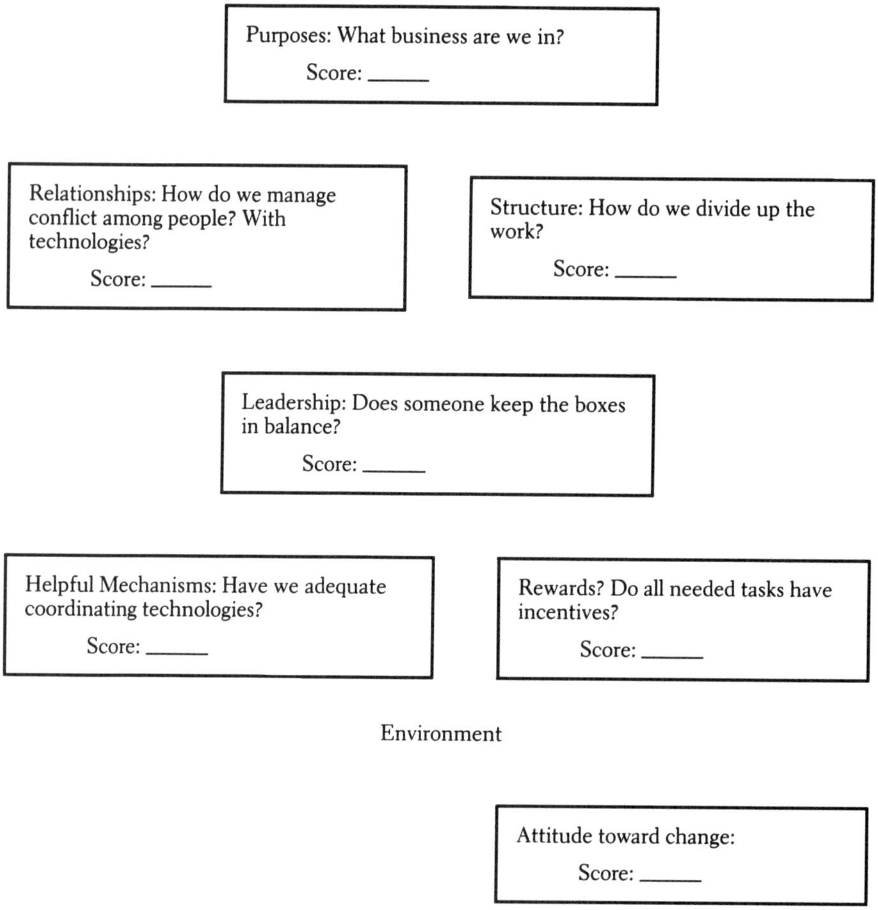

Purposes: What business are we in?

Score: _____

Relationships: How do we manage conflict among people? With technologies?

Score: _____

Structure: How do we divide up the work?

Score: _____

Leadership: Does someone keep the boxes in balance?

Score: _____

Helpful Mechanisms: Have we adequate coordinating technologies?

Score: _____

Rewards? Do all needed tasks have incentives?

Score: _____

Environment

Attitude toward change:

Score: _____

Source: Robert C. Preziosi, *The 1980 Annual Handbook for Group Facilitators* (San Diego: University Associates, 1980).

discussed only in terms of how it is perceived by its members. Consequently, an organizational climate can be perceived as supportive, conducive (or stifling) to achievement, and so forth. Once the instrument is administered and scored, the manager or facilitator develops a matrix that identifies the motives each individual in the organization perceives as driving the organization or department.

Pareek points out six motives that are appropriate in developing a framework that "facilitates analysis of the connection between organizational climate and motivation."[16]

- *Achievement.* This motive is characterized by a concern for excellence, competition in terms of standards set by oneself or others, the setting of challenging goals, and persistance in trying alternative paths to one's goals.

- *Affiliation.* Affiliation is characterized by establishing and monitoring close personal relationships; an emphasis on friendships; and expression of one's emotions.
- *Expert Influence.* Here we find a concern for making an impact on others, a desire to make people do what one thinks is right, and an urge to change people and situations.
- *Control.* Control is characterized by a concern for orderliness, a desire to be informed and to monitor events and take corrective action, and a need to display personal power.
- *Extension.* Extension is characterized by a need to be relevant to large groups, a concern for others, and an interest in superordinate groups.
- *Dependency.* Dependency is a desire for others' help in developing oneself, a need to check with others (such as experts or people who have higher status, and so on), a tendency to submit ideas for approval, and an urge to maintain a relationship based on the other person's approval.

Pareek combined dimensions of organizational climate proposed by Likert[17] with those proposed by Litwin and Stringer[18] and arrived at twelve processes or dimensions of organizational climate that relate specifically to motivation: Orientation, Interpersonal Relationships, Supervision, Problem Management, Management of Mistakes, Conflict Management, Communication, Decision Making, Trust, Management of Rewards, Risk Taking, and Innovation and Change. It is the way these twelve dimensions operate in an organization that indicates the underlying motive of top management. The MAO-C also indicates the principle motive of an organization and how that motive is sustained. By combining the twelve dimensions with Pareek's six motives, we are able to design a matrix that helps us diagnose the motivational climate of an organization.

Organizational Norms Opinionnaire

In chapter 5 we discussed goals and values and the role they play in the effectiveness (or ineffectiveness) of an organization. Organizational effectiveness also demands a variety of behaviors. Mark Alexander[19] and Allen and Pilnick[20] point out that there are required and emergent behaviors. Required behaviors are not necessarily those behaviors that are in effect. Emergent behaviors, on the other hand, have a much greater effect on the life of an organization. For example, a required behavior of prison staff is to stay aloof from inmates. Sharing personal information with inmates is also forbidden. As one moves up the seniority ladder, this norm can be ignored to a certain extent. However, whether it is existent or emergent, one behavior demanded of everyone on the corrections staff is to respond to a fellow worker's call for help. Ignoring this norm can result in strong social sanctions against the offending officer.[21]

Behavioral scientists have found that emergent organizational behavior is determined in large part by the formation of behavioral norms within working groups in the organization. Alexander points out that norms are the "oughts" of behavior. They are acceptable behavior as prescribed by the work group.

These norms can be either positive or negative. Positive norms support organizational goals and foster behavior directed toward these ends. Negative norms do just the opposite. They promote behavior that works against the attainment of organizational goals. For example, a court administrator announces that a goal has been established to complete 90 percent of all pre-sentence investigations (PSI's) in five working days (a positive norm), when the norm has been five to six weeks. Since completing PSI's in such a short time requires more effort, the Investigative Unit announces that such a goal is unrealistic and cannot be met (negative norm). Thus, the competent manager must be alert for a clash between norms and behavioral expectations.

Alexander[22] separates organizational norms into ten categories:

- *Organizational and Personal Pride.* These norms are associated with an employee's identification with and pride in his or her organization. Negative norms are associated with an "us-them" attitude toward the organization and its goals.
- *Performance/Excellence.* Norms in this category are associated with behavior that either strives for excellence or accepts mediocrity. Negative norms are reflected in an acceptance of mediocrity, and positive norms stress improvement in performance.
- *Teamwork/Communication.* These norms stress cooperation and working together. Negative norms stress secrecy and the belief that for one person to "look good," someone else must "look bad." Positive norms stress sharing information and working together.
- *Leadership/Supervision.* Leadership norms promote or detract from the effectiveness of supervision. Negative norms reflect an attitude that a supervisor must act as a police officer, and positive norms stress that the supervisor must be coach, cheerleader, and helper.
- *Service Quotient/Cost Effectiveness.* This norm in the private sector determines people's attitudes toward profitability. In corrections it determines employees' attitudes toward the level of service given. Positive norms encourage employees to save money and to maximize taxpayers' satisfaction. Negative norms foster a lack of concern for bottom-line performance.

- *Colleague and Associate Relations.* Norms in this category determine the quality of relationships between fellow employees. Positive norms lead to strong, amiable interpersonal relationships. Negative norms lead to an individualistic or a nonsupportive organizational climate.
- *Client Relations.* Norms in this category determine behavior that affects how clients and inmates are treated. Positive norms lead to minimal client/inmate dissatisfaction, and negative norms lead to the view that clients and inmates are "scumbags" deserving of mistreatment.
- *Innovativeness and Creativity.* Norms in this category lead to original and creative behavior. Positive norms stimulate new ideas and positive change. Negative norms lead to preservation of the status quo and discourage experimentation.
- *Training and Development.* Positive norms in this category view training as essential to organizational effectiveness. Negative norms hold that training is all right but nonessential to the day-to-day operation of the organization.
- *Candor and Openness.* The norms in this group promote freedom of communication between all levels of the organization, vertically and horizontally. Positive norms promote a high degree of trust and lead to open communication. Negative norms result in a closed and guarded attitude in interpersonal communication.

The Organizational Norms Opinionnaire serves several valuable purposes, such as organization assessment and diagnosis, team building, and management development.[23] By establishing an organization profile, which is a snapshot of organizational strengths and weaknesses, it allows the OD consultant or the manager to initiate necessary changes in the organization.

Disadvantages and Advantages of Instruments

While the use of instruments in the field of OD is widely accepted, they have some disadvantages.[24]

- Instruments often make people fear that they have been exposed or that someone is trying to read their minds.
- Instruments tend to encourage those who are part of the OD process to depend on the facilitator for leadership rather than sharing it among themselves.
- Instruments can dissipate useful tension that could be put to good use.
- Instruments sometimes generate nitpicking in which the respondents question reliability, validity, or relevance.
- Instruments can generate hostility from respondents who think the instrument is irrelevant, time-consuming, and useless.
- Instruments can supply an overabundance of information that the manager or facilitator will find hard to use.

Using such instruments also offers several advantages.

- Instruments give participants some construction and terminology that is useful in examining their behavior and others' behavior.
- Instruments allow participants to be given feedback about personal behavior in a group setting.
- Instruments allow latent issues to surface.
- Instruments give feedback that allows individuals to compare themselves with others.
- Instruments allow feedback to be shared in a nonthreatening way.
- Instruments allow longitudinal assessment of change in a group or an organization.

Avoiding the Disadvantages of Instruments

Managers should make an effort to remove any mystery surrounding the instrument by

1. discussing the margin of error and any other factors that contribute to less-than-perfect results,
2. allowing the participants to review the instrument and to learn how scores are computed, and
3. showing respondents how the instrument is related to everyday choice-making experiences.

The manager or facilitator can make sure enough time is made available for processing the data by

1. giving respondents the time to talk about their scores and compare their scores to others, and
2. emphasizing and legitimizing people's different lifestyles, orientations, and perspectives.

Interventions

Planning for Change

Klofas, et al.,[25] are pessimistic about the prospect for change in criminal justice agencies. They cite the paramilitary structure of those agencies as the primary reason for their pessimism, along with the folklore and routines of individual agencies. While Klofas, et al., have a point, change at times happens of necessity. It is sometimes forced by a calamity such as the New Mexico State Prison riot in 1980. Change can also be brought about through a change in political leadership or through a need to update policies and procedures.

One should keep the following two considerations in mind when viewing the organization

FIGURE 8.3
Typology of Change According to Depth of Intervention

System-wide Approaches
Contingency theories of organization design
Survey feedback and development
Organizational confrontation meeting
Collateral organization
Quality of work-life programs
Grid organizational development (The six-phase grid OD
    program covers almost every level but is placed here for
    the sake of convenience and clarity, since it involves a
    total system-wide effort.)

Individual-Organizational Interfaces
Job design
Decision centers
Role analysis
Management by objectives

Concern with Personal Work Style
Process consultation
Third-party intervention
Team building
Managing interdepartmental and intergroup relationships

Intrapersonal Analysis and Relationships
Life and career-planning interventions
Laboratory training
Encounter groups
Personal consultation

Source: Edgar F. Huse, *Organization Development and Change* (St. Paul: West Publishing Company, 1980). Permission granted.

and the possibilities for change. First, is the organization ready for change? In many instances, the manager will know that change is necessary, and the diagnostic instruments will verify that need. What is not so easily understood by members of the organization is that they will function more productively, or more efficiently, if the change occurs. This means that the manager must "sell" the need for change to organizational members. If they are aware of the need for change and are supportive, then at least half the battle is won. In all probability, however, organization members will already know that change is needed. The key is how the manager goes about actually implementing change.

If change is to be lasting, it's important that all members support the change. At the very least the manager must gain the support of the executives and department heads in a large organization. In a small organization, the support of all employees should be solicited. For example, suppose that the governor and the commissioner of corrections agree that a sweeping change is necessary in the Department of Corrections. The commissioner should begin by calling together all wardens, superintendents, and field office managers for a closed-door session to discuss the need for change. Effective leadership and team-building skills would not only allow the commissioner to gain the group's acceptance of his or her ideas but also allow the group to assume some ownership of the ideas. In this way group members would be inclined to return to their home offices or institutions and "sell" the program or change for the commissioner.

Second, it is necessary to establish internal ways to manage, monitor, and maintain the change process. Managing the change process is difficult because, as the saying goes, if something can go wrong, it will. Therefore, it is imperative that someone watch over the process and be accountable for it. In many instances, the chief of planning and research will be the most sensible choice for this function because he or she will be responsible for monitoring agency programs and/or attaining stated objectives. Since the two functions may be linked, this person would seem to be the most likely selection.

Regardless of who is responsible for the project, he or she should be an employee whose opinion is listened to and respected. If in-depth intervention is necessary, bitter pills may go down more easily if administered by such a person. Thus, for example, interventions that deal with value-laden issues may be managed more easily by a respected executive who employees believe has paid his or her dues.

Roger Harrison[26] defines depth as the degree to which the intervention is aimed at the individual rather than the organization itself. The deeper the intervention, the more likely it is to involve private and personal information. Using Harrison's model, Huse[27] developed a list of interventions according to their depth. An examination of these interventions and the level to which they are to be applied will give the manager some notion of how to proceed.

Individually Focused Interventions

W. Warner Burke[28] calls our attention to six areas of consideration in individually focused interventions.

Recruitment and Selection

Recruiting is the process of finding interested, capable persons who require a minimal amount of supervision. In the field of corrections, two obvious sources of potential employees are colleges and universities and the military. Both sources are likely to produce capable, motivated individuals who have proven themselves in one way or another.

Selection, according to Burke, is the process of reaching a final decision. He suggests a four-step process for recruitment and selection that has applicability for corrections:[29] (1) individual interview; (2) a battery of psychological tests; (3) a test of applicant's ability to differentiate between effective and ineffective supervision; and (4) a tour of the institution or other facilities.

Training and Development

Training and development in the field of corrections are never-ending tasks. Corrections is one of the few jobs where line staff are supervisors of other human beings. Thus, it is necessary for all staff to be keenly aware of the principles of effective interpersonal communication and for that knowledge to be reinforced and updated periodically. Many other individual specialties need to be attended to, such as casework methods, counseling skills, locksmithing, food service, searches, inmate supervision, contraband control, drugs, and so forth.

Career Development

Prior to promotion, the individual or the individual and the organization decide whether or not the employee will remain a specialist or become a generalist. Very few corrections or court systems have anything approaching systematic career development. Usually movement up the organizational ladder results from random opportunities. Many organizations state that they are interested in career development and allow for such things as assignment rotation between line and support functions and minimal supervisory training. However, once the employee reaches a supervisory position, the organization needs to pay attention to developing leadership, decision-making, motivational, and other management skills as well as fostering understanding of the policy process.

Counseling

The role of manager/counselor is a difficult one. However, it is a necessary role if employees are to help further organizational goals with minimal conflict between these and personal goals. This is particularly true in a prison or correctional institution, where many jobs require intense interaction with inmates and a few require very little or no contact with inmates. Lombardo[30] found in his study that correctional officers sought jobs in prison that fit their personalities. Thus, some obtained jobs in a tower and had no inmate contact while others sought out jobs that demanded more personal interaction, such as those in the cell house. The key to employee development is that the manager, as an OD practitioner, adopt an approach to counseling and stick with it, be it transactional analysis,[31] reality therapy,[32] or rational emotive therapy.[33]

FIGURE 8.4
The Effects of Design Strategies on Core Job Dimensions

Change Principles	Core Job Dimensions
Combining tasks	Skill variety
Forming natural work units	Task identity
Establishing client relationship	Task significance
Vertical loading	Autonomy
Opening feedback channels	Feedback

Source: J. R. Hackman, "Work Design," in *Improving Life at Work,* J. R. Hackman and J. L. Suttle, eds. (Santa Monica: Goodyear, 1977), p. 136.

Job Design

Job design in criminal justice is taken for granted.[34] That is, correctional officers guard inmates, probation officers counsel and supervise probationers, and prison caseworkers counsel and write progress reports. But the validity of such job design is questioned by research. Klofas and his colleagues point out that organizations need to get away from "taylorism" in job design. That is, job design needs to move away from assigning specific, narrowly defined tasks to assigning jobs that allow for self-actualization, initiative, and responsibility.

If we are going to have more satisfied employees, we need to attend to job design variables that foster job enrichment. Hackman, et al.,[35] identify five principles for job design.

- Form natural work units.
- Combine tasks so that skill variety and task identity can be maximized.
- Establish client relationships—that is, establish direct contact between worker and client and provide some means for the client to judge the quality of the product or service.
- Load the job vertically—give the worker as much responsibility as possible over how the job is to be done.

- Open feedback channels—give the worker as much direct information as possible about his or her performance.

Hackman[36] combined these principles with five core job dimensions. Figure 8.4 illustrates how these principles affect job design.

Layoffs, Reductions in Force, and Firings

It's unlikely that layoffs or reductions in force will occur on a large scale in the corrections field, but it is a fact of life in the private sector as the economy expands and contracts. However, as budgets shrink, reductions in force may become more common. For example, in May 1991 newly elected Governor Edgar of Illinois, in an effort to pare the budget, announced that all but seven parole officers would be laid off.[37] Subsequent negotiations between the employees' union, the Department of Corrections, and the General Assembly resulted in most of these positions being reinstated. However, fifty-eight other positions were cut.

It may well be that reductions in force (RIFs) and terminations in jobs will become a fact of life, although the trend right now seems to be in the opposite direction. But perhaps one day the public will begin to raise a hue and cry for an alternative to the expense of keeping so many people in prison. At that point, managers will need to have the skills to help employees cope with a loss of income and the loss of a sense of belonging; this includes demotion as well. Ways of aiding employees who have suffered the personal setback of being fired or demoted include sensitivity and support groups and help in finding other work.

Large System Change

At some point in every corrections executive's career, the opportunity or need to become involved in large system change comes about. There are many examples of large system change. Occasionally, one hears of the termination of a CEO and the subsequent search for a replacement. Meanwhile, lacking the vision and direction of a permanent manager, the agency drifts off track, and the new CEO must spend a good deal of time on organizational development.

Usually when a new "boss" is brought in to repair a damaged agency, he or she is on the job a few weeks when the revelation comes like a thunderbolt. "They didn't tell me everything when I interviewed for this job," the new boss tells her- or himself as panic sets in. The temptation to begin looking for a new position before everything is unpacked is very strong. But usually the new boss stays on and goes about the chore of rebuilding the agency in a haphazard way, often finding that her or his well-intentioned efforts are unsuccessful.

Knowing where to begin is important. There has been some discussion in the literature supporting beginning at the top.[38] Beckhard and Harris[39] suggest four places that may be appropriate as a starting place:

- the top management or top of the system;
- management-ready systems—those groups or subunits known to be ready for the change;
- "hurting" systems—a special class of ready systems in which conditions have created acute discomfort in a previously unready system; and
- staffs—subsystems that will be required to help implement later interventions.

Implementing Change

There are six phases for large system change:[40]

1. *diagnosis*—determining the needs of the organization and what the problem areas are;

2. *goal setting*—determining what the end result of the change will be;
3. *transition state*—will there be a "new look" or a "new" way of doing things until the change is complete?
4. *strategy for change*—determining the action plan and what interventions are needed;
5. *evaluation*—measuring the change and its impact; and
6. *stabilization*—getting on an even keel and establishing stability and flexibility.

In bringing about large system change, the CEO needs to consider his or her time and limitations. The CEO cannot do all things and be everywhere at once. It is therefore important that a trusted individual or team be selected to manage the change process. It is not important that all team members be criminal justice veterans, but it is important that they be loyal and knowledgeable about the task at hand; that is, capable communicators, skilled at OD, and capable of carrying out the orders of the CEO. The concept of the policy organization discussed in chapter 6 is applicable to large system change.

Summary

Organization development is a conscious, planned development of an organization's capabilities so that it can attain and sustain an optimum level of performance as measured by efficiency, effectiveness, and health.[41] Any organization can go off track or need to improve operational effectiveness.

One does not practice OD, however, by writing memoranda. One begins by pursuing a path that includes diagnosis; establishing goals; determining what the new organization will look like; and determining a strategy to bring about change, evaluate the effectiveness of the change process, and assure stabilization. Failure to proceed logically and methodically will doom most attempts from the start.

Reviewing the Case

The Santa Clara County Department of Corrections has undergone an ordeal familiar to many organizations. The director has resigned after a tumultuous period, and employees and inmates have probably received less attention than they deserve. Assistant Director Conroy must attempt to hold the organization on course until a new director is selected.

When the new director arrives he or she will need to get acquainted with the community, the organization, and the individuals responsible for making things work. The next step will be to determine what needs to be fixed. One way of doing this is to have department heads administer one or two instruments such as the Organizational Diagnosis Questionnaire (ODQ) and the Organization Norms Opinionnaire. The director will then need to meet with top managers to discuss the results and to determine the depth and breadth of possible interventions. Once that is accomplished he or she will need to assign the respon-

sibilities of bringing about the necessary interventions, evaluating the change, and assuring that stability is achieved.

The coming months will not be easy, but positive change can be implemented, and the trust of the board of supervisors can be regained. It will require many OD skills as well as patience and vision.

For Further Study

W. Warner Burke, *Organization Development and Practice* (Boston: Little, Brown, 1982).

Michael E. McGill, *Organization Development for Operating Managers* (New York: AMACOM, 1977).

University Associates, *Annual Handbook for Group Facilitators* (San Diego: University Associates, 1972–1990).

Key Terms

Organization Development
Norms
Diagnosis
Strategy for Change

Herzberg's Motivators and Hygiene Factors
Intervention

WORKING THROUGH AND WITH OTHERS

PART IV

The art of management is being able to work through and with others. The manager does not function in a vacuum; he or she must depend on those under his or her supervision to successfully reach organizational goals. Up to this point we have discussed a number of issues that skirt that of how the manager can succeed in carrying out the mission of the organization.

The theme of Part IV is pointed out in chapter 9, "Motivation." If we are to be successful as managers we must motivate others to live up to their potential and help them find a good fit between personal and organizational objectives. Chapter 9 explores motivation and how human needs influence performance in the organization. Communication is touched upon as the primary tool for motivation.

Chapter 10 is concerned with groups within the organization. Emphasis in this chapter is on using groups to further the aims of the organization. Both formal and informal groups are discussed and how the manager can use them to benefit employee needs and the organization.

Chapter 11 delivers the message that not all managers are leaders and not all leaders are managers. In a perfect world there would be no difference, but as we know, this is not the case. Leadership is usually viewed as a matter of charisma, but as chapter 11 explains, leadership is multifaceted. The chapter explores leadership and gives the reader hints on how to improve leadership effectiveness through various behaviors.

Organizational excellence is not achieved through individual efforts alone. Teamwork is an essential ingredient, as are motivated workers. As a working environment corrections is extremely harsh. If the organization is to achieve excellence and serve the taxpayer, the manager must be able to effectively work through and with others.

Motivation

Case Study: Despite Professional Gains, Life Behind Bars Is Still Highly Stressful

REIDSVILLE, Ga.—To be a guard in a Georgia prison is to spend at least a third of your life behind bars.[1]

Ask guards to describe their jobs and many say that while they feel part soldier, part minister, and part referee, they have more in common with prisoners than with anyone else. Dressed in state-issue uniforms, fed the same food, the guards and the guarded both must live with a constant potential for violence—all behind a locked door.

"We're like the inmates. For eight hours a day, we're locked in prison, too," said Robin Todd, a three-year veteran of the Georgia State Prison (GSP) here, who, like most of her colleagues, prefers the title correctional officer—or CO—to guard.

The Georgia Department of Corrections recognizes the stress of the job and is attempting to upgrade the image of the officers. There are indications that its efforts are bearing fruit. The campaign is part of a broader effort to recruit more-educated, better-trained officers to the force of 3,500—a new era of correctional officer.

"Brutality, incompetence—the old 'Cool Hand Luke' guard that kicked butt and took names—can't exist in today's correctional environment," said Tony Turpin, the former president of the Georgia Correctional Officers Association, the fraternal "voice" of the officers. "I won't say we don't have any of that type, but that's not what we're looking for. We're looking for professionals."

Some officers say traditions of discrimination persist. CO Ronnie Shuemake is one of the new generation, a twenty-nine-year-old black army veteran with five years' correctional experience. He points out that for many of the 1,400 blacks who comprise 40 percent of Georgia's officers, staying motivated is a challenge.

"We black officers would like to have something to look up to," he said, noting that while the department has been good about hiring more black officers, it has frequently failed to place blacks in management positions. "Right now [at GSP] we don't have anyone higher than a counselor. The inmates are not used to seeing you in positions of authority. And what do we have to look toward to?"

The women COs—who comprise one-seventh of the force—also face problems. They are not allowed jobs that include contact with GSP inmates. They work in control centers and other noncontact jobs. However, they feel that before working the cell block they need to fight for respect from their male colleagues.

"This is an all-man's world. You have to prove yourself again and again," said Todd, who says consistency is her unofficial credo. "The inmates will expose themselves. Masturbate in front of you. You just have to stick to discipline and be firm but fair."

At GSP, officers encounter the "baddest of the bad": maximum-security inmates convicted of every possible crime. Under federal court order, the once overcrowded and riot-ridden prison has been transformed into a relatively ordered environment, with single-person cells and a ratio of three officers for every four inmates, a much more equal number than at other Georgia facilities.

But officers say GSP is still the place where nerves fray fastest. GSP, they say, is a good place to measure how the jailkeepers are coping.

"The time of the guard with a shotgun, tobacco juice dribbling out of his mouth, beer belly like he's nine months pregnant, is gone," said CO Jimmy Bland, who is one of many former farmers wooed to GSP by the regular paycheck and the state benefits. "You may have a man in here still chewing tobacco, but he's a dignified tobacco chewer."

Dignified or not, correctional officers don't receive the same perks as other law enforcement officers. Georgia state troopers, for example, may retire at the age of fifty-five after twenty years of service. COs must hold out till age sixty-five or until they have served thirty-four years.

Troopers who are seriously injured in the line of duty may receive full medical retirement benefits—no matter how long they've served on the force. By contrast, a CO with a similar injury gets 180 days' paid leave. Unless he has served thirteen years, four months, he cannot receive medical retirement and must draw workmen's compensation.

Salaries are another issue. While the starting salary for Georgia CO's has risen $4,000 since 1981, it is still less than what a federal correctional officer makes. State officers start at less than $15,500 and stop at about $36,000, compared to a range of about $17,000 to $60,000 in the federal system.

"People like it here," Bland said. "But if a federal penitentiary opened up next door, a lot of people would leave [GSP] simply because of the pay."

Officers admit that these inequities hit harder because of the nature of their work and the constant potential for violence. Stress is a fact of life. Officers have no lunch or coffee breaks. Hours pass with no glimpse of the sky, and visits to the bathroom are permitted only if a relief officer is called to fill in—which in many understaffed institutions is nearly impossible. Eight hours a day, often six days in a row, officers must absorb the pressure without interruption.

The intensity takes its toll. "The number one killer of correctional officers is heart disease," said Turpin, who was recently made a deputy warden in Macon after nearly seven years as a CO. "You have high rates of alcoholism, ulcers, migraine headaches, divorce, financial problems. You take a low salary combined with a drinking problem or child-support payments, and it all fits into a puzzle. And job stress is the major cause of that."

Stress management is now part of basic training for CO's. But Turpin acknowledges that there is no single cure. Everyone must find a remedy—hobbies or music or exercise—or risk their lives. Turpin says he "slapped a golf ball all over the place."

Shuemake works a second job. "I get off from eight hours here, go home, shower, eat, and go to work for six more hours," he said, adding that bagging groceries at a local supermarket is the perfect therapy. "When you're doing something, it's harder to think about it. It's a cooling-out period."

Officer Todd points out, "It takes a while after work to be able to handle your family." Like many officers, she met her future spouse, a GSP sergeant, behind bars. "It can be stressful on a relationship if the person doesn't understand. If he was not working here, I'm sure it would be difficult."

Motivation in a Correctional Environment

The correctional organization (especially the prison) is perhaps one of the most difficult in the world to work in. The employee is daily subjected to threats, innuendo, and intimidation from inmates or clients. The public rarely understands what the employee does, and fellow criminal justice workers often either do not understand the nature of the work or equate the corrections employee with the inmate or client. In addition, corrections employees see many more failures than successes among their clients. There is no position in the private sector comparable to that of the jailer or correctional officer, yet as a line employee he or she is expected to have the skills of a supervisor.

How do we motivate employees trying to do such an impossible job? The remarkable thing is that we are able to attract many dedicated, competent people who, often in spite of corrections supervisors and executives, are motivated to do a good job.

Motivation Defined

Motivation is variously defined as a motive with a strong emotional association that arises from the individual's reaction to anticipated goal attainment and is based upon past association of certain cues with pleasure or pain;[2] as an inner state that causes a person to behave in a way that ensures the accomplishment of a goal;[3] and

as the internal drive to accomplish a particular goal.[4] In other words, motivation is what makes people want to work.

The thread that unites each definition is the notion that motivation often comes from within. That is, the person desires to accomplish a goal and perceives some kind of reward for accomplishing that goal. The reward can be existential, that is, a positive feeling about oneself, or it can be external, such as a pay raise or personal recognition. The problem for correctional executives and middle managers is how to instill and maintain that desire in the employee in spite of the harshness of the work environment.

Motivation and Human Needs

Maslow's Hierarchy of Needs

Maslow's Hierary of Needs[5] was discussed in chapter 8. The theory rests on the assumption that people have a number of needs and that unsatisfied needs motivate behavior. These needs are arranged in a hierarchy. That is, a lower-level need must be satisfied before a higher-level need can be satisfied. The needs for shelter, food, clothing, and sex must be satisfied before the next higher level of need (for safety and security) can be attended to, and so on up the hierarchy to the need for self-actualization, which Maslow defines as the need for personal growth. Self-actualization is fulfilling one's potential or working at one's fullest capacity. Each person's journey to self-actualization is unique. Few of us achieve a true state of self-actualization, because we are always

FIGURE 9.1
Maslow's Hierarchy of Needs

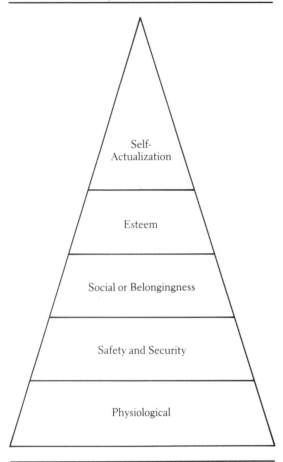

Self-Actualization

Esteem

Social or Belongingness

Safety and Security

Physiological

establishing new goals, which in turn start us on new journies.

One must put Maslow's theory into perspective when discussing corrections work in a prison such as the Georgia State Prison. One could say that the employee is placing the security of income over higher-order needs. It may well be that the daily grind composed of danger, tedium, and harshness arrest some employees' journey to self-actualization and that without creative programs that enhance the sense of belonging and self-esteem, some employees are unable to do much more than simply psychologically survive.

Argyris's Developmental Continuum

Chris Argyris[6] points out that personality has energy and that energy is located in the need systems of the personality. Energy is ready to bubble over to release itself. But as long as the boundary of the need system is strong enough, the energy will not release itself in useless activity. Put another way, so long as the pressure (energy) is not too great, the boiler will not burst.

Each individual's level of energy is different, but the deeper (the more important) a need, the more potential energy there is to release. Argyris views these needs as being located along several continua. He postulates that individuals develop along the following lines:

1. from a state of passivity as infants to a state of increasing activity as adults;
2. from a state of dependence upon others as infants to a state of relative independence as adults;
3. from being capable of behaving in only a few ways as an infant to being capable of behaving in many different ways as an adult;
4. from having erratic, casual, shallow interests as an infant to having deeper interests as an adult;
5. from having a short time perspective as an infant to having a much longer time perspective as an adult;
6. from being in a subordinate position in the family and society as an infant to aspiring to occupy an equal and/or superordinate position relative to peers as an adult; and
7. from a lack of awareness of self as an infant to an awareness of, and control over, self as an adult.[7]

Maslow's Needs Hierarchy	*Physiological Needs.* According to Maslow, the needs for food, shelter, clothing, and sleep are lower-order needs. In most work environments these needs are rarely considered because one assumes that they are being met. Many people take jobs as corrections officers in order to meet these needs for themselves and their families. Many have no intention of remaining on the job after the economy improves, for example, and they are able to return to their "real" jobs.
	Safety and Security Needs. We all desire a measure of order and safety in our lives, and to achieve them we look to the familiar and avoid the unknown, if possible. Generally, this need is met through individual compensation, but in corrections, there is always the possibility of being injured. Thus, organizations need to recognize that ensuring predictability through written policies and procedures is important, as are retirement and survivors' benefits. In addition, civil service jobs are desirable for the job security they offer. Recently, however, many state budgets have fallen under the ax, and corrections employees have also felt the pain of job insecurity.
	Social Needs. The two needs discussed above deal with physical survival. Social needs relate to companionship, love, and friendship. Many correctional institutions have employees' clubs of some sort that enable staff to gather together periodically for potluck suppers, dances, and other social activities that meet these needs. Many institutional executives realize the value in wandering around the institution occasionally and sharing coffee or soft drinks with staff. Available research points out that our need for affection, attention, and belonging is as important as our need for food and water. When staff have a strong sense of belonging, they are more productive and more vigilant.
	Esteem Needs. Self-esteem refers to how one feels about oneself. This can be positive or negative. One's co-workers and supervisors have a lot to do with self-esteem. We all need to feel good about ourselves, and when we do, we usually perform well on the job. When we do not, we usually perform poorly and may even cause co-workers to perform poorly.
	Self-Actualization Needs. Self-actualization refers to our desire to maximize our potential. This state is rarely achieved because it is a very individualized matter. We constantly set new goals for ourselves that allow for new levels of expression. Each person's search for self-actualization is unique. For example, after being discharged from the military a young man or woman may take a job at a local prison. He or she may struggle to earn a bachelor of science degree at a local college or university and then apply for a counselor's job. The employee periodically establishes new goals, and he or she may ultimately retire as a warden. Upon retirement, the individual may take a position as an elementary school counselor in the inner city. Thus, in this example, the self-actualizing person may actually hold several jobs and two or three careers in a lifetime. Thus, in order to meet the need for self-actualization on the job, managers need to be creative and flexible.

Thus, individuals develop along several continua, and their level of need on each continuum is individualized according to one's personality. Unlike Maslow's hierarchy, Argyris's developmental trends are not arranged in any order. They only represent an individual's developmental status at any point in life.

Motivation Models

Two of the several models of motivation are presented here to illustrate how motivation affects our lives and work. The two models are: (1) the Needs-Goal Model and (2) the Vroom Expectancy Model.

The Needs-Goal Model of Motivation

This model focuses only on the organism's need and its fulfillment of that need. Motivation begins with a need. "This need is then trans-

FIGURE 9.2
The Needs-Goal Model of Motivation

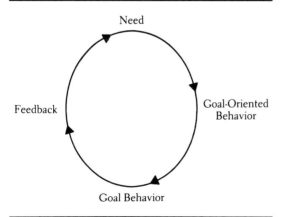

FIGURE 9.3
Vroom's Expectancy Model

Valence = Perceived Value of Results Perceived Probability that Results Will Be Realized

formed into behavior directed at supporting, or allowing, the performance of goal behavior to reduce the felt need."[8] Presumably, the goal-directed behavior will continue until the need is fulfilled. Thus, an individual who feels cold will put on a jacket or other garment to protect her- or himself from the cold. Once the desired level of comfort is achieved, the goal-directed behavior will cease and will begin again only in the case of renewed discomfort.

The Vroom Expectancy Model of Motivation

Few people will dispute that motivation is a good deal more complicated than the Needs-Goal Model depicts. In addressing these complexities, Vroom[9] posits that felt need causes behavior. However, he further suggests that motivation strength (valence) is "based not on [desired goals'] intrinsic properties but on the anticipated satisfaction or dissatisfaction associated with other outcomes to which they are expected to lead."[10] Thus, as one's desire increases or decreases, motivation strength will fluctuate accordingly.

This situation is illustrated by the case of the probation officer who has been informed that there will be an opening next year for an addictions specialist and that if she will obtain the necessary certification, she can have the position at a $2,000 increase in salary. Assuming that the probation officer needs the money, her motivation strength is determined by:

1. the value the probation officer puts on $2,000 per year;
2. the probation officer's perception of the probability that she could complete the certification course on time and perform the job satisfactorily;
3. the value the probation officer places on being an addictions specialist.

As the value the probation officer places on $2,000 per year goes up, the higher the value she will assign to being an addictions specialist, and as her perceived probability of satisfactorily completing the certification course increases, the strength of her motivation is said to increase.

Meeting Human Needs

In the late 1950s Frederick Herzberg and two colleagues[11] published a study that surveyed 200 engineers and accountants. Specifically, these individuals were asked about events or situations at work that resulted in significant improvement or reduction in job satisfaction.

Motivational Factors (Job Satisfaction)

Herzberg, et al., found five factors that stand out as strong determinants of job satisfaction: achievement, recognition, the work itself, responsibility, and advancement.

They point out that while these factors motivate employees, their absence does not necessarily lead to job dissatisfaction. Further, when recognition appeared in a high number of events, it referred to recognition of achievement rather than to recognition as an individual or as a human relations tool. One final note: the factors of the work itself, responsibility, and advancement are of greater importance for last-

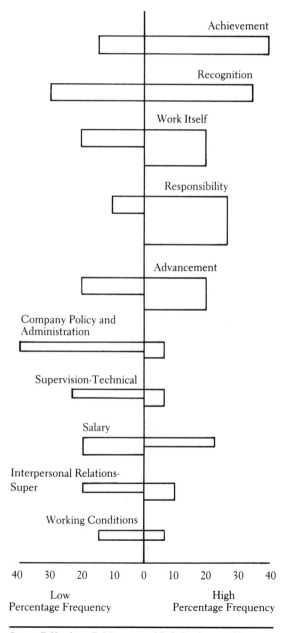

FIGURE 9.4
Comparison of Motivational Factors and Maintenance Factors

Source: F. Herzberg, B. Mausner, and B. B. Snyderman, *The Motivation to Work* (Wiley, 1959).

ing change in attitudes than the factors of achievement and recognition.

Maintenance (Hygiene) Factors (Job Dissatisfiers)

When the factors that determine job dissatisfaction were examined, an entirely different picture emerged. While these factors were also unidimensional, they served only to bring about dissatisfaction and were rarely present in events that led to positive job attitudes. Unlike the motivational factors (satisfiers), the **maintenance factors** (dissatisfiers) consistently produced short-term changes in job attitudes.

The maintenance factors are: company policy and administration, supervision, salary, interpersonal relations, and working conditions.

Motivational factors are those elements above and beyond what one ordinarily expects from a job; however, when maintenance factors are lacking in a job, they tend to assume even greater importance.[12] Correctional workers like to feel that they are getting something other than a paycheck for their efforts. If they feel cheated out of recognition or opportunities for advancement or find the work itself demeaning or unfulfilling, they probably will begin to ask for greater fringe benefits, higher pay, or more liberal sick-leave policies. This is not to say that these points are not important. They should be maximized in order to seek and retain the best-qualified people for the job. That is just the point. If executives and supervisors fail to recognize the importance of **motivational factors**, valuable time and effort will be expended dealing with employee concerns in the area of **maintenance factors.**

Figure 9.5 illustrates the findings of the study done by Herzberg, et al. The length of the box represents the frequency with which the factor appeared, and the width of the box represents the period the attitude toward the job lasted, which could have been from a few weeks to years.

FIGURE 9.5
The Communication Process

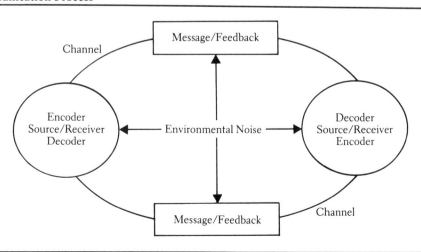

Strategies for Motivation

Communication

Communication is the transmission of ideas, information, skills, and emotions through symbols such as words, pictures, gestures, and so forth. Clampitt[13] points out that many managers are Arrow managers; that is, they tend to be straightforward and results-oriented. To these managers communicating is something like shooting an arrow at a target. They attempt to imbed an intact message in the target. They see communication as a one-way activity based primarily on the skills of the sender. In other words, according to Clampitt, the focus is on the sender of the message. This type of manager is often found in corrections.

Clampitt identifies two other approaches to communicating: the Circuit approach and the Dance approach. In the former, the managerial approach to communicating is on "networking," "going with the flow," and "making connections." Circuit managers stress feedback over response, relationships over content, and understanding over compliance. They view communication as a two-way process involving an active sender and receiver.

Those who use the third approach to communication, the Dance Approach, believe that effective communication can only be determined in light of the communicator's goals, whatever they may be. They view communication as a patterned activity involving the coordination of meaning, and coorientation (one's ability to anticipate another's cues, actions, and responses) and as a set of skills, some of which are not a part of one's consciousness.

Certainly the effective communicator uses all methods to communicate clearly, concisely, and coherently. Criminal justice seems to attract people who are action-oriented, people who expect results and often see situations as either black or white. Clampitt's three communication approaches shed some light on why some managers are successful communicators and some are not. Arrow and Circuit communicators do not share the Dance communicator's ability to account for the complexity of organizational situations; rather, they focus on immediate results.

Archambeault and Archambeault[14] point out that communication is written, verbal, and nonverbal. Written communication refers to all information transmitted through the written word. It should be carefully considered and planned before being finalized and distributed. Verbal communication, or oral communication, is the most frequently used form of communication in any organization. All employees use both formal and informal verbal communication depending on the situation and setting. Nonverbal communication refers to the transmission of feelings, attitudes, or meanings through body language such as posture, gesture, and tone of voice. Just as we use punctuation in our written communication, we use nonverbal communication to punctuate and accent our verbal communication.

The effective manager realizes the value of good communication. He or she sees communication as a two-way process involving a sender and a receiver. Communication can be blocked or distorted by extraneous "noise" such as bias, semantics, and subjective interpretations.

Internal Organizational Communication
Internal organizational communication is composed of both formal and informal communication channels. Both figure into the motivation process because they may be used to keep organization members informed about what is going on in the organization. There is a relationship between the formal and informal communication systems in that formal systems rarely satisfy the informational needs of organization members.[15] As a consequence, these individuals develop informal contacts through the grape-

The Woodshed	In 1981 David Stockman, then director of the Office of Management and Budget (OMB), made some remarks during an interview that President Reagan felt reflected poorly on him and his economic policies. Mr. Stockman's well-publicized trip to "the woodshed" for a chewing out* vividly calls our attention to the often necessary and always unpleasant task of chastising and correcting a subordinate. This is colloquially called an "ass chewing."
	Some people have been able to elevate this process to an art. Anyone who has worked in corrections has at one time or another had to endure such an ordeal. We may have left the office of the manager angry, insulted, and frustrated that we could not fight back without losing our job; but on the other hand, we may also have recognized that we deserved correction and that we had learned something.
	What makes the difference between the two attitudes is the way the manager administers a talking-to. Some managers are unable to correct employees without personally attacking them. Others raise their voices and use epithets to get their point across. Neither is necessary. While the following guidelines are helpful in daily communications with subordinates, they are especially valuable for the manager to keep in mind when he or she is conducting a one-on-one session with an employee.
	■ Be descriptive of the behavior that you are criticizing. If evaluation is necessary, be sure to avoid evaluating the individual. ■ Stick to solving problems and avoid the appearance of exerting personal control. ■ Maintain an air of empathy. If the employee's poor performance is the result of other personal problems, you need to understand them and to be prepared to help resolve them. ■ Maintain an air of equality. Avoid any implication of smug superiority.
	*Time, December 7, 1981, V. 118, No. 23, p. 19.

vine to obtain the kinds of interesting information that are unavailable through formal channels.

The Formal System. The organizational chart best depicts where the formal lines of communication lie. The major forms of formal communication are: downward communication, upward communication, and horizontal communication. **Downward communication** serves several purposes, among which are sending or-

ders down the hierarchy and providing job-related information to organization members.[16] On the other hand, a heavy reliance on downward communication reflects a Theory X orientation toward employees and inhibits upward flow of reliable information.

Upward communication flows from employees upward, ultimately reaching the appropriate level. Upward communications serves several important functions within the organization:

- It provides management with feedback about current organizational issues and problems.
- It is management's primary source of feedback in determining the effectiveness of downward communication.
- It relieves tension by allowing employees to share relevant information with superiors.
- It encourages employee participation in organizational processes, thereby enhancing organizational cohesiveness.[17]

Horizontal communication is basically peer communication. It enhances the functioning of an organization by aiding in problem solving, providing mutual support, and facilitating the sharing of information.

The Informal System. In addition to the formal communication system, an informal system emerges that is a result of interaction within the organization. The informal system is a message system that develops between members of the organization and is not necessarily prescribed by the formal structure.[18]

Individuals have a great need for meaning in their lives, and the informal communication system contributes to that meaning by allowing the organization member to have reliable, relevant, and in-depth information. The grapevine, as it is often called, provides members with interesting information that is usually not available through formal channels. This information helps members understand organizational life and strategically direct their own activities.

Information also means power.[19] Individuals who possess information and are willing to use it usually have power and influence. For example, the department head in charge of the correctional officers, variously called captain, major, or even colonel, is often the most powerful person in a prison. The reason for this is that he or she not only commands the largest number of employees but also is the destination

of a great deal of information. Most of the information is trivial, but some of it is power-enhancing. Therefore, the effective manager needs to recognize the existence of informal power that is sometimes equal to his or her formal power. The struggle occurs when an unscrupulous individual is in a position of authority and uses informal power to advance a personal agenda. These "Machiavellian" types can make life most uncomfortable.

On the other hand, informal communication channels are not inherently bad for the organization; rather, they are potentially useful to the manager.[20] Informal communication networks are useful because:

1. Information passes along the grapevine rapidly.
2. Informal communication channels are relatively distortion-free. This is not to say that messages are always accurate but rather that information generally changes less than it does along channels of formal communication.[21]

Managers can benefit from the grapevine by using it as a supplement to formal channels of communication. Further, the grapevine can bolster the formal power of the chief executive and supplement formal communication, thereby negating lies, rumors, and innuendo.

Theory X—Theory Y

In chapter 2 the reader was introduced to McGregor's Theory X and Theory Y. Douglas McGregor[22] identifies two approaches managers often use when dealing with subordinates—the Pessimistic View and the Optimistic View.

The Pessimistic View
According to Theory X, people really do not want to work. They need to be pushed, closely

supervised, and threatened with punishment before they accomplish anything. Further, because workers have little or no ambition they avoid responsibility while at the same time seeking responsible positions. While this view is rarely stated so explicitly, it is clearly implied in managers' actions as well as in organizational policy and practices. Reece and Brandt[23] point out that there are two major drawbacks to Theory X. First, Theory X reflects a pessimistic view of human nature because managers and executives who adhere to it believe that punishments and rewards are the only ways to deal with employees, and usually punishments more than rewards. Many times one sees a memorandum to employees ending with the statement: "Failure to comply will result in . . ." Clearly this manager does not expect employees to respond promptly or completely to directives.

Second, adherents to Theory X create a negative attitude toward workers. Managers who view employees as lazy, incompetent, and unwilling to accept responsibility often treat employees with suspicion, distrust, and little respect. Their style of management usually rests upon fault finding, blame, and reprimands.

The Optimistic View
Theory Y is based on a more generous view of human nature. According to this theory, work is as natural as play or rest; workers can exercise self-direction and do not need to be threatened; workers have the capacity to be imaginative and creative and to seek responsibility; the intellectual capacities of most workers are only partially utilized.

Managers who accept Theory Y are interested in employees' concerns. They solicit employees' input and attempt positive means of motivation. The concept of Functional Unit Management (FUM) will be discussed in chapter 15. FUM is an excellent management tool for those who accept Theory Y. Through FUM the unit manager and the assistant warden have

the opportunity to delegate responsibility and to become closely involved with employees. Everyone in the unit works together as a team, and the emphasis is on getting the job done. In short, FUM fosters a healthy, two-way relationship where employees want to give more.

The primary reason for managers to adopt a Theory Y orientation is that it more successfully meets human needs in the workplace. Through Theory Y, workers' needs for recognition, responsibility, and a sense of growth are met. **Theory Z** (discussed more thoroughly in chapter 10) is an outgrowth of Theory Y in that it assumes that the best management includes workers of all levels. Employees of Theory Z type organizations have a sense of belonging because of the group decision-making process and lifetime employment. Workers in these organizations are likely to perform their tasks conscientiously and enthusiastically.

Critics point out that civil service is lifetime employment. Perhaps it is and perhaps it isn't. Regardless of one's stance, civil service does offer job security. Therefore, there is room to argue in favor of a management approach such as Theory Z in the field of corrections.

Job Redesign

Individuals do not work in a vacuum. Rather, they work in organizations where many jobs contribute to accomplishing organizational objectives. **Job design** is the attempt to plan all structural and social aspects of a job and its impact on individuals and on the organization as a whole.

A correctional organization exists to protect the community. A prison holds sentenced offenders until the time of their release, and in the interim, offers certain programs to meet the needs of the inmates in the areas of counseling and education, for example. A probation and parole agency is responsible for supervising the offender while he or she is at large in the community; the probation agency serves the needs of the court in regard to investigating the background of the offender. Community release centers also protect the community and in addition provide a degree of custody for the offender. These diverse aims occasionally confuse managers when they go about the task of job design.

The nature of individual positions is predetermined by the objectives or goals of the organization. There are many unhappy employees in correctional organizations because executives have attempted to superimpose one standard for a position regardless of whether it is in a maximum security institution or in a work-release center. The result is a measure of role conflict and organizational strife. For example, the corrections officer in an institution is measured by his or her ability to prevent escapes and fights between inmates. Rarely is the officer chastized for failing to counsel inmates.[24] On the other hand, the job description for an officer working in a work-release center is very nearly the same as that for an officer working in an institution. However, the officer in a work-release center is constantly bombarded with encouragement to be more conciliatory and more interested in counseling inmates and is expected to perform a variety of tasks that support the social-work aspects of the job.

Over the years there has been increased interest in job design and redesign. There are at least three major approaches to job design or redesign.[25] The first is the **Methods Analysis Technique**. This approach has its roots in Scientific Management as expressed by Frederick Taylor and Frank and Lillian Gilbreath. Most corrections agencies design their jobs from this perspective. However, the advent of Functional Unit Management has the potential to change how many corrections jobs are designed.

The second approach is **Human Factors Engineering**. This approach has its roots in the need to consider such human characteristics as physical, sensory, perceptual, and cognitive abilities. The thrust of this perspective is to design equipment and facilities so they are user-friendly. This approach, too, has not been lost on corrections planners and architects, as a comparison between the old linear-surveillance jails and the new-generation jails makes clear.

The third major approach to job design is **job enrichment**. Maslow addresses this approach when he points out that as one need is fulfilled it is replaced by a higher-order need. Thus, one is continually striving to achieve full potential. Herzberg, however, is more to the point. He calls our attention to the fact that job satisfaction and job dissatisfaction are not opposite ends of a continuum but rather separate factors. According to Herzberg, if the hygiene factors are inadequate, job dissatisfaction will result. If they are adequate, the worker is able to avoid dissatisfaction but will not achieve satisfaction. Job satisfaction occurs when certain motivators are present.

Recent Corrections Job Design Strategies

Klofas, et al.,[26] summarize what we know about job design efforts in the field of corrections. It may be surprising to some, but correctional managers have a history of innovation in the area of job design. One of the earliest efforts occurred at the Norfolk Prison Colony in Norfolk, Massachusetts.[27] While some officers controlled the perimeter of the colony, others assumed additional tasks related to casework and counseling. There have been other efforts since then: for example, distributing probation caseloads by the amount and type of supervision required; developing skill areas so that various probation officers have particular specialties that allow them to "broker" services in the community; and encouraging officers to plan the operation of a new jail and to develop and write policies and procedures. In institutions, the most progressive attempt at job redesign in recent history has been the development of Functional Unit Management. Under the unit management scheme, staff in the unit work as a team. Specialty lines are often blurred; for example, everyone is concerned with security, officers counsel, case managers turn keys, and secretaries attempt to do most everything. In another example, as a measure to alleviate overcrowding in an institution in Alabama, inmates were released to the community, where they were supervised by correctional officers. Research indicates that the officers felt a higher level of job satisfaction and personal accomplishment. Zupan[28] documents the contribution of new-generation jails to job redesign and the positive effects of direct-supervision jail units on staff and inmates.

The above examples clearly address the motivation factors in Herzberg's model. That is, they contribute to a sense of achievement, recognition, and responsibility and offer opportunity for advancement. Herzberg is a strong supporter of job design;[29] however, he differentiates between **vertical loading** and **horizontal loading**. Vertical loading refers to increasing the level of responsibility, challenge, and meaningfulness of the job. Horizontal loading, on the other hand, refers to increasing the variety or diversity of job activities that are essentially the same skill level as those that are already part of the job. Herzberg argues that vertical loading contributes to job satisfaction because of its motivational features.

Human Relations

It is difficult to motivate employees in corrections. However, we must keep trying. Some managers have the impression that workers in general have experienced declining motivation. Grant[30] lists ten reasons for the perceived decrease in employee motivation. They include greater instability and increased diversity of values, more guaranteed rewards, inability of re-

wards to satisfy emerging needs, a disappearing work ethic, reduced costs of failure, rising income and progressive taxation, more group production and problem solving, decreased employee loyalty, less supervisory power, and shorter time perspectives. Taken separately, these reasons do not add up to much, but Grant argues that the decline is not due to any single reason and that in the long run, lost ground may never be recovered.

Odiorne[31] calls for organizations to emphasize strategic concerns in order to motivate employees and to contribute to job satisfaction. He offers ten areas of strategic concern to the manager. Among them are:

- *Management by anticipation.* Instead of reacting to situations, managers need to be sensitive to the environment in order to be proactive.
- *Relating people to the organization.* Demands by women, minorities, the handicapped, and gays will not abate. We need to forget our arguments about why things cannot be done and focus on new paradigms.
- *The motivational aspects of physical plant design and layout.* Corrections managers must focus not only on the cost-effectiveness and motivational aspects of work and work life but also on safety.
- *More use of work teams.* Building and using primary groups or work teams allow the personalization of work.
- *Better strategies for managing managers and professionals.* Management practices used with poorly educated factory workers have been carried over to middle-class professionals, resulting in alienation and a sense of powerlessness and ineffectiveness and a loss of morale. We must develop programs that accommodate and encourage these people, define challenging goals, give them control over their resources, and allow more freedom.

- *Treating employees with respect.* Drop our Theory X assumptions and view employees as assets that need to be guarded, encouraged, and developed.
- *Decentralization.* Breaking down large, impersonal organizations creates pockets of individual decision making and ties responsibility and results to the individual effort.
- *More sociotechnical systems.* In the coming years we need to encourage the development of joint management-labor groups to advise management on everything from problem areas affecting both groups to employee recreation programs.
- *More training/education.* Training changes behavior, raises personal expectations, and motivates.

Employee Programs

Many programs attempt to address the motivational needs of employees. In corrections there are constraints imposed by the nature of the organization, such as clientele, the need to be a twenty-four-hour agency, security needs, and so forth. Nevertheless, the innovative manager can formally recognize the employee, account for a changing work-force and personal needs, as well as allow employees to have input into decision-making processes. Three such programs are discussed below.

Employee of the Month (or Quarter)
This is a rather simple program to implement, and it should be part of the employee-evaluation program. It is a vehicle that provides for the recognition of those who have improved the operation of the organization by submitting effective ideas, by performing in a way that is consistently superior, or by doing something above and beyond what the job requirements call for.

Organizations that use this approach often contract with a local portrait photographer for an eight-by-ten color photo of the employee, which is put on display in the lobby or other prominent place. Beside the portrait is usually a plaque with space for the names of all employees of the month (or quarter) to be engraved along with the dates of the honor. Other motivational "perks" are offering nearby parking for the employee's car or a gift certificate to a favorite restaurant for the employee and spouse or friend. In more rural areas, local newspapers often publish the employee's name and record his or her accomplishment. This program can be an important vehicle for recognizing deserving employees.

Flextime
Flextime is any work schedule that deviates from the traditional forty-hour, five-days-a-week schedule. Douglas L. Fleuter[32] points out that flextime has many advantages: (1) a gain in productive hours worked, (2) increased production, (3) increased job satisfaction, (4) back-up training for supervisors (forced delegation of responsibility), (5) reduction in early-morning tension, (6) more efficient planning of their day by employees, and (7) decreased traffic congestion.

Naturally, not all of these advantages are available to corrections managers. For example, probation and parole officers may already work a flextime schedule. But if not, they could spend a portion of their week on the streets and be in the office on some evenings in order to accommodate client work schedules.

Institutional support staff and counselors and case managers could be allowed flexibility in establishing work hours that meet personal needs and the needs of the institution. It's entirely feasible for corrections officers to have hours that do not conform to the traditional forty-hour work week. Some states and jurisdictions have implemented a four- and-three schedule. That is, officers work ten or twelve hours per day for four days and are off for three days. There are other variations that allow for more leisure time.

Quality Circles

A Quality Circle is a voluntary group of eight to twelve employees who perform similar work and who meet on a regular basis (on company time) to identify, analyze, and develop solutions to a variety of work-related problems.[33] The Japanese have successfully used Quality Circles in industry, and the notion is gaining popularity in the United States. While Quality Circles have been used primarily in manufacturing, they also have been successfully used in banks, hospitals, and service organizations.[34] Organizations that use Quality Circles do so because they agree with Herzberg's conclusions on motivators and increasing job satisfaction and improving task performance.[35] Quality Circles are particularly suited to correctional organizations because of employees' common interests and the need to share information. Correctional institutions already use a form of Quality Circle. It is called a shift, and Quality Circle time is called roll call. After posts and the names of personnel working the posts are called out, many supervisors ask for discussion. Often officers identify problem areas or inmates having problems, and solutions to ongoing problems are analyzed and discussed. Clearly, the concept can be broadened to other areas of the organization.

Quible[36] suggests several guidelines for implementing and operating Quality Circles.

- Members of a circle should have a common job function.
- Participation in the circle should be voluntary.
- Meetings should be held regularly—not just when problems occur.
- Each member must participate.
- Top management must support the Quality Circle.
- Circles should concern themselves only with work-related problems.

- Impact of the circles' implemented recommendations should be monitored and measured, if possible.

Implementation of Quality Circles requires commitment from top management and a dedication to improving organizational communication. The concept is an exciting and dynamic one that promises to improve employee productivity and enhance job satisfaction.

Summary

The correctional environment is a stressful one in which to work. The capable manager must try to motivate employees and should be aware that he or she is looked up to as a cheerleader and coach. Motivation has been defined several ways, but basically it is the art of allowing people to work.

In motivating employees, managers need to be aware of employees' needs and realize that working is also a social experience. People's needs range from basic physiological ones to the need to fulfill their potential. Argyris argues that development and the ability to fulfill those needs range along a continuum. Motivation is congruant with need fulfillment in that individuals attempt to fulfill unmet needs.

Herzberg identifies two types of needs of workers: Hygiene Factors and Motivation Factors. Hygiene Factors contribute to job dissatisfaction, but when absent, do nothing to contribute to job satisfaction. Motivation Factors contribute to job satisfaction. Examples of Motivation Factors are achievement, recognition, and advancement.

Communication fits into Herzberg's model in that the manager who has good communication skills is better able to motivate employees. The effective manager also knows how to use the formal and informal communications systems in the organization. Job design and employee programs that motivate and satisfy social needs of employees contribute to production, service, and job satisfaction. Finally, motivation extends beyond simply allowing others to work or supporting them as they face the pressures of work. Motivation means encouraging subordinates to be creative in their decision making and innovative in problem solving.

Reviewing the Case

The Georgia Department of Corrections is facing a formidable task. Corrections workers are being asked to undertake a stressful, thankless job for low pay and poor benefits. How do the wardens, superintendents, and other executives build and maintain motivation?

Assuming that salaries and benefits will rise somewhat, the commissioner of corrections realizes that performance and motivation will improve if the staff are given the responsibility for making certain decisions on the job. That responsibility will be gladly accepted if there are clear and precise policies and procedures. In addition, employees must feel that there is an opportunity for growth, advancement, and recognition, among other factors. Certain social needs must also be met. The commissioner realizes that work is a social experience, that he must make an effort to meet employees, and that employees must have the opportunity to forge social links through sports teams or other groups.

For Further Study

Barry L. Reece and Rhonda Brandt, *Effective Human Relations in Organizations,* 3d ed. (Boston: Houghton Mifflin, 1987).

R.C. Huseman, C.M. Logue, and D.C. Freshley, eds., *Readings in Interpersonal and Organizational Communication* (Boston: Holbrook, 1973).

Linda Zupan, *Jails: Reform and the New Generation Philosophy* (Cincinnati: Anderson, 1991).

Key Terms

Motivation

Vroom Expectancy Model

Maintenance Factors

Job Design

Needs-Goal Model of Motivation

Motivation Factors

Dance Approach to Communication

Quality Circle

The current jail in Muscatine County is inadequate. Unfortunately, many jails are inadequate and were designed to hold fewer inmates than they presently hold. The Muscatine County Jail is no different. There have been many policy problems in the Sheriff's attempts to construct a new one. (*Photo courtesy of Ron Duzenberry.*)

The Multnomah County Detention Center is an excellent example of planning, design, and effective policy implementation. It is a positive addition to the central business district and represents the best in community intentions. (*Photo courtesy of William Wood.*)

The Larimer County
Detention Center is
an example of
Theory Z in action.
The staff have been
willing to innovate
and the supervisors
and commanders
realize that staff are
the county's most
precious resource.
(*Photo courtesy of
Sandra L. Schilling
and Leslie L.
Johnson.*)

The Panopticon was
designed by Jeremy
Bentham. The
concept allows for
one officer to
supervise a number
of inmates in their
cells from his post at
the center of the cell
house. (*Photo
courtesy of Illinois
Department of
Corrections.*)

Of the four original Panopticon cell houses at the Illinois State Penitentiary at Stateville, only one remains. They were deemed beyond repair and the third one was razed in 1986.
(*Photo courtesy of Illinois Department of Corrections.*)

The Federal Correctional Institution, Milan, Michigan, is an example of the Self-Enclosed Design in prison architecture. Notice the central courtyard around which are found inmate housing and administrative offices. The outside wall of the cell house/office serves as the outside wall as well. Until the mid-1970s the buildings to the left did not exist. (*Photo courtesy of U.S. Bureau of Prisons.*)

The U.S. Penitentiary, Terre Haute, Indiana, is an example of the Telephone Pole Design in prison architecture. Notice the long central corridor terminating in two cell houses forming a "Y" at each end of the corridor. Other cell houses and buildings serving a variety of functions, such as dining hall and hospital, are at forty-five degree angles from the corridor. (*Photo courtesy of U.S. Bureau of Prisons.*)

CMF Vacaville is a good illustration of architecture that is not depressing to the spirit. CMF is a medical facility that houses a variety of custody classifications and serves the medical needs of inmates within the California Department of Corrections.
(*Photo courtesy of California Department of Corrections.*)

The Federal Correctional Institution, Morgantown, West Virginia, is the site of the beginning of the movement to unit management. Its open, campus-like setting and population of youthful offenders serving sentences for less serious offenses combined to create an ideal beginning for the movement. (*Photo courtesy of U.S. Bureau of Prisons.*)

Control centers are busy places where the responsibility for the institution is in the hands of one or two officers. This photo of the control center at the CCA Santa Fe Detention Center illustrates that in a well-managed, private institution, one is unable to distinguish between a private facility and a public one. (*Photo courtesy of Corrections Corporation of America.*)

Managing the Informal Organization

Case Study: Prison Guards' Problems Prompt Union's Creation

Prison guards and other correctional workers make up less than one-tenth of the state work force, yet they file a third of the state employee personnel appeals each year.[1] The disciplinary suspension rate is high, as is the risk of inmate lawsuits.

Overcrowded prisons and understaffing combine to create dangerous working conditions, corrections officers say, while they remain wary that any use of force will bring swift disciplinary action against them.

"The solution is always to suspend the officer and let him file a grievance," said Rodney Parker, who has worked six years at the Maryland Penitentiary. "The administration is not listening to us."

There is a good deal of frustration among penal employees and that has sowed the seeds for the formation of the Maryland Correctional Union (MCU). Unlike the three unions now representing all types of state employees, MCU will restrict its membership recruiting to the 6,000 workers in the state corrections division.

That focus will be the source of the new union's organizing appeal as well as of bargaining power with state authorities, predicts Rick Silva, field services director of MCU.

"When there's one union recognized as representing these workers, the administration and legislators will have to listen," said Mr. Silva, who worked for a dozen years with corrections workers as a representative of the rival Maryland Classified Employees Association.

"And with better lines of communication, we hope to work out many of the job-related problems before they escalate to formal grievances."

"We've seen a deterioration of the rights of correctional employees," he said. "They have as little rights as an inmate."

Corrections workers feel that their goals have been thwarted in the past by the lack of a single voice and by unions that have not effectively represented their unique needs. Officers had a chance to gain important security and staffing changes in 1984 with their "sick-out" action following the fatal stabbing of Officer Herman Toulson at the Maryland Penitentiary, but while one state employee union was pressing the job action, another was publicly declaring that it was over. That effectively broke the pressure on authorities to do anything, stated one authority.

MCU hopes to build a core of members from some 850 city jail employees who will become state employees July 1, 1991. Some jail employees are now represented by the City Union of Baltimore, which like MCU is an affiliate of the American Federation of Teachers. Collective bargaining is the main priority of MCU and to gain an acceptable contract for correctional employees.

The goal of the union is to obtain better pay and benefits for workers. This may be a difficult task at any time, but the economy and the fact that two other unions are attempting to organize workers complicate matters.

Introduction

The Hawthorne studies, discussed in chapter 2,[2] clearly reveal the importance of groups in the workplace.[3] Every organization is a patchwork of groups,[4] and an individual can belong to several groups at the same time. For example, an institutional case manager, or counselor, is first of all a member of a department or functional unit. At the same time, however, he or she can be a member of a special task force for the warden, part of a small group of employees who enjoy each other's company, and a member of the employees' club. His or her role in each group is different. There are **formal** and **informal** groups, and in each group the members interact and influence one another.

The Informal Organization as Part of the Formal Organization

Allport[5] describes a J-shaped curve in the distribution of human behaviors. He points out that we need to begin by viewing the range of human behavior as distributed along a normal bell-shaped curve. However, behaviors can deviate from this range. Sometimes they follow something like an inverted J curve. That is, most individuals behave at the norm, others operate away from the norm in one specific direction, and a few operate away from the norm in the other direction. Behavior tends to conform to the J-shaped curve because sanctions are strictly applied to one side of the behavior range rather than the other.

To illustrate, several years ago a unit manager at a Midwestern penitentiary was often late coming to work. The associate warden, whose office overlooked the entrance, was incensed that the unit manager arrived persistently late and called him in for a reprimand, refusing to listen to an explanation. What the associate warden didn't see (because he was most often the first leave at 4:00 P.M.) was the unit manager leaving almost every day between 5:00 and 6:00 P.M. and devoting many Saturdays and an occasional Sunday to his job. As a consequence, the unit manager was faced with the choice of arriving on time and leaving at 4:00 P.M. or arriving on time and staying late to deal with issues that could only be handled after the inmates returned from their work assignments. The second choice, of course, would take even more time away from family and home. The point here is that sanctions are rarely applied to those who arrive early for work (often to sit around and drink coffee), but they are often applied to those who are persistently late for work. In the above example, behavior is shaped to conform to the wishes of the executive.

Likert's System of Management

In determining organizational behavior, Likert[6] points out that the informal structure of an organization is more important than the formal structure. He suggests some important aspects of the informal structure that can be used to

FIGURE 10.1
Arriving at Work

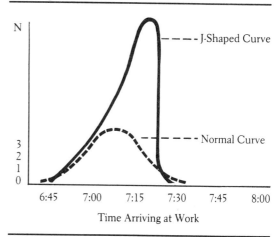

Time Arriving at Work

modify, supplement, or replace the more traditional structural designs used in business and government. His suggestions are based upon his own research into the following organizational and performance characteristics.

- Leadership processes
- Character of motivational forces
- Character of communication processes
- Character of interaction-influence processes
- Character of decision-making processes
- Character of goal setting or ordering
- Character of control process[7]

Wieland and Ullrich explain:

Likert divides each continuum upon which responses can be made into four intervals, each of which is related to a different style of management. In completing the questionnaire, an individual is asked to place a mark on the continuum at the point which best describes the organization under investigation. Responses which fall to the left of the center of the continuum are

FIGURE 10.2
Likert's Management Systems

Exploitative Authoritative	Benevolent Authoritative	Consultative	Participative Group
system one	system two	system three	system four

Source: Rensis Likert, *The Human Organization: Its Management and Value* (New York: Harper & Row, 1967).

indicative of an authoritative system of management while those which fall to the right of center indicate a system which is more participative.[8]

Likert found that the lowest-producing departments fall to the left of the continuum and the highest-producing departments to the right; that is, the latter can be described as system three or four organization. Further, when employees were asked what kind of organization they worked in, they usually described a system two or three. When asked to describe the kind of organization they would like to work in, they usually described a system four.

According to Likert, three characteristics appear to explain the success of system-four management: supportive relationships, group decision making and group methods of supervision, and high performance goals for the organization.

The Linking Pin Function

The success of system-four organizations demonstrates that the organization is a tightly knit, effectively functioning social system. This system is composed of interlocking work groups with a high degree of group loyalty among its members and favorable attitudes and trust between superiors and subordinates. System-four management recognizes and requires a work group that involves a superior and all of his or her subordinates. Each subordinate, in turn, is a superior for subordinates at the next lower level in the organization. Consequently, the organization is comprised of overlapping groups with managers at every level, except the highest which serve as linking pins between two groups.

The groups function as formal groups, although they have some informal group characteristics, such as friendship and proximity. Each member of the group is involved in decision making, and group members function in such a way that communication is open and problems can be openly examined. In correctional organizations, the functional unit comes closest to system-four management, and at the lowest level the unit manager is the linking pin. The unit managers, with the assistant warden, serve as another work group that reports to the warden. Properly executed, functional unit management provides for supportive relationships and group decision making and is able to establish high performance goals.

System Four and Theory Z

All of this sounds suspiciously like Ouchi's Theory Z,[9] which was briefly discussed in chapter 9. Ouchi studied Japanese manufacturers in an attempt to explain why they have continued to outpace U.S. manufacturers. He was able to identify three primary dimensions that seem to determine success. It should be noted, however, that Japanese culture may have characteristics that foster Theory Z, such as homogeneity, group cohesiveness, emphasis on the group over the individual, and so on. Nevertheless, Ouchi points out that these same characteristics may also apply to successful U.S. firms.

Lifetime employment is the most important determinant of success and most salient aspect of Japanese corporate life. Ouchi esti-

FIGURE 10.3
The Linking Pin Function

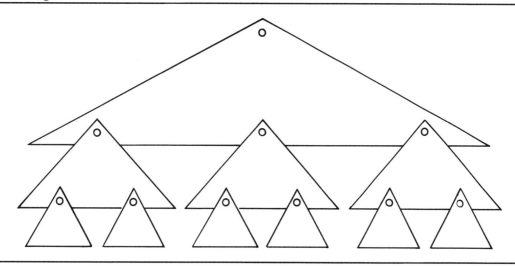

mates that perhaps 35 percent[10] of Japan's work force is promised lifetime employment. Hiring is conducted once a year, promotions are from within, and termination will not occur unless the employee is convicted of a crime. Once the employee reaches age fifty-five, he or she retires and is paid a lump sum amounting to five or six years' salary. Interestingly, there is no pension or social security, which is perhaps why the Japanese have one of the highest rates of personal savings in the world. Retirement is augmented by the Japanese system of *Zaibatsu*, whereby upon retirement the employee is shipped off to a satellite firm where he or she may work part-time for up to ten years. Thus, the employee is able to augment his or her retirement pay and at the same time make way for younger employees. There is no need for the government to enter the picture.

The second dimension is **evaluation and promotion**. In a Japanese Theory Z organization, the employee is not formally evaluated until he or she has been employed for ten years.

In the meantime, the employee will receive exactly the same promotions as others who began work at the same time. The drawback of this practice, of course, is that the employee has no incentive to make great, creative leaps or innovations; on the other hand, he or she is also not inclined to seek career advancement at the expense of someone else. Ouchi[11] notes that this career advancement is painfully slow but that the process promotes an open attitude by employees toward cooperation, performance, and evaluation. What makes the system work so well is that employees are members of as many as eight or so work groups. Research tells us that membership in work groups more than any other factor influences employees' attitude, behavior, and motivation. In other words, we care what peers think, and feelings of kinship shape our behavior.

The third dimension is that of **nonspecialized career paths**. One fundamental difference between Japanese and American employees is that the latter conduct their careers between organizations but within a single specialty, whereas the former conduct their careers between specialties but within a single organization. As explained earlier, in Japan a new college graduate is employed along with a number of others. He or she will work for ten years before undergoing a formal evaluation. During that time he or she is transferred from one area of specialty to another, so that by the first evaluation, the employee is acquainted with all aspects of the organization and perhaps the industry. By the time the employee reaches the peak of his or her career, he or she understands how every function, every specialty, and every office or department fits into the whole organization. The obvious advantage is that employees' skills and commitment to the organization are developed to the maximum.

Lifetime employment, evaluation, and job rotation are only a few of the characteristics that drive an organization to excellence. This brief look at Theory Z may enable the reader to draw some conclusions about U.S. industry and service organizations. Now let us attempt to place the foregoing discussion in the context of corrections.

The Corrections Z

In some ways corrections organizations qualify as Theory Z organizations. First, lifetime employment in corrections is fairly well assured as long as the employee does his or her job and remains free of criminal convictions. Many people enter civil service after college or military service and stay until retirement. The fact that salaries are a matter of public record may promote cooperation and lessen the "guerrilla" warfare witnessed in many private sector organizations.

Many correctional organizations do not have a way of evaluating employees. This is particularly true of smaller county units such as jails and probation agencies. But where it does exist, evaluation assures that excellence is rewarded and that those who perform poorly can be motivated to improve or be terminated according to policy.

Workers on nonspecialized career paths may be the most problematic because managers often do not look forward to directing and training employees who are unfamiliar with the job. In addition, unions may object to job rotation if agreed-upon procedures are violated, especially where seniority is an issue. However, it is safe to assume that employees in correctional organizations that use job rotation appear to have a higher level of competency, less burnout, and a greater commitment to the organization. Functional Unit Management shows the value of job rotation. Assuming that all jobs below that of unit manager are specialties, then the unit manager position is that of generalist. If the unit manager has not had the opportunity to learn a variety of jobs before assuming that position, he or she will certainly have the chance afterwards. The manager may then transfer out to other unit manager positions, to another comparable non-unit manager position, or to the position of assistant warden.

Likert points out that people prefer to work for organizations in which they share decision making and that foster close, supportive relationships and high performance goals. Tom Peters[12] provides helpful advice for the corrections manager when it comes to groups in the workplace:

- involve everyone in everything, and
- use self-managing teams.

In regard to the first, there may be limitations such as the security necessary to conduct an investigation, but in terms of management, everyone should be involved. Through examples[13] Peters illustrates how progress in the work organization he cites continued and even accelerated when line employees were allowed input. Peters admonishes managers to do *something* to stimulate involvement.

The second piece of Peters's advice is remarkably suited to corrections. Self-managing teams should be the basic unit of any correctional organization. Employees who are adequately trained, compensated, and team-oriented can move mountains. The curious thing about paramilitary organizations is that they can stifle teamwork and involvement or they can foster it. Just ask any United States Marine and any employee of a major penitentiary about teamwork and commitment and compare their responses. Peters's point is that front-line supervision must widen the span of control, or self-management will not work.

Corrections employees are no different from employees in the private sector. They want the chance to be creative, to share in decision making, and to strive for lofty goals. The best way to achieve this is to create a Theory Z organization that is characterized by involvement at all levels and by the use of self-managing teams.

The Larimer County Detention Center clearly reflects a Theory Z orientation, and the facility appears to be managed most effectively. But what about those correctional organizations that appear to have Theory Z characteristics but are poorly managed? DiIulio criticizes Michigan's responsibility model by pointing out that it does little "to promote organizational morale and much to stimulate among correctional officers a feeling of animosity toward the 'brass' at headquarters in Lansing."[14] Further, officers have little respect for the organization and its policies and have "no clear sense of mission."[15] In another discussion DiIulio states that "the California consensual model of correctional management presents us with no coherent pattern of correctional principles and practices."[16] Yet both the California Department of Corrections (CDC) and the Michigan Department of

Corrections (MDC) fit the descriptions of the Corrections Z given above. They both offer "lifetime" employment and both (presumably) have employee evaluation procedures. But here the "Z" begins to break down. Unions make life difficult for the administration by pointing out its shortcomings (true or not), by failing to provide a supportive work environment, and by failing to solicit input from the rank and file. In short, both the CDC and MDC fail to involve all levels of the organization in decision making.

Farmer[17] documents the experience of Walpole State Prison in Massachusetts, which moved from a disorganized, dangerous place in which to work or serve time to an organization that at least approximated a Corrections Z orientation. This was accomplished by the implementation of Unit Management. According to Farmer, "Each unit team works cooperatively in a participatory management style which has resulted in higher morale and commitment to purpose."[18] It appears that the HVMF of the Michigan Department of Corrections, according to DiIulio's description, falls into what Likert calls a system-two organization; that is, an organization characterized by a lack of trust, little communication between superiors and subordinates, relatively little teamwork, and decision making located at the top of the organization only.

Groups in Organizations

Groups Defined

The effective correctional manager must have a good understanding of the group and how it relates to the organization. For the purposes of this chapter, a group is understood to be made up of two or more people who interact and mutually influence each other.[19] Gibson, Ivancevich, and Donnelly[20] point out that there is no generally accepted definition of *group*. They surveyed the literature and found that understandings of what a group is fall into four categories:

1. *Perception*—group members perceive that they are members of that group.

2. *Organization*—the group is viewed relative to organizational characteristics. That is, there is a standard set of role relationships among members, and the group has a set of norms that guide conduct.

Theory Z in Action	In October 1983 the Larimer County (Colorado) Detention Center took advantage of the opportunity to move into the 1990s. It did so by opening a new direct-supervision jail and by implementing a radical change in management style.
	For centuries jails have been constructed and operated as a means to control and hold prisoners with very little thought given to management. Along with the change in philosophy from a linear—intermittent-surveillance jail philosophy—to a direct-supervision approach came a change in philosophy toward staff. The new approach to management draws upon Theory Z for its substance and style.
	Staff and inmates at the center believe in and practice a participatory team-management approach at all levels within the organization. This begins with the inmates' involvement in inmate council meetings, where, through a representative from each inmate housing area, they have the opportunity to voice concerns and offer suggestions to improve their stay at the Larimer County Detention Center.
	This management philosophy works because it establishes lines of communication between the inmates and staff. Open communication between staff members is just as diligently sought. At every level there is cooperation and comanagement between inmate services and security staff, up to and including two facility administrators who are of equal rank and make all decisions jointly for the benefit of the facility. This peculiar but effective management style is encouraged through pod meetings, where officers from a particular work area make their own proprietary decisions on how to manage their pods. The officers are encouraged to make decisions at their levels. They forward notification of any major changes to their supervisors for "bottom-up" implementation. Supervisors from each unit hold monthly team meetings, where everyone has the opportunity to help solve problems within the group.
	No management style is the "one best way," but the staff of the Larimer County Detention Center have demonstrated their willingness to consider and experiment with new ideas. Through it all, their ultimate goal is to manage inmate problems effectively and to make the staff aware that they are the organization's best resource.
	Source: Sandra L. Schilling, Captain, Leslie L. Johnson, Captain, Larimer County Detention Center.

3. *Motivation*—the group is viewed as an entity that satisfies certain needs of its members.

4. *Interaction*—the group is characterized by face-to-face communication, and the group is small enough that each person is able to communicate with all other members over a period of time.

In this chapter, a group is defined as:

Two or more employees who interact with each other in such a manner that the behavior and/or performance of a member is influenced by the behavior and/or performance of other members.[21]

Kinds of Groups in Correctional Organizations

Excluding inmate groups, there are basically two kinds of groups in correctional organizations: formal groups and informal groups.

Formal Groups

A formal group is one that is established to further the mission of the organization. In a jail, for example, one formal group is composed of employees who function as officers. Their job is to provide security and to maintain institutional tranquility. Another example is that of a chief probation officer who forms a standing committee whose purpose is to advise him or her on matters of concern to the community. Thus, the demands of the organization have led to the formation of two different groups. Specifically, there are two types of formal groups: command groups and task groups.[22]

Command Group. The command group is specified by the organization chart. Members of such a group report to a supervisor, who in turn reports to someone else. The authority re-

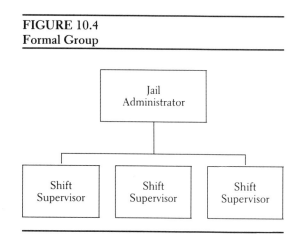

FIGURE 10.4
Formal Group

Jail Administrator

Shift Supervisor

Shift Supervisor

Shift Supervisor

lationship between the shift sergeant and his or her subordinates constitutes a command group.

Task Group. Members of a task group work together to complete a particular task or project. In the example used above, the chief probation officer requests that five or six probation officers and staff meet with him or her once a month to discuss the organization and the attitudes, perceptions, and community corrections needs of the community. The chief probation officer will then be able to discuss programs and problems more intelligently with the judges and to gauge the impact of programs more sensitively. Task groups are often called committees. They are valuable for four reasons.[23] First, they allow organization members to exchange ideas; second, they allow members to generate suggestions and recommendations for other organizational units; third, they encourage members to develop new ideas for solving existing organizational problems; and fourth, they assist in the development of organizational policies.

Informal Groups

Informal groups arise naturally as a result of the work situation and in response to social needs. Two types of informal groups are identified.

FIGURE 10.5
Informal Groups

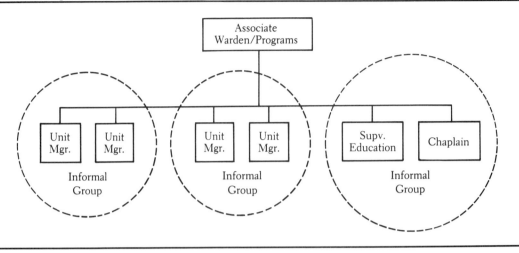

Interest Group. Employees may band together to address a particular issue; for example, to press for higher wages or better benefits. Once the need is met, such groups often disband.

Friendship Groups. Many groups form because of common interests such as church and hobbies or because of a similarity in age. Friendship groups extend their activities to off-work hours and tend to change over time.

Allcorn's Typology

Seth Allcorn[24] identifies four types of groups that managers need to be aware of if they are to understand the psychodynamics of organizations. The four types are: the homogenized group, the institutionalized group, the autocractic group, and the intentional group. According to Allcorn, the first three arise as a defensive mechanism to anxiety that arises from group membership. Change, he asserts, is driven by individuals' need for security and self-esteem

and by threats to the group's existence that stem from the operating environment.

The Homogenized Group. This is the most primitive of the three defensive groups. Participation is unrewarding and members perceive a lack of direction, leadership, and task or agenda and behave accordingly. There may be some hostility toward other members of the group, and group culture discourages members from offering leadership or direction. Homogenization occurs when the individual's need to be valued by others is not satisfied. Fear and anxiety result. There is a lack of connectedness to others, and members react by psychologically, and sometimes physically, withdrawing.

The Institutionalized Group. Members of this group control their anxieties by creating an external defense system. The result, according to Allcorn, is a hierarchical organization that regulates interaction between members and provides nonthreatening leadership by specifying the degree of power and authority a leader will have. Rigid routines are devised to control members' actions. Members are lulled into the belief that they are members of a stable, predictable environment where everyone is equal. Productivity is of secondary importance, but work is accomplished because everyone rigidly follows the rules.

The Autocratic Group. The anxieties of the autocratic group are addressed by identifying a powerful, charismatic leader who everyone believes will ensure their security. The organization, or group, is dominated by a leader who provides direction, rewards, and punishments and who maintains as much control as possible. Selected admirers may be elevated to important positions. Ultimately, however, followers learn that the leader is only human, and aggression from the more frustrated and anxious members may lead to the leader's removal. Autocratic group members can be productive and even achieve great success, but it is just as likely that members may follow a leader down the wrong path.

The Intentional Group. Unlike members of the first three groups, those who belong to intentional groups are relatively free of the need to defend themselves from other members' aggression. They understand their feelings and behavior and participate in the group's work. They are able to deal with group fantasies, unconscious motivations, personal needs, and defensive behavior. Conflict is acknowledged and members have little need to resort to psychological defenses.

Why People Form Groups

Groups form for a number of reasons. Formal groups are constructed to meet organizational needs such as meeting organizational objectives. Informal groups form in order to meet human needs. Some of the reasons informal groups form include personal needs, proximity, attraction, goals, and economic considerations.[25]

Satisfaction of Needs. Maslow calls our attention to a hierarchy of needs.[26] The security, social, esteem, and self-actualization needs of some employees can be met by affiliating with a group or groups.

Security. Being a member of a group gives a sense of security, especially when the individual is a new employee or is making demands on management. Unions sense this purpose and in the past twenty-five years public employees, including corrections employees, have felt it necessary to affiliate with a union in order to press demands for higher pay, better benefits, and so forth. On a less cosmic scale, corrections employees feel the psychological need to affiliate with a group of peers because of the dangers they face daily. They would indeed have a lonely existence without the security of a group of fellow employees from which to draw strength.

Social. There is a fuzzy line between the security needs and social needs of the employee who daily faces inmates, parolees, or probationers. People's gregarious nature fosters a need to belong to a group. This is true both on and off the job, as is evidenced by the abundance of service organizations, special interest clubs, and the like. However, in the prison and in parole and probation agencies, there is more to it. Kauffman[27] discusses the social effects of prison employment and the isolation suffered by officers. The officers she spoke to saw more of each other, both on and off duty, than of their families. It is clear that in some instances the social needs of the individual are met by work groups that become social

TABLE 10.1
The Cultures of the Four Workplace Groups

Homogenized Group	Institutionalized Group	Autocratic Group	Intentional Group
All members have equal *status*, with no clear individual *roles*.	Each member is assigned a particular *role* and *status* and given guidelines for changing the role and status.	All members are assigned *roles* with *status*, but no clear guidelines are provided for self-advancement.	All members assume and accept *roles* and *status* based on the needs of the group and the leader.
No *leader* is acknowledged to exist or permitted to arise.	*Leadership* is designated by the group's operating structure.	The *leader* is viewed as omnipotent and is clearly in control of the group.	A permanent *leader* may be found among the members or *leadership* may be passed among members based on each person's unique ability to lead the group at the time.
Autonomous behavior such as the offering of ideas is either attacked or not supported by others.	*Autonomous behavior* such as the offering of ideas is controlled by procedures.	*Autonomous behavior* such as the offering of ideas may be rewarded or punished by the leader, who may offer no reason for his or her decision.	*Autonomous behavior* is acknowledged as valuable as long as it contributes to the group's purpose.
Members are unable to find a *direction for the group*.	The *direction of the group* is limited by the organization structure.	All skills for *directing the group* are held by the leader.	Members actively participate in offering *direction* to the group.
The group acts as though time and the environment had been temporarily suspended and as if there were nothing more than the group's experience.	*The group acts as though* the organization were in control of events and the process and as if work were to be accomplished as planned.	*The group acts as though* the leader will take care of everything if he or she is permitted to do so.	*The group acts as though* all members were responsible for the group's work and leadership.
Some group members may be *singled out and stigmatized* for their willingness to express their feelings and thoughts. They may be coaxed into increasing emotionalism until they are rendered incompetent and discarded.	Some group members may be *singled out and praised* for participating in the group as expected, or they may be *publicly punished* for deviating.	Some members may be *singled out for rewards* for actions the leader finds supportive, or *punished for deviations* from the leader's expectations.	Contributions of members are *acknowledged by the group* as a whole.
Little *work on the group's task* is accomplished and no plans are made to do any work.	*Work on the group's task* is accomplished as specified by the organizational work process.	*Work on the group's task* as specified by the leader is accomplished according to the leader's instructions.	*Work on the group's task* becomes the responsibility of all the members, with no one individual (including the leader) assuming complete responsibility for the work.

Source: Seth Allcorn, "Understanding Groups at Work," *Personnel*, Vol. 66 (August, 1989), p.33.

groups and that group affiliation enables the individual to cope with his or her environment and may even enable the individual to arrive at a self-identity.

Esteem. Certain work environments have a work group that carries a good deal of prestige. Consequently, for employees who have a high need for esteem, membership in a group of this sort can bring a good deal of satisfaction.

Proximity and Attraction. Proximity refers to physical closeness. Attraction refers to the appeal one person has for another because of appearance, attitudes, or similar motivations. People who work together have the opportunity to exchange ideas, thoughts, and information about a variety of topics that range from on-the-job to off-the-job topics. Once interest is aroused, people may form a group to sustain interaction.

Goals. The goals of a group are sometimes reason enough for an individual to join. For example, a person may apply to join the institutional emergency response team. The individual may see the need for such a group, agree with its aim of quelling insurrection, and enjoy the comraderie and physical fitness regime required for membership in such a group.

Economic considerations. Groups form also because members (or potential members) see economic gain resulting from their membership. Nonunion employees may join a union to pressure management or legislators for pay raises. Obviously, public sector employment presents few opportunities to join groups for economic reasons. However, the initial application to join the organization is made for economic reasons: steady employment and little chance of being furloughed.

To repeat, people join groups for many reasons. In the corrections organization the effec-

tive manager will recognize groups and try to further organizational aims through informal groups. Committees, task forces, and work groups are all formed for this purpose. Informal groups can also be used to aid the organization. In an earlier chapter, the grapevine was discussed as a means of communicating with organizational members. Without informal groups, the grapevine would not be as effective. Another important point to remember is that groups meet the needs of employees. In corrections these needs usually revolve around personal security, group solidarity, and social/esteem needs. Thus, the manager who ignores or fails to accommodate these needs does so at great risk to his or her job.

Determining Group Existence

Groups impact the productivity and pace of organizational life. The manager must take that impact into consideration in the daily life of the organization. Consideration includes (1) determining group existence and understanding the evolution of informal groups,[28] (2) the level of tolerance and freedom in the group, and (3) the type of leader.

Relationship Patterns

One of the more important steps a manager needs to take is to determine what groups, other than formal groups, exist in the organization. Because we participate daily in informal groups, we often perceive what goes on as random and spontaneous. However, even in the most relaxed and unstructured groups, established patterns of relationships develop that are ranked in relationship to each other. **J. L. Moreno**[29] developed a method of analyzing group status. His technique is a simple yet effective diagnostic tool that aids the manager in determining group existence.

Briefly, each member of a group votes on his or her preferences for one another. The voting is based on preferences in specific situations. For example, members of a prison correc- tional officer force might be asked the following questions:

■ With whom would you prefer to work?

FIGURE 10.6
A Sociogram

A sociogram of ten employees. Each employee is represented by a circle and the number shows the votes each received in the balloting. Arrows indicate the direction of choices. Solid lines represent two-way preferences and broken lines indicate one-way preferences. Employees A, B, and I represent a triangle, J is a star, and F is an isolate.

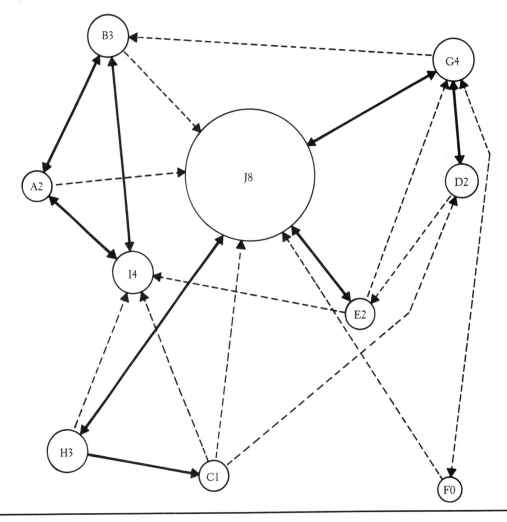

- With whom would you most like to have the same days off?
- Who would make a good supervisor?

Each employee is usually asked to list three preferences for each question.

Analysis of the results reveals that some persons receive a large number of votes. These are the **stars**. Those who receive very few or no votes may be termed **isolates**. There are those who vote for each other (**mutual pairs**), and sometimes a **triangle** emerges. This is an effective method of identifying cliques. It can be used to keep people apart who are unproductive when together or to group informally those who are supportive of each other and the administration.

SYMLOG

A fairly recent innovation in the study of groups has been developed by Robert F. Bales and Stephen P. Cohen.[30] SYMLOG is an acronym for SYstem for the Multiple Level Observation of Groups. Bales and Cohen say that SYMLOG is "a set of methods for the study of groups— groups of many kinds, but basically small, natural groups, such as families, teams, or classroom groups, where the personalities of the specific persons involved and their relationships with each other are the focus of interest."[31]

SYMLOG is designed so that in its most compact form, one person can be used by another for the study of a single group in order to more fully understand the group and to more easily work with it. The rating method provides a systematic way of allowing a person to capture another from memory. As a consequence, questions may be raised and perhaps insight generated as to that person's performance and/or behavior even when he or she is not present.

The rating is rather complicated, and computerized scoring has been developed to aid the user. Scoring is different from rating in that with the former, one must be able to make detailed observations in the course of group members' interaction. Scoring usually requires some arrangements with group members to make either observations or a video recording.

While SYMLOG requires training and takes longer than the usual rating method, "it has the advantage of richness of detail and particularly tends to give insight into the way in which different kinds of topics the persons in the group talk about affect relationships in the group."[32]

The Staff-Client Interface

The discussion so far has been confined to staff and the manager's ability to effectively work with formal and informal groups in the organization. Probation and parole agencies are not faced with the formidable task of managing an institution, but they are expected to balance the dual roles of law enforcement and social work. Occasionally a probation officer is injured or even murdered in the line of duty. Fortunately, these incidents are rare. Nevertheless, the task of managing an institution is most difficult in terms of inmate and staff relationships.

Prisons today are characterized by segregation. John Irwin[33] points out that prisoners distrust most other prisoners and that the obvious racial division between black and white prisoners illustrates the hatred between them. This hatred may also extend to correctional officers,[34] necessitating a good deal of work on the part of managers and executives in the area of multicultural training.

Gangs have also heightened the tension in today's prisons. The concomitant escalation in violence has resulted in a new convict identity.[35] The new identity stresses toughness and being able to take care of oneself as well as having the "guts" to prey upon weaker inmates.

FIGURE 10.7
S Y M L O G

General Behavior Descriptions

Your Name _____   Group _____

Name of person described _____

		Circle the best choice for each item:		
		(0)	(1)	(2)
U	active, dominant, talks a lot	not often	sometimes	often
UP	extroverted, outgoing, positive	not often	sometimes	often
UPF	a purposeful democratic task leader	not often	sometimes	often
UF	an assertive business-like manager	not often	sometimes	often
UNF	authoritarian, controlling, disapproving	not often	sometimes	often
UN	domineering, tough-minded, powerful	not often	sometimes	often
UNB	provocative, egocentric, shows off	not often	sometimes	often
UB	jokes around, expressive, dramatic	not often	sometimes	often
UPB	entertaining, sociable, smiling, warm	not often	sometimes	often
P	friendly, equalitarian	not often	sometimes	often
PF	works cooperatively with others	not often	sometimes	often
F	analytical, task-oriented, problem-solving	not often	sometimes	often
NF	legalistic, has to be right	not often	sometimes	often
N	unfriendly, negativistic	not often	sometimes	often
NB	irritable, cynical, won't cooperate	not often	sometimes	often
B	shows feelings and emotions	not often	sometimes	often
PB	affectionate, likeable, fun to be with	not often	sometimes	often
DP	looks up to others, appreciative, trustful	not often	sometimes	often
DPF	gentle, willing to accept responsibility	not often	sometimes	often
DF	obedient, works submissively	not often	sometimes	often
DNF	self-punishing, works too hard	not often	sometimes	often
DN	depressed, sad, resentful, rejecting	not often	sometimes	often
DNB	alienated, quits, withdraws	not often	sometimes	often
DB	afraid to try, doubts own ability	not often	sometimes	often
DPB	quietly happy just to be with others	not often	sometimes	often
D	passive, introverted, says little	not often	sometimes	often

Source: Copyright © 1980 by The Free Press, A Division of Macmillan Publishing Co., Inc.

Loyalties are to one's gang, not to fellow inmates. This new convict identity has placed additional strain on prison staff.

Lombardo[36] investigated prison officers and found that officers differ in their approach to inmates. How effective they are depends on many variables, including authority, rule enforcement, and social distance. Hence, social distance is often great, as evidenced by negative remarks on the part of officers. It seems reasonable to assume that when there is a measure of social distance between staff and inmates, inmate violence and rebelliousness will result,

causing a further widening of the social distance between staff and inmates, and so on, in a never-ending downward spiral.

In the Huron Valley Men's Facility (HVMF),[37] where staff and officers are treated with overt disrespect in the form of cursing, insolence, threats, and disobedience, the result is an institution where staff and inmates live with uncertainty as to the outcome of almost every social exchange. The results are social disorganization, violence, and fear. DiIulio is correct in saying, "Prison order is good and a necessary precondition for other valued aspects of prison life."[38]

It is against this backdrop, or because of it, that much of the informal staff organization in prisons exists. The two worlds of staff and inmates exist side by side, each mirroring the other, and with few points of interpenetration. The manager's task is to keep one eye on the staff organization and the other on the inmate organization.

Summary

Groups are defined as two or more people who interact and mutually influence each other. Basically, there are two kinds of groups in organizations: formal and informal. Formal groups are established to further organizational goals. Informal groups exist as a result of social needs. Groups form for a variety of reasons, usually revolving around security, social and esteem needs, proximity, mutual goals, and economic needs.

Research indicates that employees usually report that they work in organizations that are impersonal, autocratic, and characterized by poor interaction and one-sided decision making. They also report that they would prefer working for an organization that is just the opposite. Ouchi's Theory Z organization appears to have the qualities that workers seek in an organization.

The effective manager can analyze groups in the workplace. Sociometric methods and a more recent innovation, SYMLOG, are two instruments that can identify groups and their qualities and dynamics. Armed with such information, the manager can make more accurate decisions centering on work groups, employee proximity, and even shift assignment.

Reviewing the Case

The Maryland Department of Corrections has a problem. Correctional officers and other employees do not believe that the administration is supportive of their efforts on the job and are of the opinion that the organization is a matter of "us" against "them." In this instance a group of employees has formed to address the issues of pay and the grievance procedure. The formation of a union addresses security and economic needs.

The secretary of the department could have headed off any problems by recognizing that employees have such needs. It is important for employees to feel that they are accepted and that the administration supports them. This could have been accomplished by periodic formal meetings with lower-level employees; by encouraging executives to meet with and listen to subordinates; and by forceful, decisive action in the courts, administrative hearings, and the legislature. The result of the perceived inaction and lack of support has been divisiveness and suspicion on both sides.

For Further Study

Rensis Likert, *The Human Organization: Its Management and Value* (New York: Harper & Row, 1967).

Tom Peters, *Thriving on Chaos: Handbook for a Management Revolution* (New York: Harper & Row, 1987).

Marvin E. Shaw, *Group Dynamics: The Psychology of Small Group Behavior*, 3d ed. (New York: McGraw-Hill, 1981).

Key Terms

Groups	SYMLOG
Informal Groups	Formal Groups
Theory Z	Linking Pin

Leadership

Case Study: New Prison Is Pretty, but Not Peaceful

Salmon is the soothing color of a new residential development on the Gulf Coast.[1] About 1,400 people live, work, and play in the intimate two-story community on four artificial lakes just south of this subdued town of unspoiled beaches. Already the development is full, and the outdoor basketball courts are the social center.

The citizens of Florida pay for this $33 million project. And they are paying the room and board of every resident: about $3 million a year. This is one of Florida's newest, biggest, most secure prisons, designed to handle the state's meanest, most aggressive outlaws. But it has not been an easy infancy for the eighteen-month-old Charlotte Correctional Institution, built just east of Interstate 75 about ten miles north of Fort Myers in one of the state's fastest-growing regions.

But the prison's state-of-the-art technology has produced state-of-the-art glitches: inmates slithering through too-big food slots in their cell doors; cell doors popping open frequently and unexpectedly, as though some prison poltergeist were flipping electronic switches in the central control room.

Other problems point to prison employees and inmates: In September five guards were charged with beating prisoners or lying about the beatings in reports. They remain on the job while an investigation continues. One inmate lost a testicle after a struggle with some officers.

That same month, an inmate from Miami, in the worst of at least four stabbings at the prison last year, was killed by another inmate with a homemade knife.

"Bad Publicity"

"I think there are more problems than there should have been," Bill Booth, regional director for the Department of Corrections, said of the Charlotte prison. "But I think it's gotten more than its share of bad publicity."

Booth concedes he can't remember the last time even one prison officer in his region was arrested for inmate abuse. "It's a pretty drastic measure," he said, "and it usually gets everyone's attention when it occurs."

Former Governor Bob Martinez made the need for prison beds a prominent theme in his one-term tenure. The people of Florida, he said, wanted criminals behind bars and wanted them to stay there for the duration of their sentences. In the past decade, the legislature has approved prisons to hold 25,000 more inmates. During that time, Florida's prison population has more than doubled to 42,000 in forty-three major prisons.

The Charlotte prison, one of four in the state designed to hold the toughest criminal men, opened its single-cell doors in six dormitory-style houses in August 1989. The prison, painted in pastels, looks not unlike a small, modern college campus, opening onto a green courtyard with walkways that spread like tributaries across the well-kept lawn.

There's one correctional officer for every six or so inmates. Three prisoners have escaped so far; two were quickly recaptured. Two of the escapes occurred when prisoners were outside the main gate on work details; one got away. The third prisoner jumped two fences to escape but was caught the next day.

There's little need for keys in this prison; virtually everything is operated by computer in a see-through control room that sits in the center of each two-story dorm. Each cell houses one or two inmates. This high-tech system minimizes contact between officers and inmates.

Officers punch buttons to open doors. They flick switches to turn on showers. For inmates not allowed to leave their cells, a thermometer gauge attached to food carts automatically checks the temperature of each meal. If it's cooler than 110 degrees, the food goes back to the kitchen.

Prison Scene

On the other side of the cafeteria building, a half-dozen prisoners sit on some bleachers. They all have the same complaint about Charlotte, a complaint quickly validated by officers and administrators.

"There's nothing to do," one says. "No schools, no weights, no Jaycees," adds another.

Too much "idle time." How much that accounts for Charlotte's problems is debatable, but everyone agrees it is an important factor. Older prisons have more activities—college classes, weight rooms, Jaycees, support groups like Alcoholics and Narcotics Anonymous, PRIDE work programs where inmates make eyeglasses, dentures, and cabinets.

At Charlotte, between 200 and 300 inmates are assigned to keep the grounds clean. The result: very clean grounds and a lot of spare time for a lot of inmates.

"They're just going to be in each other's way," said E. C. Dobson, acting superintendent. "We don't have meaningful jobs to assign the inmates."

Most of the inmates spend much of the day confined to their cells or a day room. Those being disciplined at Charlotte have fewer privileges than people on Death Row; they have seven minutes twice a week to take a shower and get two hours a week of exercise. About 200 better-behaved inmates enjoy more freedom. They live in two "open population" dorms that look like minimalist boot camps with rows of neatly made, single bunks. They move around the prison grounds, playing sports, washing laundry, cooking and cleaning, cutting the grass.

"The facility was constructed to house the inmates," said former superintendent Dean. "There were budget considerations. No money was available to provide any programs or activities."

So one activity has been fighting.

From January through November of 1990, forty-two assaults among inmates were reported at Charlotte. At the other high-security prisons in the state, the number of assaults ranged from fourteen to eighty-nine.

Lt. J. T. Tompkins, Charlotte's administrative chief, says Charlotte has a "remarkably lower violence rate" than the two other high-security prisons he's worked at in Florida. Charlotte's violence peaked on September 8 when inmate Keith Jackson, twenty-nine, was stabbed four times on the rec yard during an argument. It was one of three prison slayings in

Florida in 1990. Officials say they expect murder charges to be filed against one or two inmates.

Less than two weeks later, on September 18, the officers were charged with misdemeanor battery or lying in reports, following a long investigation by the Department of Corrections. Four inmates were abused, the probe concluded. Charges against two of the officers were dropped in December, but more charges, including some felonies, may still be filed, said prosecutor Robert Ford.

Inmate's Problems

Inmate Charles Curry's troubles began when an officer accused him of trying to break into a food line, said Ford. Curry demanded to talk to a lieutenant; a scuffle with officers occurred as he tried to enter the lieutenant's office without permission, Ford said.

Curry was eventually taken to a hospital where his badly swollen testicle was surgically removed. That's one of the incidents Ford is still investigating. Prison officials decline to discuss details of the incidents, saying the matter is in the hands of state prosecutors. Instead, they talk about progress at the prison.

Workers have welded bars across the food slots so inmates can't slip through anymore. And they tinkered with the computer software to keep the cell doors closed. A private college is offering limited classes at the prison and administrators hope to schedule some AA meetings.

Dobson, the acting superintendent, has asked the state's nonprofit prison work group to set up a program at Charlotte as it has at twenty-three other Florida prisons.

"I really see this institution as being successful so far," Dobson said. "It's not as easy as someone on the outside looking in may think."

Introduction

Prisons need effective leadership today more than ever before in the history of corrections. In an era of shrinking budgets, exploding prison populations, and a more sophisticated and better-educated work force, the corrections manager needs to be a leader as well as a manager. As we shall see, this is an important distinction.

DiIulio[2] notes that the literature cites nothing remarkable about correctional leadership and organizational culture. However, he sees certain "interlocking patterns" of "successful" correctional managers. He points out that successful leaders inspire a vision among subordinates and focus on results and performance, get out of the office and walk around, and make significant alliances with key constituencies. DiIulio also points out that while these managers rarely innovate, when they do the results are far reaching. We shall explore these themes, and others, in this chapter.

Diluio fails to mention the differences between managers and leaders. The literature on corrections is replete with accounts of both charismatic and incompetent leaders. The student of criminal justice is led to believe that criminal justice supervisors and executives fall into one group or the other, with no middle ground. Toch sums up DiIulio's view of correctional leadership:

> He envisages a mix of pre-bureaucratic organization at the top and bureaucratic organization at the bottom. His conception of an ideal-type head of a correctional agency is a well-connected leader who promiscuously attends to quotidian details and freely intervenes everywhere. DiIulio's rank and file, by contrast, are a tightly controlled army that follows minute prescriptions to the letter.[3]

The effective correctional executive is both a good manager and a leader. As Commissioner Beto[4] and Warden Ragan[5] both learned, it is important to do the right thing as well as to do things right. Leadership skills are not innate, though we like to think so. They can be learned. This chapter explores leadership and sheds light on issues important to effective leadership.

Defining Leadership

There is no commonly accepted definition of leadership,[6] but when we talk about leadership in everyday conversation, we are usually referring to the process of moving a group of people in one direction or another through mostly noncoercive means or to people who are in roles where leadership is expected.[7] Leadership is also defined as the art or process of influencing people to strive willingly and enthusiastically toward the achievement of established group goals.[8]

Burns[9] identifies two types of leadership: the **transactional** and the **transforming**. Transactional leadership is an exchange of one thing for another: jobs for votes, doing a good job for a bonus, and so on. He points out that this approach comprises the bulk of relationships between leader and follower in such groups as legislatures and political parties. The second type of leadership, transforming leadership, is more complex and more potent.

> The transforming leader recognizes and exploits an existing need or demand of a potential follower. But beyond that, the transforming leader looks for potential motives in followers, seeks to satisfy higher needs, and engages the full person of the follower. The result of transforming leadership is a relationship of mutual stimulation and elevation that converts followers into leaders and may convert leaders into moral agents.[10]

Further, Burns identifies moral leadership in terms of followers, for one cannot gain a true perspective of what leadership is until it is viewed through the eyes of the followers. He points out that moral leadership emerges from and always returns to "the fundamental wants and needs, aspirations, and values of the followers."[11]

Theories of Leadership

The Trait Approach

We often speak of the "born" or "natural" leader, and our thinking about leadership is saturated with the idea that some people have in-born abilities to lead. Much of the early work of scholars also reflect this bias. They attempt to describe successful leaders as accurately as possible, believing that if certain traits can be identified, the people who possess those traits can be boosted into leadership positions.

There are a number of studies that attempt to identify leadership traits. Stogdill concludes that the following traits are associated with leadership:

- intelligence, including judgment and verbal ability;
- a history of achievement in scholarship and athletics;
- emotional maturity and stability;
- dependability, persistence, and a drive for continuing achievement;
- the skill to participate socially and to adapt to various groups; and
- a desire for status and socioeconomic position.[12]

The idea that specific personality traits are associated with leadership has been found to be without basis. After all, Mahatma Ghandi is considered to have been a great leader, but he was a very small, unathletic, frail man with no desire for status or socioeconomic position. On the other hand, Adolph Hitler can also be considered a leader, but he was reportedly socially inept and had few, if any, past achievements in scholarship and athletics, to say nothing of his instability and emotional immaturity. Nevertheless, both men motivated and inspired millions. It is obvious that examining leadership is much more complex than simply identifying the traits of successful leaders.

Contingency Theories

Contingency theories focus on the situation rather than the individual. The assumption is

that each instance of successful leadership is a different mix of leader, followers, and situation. This interaction can be expressed by the formula: SL = f(L, F, S).

SL = successful leadership
f = function of
L = leader
F = follower
S = situation[13]

By looking at the formula we understand that successful leadership depends on the leader, the followers, and the situation and that each element must be appropriate for the others. For example, the successful warden of a prison is going to approach quelling a disturbance differently from working with assistant wardens and department heads in developing objectives for the coming year. In the former, the warden would assume a more authoritative, decisive approach; in the latter, he or she would be participative and function as a salesperson and coach rather than an autocrat.

Fiedler's Contingency Approach

Fiedler[14] points out that a leader is dependent upon three major situations. First, the relationship between leader-follower is built upon trust and affection. Put another way, the leader who is better liked by subordinates is more successful in achieving organizational goals. Second, the task structure of the organization either aids or hinders the leader. In other words, the more clearly directions and procedures are spelled out, the easier it is to lead. Prisons and other corrections organizations often have ill-defined task structures, and the looser the structure, the greater the probability of ineffective leadership. This is a strong argument in favor of a well-written mission statement and clearly articulated policies and procedures. Finally, the leader's position power is important. He or she must have the authority to hire and fire subordinates. Leader's with high position power are able to hire and fire at will; those with low position power cannot.

Path-Goal Theory

The path-goal theory of leadership suggests that the primary function of the leader is to clarify and establish goals with subordinates, to help them find the best path for achieving goals, and to remove any obstacles along the path. Robert J. House[15] has developed a path-goal theory of leadership that identifies situations in which the leader's consideration or initiating structure is an important determinant of performance or motivation.

House's research is derived from an expectancy model of motivation (see chapter 9). His model identifies five crucial components of subordinate motivation:

1. the intrinsic rewards of work-related activities;
2. the intrinsic rewards of task accomplishment or work achievement;
3. the extrinsic rewards that follow or depend upon level of work achievement;
4. the clarity of the "path" or "plan" by which work behavior culminates in achievement; and
5. the subjective probability that various extrinsic rewards depend on achievement.[16]

In addition, Koontz, O'Donnell, and Weihrich's[17] expectancy theory (of which path-goal theory is a derivation) suggests that other factors must be considered, such as characteristics of the followers and the work environment. Suc-

FIGURE 11.1
Path-Goal Approach to Leadership Effectiveness

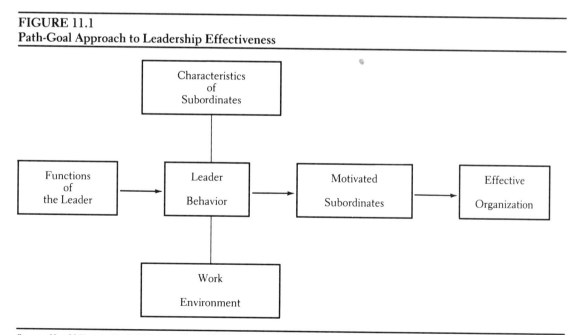

Source: Harold Koontz, Cyril O'Donnell, Heinz Weihrich, *Essentials of Management* (New York: McGraw-Hill Book Company, 1986), p. 413. Permission Granted.

FIGURE 11.2
Four Fundamental Leadership Styles Based on the OSU Studies

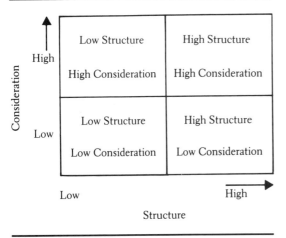

Source: Samuel C. Certo, *Principles of Modern Management: Functions and Systems,* 3d ed. Copyright © by Allyn and Bacon, Reprinted by permission.

cessful leadership, according to path-goal theory, is situational, and the belief in only one correct theory of leadership is incorrect. Leader behavior is categorized into four groups.

- Supportive leadership considers the needs of subordinates, shows concern for their well-being, and creates a pleasant organizational climate.
- Participative leadership allows subordinates to influence the decisions of their superiors and can result in increased motivation.
- Instrumental leadership gives subordinates rather specific guidance and makes clear what is expected of them. Thus, to a large degree the leader plans, organizes, coordinates, and controls.
- Achievement-oriented leadership involves establishing challenging goals, seeking improved performance, and having confidence that subordinates will achieve high goals.[18]

Leadership in General

The OSU Studies

The OSU (Ohio State University) studies[19] are a series of investigations that determined that leaders exhibit two main types of behavior: **structure behavior** and **consideration behavior.** Structure behavior specifically details what the relationship between leader and follower will be and promotes well-defined procedures for accomplishing organizational objectives. Consideration behavior reflects trust, friendship, warmth, and respect for the followers. This is usually the type of behavior found in Theory Z organizations (see chapter 10).

The OSU studies resulted in the development of a model illustrating four fundamental leadership styles. Figure 11.2 depicts this model and the four leadership styles. It is easy to recognize supervisors and executives we have known from the figure. For example, the high-structure, low-consideration quadrant illustrates the warden who emphasizes procedure and operates by the book and makes no attempt to maintain a personal relationship with followers.

Leadership Effectiveness

In 1981 the Iowa State Penitentiary at Fort Madison was an unpleasant place to work or serve time. A series of disturbances and a class action suit by the inmates forced change. The Iowa Department of Corrections hired Crispus C. Nix, a newly retired colonel from the Disciplinary Barracks at Fort Leavenworth, as the new warden. Warden Nix was given the challenge of implementing the changes ordered by the court. He was well trained to meet this challenge. He knew that leadership depends on the situation and that no single style is more effective than another. Experience told Warden Nix

FIGURE 11.3
Life Cycle Theory

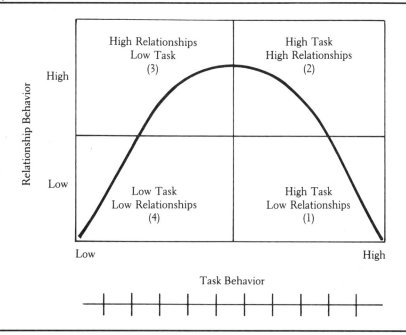

that what works in one situation may not work in another.

The life cycle theory of leadership gives us a hint as to what approach may work in such a situation. The theory is based on the same type of leadership behaviors that the OSU studies describe, but in this case they are called *task* rather than *structure* and *relationship* rather than *consideration.* This theory develops the idea that as the maturity of the followers increases, appropriate leadership behavior requires less structure (task) and less support (relationship).[20]

The cycle is illustrated by figure 11.3. To begin, follower maturity is defined as followers' ability to perform their jobs independently, their ability (and willingness) to accept additional responsibility, and their desire for success. In the illustration, follower maturity is represented by the curved line. As the line runs from right to left, the followers' maturity in-

creases. Thus, the theory proposes that the leadership style to be used is dependent upon the maturity of the followers.

In Warden Nix's case, let us assume that upon his appointment, he determined that employees were burned out, weary of constant emotional and physical battles, and unwilling to accept any more responsibility than necessary and that they defined success as simply going home after work. He may have begun his tenure with a high-task, low-relationship attitude. In this instance he would have begun by assuring that policies and procedures were sound and in place, that the emergency response team was adequately trained, that job descriptions were up-to-date, and that the mission statement was well thought out. He would have given little thought to relationship behavior except to communicate his vision and to recognize outstanding performance.

As time passed and the job-related maturity

of the workers increased, he may have shifted his leadership behavior to high task and high relationship, while continuing to keep an eye on task completion. Still later, as worker maturity continued to increase, he probably shifted his leadership style to high relationship and low task. He would then have been able to call upon the trust and respect that had been built up previously and to de-emphasize task behavior. As followers were able to cope with job-related problems more effectively, he was able to focus on more strategic concerns.

Finally, in our illustration, the employees reached maximum maturity and Warden Nix was able to de-emphasize both task and relationship behavior. The staff were able to do their jobs without close supervision, and relationship behavior was used to nurture relationships that had developed over time.

The above example is simplified for illustrative purposes, but it should be noted that the idea of maturity resembles Chris Argyris's immaturity-maturity continuum[21] covered in an earlier chapter. Argyris argues that as a person matures he or she moves from a passive to an active state, from dependency on others to a state of relative independence. The continuum emphasizes psychological maturity in the form of personal growth and development. As it turns out, Warden Nix's perceptions were right on target, and his ability to adapt his leadership style resulted in the Iowa State Penitentiary becoming a relatively quiet and stable maximum-security institution, even after his retirement.

The Managerial Grid

Robert R. Blake and Jane S. Mouton[22] conceived the **Managerial Grid**. It is based upon two management-style dimensions: concern for people and concern for production. In corrections, production may be viewed as units of ser-

vice, degree of security, quality of programs, and so forth. Concern for people may be viewed as safety of personnel, quality of the environment, pay level, and the like.

The grid clarifies how the two concerns mesh. One concern is for getting results and a second is for people as distinct individuals. A third concern is for how one uses the hierarchy to achieve production with and through people.[23] While there are eighty-one different leadership styles in the grid, Blake and Mouton point out five styles that are of greater importance than others.

Blake and Mouton use the phrase "one best way" in reference to the 9,9 style of management. They state, "Involvement, participation, and commitment of those concerned with decision making and problem solving [are] the basis of teamwork."[24] Clearly, Blake and Mouton address the same issues as proponents of Theory Z and Likert's System Four.

Leadership and Decision Making

The decision-making process is discussed at greater length in chapter 14. By way of introduction it can be stated that the situation and the leadership style are important ingredients of organizational effectiveness. Tannenbaum and Schmidt[25] assert that the situation is of critical importance when a leader makes a decision. This lends credence to the idea that there is no one best way to lead—it all depends on the leader, the followers, and the situation. Figure 11.4 illustrates a continuum in which leadership behavior is linked to the amount of freedom given to subordinates.

Managers to the left of the model exercise high control and allow subordinates little freedom in decision making. Managers to the right exercise little control and allow subordinates maximum freedom in decision making. One should not infer

FIGURE 11.4
Continuum of Leadership Behavior

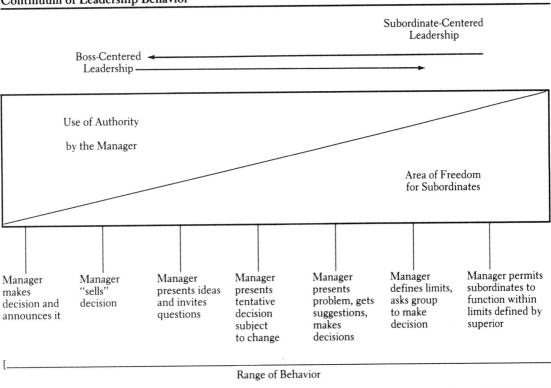

Source: Robert Tannenbaum and Warren H. Schmidt, "How to Choose a Leadership Pattern," *Harvard Business Review* (March/April 1958), p. 96. Permission granted.

from the model that some managers always announce a decision and others simply announce limits and then let subordinates make decisions. On the contrary, it should be obvious that different styles are appropriate for different situations. Earlier the formula SL = f(L, F, S) was given to illustrate how effective leadership is dependent upon the particular mix of leader, followers, and situation. Since leaders spend a good deal of time making decisions, it is reasonable to allow subordinates freedom to make decisions in areas covered by their job description, thus freeing the manager for more strategic concerns.

For example, a superintendent or warden whose institution has been struck by a calamity such as a tornado or terrorist bomb would not normally be inclined to sit down with subordinates and discuss alternatives and perhaps take a vote. He or she must give orders that must be executed immediately, with no discussion. On the other hand, it is useful to involve subordinates in decisions about a housing policy or what to do with known HIV-positive inmates. The warden may state explicitly that he or she wants to hear everyone's views or simply set the limits and ask for a decision.

Leaders and Managers

In the introduction to this chapter it was pointed out that management and leadership are not the same. Management is "the design of an environment in which people working together in groups can accomplish objectives."[26] Hicks and Gullett[27] point out that the mix of work that a manager performs varies according to the manager's place in the organization. Put another way, the higher up the manager, the more time he or she devotes to decision making and strategic management concerns; managers at a lower level may devote more time to somewhat technical matters.

Leaders, on the other hand, are not dependent upon organizational level. Managers primarily manipulate and allocate resources, and their concerns are broad in scope. Leaders have an intangible quality that emphasizes behavioral issues. Figure 11.5 illustrates that not all managers are leaders and not all leaders are managers. As Bennis states, "Leaders are people who do the right thing; managers are people who do things right."[28] This is an important distinction. Both roles are crucial, but it is the leader who is capable of leading an organization to greatness or to significant accomplishments. Jacobs[29] calls our attention to this distinction when he points out that the management at the Illinois State Prison at Stateville, after the departure of Warden Ragan, moved toward a more corporate approach. While Stateville was never a great organization in terms of management, Jacobs makes clear that Warden Ragan had strong leadership qualities. He ruled the institution through force of personality and charisma. He did all the right things.

The Eye of the Follower

The term *follower* in criminal justice connotes a weak, indecisive person. We all want to be leaders. Leaders are the ones who accomplish things and often go on to greatness. But in another sense, we are all followers. The department head follows the assistant warden, the assistant warden follows the warden, and so on, right up to the governor, who follows the electorate and is accountable to the voters.

Without followers, leaders cannot lead. They are solitary heros if not comic figures.[30] Effective leadership depends on both the follower and the leader, and it is the follower who determines who is the leader. Kouzes and Posner[31] investigated perceptions of leaders nationwide. They asked over 10,000 managers from private and public organizations what they admired or looked for in leaders. They found, with striking regularity, that people want leaders who are honest, competent, forward looking, inspiring, and credible.

Honesty

We want to be sure that we can trust our leaders and that they are worthy of our trust. We ask ourselves, "Is this person truthful and ethical?" "Does he or she have high principles?" These

---

FIGURE 11.5
Managers and Leaders

Managers Who Are Not Leaders

Leaders Who Are Not Managers

Effective Managers and Leaders

are not easy questions to answer, but Kouzes and Posner found that the answers are in the leader's behavior. In other words, followers will listen to the leader's claims to honesty and high principles, but they need to see these qualities to believe in them. The leader must demonstrate congruence between stated beliefs and action.

Competence

The second most valued attribute in a leader is competence. If we are going to follow someone, we must be sure that the leader knows what he or she is doing. We must see that person as capable and effective rather than merely technically competent. The area of competence varies with the rank of the leader. For example, a department head must demonstrate a level of technical competence and be able to work effectively with others. On the other hand, a warden or chief probation officer must demonstrate proficiency at policy and strategic planning as well as be able to work with others.

Looking to the Future

We expect our leaders to have a sense of direction and a concern for the future of the organization. While we can call this a vision or a calling, we do not expect an organizational messiah. We simply expect our leaders to know where they are going so that we may also set our course.

Inspiration

The fourth most important trait we look for in our leaders is inspiration. We expect leaders to be enthusiastic, energetic, and positive about the future. Leaders must be both coach and cheer-

leader. Some people are uncomfortable with inspirational leaders, but make no mistake—the warden or chief probation officer who has a vision of where the organization is going, who is enthusiastic, and who is able to communicate that vision is going to be successful.

Credibility

Credibility is the foundation upon which rest the other four traits. When we decide that leader is credible, we are able to "buy into" the leader's vision and to entrust our work lives and our careers to that person. However, credibility is fragile. Leaders earn it bit by bit over the years, but it can be lost in an instant. It is the leader's most precious asset and must be guarded very carefully.

Leadership Practices

Kouzes and Posner[32] also point out that leaders establish and maintain credibility by their actions. They discovered five fundamental practices that enable leaders to earn followers' confidence and to get things done.

- *Challenging the Process.* Leaders innovate and experiment and are willing to change the status quo in order to improve the organization.
- *Inspiring a Shared Vision.* Leaders are able to look past the horizon and to envision a future fraught with possibilities. They have good communication skills and are able to share that vision with others.
- *Enabling Others to Act.* Leaders stress collaborative goals and infuse people with a strong sense of responsibility. They foster spirit-developing relationships based on mutual trust. They involve others and make them feel strong and capable.

- *Modeling the Way.* Simply put, leaders are role models who are clear about their values and beliefs. They are able to keep people and projects on course by behaving consistently, making it easy for others to achieve goals.
- *Encouraging the Heart.* Leaders encourage people by recognizing contributions to the common vision. They recognize accomplishments and find ways to celebrate them.

Leadership is a unique and special relationship between leader and followers. Perhaps that is why there are so few true leaders. Special attention must be paid to that relationship because it requires hard work to build and maintain the trust that is necessary.

Get to know subordinates. This is associated with what is called walk-about management. Only by interacting with employees; by sharing a cup of coffee with them; by being interested in their concerns, values, and beliefs can the leader serve employees' interests and at the same time those of the organization. Many wardens would be surprised at how much mileage can be gained by a 2:00 A.M. visit to the institution just to talk and have a cup of coffee on post with a few of the officers.

Stand up for your beliefs. We appreciate people who are willing to take a stand. Confusion over where the leader stands creates stress and indecision among employees. Rigidity can be avoided by talking to followers and actively listening to and empathizing with what they are saying.

Be eloquent. Eloquence is an art that can be learned and cultivated. If leaders are to motivate others they need to be able to communicate their excitement about their vision. A leader should tell stories; relate anecdotes; enable others to envision, see,

hear, and feel what she or he is experiencing. When a leader is able to communicate a dream to others, it will live on.

Lead by example. Leaders are role models to whom we look for cues for our own actions. Leaders set the example.

Conquer personal frailties. Because we are only human, it is difficult to live up to the practices discussed above. The real struggle is within ourselves, and only a few of us are willing to keep up the fight. We need to constantly ask ourselves, "How am I doing?" "How are the others interpreting my actions?" and "Am I prepared in all ways to lead the organization where it needs to go?" Conquering oneself begins with a value system and code of personal ethics set in granite. This will be discussed more thoroughly in chapter 17.

On to the Future

Warren Bennis is a leading scholar in the area of leadership, and his contributions to what we know about leadership and its dynamics are too numerous to mention. Beyond that, he has a flair for capturing ideas and illustrating them in easily understandable ways. In *Why Leaders Can't Lead* he quotes a character from an E. B. White story.[33] The character states, "I predict a bright future for complexity. Have you ever considered how complicated things can get, what with one thing always leading to another?" Just in case the corrections manager thinks that things will get simpler or easier, Bennis points out some current randomly chosen problems in the United States. A few other complications have been thrown in for good measure.

Accelerating change
Aging inmate population

AIDS

Balkenization of U.S. society and/or the end of consensus

Big government, big media, big corporations, big everything

Bureaucracy

Continuing hunger

Corporate scandals

Crisis of public education

Eclipse of the community

End of the "Melting Pot" hypothesis

Failure of "bigness"

Fragmentation of life, work, ideas, solutions, world views, family

Gangs

Gay activists

Government—city, county, federal

Greed

Gridlock—freeway, corporate, personal

Hedonism

Homelessness

Hypocrisy of corporate America

Illiteracy

Inept managers

Legal and illegal coverups

Media

Moral/Spiritual decline and/or rise

New concepts of growth

New concepts of no growth

People unable to realize their potential, or "people are no damned good"

Poverty

Privacy and secrecy

Restrictions of freedom

Shift toward conservatism

Shift toward liberalism

Taxes

Technology

Third World

Twilight of the hydrocarbon era

Wall Street

Welfare

Women's Movement

Work

Summary

Talk to any executive about the problems facing the corrections organization and you will get the same story: overcrowding, underbudgeting, and a host of other problems ranging from AIDS to gangs. Unquestionably, the world of the corrections executive has changed. If there is a reason to join the doomsayers in their handwringing, it is most certainly that most correctional managers were trained during a time when the traditional paramilitary approach to management was believed to be the solution to any problem that might arise. All too often leadership in the average prison or probation agency has consisted of nothing more than attempting to resolve the day-to-day problems that might disrupt the status quo. However, in the last ten years the game has changed. Never before have corrections managers faced so many challenges. If we do not come to grips with those challenges, we will have failed in our duty to the taxpayer, ourselves, and those who are placed in our custody.

Leadership is defined as the process of influencing people to do wholeheartedly something they would not have ordinarily done. The trait approach to leadership has been rejected in favor of the situational approach. Blake and Mouton go even further and espouse an approach to decision making and leadership that is team oriented and characterized by interdependence, respect, and trust. Path-Goal theory holds that it is the responsibility of the leader to clear the way for subordinates so they can complete assigned tasks without difficulty.

Not all managers are leaders and not all leaders are managers. Managers are concerned with doing things right and leaders with doing the right thing. Followers look for certain qualities in leaders: honesty, competence, a sense of direction, inspiration, and credibility. Leadership is a unique relationship between the leader and her or his followers. It is nearly impossible to be looked up to as a leader if one has failed to conquer oneself and is not yet ready to set an example.

Reviewing the Case

The Charlotte Correctional Institution is a new facility that has experienced problems of underfunding, violence, and a lack of inspirational leadership. A new warden must recognize that the situation demands someone who understands the dynamics of leadership. There are already enough specialists to assure security and the completion of case management tasks; obviously, another specialist is not needed.

Successful leadership in this situation hinges on the perception of the staff. The warden must be someone who is honest and willing to discipline those who abuse their positions; he or she needs to demonstrate competence by being able to work with staff in identifying goals for the institution and how to achieve them; he or she must have a vision and be able to

passionately share it; and finally the warden must be credible and a role model.

Clearly, this person is unique, and most applicants will fall short. Many similar institutions may have the same problem.

For Further Study

James MacGregor Burns, *Leadership* (New York: Harper Torchbooks, 1978).

Warren H. Bennis, *Why Leaders Can't Lead: The Unconscious Conspiracy Continues* (San Francisco: Jossey-Bass, 1989).

Warren H. Bennis, *An Inverted Life: Reflections on Leadership and Change* (Reading, Mass.: Addison-Wesley Publishing Company, 1993).

Key Terms

Situational Leadership	**Follower Maturity**
Leadership Credibility	**Contingency Approach**
Managerial Grid	**to Leadership**

THE MANAGER AND THE ORGANIZATION

PART V

Part IV discussed the notion that if an organization is to accomplish stated objectives, the manager must be able to effectively work through and with others. Part V centers around the idea that the manager must have an idea where he or she wants the organization to go and how to allocate resources to get there. Chapter 12 discusses planning how the organization will get to where it wants to go and organizing resources for the pursuit of stated objectives.

Chapter 13 points out that in order for something to happen the way it is supposed to, the manager must control the processes, such as by measuring performance and results. Technology, design of facilities, and information management are discussed.

Planning, organizing, and controlling invariably involve decision making. In chapter 14 a decision is defined as a choice between two or more alternatives. How that decision is reached is critical to organizational effectiveness. Decisions are either programmed or nonprogrammed and are subject to certain conditions. The manager can improve conditions for sound decision making.

Planning and Organizing

CHAPTER 12

Case Study: Strategic Planning in the Federal Bureau of Prisons

To the Bureau of Prisons, strategic planning is a way to bring focus and attention to issues of common concern, to enhance communication, and to aid in setting priorities.[1] Strategic planning was introduced as a management initiative that could involve all managers and employees in determining our future directions. Through strategic planning we seek continuous improvement and efficiency in accomplishing our mission and by fully involving the entire work force we seek to empower staff at all levels.

Although the executive staff portion of the planning process is conducted in July, strategic planning in the bureau is a year-round activity encompassing activities that are aimed at gathering information from and fostering participation at all levels of the organization. We have dubbed this the **Strategic Management Cycle**, and our desire is to continuously improve the way the bureau delivers services and makes effective use of tax dollars.

Strategic planning is simple. It involves taking a look at four areas in the organization and the various subunits:

What it does (its mission and core values)
What it wants (goals/objectives)
What it's got (its resources)
What it faces (obstacles and circumstances)

The Flow of Strategic Planning Information

The Bureau of Prisons' strategic planning process is neither "top-driven" nor "bottom-driven." Strategic issues are identified at all levels of the organization. The executive staff of the bureau identifies the goals and objectives that set the direction for the entire agency, and each level participates in the development of objectives that direct our energies toward achieving these strategic long-term goals.

Although we begin this explanation of the cycle at the line-manager level, the planning process neither begins nor ends there. But an explanation of a cycle has to begin somewhere.

Line managers, in consultation with line staff, are asked to identify critical issues (circumstances) through the various examinations of the existing program and services, including the processes of management assessments and operational reviews. These critical issues are communicated during planning meetings and staff retreats and analyzed/prioritized/consolidated by wardens and the institution's upper management. Additional critical issues are developed by regional administrators and central office administrators during meetings and divisional management assessments.

Critical issues are discussed by the executive staff at planning retreats and during executive staff meetings. During these meetings, the director and the executive staff review the status of the agency and the circumstances surrounding individual employees and the agency. They also identify critical issues and key indicators suggesting probable future events that will impact on the agency. This review results in promulgation of the annual goals and major budget themes. These goals and budget themes are produced, in part, by linking together the planning activities of the central office divisions, regional offices, institutions, and institutional departments.

Regional and institution managers develop strategic plans for the implementation of the annual agency-wide goals as well as for goals developed as a response to the unique feature of the regional or institutional environment.

The BOP Planning Cycle

The Bureau of Prisons planning cycle provides a structure for linking together the information flow of planning activities

bureau-wide. It also promotes planning and goal-setting accomplishment as a "process."

March—Wardens Submit Issues for Next Year. Wardens review
current goals and identify strategic issues for the regional
director for review at the next executive staff planning
retreat.

May—Management Assessments Are Completed. Central office administrators, with assistance from their counterparts in the regions, complete management assessments
and identify proposed strategic issues for the ensuing fiscal year.

June—Wardens Conference. The Wardens Advisory Groups
(WAG) review and discuss management assessment results, strategic issues submitted in March, and other issues
identified by central and regional office administrators.

July—Executive Staff Strategic Planning Retreat. The executive staff meets to identify strategic issues and establish
overall goals for the BOP. WAG input regarding management assessments and strategic issues identified by wardens and central regional office administrators is provided. Tentative budget themes for the "spring call" (two
years out) are identified.

August—BOP Goals Announced. The overall goals for the
BOP are announced.

September 1—Central Office Divisions Announce Objectives.
Divisions identify specific objectives to accomplish BOP
goals and other divisional goals. Management assessment
information, divisional planning retreats, and WAG feedback on strategic issues aid in the development of divisional goals.

September—Regional Wardens Meetings. Wardens meet in
their regions to review new BOP goals and to identify
specific objectives to help achieve them. In addition, the
regional director, wardens, and regional administrators
identify specific regional goals, objectives, and resources
to support those goals.

October 1—Regions Announce Regional Objectives. Regional
directors announce the objectives developed to support
the BOP goals. In addition, regional directors announce
regional goals and objectives developed at the September
regional wardens' meetings.

October 15–30—Institution Strategic Planning. Institutions formulate local objectives in support of BOP goals and develop
local goals and objectives to address institution issues and

regional goals. Planning retreats provide staff from every department an opportunity to jointly discuss and prioritize overall institution goals and objectives. Program and operational review findings, character profile information, social climate and key indicator data are primary information sources for reviewing internal strengths and weaknesses. Local goals constrained by lack of resources should be reported to the regional director for review. The priority of the unfunded goals will be evaluated by the executive staff in conjunction with their January discussion of major budget themes for the "spring call" (two years out).

October 30—Institutions Announce Objectives. Institutions disseminate goals and objectives to institution staff and the regional office. Other area concerns such as community relations boards and local law enforcement offices should also be informed. Goals requiring advance procurement planning are to be coordinated through the regional office.

November—Major Budget Theme Development. Assistant directors and regional directors begin to solidify potential budget themes for the "spring call." The budget themes should be based upon input from wardens, regional administrators, central office branch chiefs, and the strategic issues discussed at the July planning retreat.

January—Executive Staff Selects Budget Themes. The executive staff selects major budget themes from the input received from assistant and regional directors in November.

The Bureau of Prisons planning cycle for the calendar year is consistent with the information flow described above. The timing set out in this calendar is not a fixed process and may change as complementary planning cycles are continually adjusted. It illustrates, however, the way information links up at all levels to define the agency's goals, objectives, new initiatives, and the annual budget requirements. It is important to remember that strategic planning is not a futurist activity. It is through strategic planning that managers are able to assess the circumstances surrounding them in order to make the best decision today in light of tomorrow's probabilities. A manager who suggests that he or she does not have time for strategic planning because of the pressures and demands of today is doomed to rely on nothing more than an unprepared, intuitive guess—with a high risk of the gambler's failure.

Introduction

Planning can be defined as the process of arranging future activities in order to accomplish a particular objective. Certo[2] defines planning as "the process of determining how the organization can get where it wants to go." Donnelly, Gibson, and Ivancevich state that "the planning function includes all the managerial activities which lead to the definition of goals and the determination of appropriate means to achieve these goals."[3] Donnelly, et al., also assert that the planning function can be broken into four parts:

1. establishing goals and fixing their priority;
2. forecasting future events that can affect goal accomplishment;
3. making the plans operational through budgeting; and
4. stating and implementing policies that direct the organization's activities toward the desired ends.

Generally speaking, all planning is directed toward improved decision making. Improved planning and the resultant improvement in decision making has several benefits:

- Programs and services are improved. The ultimate goal for any correctional organization is service: service to the community and the provision of security, creature comforts, and/or programs to inmates or clients.
- The ability to identify and analyze problems is improved. Adequate planning generates data and information that can be used to improve decision making.
- Planning demands that clear and attainable objectives be established. Once objectives are established, the procedures to attain them can be specified, as can the linkages between the objectives.
- Cooperation and coordination between the various units or departments are improved.

It is remarkable that prisons work at all. If an institution is to function effectively, all departments must work together in order to achieve the institutional mission.
- Planning allows for effective allocation of resources. In an often resource-scarce environment, it is imperative that the manager establish priorities for the allocation of resources.

Overall, planning decreases risk within the organization. Planning ensures the safety and well-being not only of staff and inmates but also of the community. It decreases the risk that requested funds will be cut for the coming year, if cutting them would be detrimental to the organizational mission. Planning also decreases the risk involved in accomplishing stated goals; and finally, planning decreases the risk that the careers of aspiring, upwardly mobile executives and midlevel managers will be terminated.

There are other reasons for planning. As previously pointed out, planning allows the chief executive to coordinate decision making. Traditionally, prisons have been custodially oriented institutions, where all decisions are subordinated to the custodial model. In recent years, however, the corporate model of management in corrections has been noted.[4] Thus, in the evolution from charismatic model to corporate model, departments in the organization are likely to be managed by competent men and women who are able to make a contribution to the organization but whose functions may be perceived as conflicting with the custodial function.

Planning also forces the executive staff to formulate objectives. Pursuing those objectives requires a coordinated effort throughout the organization, with thought given to decisions that affect the organization. Finally, planning forces the staff to be future-oriented. So many times in a correctional institution one hears a staff member state, "It will work out," or "Why worry? Nobody is going anywhere." Such statements do not reflect the thoughts of planners. The advantage of planning is that staff are required to look to the future, anticipate problems or issues, and ponder possible solutions before problems erupt.

The State of Corrections Planning Today

Burt Nanus[5] calls our attention to the fact that criminal justice agencies tend to be reactive rather than future-oriented in their decision making and operations. Drawing upon his business background and education, he offers a model that organizes the planning function. If his advice had been taken seriously by corrections agencies over the last several years, many of the problems they face today might have been avoided. After reminding us that the planning process is complex, Nanus states that the five types of planning shown in figure 12.1 should occur in a continuous and systematic fashion.

One is forced to ask, tongue in cheek "Did anyone listen to Burt?" The answer is, hardly anyone.[6] There are a few scattered examples of excellence in planning, but largely the picture is gloomy. Table 12.1 shows the current state of planning in most state departments of corrections as well as in New York City, Philadelphia, and Washington, D.C.

Forty-three departments of corrections responded to a questionnaire mailed to them in the spring of 1990.[7] The size of the organizations responding range from very large to very small. In spite of the diversity of responding departments, all CEO's who responded either agreed or strongly agreed that planning is important to the future of their agencies. The difference in the strength of their agreement apparently lies in the amount of resources devoted to the function of planning.

Some agencies do not have a separate planning department. Most respondents have a planning department as well as a published mission

FIGURE 12.1
A General Model for a Criminal Justice Planning Process

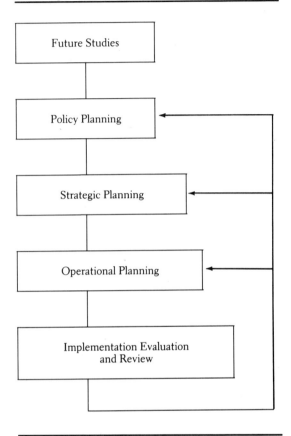

Source: Burt Nanus, "A General Model for a Criminal Justice Planning Process," *Journal of Criminal Justice*, 2:4 (Winter 1974), pp. 345–56. Permission granted.

statement and master plan. Beyond that, the survey shows a mixed emphasis on planning. For example, in an attempt to determine the depth and breadth of the planning process, the question was asked, "Do you have long-range plans for increasing numbers of inmates with histories of drug and alcohol abuse, gangs, AIDS, and increasing numbers of elderly inmates?" There are slightly more no answers than yes (112 no and

91 yes), and it appears that most departments are prepared to meet the demands of drug and alcohol abuse as well as AIDS. Geriatrics and, surprisingly, gangs are not so well addressed, and the size of the overall budget appears to have little to do with planning in those areas. Additionally, interface with other agencies that could help in the planning process is nearly nonexistent, as is training for the planners. Based upon the survey, two examples of excellence emerge—in Minnesota and North Carolina. Montana, Mississippi, and Missouri came in a close second. Texas gave many correct answers, but their problems are well known. Other states with big budgets and large inmate populations may be reacting to day-to-day problems.

This is a curious state of affairs when over 60 percent of CEO's surveyed strongly agree that the planning function is important and over 90 percent agree or strongly agree that the planning function should be stressed at every opportunity. One wonders whether there is a clear understanding of the planning function or whether it is a matter of budget.

Management by Objectives

In any organization it is important to keep on track and to work toward goals. Whether goals are established by work teams, departments, or the organization as a whole, it is important to involve everyone in the process. Once goals or objectives are established they offer a yardstick against which to measure the organization's progress over time.

Management by Objectives (MBO) is "a well-known philosophy of management that assesses an organization and its members by how well they achieve specific goals that superiors and subordinates have jointly established."[8] There is some discussion in the literature in regard to whether or not MBO should be a top-down or a bottom-up approach. In a top-down approach objectives are formulated by top management and then imposed on line and supervisory staff. In a bottom-up approach objectives are formulated by supervisors and line staff and given to top management.

The consensus seems to be that a compromise is best. Organizations have multiple goals that compete and sometimes appear to be incompatible. This is especially so in a correctional organization where the interests of management, staff, and inmates often conflict and those conflicts must be resolved and priorities established. One author has concluded that organizational objectives should be treated "as fiction produced by an organization to account for, explain, or rationalize its existence to particular audiences rather than as valid and reliable indications of purpose."[9] Thus, it is important to involve as many staff as possible and to develop a living document that reflects the real organization and not an organization the managers think a particular audience wants to see.

Establishing Objectives

The MBO process is a lengthy one that may require years to put firmly in place. Objectives need to be reviewed periodically so that progress or attainment can be ascertained, and everyone in the organization should feel some ownership of the program.

According to Certo,[10] managers can increase the quality of their objectives by following certain guidelines:

1. Managers should allow the people responsible for attaining the objectives to have a voice in setting them. In corrections, line staff often have a better feel for conditions than top management; therefore, their input is crucial if work-related problems faced daily by line staff are going to be translated into meaningful objectives.

2. Managers should state objectives as specifically as possible. Precise language minimizes confusion. Further, objectives should be unambiguous, prioritized, measurable, and, most of all, attainable.

3. Managers should relate objectives to spe-

TABLE 12.1
Corrections Planning Today

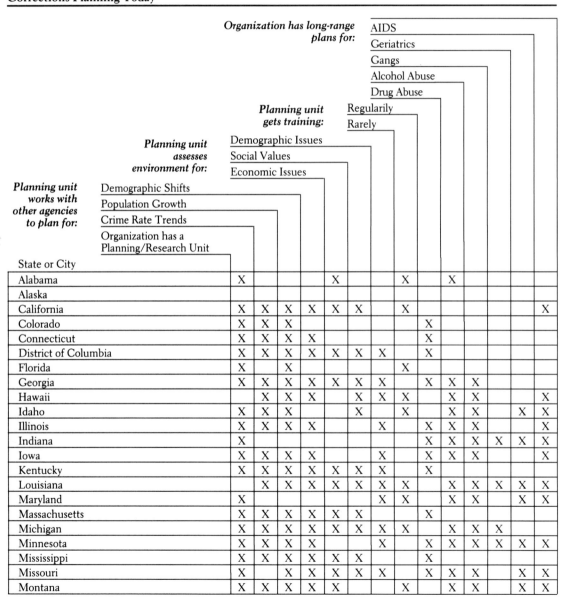

State or City	Organization has a Planning/Research Unit	Crime Rate Trends	Population Growth	Demographic Shifts	Economic Issues	Social Values	Demographic Issues	Rarely	Regularly	Drug Abuse	Alcohol Abuse	Gangs	Geriatrics	AIDS
Alabama	X			X		X		X						
Alaska														
California	X	X	X	X	X	X		X						X
Colorado	X	X	X						X					
Connecticut	X	X	X	X					X					
District of Columbia	X	X	X	X	X	X	X		X					
Florida	X		X						X					
Georgia	X	X	X	X	X	X	X		X	X	X			
Hawaii		X	X	X		X	X	X		X	X			X
Idaho	X	X	X			X		X		X	X		X	X
Illinois	X	X	X	X			X		X	X	X			X
Indiana	X								X	X	X	X	X	X
Iowa	X	X	X	X			X		X	X	X			X
Kentucky	X	X	X	X	X	X	X		X					
Louisiana		X	X	X	X	X	X	X		X	X	X	X	X
Maryland	X						X	X		X	X		X	X
Massachusetts	X	X	X	X	X	X			X					
Michigan	X	X	X	X	X	X	X	X		X	X	X		
Minnesota	X	X	X	X			X		X	X	X	X	X	X
Mississippi	X	X	X	X	X	X			X					
Missouri	X		X	X	X	X	X		X	X	X		X	X
Montana	X	X	X	X	X			X		X	X		X	X

cific actions whenever necessary. Specific actions eliminate the need for guesswork on the part of those responsible for achieving the objectives.

4. Managers should pinpoint expected results. Employees will know when they have

---

TABLE 12.1 (*Continued*)
Corrections Planning Today

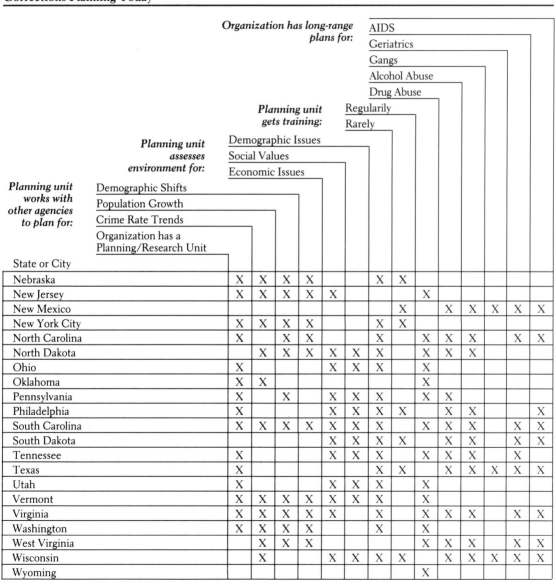

Column groupings:
- *Planning unit works with other agencies to plan for:* Demographic Shifts, Population Growth, Crime Rate Trends; Organization has a Planning/Research Unit
- *Planning unit assesses environment for:* Economic Issues, Social Values, Demographic Issues
- *Planning unit gets training:* Rarely, Regularly
- *Organization has long-range plans for:* Drug Abuse, Alcohol Abuse, Gangs, Geriatrics, AIDS

State or City	Org. has Planning/Research Unit	Crime Rate Trends	Population Growth	Demographic Shifts	Economic Issues	Social Values	Demographic Issues	Rarely	Regularly	Drug Abuse	Alcohol Abuse	Gangs	Geriatrics	AIDS
Nebraska	X	X	X	X				X	X					
New Jersey	X	X	X	X	X				X					
New Mexico									X	X	X	X	X	X
New York City	X	X	X	X				X	X					
North Carolina	X		X	X					X	X	X	X	X	X
North Dakota		X	X	X	X	X	X		X	X	X	X		
Ohio	X				X	X	X		X					
Oklahoma	X	X							X					
Pennsylvania	X		X		X	X	X	X	X					
Philadelphia	X				X	X	X	X	X		X			X
South Carolina	X	X	X		X	X	X		X	X	X	X	X	X
South Dakota					X	X	X	X	X	X	X		X	X
Tennessee	X				X	X	X		X	X	X		X	
Texas	X				X	X		X	X	X	X	X	X	X
Utah	X				X	X	X		X					
Vermont	X	X	X	X	X	X	X		X					
Virginia	X	X	X	X	X				X	X	X		X	X
Washington	X	X	X	X					X		X			
West Virginia		X	X	X					X	X	X		X	X
Wisconsin		X			X	X	X	X	X	X	X	X	X	X
Wyoming									X					

achieved results. Completion of a cell house renovation before the deadline is something to celebrate; an increase in the number of G.E.D. certificates awarded is an achievement of which the education department can be proud.

5. Managers should set goals high enough that employees will have to strive to meet them, but not so high that employees become discouraged and give up trying. Supervisors and wardens want employees to work hard, but not burn out, when trying to achieve goals.
6. Managers should specify when they expect goals to be achieved. Stated time frames are important so that employees can pace themselves.
7. Managers should set objectives only in relation to other organizational objectives. Keeping a close eye on the larger picture will keep conflicting objectives to a minimum.
8. Managers should state objectives clearly and simply. Understandable and concise language should be used when communicating a goal to the organization.

While there may be problems in formulating and implementing an MBO program, Kast and Rosenzweig point out that

> management by objectives programs have been used successfully by a number of business organizations to integrate organizational and individual goals. The most successful programs appear to be those that emphasize a total systems approach to MBO and take into consideration its impact on all of the organization's subsystems.[11]

Hidden Dangers in Planning

Often planning is doomed to failure even if the chief executive supports planning activities.

Paul J. Stonich[12] calls our attention to three reasons why planning efforts fail.

1. A focused approach to planning is often lacking. Organizations often concentrate on specific actions and decisions but fail to develop a planning system that brings important issues to the attention of the planners.
2. Many formal planning systems do not concentrate on actions or decisions that managers can take today to influence performance tomorrow. Instead, Stonich points out, technicians take over and emphasize overly analytical techniques, statistics, and other analytical tools that have no meaning for the action-oriented manager.
3. Many organizations are guilty of separating formal planning from the rest of the management systems, which include organization, communication, reporting, evaluation, and performance review. If planning is to be effective, it must be an integral part of the total organization.

Overall, planning offers distinct advantages if it is used properly and if executives are able to delegate and do not devote an inordinate amount of time to it. If processes are kept simple and planning flows from a coherent MBO program, then the obvious conclusion is that the advantages of planning certainly outweigh its disadvantages.

Managing the Planning System

Steps in the Planning Process

The planning process contains seven steps. It is difficult to put them in order because they are interrelated.[13]

1. Identify the planning manager/coordinator. While the chief executive must focus

FIGURE 12.2
Managing the Planning System

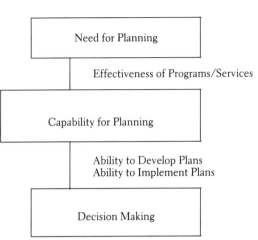

on long-range strategic planning, he or she cannot, in most cases, spend the bulk of his or her time on planning and implementation. Therefore, it is important to identify one person who will be responsible for managing the planning unit and acting as the liaison with the various departments during all stages of the process, particularly during the implementation process.

2. Identify and state institutional/organization objectives. It is necessary to clearly spell out the objectives of the organization in order for the planning process to begin.

3. List ways to achieve the objectives. In a correctional environment there is often more than one alternative.

4. Choose the best way to achieve the objective. Choosing the best way includes examining inmate and staff concerns as well as possible external restraints, such as court decisions or pending legislation.

5. Identify the department head who will be responsible for reaching the objective. Accountability is vital, so it is important for department heads to know what they are supposed to do and when they are supposed to do it.

6. Develop plans to pursue the chosen alternative. Once an alternative is chosen, the responsible department head must develop strategic and tactical plans.

7. Put the plans into action. Obviously, there is no benefit to the organization until the plans are put into action. All plans need to include strategic and tactical strategies that include the entire organization.

Tools for Planning

The survey noted earlier in this chapter calls our attention to the fact that many systems are dangerously overcrowded. Obviously, when an institution or a department of corrections is overcrowded, it tends to be reactive rather than proactive, and all too often pays little attention to strategic planning. Instead, all planning resources are directed at resolving one crisis after another.

For example, as the introductory essay by Babe Crockett of the U.S. Bureau of Prisons illustrates, if the warden and the central office are part of an effective planning unit, they begin each planning year by establishing the relationship between prison population, prison conditions, and economic and social indicators. Secondly, they attempt to determine the impact of new legislation, social trends, and demographics on projected inmate populations and needed programs. Third, they estimate the potential for developing new institutions. Finally, they evaluate existing programs to determine whether they should be continued. Effective planners need to be armed with tools that further their ability to do the job well.[14]

Core Knowledge

The corrections planner needs a thorough knowledge of corrections philosophy, procedures, and trends in corrections programs and treatment. This means that the individual should have a minimum of a bachelor's degree in criminal justice or a related field.

Sources of Criminal Justice Data and Information

Crime statistics are notoriously unreliable. This results from several factors: reporting varies from one jurisdiction to another, reporting is often voluntary for each agency, and often changes in reporting further distort the statistics. Nevertheless, there are information sources available to aid the planner. These include:

United States Census
United States Census of Manufacturers
National Crime Survey
Uniform Crime Reports (UCR)
Vital Statistics of the United States
National Institute of Justice
National Sheriff's Association
Sourcebook of Criminal Justice Statistics
Various state and local reports

Tools for Scheduling Activities and Resources

Scheduling is the process of compiling lists of tasks as well as of the people and resources necessary to complete them. Two well-known scheduling techniques are Gantt charts, introduced in chapter 2, and the Program Evaluation and Review Technique (PERT).

Gantt Chart

The Gantt chart, developed by Henry L. Gantt, is essentially a bar graph that shows the time allotment on the horizontal axis and the scheduled resource on the vertical axis.

The chart in figure 12.3 depicts Jack, Jim, and Wendy assigned to tasks related to opening a new institution. Jack is on schedule in completing his tasks; Jim is one day behind on his task. Wendy, however, has completed her task ahead of schedule and has begun to work on a related task.

A Gantt chart serves several purposes. First, the chart can be used to gain an overview of what tasks are to be completed, when they are to be completed, who is to work on them, and what, if any, resources are to be used. Second, correctional managers may use the Gantt chart to help coordinate organizational resources. Finally, the chart can be used to establish worker output. If workers are completing tasks more quickly than expected, for example, adjustments can be made.

Program Evaluation and Review Technique (PERT)

PERT is a group analysis and charting procedure that begins by determining the sequences of dependent activities. In 1958 the management firm of Booz, Allen, and Hamilton developed PERT to plan the procedures and processes required to complete the Polaris Missile Project. The U.S. Air Force, and then the civilian sector, adopted PERT, often under different names, to help them complete complicated projects.

There are four advantages to PERT:

1. It streamlines production.
2. It helps assure that projects will be completed within budget.
3. It promises optimum use at all times of personnel and material resources.
4. It accepts uncertainty as part of the system.

The PERT network contains two elements: activities and events. Activities are specified be-

FIGURE 12.3
Gant Chart

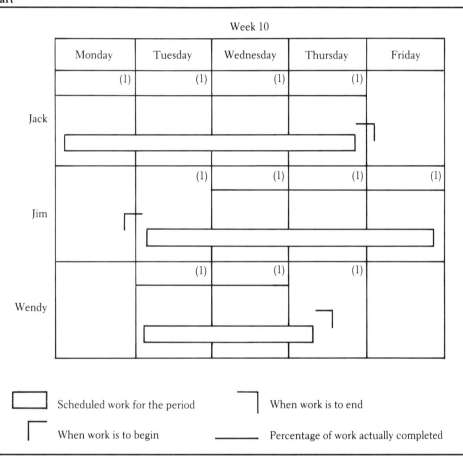

Week 10

	Monday	Tuesday	Wednesday	Thursday	Friday
Jack	(1)	(1)	(1)	(1)	
Jim		(1)	(1)	(1)	(1)
Wendy		(1)	(1)	(1)	

☐ Scheduled work for the period   ⌐ When work is to end

⌐ When work is to begin   ──── Percentage of work actually completed

haviors and events are completions of major tasks. Certain activities are assigned for each event, and these activities must be completed before that event can materialize. PERT charts are always illustrated from left to right to show how the events are interrelated. In addition, the time frame is presented on the solid lines, in parentheses.

On a PERT chart the critical path is the sequence of events and activities that takes the longest time. If problems arise, critical path analysis highlights those areas where remedial action needs to be taken to maintain the overall program schedule. Figure 12.4 depicts the critical path to completing a simple activity and shows the difference between events and activities. It doesn't take much imagination to realize how complicated PERT charts could be for opening a new institution. In that instance, there would be many, perhaps several hundred, activities noted, thus helping the planners keep on track.

FIGURE 12.4
Transporting the Prisoner

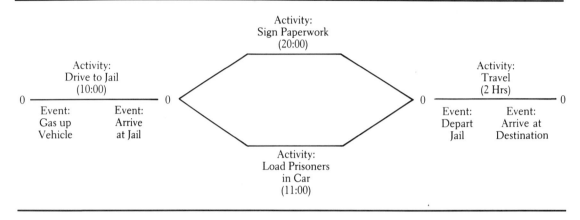

There are four primary steps in designing a PERT network:

1. List all activities and events for the project and the sequence in which these activities and events need to be completed.
2. Determine how much time will be needed to complete each activity and event.
3. Design the PERT network using the information in steps one and two.
4. Identify the critical path.

Who Plans?

The answer to the question of who plans is very simple—anyone who wants to succeed. This is not to suggest that corrections executives do not want to successfully pursue the mission of the organization or to have a successful career; quite the contrary. However, in the field of corrections, there are some built-in impediments to planning that do not exist in the private sector. As Nanus points out:

The main problem seems to be that individual criminal justice agencies tend to be reactive rather than future-oriented in their decision-making operations. Systematic and comprehensive long-range planning is seldom done because these agencies are constantly being subjected to short-term political pressures; their funding is based on a one-year cycle; and the problems of the moment are often real enough and quite compelling. However, even a totally reactive agency can operate even more effectively with a long-range planning perspective, as military strategic planning has often demonstrated. More important, there can be no meaningful regional or system-wide planning without individual agencies first being able to establish their own orderly, systematic, and continuous processes of setting objectives, anticipating the future, and bringing these anticipations to bear on critical present decisions.[15]

System-Wide and Local Planning

On a practical basis, planning can be broken into system-wide and local planning. **System-wide** planning refers to the planning carried out by what is generally referred to as the central office. Basically, the procedure for planning sessions at the central office level is the same as at the local level.

Usually, the central office is in the state capital, and the commissioner of correction (or secretary, as that person is called in some states) is responsible for initiating planning activities. The central office is concerned with the same issues as the local level, but on a more cosmic scale. It is also concerned with issues such as system overcrowding, new facilities, pending or needed legislation, and other kindred items. Planning activities must include not only support personnel in the central office but also the deputy commissioners and all wardens and superintendents.

Local planning is usually initiated by the CEO of the correctional institution or any similar subunit that deals directly with clients or inmates. The CEO usually wants to plan for such issues as inmate/client programs, services such as medical care or food services, and issues relating to inmate management, such as disciplinary reports. While these issues are similar to, and in many ways overlap, the responsibilities of the central office, the difference is in their impact on the day-to-day operation of the organization.

The development of local plans, by necessity, should include a variety of personnel who have knowledge of the organization and its processes. To begin, a CEO requests that all department heads meet with their personnel to develop a list of objectives for the coming year, or perhaps for a longer period of time. Once these objectives and the means to achieve them have been identified, they are submitted to the CEO, or his or her designee, to be compiled in a master list. Next, the CEO will call all department heads for a joint planning session. Often this session will be held at a location away from the institution or the offices so that participants can focus their attention on the matters at hand

without interruption. Once an organizational plan is formulated, the plan can be sent to the central office for review and for inclusion in system-wide planning.

The Chief Executive and Planning

Clearly, wardens, superintendents, chief probation officers, and commissioners are key persons whose support and active participation are crucial in developing and maintaining the planning process in any organization. The chief executive has five specific planning responsibilities:

1. to assure that a planning mechanism for the agency is developed and maintained;
2. to assure that lower-level executives bring long-range considerations to bear on operational problems;
3. to initiate, stimulate, and evaluate strategic and operational planning;
4. to lead the policy planning effort, particularly as regards the setting of objectives; and
5. to create an environment in which innovation and change are encouraged and rewarded.[16]

For the planning process to be effective, the chief executive of a correctional organization must recognize that he or she has many roles. The commissioner, warden, or chief probation officer is the recognized ceremonial head and must represent the institution or agency at various functions. He or she must assure that organization members are properly guided toward the accomplishment of organizational goals. He or she also acts as a liaison with the forces and interests outside the organization, monitors progress toward goals, and settles disputes within the organization. Finally, as a leader and manager, the CEO must assure the proper allocation of scarce resources in order to accomplish the organization's mission and achieve stated objectives.

Tactical Planning

Tactical planning is short-range planning. It usually focuses on the local organization. Certo asserts that short-range planning emphasizes current operations of various parts of the organization.[17] Usually tactical planning will extend only one year or so into the future and will emphasize important, but attainable, goals. Tactical plans are usually related to inmate management, programs, and the physical plant.

For example, the warden and the planning committee of a correctional institution may establish an objective to renovate a cell house within twelve months; another objective might relate to the excessive number of disciplinary reports for the defacing of government property. Measures will then be developed to correct the problem within a certain amount of time. Or, a chief probation officer might find that an unacceptably high number of clients without high school diplomas, or G.E.D.'s, have not enrolled in available programs. The chief and his or her planning staff can establish a goal to raise that number over the next year.

Strategic Planning

Strategic planning is long-range in scope and focuses on the larger organization; in other words, it is usually system-wide. In this case we can define long-range as three to five years or even longer, in spite of the yearly budget cycle. Strategic planning can be defined as the formulation, implementation, and evaluation of actions that will enable an organization to achieve its long-range objectives.[18]

According to Gibbons, et al.,[19] strategic planning calls for a wealth of knowledge and information in two general categories. First, the corrections planner must possess an in-depth understanding of crime patterns, social forces in crime causation, and key factors in the development of criminal careers as well as a comprehensive knowledge of correctional philosophy and practices. Second, the planner must possess a command of planning principles, concepts, and tools that can be utilized to deal with specific problems.

Since correctional institutions are an integral part of the community, the correctional manager must develop strategies that aid him or her in developing plans that meet the needs of the community. Certo[20] proposes environmental analysis to pinpoint environmental factors that influence organizational operations. According to Certo, economic issues, demographics, social values, and suppliers are critical issues to consider when developing strategic plans.

Economic Issues. Economics is the science of how people produce, distribute, and use various goods and services. Economic issues affect not only our everyday life but also public agencies. Without a steady tax base, for example, funding is apt to be decreased, and this results in the elimination or cutting of social programs. Therefore, if a recession or a downturn in the economy is on the horizon, strategic plans should be developed accordingly.

Demographics. Demographics are the characteristics of a population. Changes in the demographics of a state or region can influence a correctional organization drastically. For example, the U.S. population is aging. What effect, if any, will this phenomenon have on the need for prisons, camps, and related agencies and programs?

Social Values. Social values are relative degrees of worth that society attaches to abstractions such as patriotism, "right," and "wrong." Social values change over time and affect the operations of correctional agencies. In recent years, for example, there has been a call for harsher sentences and more stringent parole guidelines. This has placed an almost intolerable strain on correctional agencies to deliver services.

Suppliers. As mentioned in chapter 1, the correctional institution does not function in a vacuum. Suppliers are those businesses and agencies that provide the organization with goods, services, and inmates. Examples of suppliers include the courts, utilities, and food vendors. Successful long-term planning must generally include some consideration of prices and availability of supplies as well as of the flow of inmates/clients to the organization.

In the same way that a correctional agency cannot exist without input from outside sources, it cannot exist without planning how to use or process that input. However, without some form of organization, even excellent planning efforts are for nothing if there is no structure to plan and deliver services to the inmate/client. We now turn our attention to the subject of organizing to accomplish the mission of the organization.

Organizing

The U.S. Bureau of Prisons is considered a leader in the field of corrections. Structurally, the bureau is made up of a central office staff in Washington, D.C., and five regional offices in Philadelphia, Atlanta, Kansas City, Dallas, and San Francisco. Each regional director is responsible for supervising the wardens and superintendents as well as all community programs in his or her region. Ostensibly, the central office concerns itself with more cosmic matters such as budgets, legislative matters, and

research and planning as well as special cases.

In spite of decentralization, the Bureau of prisons remains a highly centralized organization, and many decisions are made at least at the regional level. The wardens and other managers often have little discretion about what they do. Most of the case management work is controlled by the "manual" and the SENTRY system (a management information system). The custodial and other departments are controlled by the threat of audits and must perform their tasks according to guidelines spelled out in the "manual." The advantage of such a tight structure is that policy is interpreted the same way at the Federal Correctional Institution, Petersburg, Virginia, as it is at the Federal Correctional Institution, Terminal Island, California. The procedures to implement and maintain those policies are also the same at all institutions in the Bureau of Prisons. There is a downside, however; continuity and sameness are often preserved at the expense of innovation and creativity.

It is difficult to get away from this type of rigidity and structure in what is essentially a paramilitary organization. The larger the institution, the more rigid and refined the structure becomes. The smaller the organization or institution, the less rigid and refined the structure.

Structural Assumptions

Certain assumptions are made when one considers how an organization should be structured.[21]

1. Organizations exist primarily to accomplish established goals.
2. For any organization, there is a structure appropriate to the goals, the environment, the technology, and the participants.
3. Organizations work effectively when environmental turbulence and the personal

preferences of participants are constrained by norms of rationality.

4. Coordination and control are accomplished best through the exercise of authority and impersonal rules.
5. Structures can be systematically designed and implemented.
6. Specialization permits higher levels of individual expertise and performance.
7. Organizational problems usually reflect an appropriate structure and can be resolved through redesign and reorganization.

Organizational Structure

In chapter 2 it was pointed out that Henri Fayol made a significant contribution to organizational theory with his "general principles of management." Several of those "general principles" are extremely relevant to organizational structure in a correctional institution.

Division of Work

According to Fayol, the object of division of work is to produce more and better work with the same effort. In a correctional institution there must be a division of work if prisoners are to be guarded and fed, problems and paperwork attended to, and payroll maintained. However, since security and watchfulness are everyone's responsibilities, it is necessary for everyone to be familiar, at least to a certain extent, with several other tasks in order to be able to fill in during emergencies. In some systems, for example, riot plans call for secretaries to take positions in certain gun towers in order to free correctional officers for more specialized and dangerous duties.

Unity of Command

The point here is that an employee should receive orders from one superior only. If this rule is violated, according to Fayol, discipline and authority are undermined and order and stability threatened.

Centralization

Fayol believed that centralization is a part of the natural order. In small organizations centralization is greater, but in larger organizations the scalar chain is interposed between the warden (or CEO) and those in the lower echelons who are responsible for executing the orders of the warden.

Scalar Chain

The scalar chain is the chain of command ranging from the highest authority to the lowest rank. The line of authority is the route followed by all formal commands and communications. Suppose, for example, that the warden receives a call from a state senator about a particular inmate and his prospective release date. The warden calls the assistant warden, who calls the records office chief. The records office chief obtains the requested information and sends it back up the scalar chain, through the assistant warden. There are exceptions, of course, that reflect the impact of informal groups and informal lines of communication (see chapter 10).

The organization chart shown in figure 12.5 illustrates the scalar chain and the formal lines of communication. Traditionally, organizational charts are pyramidal, with most authority resting at the top and the least authority resting at the bottom. In addition, the chart illustrates the departmental form of an organization and the working relationship between those responsible for executing the mission of the organization.

Departmentalization

A department can be viewed as a unique group of organizational resources established by management to perform specific organizational tasks. The process of establishing departments is called *departmentalization*. The creation of

FIGURE 12.5
Traditional Prison Organization

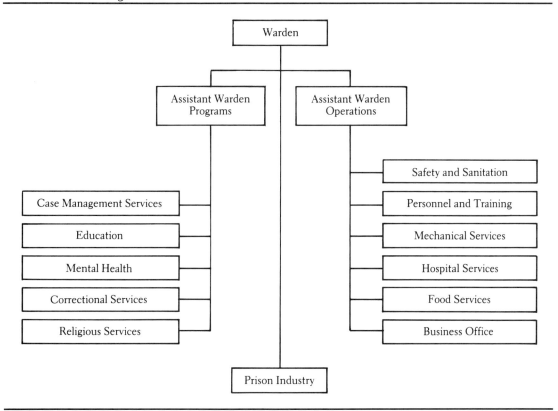

FIGURE 12.6
An Institutional Department

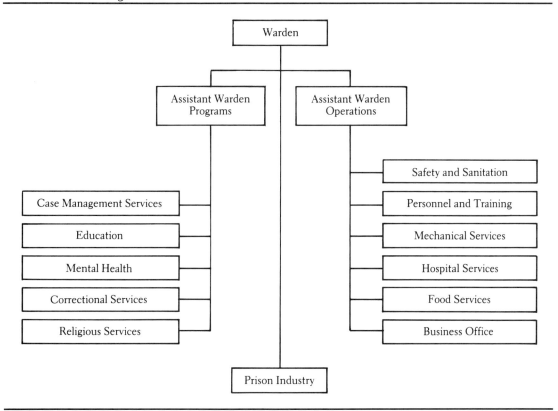

FIGURE 12.7
Mixed Probation Department

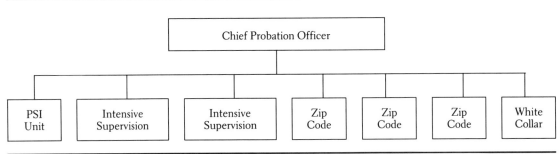

a department is based upon either tasks to be accomplished (grouping similar functions together) or the target group of the department.

One example of departmentalization by tasks to be accomplished is the Mechanical Services Department in a large prison. This department is responsible for the physical plant and is composed of various subunits, each with a supervisor who reports to the chief of mechanical services.

Departmentalization based upon target groups is common in a probation or parole office. It is not unusual for community services offices to organize resources around particular groups of people or areas of a particular jurisdiction. For example, a probation department in a populous county such as Los Angeles, California, or Cook County, Illinois, may assign probation officers by zip codes. Or, the department might be organized according to target groups, such as difficult-to-manage groups, pre-sentence reports, substance abusers, and so on.

Span of Management

The term *span of control* is frequently used in the literature, but perhaps a more accurate term would be *span of management*. As Koontz and O'Donnell point out, "The span is one of management and not merely of control."[22]

In chapter 2 it was mentioned that Moses was possibly the first public administrator on record. In the Book of Exodus, Moses' father-in-law suggested that he appoint leaders to aid him in his task, "and let them judge the people at all times; every great matter they shall bring to you, but any small matter they shall decide themselves; so it will be easier for you and they will bear the burden with you."[23] Here we see that Jethro had an organization chart in mind, and thus the formal delegation of responsibility and accountability was first documented. Today if an organization is to be successful, the span of management must be appropriate for the tasks and management style of the chief executive officer.

Henry H. Albers summarizes a report by the American Management Association that attempts to shed light on the question of how many employees a manager can effectively supervise. In a study of the span of the president, a sample of 141 companies "with good management practices" was selected. Data were obtained from 100 large companies with over 5,000 employees each and 41 medium-sized companies with 500 to 5,000 employees. The researchers found that the number of subordinates reporting to the president ranged from 1 to 24. In 9 out of 141 companies only one executive, usually an executive vice president, reported to the president. The presidents of 55 companies had a span of 10 or more. The median for the 100 large organizations surveyed was between 8 and 9; for the 41 medium-sized concerns, between 6 and 7.[24]

The results of the survey are summarized in table 12.2. It appears that there is a good deal of variation in the number of subordinates who report to the president. In fact, some authors argue that limited span of control is not the norm.[25] On the other hand, others point out that as a rule the concept of span of control closely follows that advocated by theorists.[26]

Generally speaking, the principle of span of control, or span of management as it is now called, indicates that efficiency is increased by limiting the manager's number of subordinates to no more than five or six.[27] Any more than that creates communication problems. Put another way, the more levels of organization communication must pass through, the less responsive the unit is to the manager's direction.

Span of Management in Corrections

In correctional organizations, the span of management varies from agency to agency. Few guidelines are given to the manager, but the American Correctional Association somewhat obliquely addresses this issue in its *Standards for Adult Correctional Institutions*.

2–4013. A written plan with an organizational chart describes the institutional organization, and groups similar functions, services, and activities into administrative subunits. This plan is reviewed at least annually and is updated as needed.

Discussion. The functions and number of units

may vary depending on the size and type of inmate population, the nature of the programs, the history and traditions of the facility, and the fiscal and physical resources available. The numbers and kinds of subunits, levels of supervision, and types of employees should be graphically illustrated to delineate clearly the lines of authority responsibility.[28]

Most wardens and superintendents will admit that any more than six or seven subordinates is too many. For example, the typical warden will have six to ten employees reporting

TABLE 12.2
The Numbers of Executives Reporting to the President in 100 Large and 41 Medium-Sized Companies

Number of Executives Reporting to President	Number of Large Companies	Number of Medium-sized Companies
1	6	3
2	—	—
3	1	2
4	3	2
5	7	4
6	9	8
7	11	7
8	8	5
9	8	2
10	6	4
11	7	1
12	10	—
13	8	1
14	4	1
15	1	—
16	5	—
17	—	1
18	1	—
19	—	—
20	1	—
21	1	—
22	—	—
23	2	—
24	1	—
Totals	100	41

Source: Henry H. Albers, *Principles of Organization and Management,* 2d ed. (New York: John Wiley and Sons, 1965). Reprinted by permission of John Wiley and Sons, Inc.

directly to him or her. They include such diverse positions as locksmith, secretary, and intelligence officer in addition to the assistant wardens. Given the many roles the warden or superintendent has to play, he or she must delegate as much responsibility as possible in order to effectively carry out the daily routine.

Summary

Planning and organizing are important to the success of the organization. The chief executive officer is responsible for the development and continuation of an executive planning program. Because CEO's cannot spend all their time working at planning activities, they must appoint someone as the organization planner. In order to be effective, the planner needs to have certain qualifications, including an ability to easily relate to action-oriented managers.

Most correctional organizations are structured to assure quick and easy communication and to provide security and accomplish the goals of the programs. Most corrections departments are organized along the lines of the traditional pyramid and rely upon the usual paramilitary organization to accomplish the organizational mission. This results in a strong supervisory approach, with staff not free to demonstrate initiative and creativity. Perhaps there is change on the horizon. Today many progressive organizations are moving toward decentralization as a way to better accomplish the mission of the organization and to move decisions on case management closer to the inmate or client population. Such an innovation improves the span of management and communication.

Reviewing the Case

Mr. Crockett clearly points the way for those who are interested in the planning process. The U.S. Bureau of Prisons may have one of the best planning departments of any corrections agency in the nation, and the process is clearly supported by top management. The Bureau of Prisons' approach to planning is simple: involve everyone. While the Office of Strategic Planning focuses primarily on the long term, the process stimulates planning and action by local staff in tactical planning as well. Planning as a year-round, ongoing process has enabled the U.S. Bureau of Prisons to become a recognized leader in the field of corrections.

For Further Study

Burt Nanus, "A General Model for a Criminal Justice Planning Process," *Journal of Criminal Justice*, 2:4 (Winter 1974), pp. 345–56.

Don C. Gibbons, Joseph L. Thimm, Florence Yospe, and Gerald F. Blake, Jr., *Criminal Justice Planning* (Englewood Cliffs, N.J.: Prentice-Hall, 1977).

James C. Worthy, "Organizational Structure and Employee Morale," *American Sociological Review* (April 1950), pp. 169–79.

Key Terms

Management by Objectives	Core Knowledge
	PERT
Gantt Chart	Strategic Planning
Tactical Planning	Span of Management
Departmentalization	

Organizational Control

Case Study: Control and Change in a Probation Department

As probation and community corrections agencies across the nation continue to professionalize operations, it is becoming more common for troubled systems to hire experienced administrators from outside the agency to provide objective, unbiased leadership.[1] Such reliance on new blood is generally needed when severe problems (official misconduct, criminal conduct, and so on) have been experienced by the previous administration, when no qualified successor exists within the current administration, or when no qualified successor desires to step forward and make application for the vacated position. In assuming command of agency operations from the outside, the new probation chief is presented with numerous challenges. Of supreme importance is the establishment of his or her leadership style: how controlling, how participatory should the new chief be?

This decision is influenced not only by one's individual management style but also by the programmatic efficiency or inefficiency of operations. If an agency is incompetent in meeting its mandate, the chief emphasizes team building and the establishment of quality control measures that are mutually decided on the administrative/supervisory level. This process may not necessarily be orderly or attractive, but its importance is critical as this action may be precisely what is needed and expected. At this point, immediate response and timing are paramount. If the ship is sinking, the captain does not call a ship's meeting to determine which size bucket to bail with. Swiftness of response is vital also because the initial impressions of staff will likely be long lasting. The chief is very much under a microscope, "on the bubble," at this point, and while swift, decisive action is desired, such a response without benefit of input from key staff is a significant mistake and will likely prove a costly managerial error.

While the chief hopefully brings a fresh, objective, and competent approach, he or she is at a tremendous disadvantage in not knowing firsthand the agency history and culture. Much of this knowledge can only be personally experienced and understood over time. However, key administrative and supervisory staff may greatly help the chief gain at least a superficial understanding of agency dynamics. It is important that mistakes not repeat themselves, and if the chief operates in a vacuum or under the smug premise that he or she is omniscient, trouble will be certain to surface soon.

Once some stability and mutual trust and respect have been established, some of the necessary initial controls may be relaxed; however, the chief needs to demand that quality control measures that are essential to acceptable performance remain in place. Not only is the timing of change important; equally important is the amount of change. Very few people like or embrace change, so at the initial onset, a minimal amount of change is best. A new chief probation officer on the floor is enough change in itself.

For change and control mechanisms to be accepted, they must be well explained and well orchestrated. Such a process is best accomplished by the chief emphasizing the establishment of strong, personal relationships with key advisers and confidants. Staff follow new directives and procedures at a faster and more supportive pace when they believe that their boss holds a genuine interest in their personal and professional welfare. Development of such relationships does not come by accident. The new chief should be visible, accessible, and sincerely concerned and committed to the interest of his or her agency and staff.

While some new chiefs may be hesitant about imposing strict policies and procedures, many staff will welcome and embrace such restrictions and will support them even more if they are afforded a fair and honest role in their creation. People tend to be committed to and supportive of those decisions they have had a part in creating; these change efforts also have the best chance of success.

An initial demand that should never be compromised is for honest, ongoing, two-way communication. A common thread to poor probation operations is inconsistent and underemphasized communications on all levels. Ongoing, unsolicited feedback on all levels must be the expected, consistent norm.

While much of the change process is dependent upon the chief, he or she should not be closed to suggestions or change opportunities presented by others. Again, the newly arrived chief is historically and culturally ignorant, and support of a long-time employee's suggestion or recommendation, after proper analysis, may prove to be a brilliant decision.

The personality and culture of a probation agency take time to experience and learn. No two agencies are alike. All probation operations maintain and support traits and idiosyncracies common to their specific operation. The new probation chief must respect local tradition and custom but not to the extent of hindering necessary operational controls and needed change. While harmonious working relations are desired on all levels, the function of any probation agency is to provide mandated probation services that are quality-driven and consistently delivered. Without question, that is any probation chief's main duty, and the style and manner in which that mandate is accomplished will always remain an individualized process that balances the issues of service delivery with the needs of employees.

Introduction

Controlling is a primary function of corrections managers, including department heads, project managers, chief probation officers, and the commissioner of corrections. Without the guidance of these individuals, organizational objectives would not be met. This chapter explores ways the corrections manager can control resources and activities of organization members in order to achieve stated organizational objectives.

Fundamentals of Control

In a broad sense, many of the issues discussed thus far are a part of control: budgeting, motivation, group management, planning, and leadership. For the purposes of this chapter, the managerial function of controlling is "the measurement and correction of performance in order to make sure that enterprise objectives and the plans devised to attain them are accomplished."[2] Peter F. Drucker neatly sums up the differences between control and controls:

In the dictionary of social institutions the word 'controls' is not the plural of the word 'control.' Not only do more controls not necessarily give more control, the two words, in the context of social institutions, have different meanings altogether. The synonyms for controls are measurement and information. The synonym for control is direction. Controls pertain to means, control to an end. Controls deal with facts; that is, with events of the past. Control deals with expectations; that is, with the future. Controls are analytical, concerned with what was and is. Control is normative and concerned with what ought to be.[3]

Control in the Correctional Organization

The manager must recognize that there are several (if not many) control mechanisms that must be focused on at one time. Developing a control system is often a matter of sampling and is often a function of personal bias. The difficulty is in selecting a system that controls efficiently and effectively. Overcontrol is costly and creates a host of motivational problems. Undercontrol is also costly (in a different sense) and creates a number of problems related to achievement of the organizational mission.

Max Weber[4] views bureaucracy not in terms of red tape and inefficiency but rather as a structural device that allows workers to achieve a stated purpose. Bureaucracies, according to Weber, are the most efficient means for complex organizations to meet the needs of a complex society.

Etzioni[5] offers a typology of organizations based upon compliance. He defines compliance as "a relation in which an actor behaves in accordance with a directive supported by another actor's power, and to the orientation of the subordinated actor to the power applied."[6] The typology classifies organizations according to their predominant compliance pattern. Thus, he views organizations as coercive, utilitarian, or normative.

Coercive organizations are those that rely mainly upon coercion to gain and maintain control. Etzioni points out that typical examples are concentration camps, prisoner of war camps, prisons, correctional institutions, mental hospi-

tals, and relocation centers. The greater the amount of coercion used, the higher the level of alienation among the inmates.

Throughout his discussion Etzioni's focus is upon the inmates. Very little is said of the work force that is charged with the task of keeping the inmates in the camp or prison. Perhaps the coercive nature of prisons explains, in part, the character of the staff as well as the managerial approaches adopted by some managers. If, as Etzioni asserts, coercion breeds alienation, then it is not difficult to comprehend why the work force is alienated and expresses a low level of loyalty to the organization.

Utilitarian organizations are "organizations in which remuneration is the major means of control over lower participants and calculative involvement (i.e., mild alienation to mild commitment) characterizes the orientation of the large majority of lower participants."[7] These organizations are usually industries; lower participants include blue-collar workers in factories and mines and white-collar workers in banking, finance, and so on. Also considered lower participants are professionals in, for example, research organizations and even law firms.

Normative organizations are "organizations in which normative power is the major source of control over most lower participants, whose orientation to the organization is characterized by high commitment."[8] Normative power is defined as the allocation and manipulation of symbolic rewards and deprivations by leaders. Such organizations include religious organizations, hospitals, universities, and professional organizations.

Etzioni's typology is valuable for the present discussion because it provides a theoretical backdrop against which we can compare correctional organizations to other organizations in our society. Clearly, if we view prisons as two organizations in one, the inmate organization and the formal organization, we begin to sense the schizophrenic character of the prison. Community-program organizations such as probation and work-release centers are less schizophrenic because the level of coercion is less—hence less alienation by employees and a greater commitment. Thus, in corrections at least, perhaps a typology is inaccurate and we should look at the correctional organization along a continuum from most coercive to least coercive and along which each correctional organization must fall.

Regardless of where the organization falls along the continuum, the manager must exercise control. He or she must make sure that inmates do not escape, fight, kill, or rob one another and must coordinate the efforts of staff so as to achieve the objectives of the organization (stated objectives usually flow from attempts to control the inmate population). The objectives of community-program organizations are much the same as institutional objectives, but in addition, these organizations are interested in helping the client or resident find employment, become involved in drug counseling, and so forth. These goals, however, are achieved through much less coercion.

This chapter is less about inmate control (or inmate management, as it is termed by practitioners) than about organizational control. How do we get from here to there? What will we look like as an organization in five years? How can we be sure staff is doing what they are supposed to be doing? These are questions the effective correctional manager needs to ask himself or herself every day.

The Process of Control

The control process is a sequential chain of events. Figure 13.1 illustrates the sequence of events that occurs in the control process as discussed throughout much of this text. Objectives are established, programs developed, workloads determined, and so on, all with an eye on excellence of service. There is interface at the higher level where goals or objectives are established and at the lower level where the actual work is performed.

Establishment of Standards

As figure 13.1 shows, step one is the establishment of plans. However, plans are often quite detailed, and in order to determine whether they are being adhered to, the manager should develop standards. Standards are criteria of performance[9] and the yardstick against which we measure performance. In a work-release center or a regional parole office, for example, the manager may be able to control performance through simple observation. But in a large penitentiary it is another matter; the warden or superintendent must establish a variety of standards.

The points selected for control should be the critical areas that demonstrate that the organization is moving in the proper direction. Management by Objectives (MBO) was discussed in chapter 12. Objectives established via an MBO process provide many of the standards necessary for a manager to measure an organization's performance. Thus, every objective, every activity, every policy, and the annual budget become standards against which performance can be measured. In practice, however, standards tend to be the following: physical standards, cost standards, capital standards, revenue standards, program standards, intangible standards, and goal standards.[10]

- *Physical standards.* Physical standards are nonmonetary standards used to measure consumption of materials; e.g., the prison industry's use of raw materials such as steel, plastic, and cotton. Physical standards also may reflect quality, such as numbers of disciplinary reports in a prison

FIGURE 13.1
The Cycle of Control

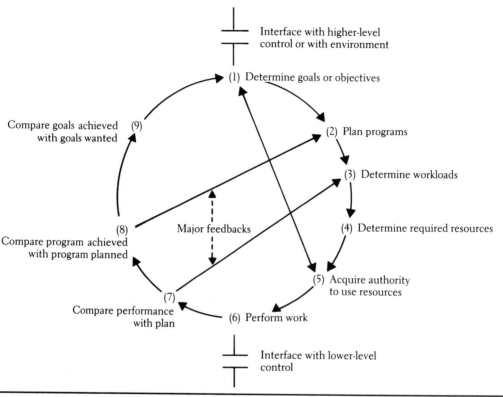

Interface with higher-level control or with environment

(1) Determine goals or objectives

(2) Plan programs

(3) Determine workloads

(4) Determine required resources

(5) Acquire authority to use resources

(6) Perform work

(7) Compare performance with plan

(8) Compare program achieved with program planned

(9) Compare goals achieved with goals wanted

Major feedbacks

Interface with lower-level control

Source: Marvin E. Mundel, *A Conceptual Framework for the Management Sciences* (New York: McGraw-Hill Book Company, 1967), p. 162. Permission granted.

or a probation officer's contacts with a client or clients.

■ *Cost standards.* While monetary measurement is a common standard, it is very difficult to establish cost standards in the field of corrections because so few people are able to compute (or divine) the true cost of services (see chapter 7). However, cost standards are often computed as daily costs to maintain an inmate in a prison or halfway house or labor costs per hour in prison industries.

■ *Capital standards.* Often this is the most overlooked item in computing the true cost

of services (see chapter 7). Capital standards relate to capital invested, such as construction. It is a most important consideration for the chief executive officer and the controller.

■ *Revenue standards.* Revenue standards are often used to measure, for example, sales in manufacturing or retail. However, in corrections such standards can be used for prison industries or for work-release residents who reimburse the state for room and board.

■ *Program standards.* A manager may be responsible for developing a new program.

Such a program may be either a community-based program or an institutional program designed to deliver a particular service or to achieve certain objectives. There will be some subjective standards regarding program success, but there will also be objective standards, such as how many residents find work or the number of hours of counseling and therapy the staff delivers.

- *Intangible standards.* Most difficult to establish are those standards not relating to physical or monetary measurements. For example, how do we measure the performance of a unit manager or a probation officer? How do we determine that a therapeutic community for inmates with a history of drug addiction is truly achieving its objectives? Corrections as a discipline is rife with intangible standards, particularly because it deals in a service and is responsible for the actions and behavior of people who would rather be somewhere else or doing something else. Thus, human relationships complicate our work life and at the same time make it more exciting.
- *Goal standards.* Complex organizations should have goals to strive for. That is why an MBO program is an important element in the search for excellence. Goals enable us to quantify most of our objectives and to measure our progress.

Measuring Performance

Everyone measures her or his personal performance. We ask, "How am I doing?" or "Am I doing as well as the next person?" Such measurement is perfectly natural, because the average person is interested in doing as well as he or she can, regardless of the payoff. Organizations also measure their own performance. The difference is that organizations need to justify their continued existence, make a profit, or receive funding from the legislature, county council, or congress.

On a level closer to home, organizational rewards are most often tied to performance. Superiors evaluate performance of subordinates in a formalized process that is repeated on a biannual or quarterly basis. Promotions, merit pay increases, and occasionally termination hang in the balance. When appropriate criteria are used to assess performance, trust is established between subordinates and superiors, and the employee is often motivated to perform at a higher level.

The same can be said of programs. When appropriate criteria are established for assessment, management can make sound decisions necessary for fine-tuning program procedures. Decisions in regard to budget requests (or deletions) are more sound, and personnel decisions—more staff or fewer staff—can be justified.

Correction of Deviations

If standards are developed that accurately reflect the structure of the organization and the mission of the organization, it is much easier to correct deviations. "Corrective action is managerial activity aimed at bringing organizational performance up to the level of performance standards."[11] In other words, the way we go about correcting mistakes or altering performance hinders or enhances the overall performance of the organization.

Correction of deviations spans the entire managerial subsystem. Managers may correct deviations by altering the budget, through the planning process, by identifying leaders, by writing or rewriting policy, and by working to improve dysfunctional work groups.

Performance appraisal in many organizations has become dysfunctional.[12] Low levels of trust, inappropriate criteria, and inappropriate discussions cause employees to be dismissive of the process. In addition, during the appraisal

FIGURE 13.2
Control and Performance

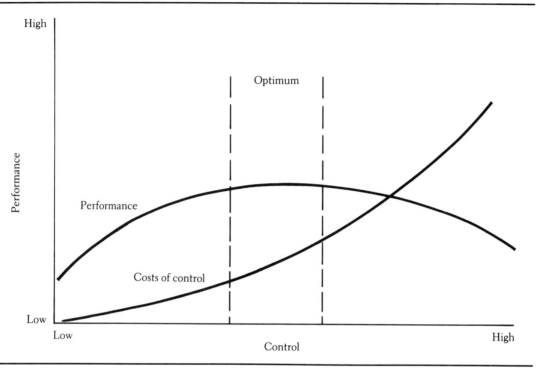

process many supervisors and executives focus on shortcomings rather than accomplishments, resulting in distrust, unhappy employees, and decreased efficiency.

Finally, control is elusive. Control in a prison or community corrections agency is necessary to assure the warden, chief probation officer, or commissioner that the job is being accomplished as he or she wants it accomplished. But the field of corrections attracts people who may rebel at too much control on the one hand but who view the lack of control as a sign of weakness and indecisiveness on the other hand. Therefore, the manager must walk a fine line, and finding that line can be difficult. Figure 13.2 illustrates the optimum area for organizational

control. Too much control results in decreasing performance, and the costs of control can escalate beyond a productive point.

Types of Control

There are three types of management control: (1) precontrol, (2) concurrent control, and (3) feedback control.[13]

Precontrol

Precontrol occurs before work is begun. Policies, procedures, and rules (see chapter 6) are examples of precontrol aimed at directing the activity of employees and eliminating undesirable work results. For example, the warden of a penitentiary orders count to be taken at certain times over a twenty-four hour period. This is to prevent escapes and to ensure that employees who supervise inmates know where they are at all times.

Concurrent Control

Concurrent control occurs while work is being performed. It relates to performance as well as material. For example, many prisons responsible for more violent and intractable inmates use what is called "three-man cover" to move inmates from one place to another. That is, three officers escort a handcuffed inmate from one place to another. The intent is to provide for the safety of the officers, the inmate, and others in the vicinity. In terms of tangible items, concurrent control relates to on-time inventory; that is, not allowing items carried in the inventory to build up or be depleted.

Feedback Control

Feedback control focuses on work that has already been completed. That is, the manager gets a report about a job or task that has been completed or, in corrections, information about a previous time period. For example, many wardens or commissioners insist on a Monday morning report. This report contains information about numbers of arrivals, releases, disciplinary actions, assaults, escapes, and so on, over the last seven-day period. In this way the manager can take action to correct mistakes and have answers for the media. Figure 13.3 illustrates the process.

An **audit**, sometimes called an inspection, is one way to maintain control via the feedback process. As used in many agencies, an audit is an inspection by a team of specialists from another part of the agency that spends one to several days reviewing and critiquing procedures and pro-

---

FIGURE 13.3
Feedback Control and Management

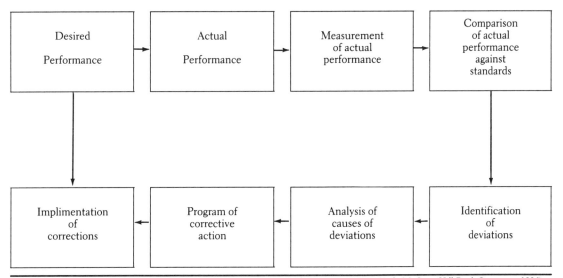

Source: Harold Koontz, Cyril O'Donnell, and Heinz Weirich, *Essentials of Management* (New York: McGraw-Hill Book Company, 1986), p. 453. Permission granted.

FIGURE 13.4

Security Audit Directives and Recommendations

Directives
1. Utilize the log of changes on the Daily Roster to account for all staff changes.
2. Post orders are required to be reviewed by staff prior to assuming the post.
3. Emergency plans require the approval of the central office.
4. Inmates entering and leaving the institution through front or rear entrances will be searched each time, occasionally strip searched.

Recommendations
1. Clarify post orders on the apprehension of individuals. No effort is made to distinguish between an escaping inmate and others.
2. Recommend construction of cabinets for storage in the Control Center in order to reduce the cluttered appearance.
3. Recommend better access to the emergency keys so they may be checked and counted daily.

grams. The team may specialize in one function, such as custodial or food service, or it may inquire into several areas. Often American Correctional Association (ACA) standards are used as the guide for inquiry. Many organizations use audits as a means to assure the commissioner that employees are following procedures. Many systems have a highly refined audit process covering several areas. In the U.S. Bureau of Prisons two of the more important audits are the Correctional Services Audit and the Unit Management Audit.

Audits are conducted on two levels: internal and external. The **internal audit** is conducted periodically by the responsible assistant or associate warden through the responsible department head. The **external audit** is conducted by the responsible assistant commissioner or regional director through regional or central office personnel responsible for that activity.

Before effective audits can be conducted, policies and procedures need to be clearly articulated and in place. Staff must be properly trained in their execution, and proper records must be main-

tained. The purpose of the internal audit is to fine-tune organizational operation and to prepare for an external audit. The purpose of the external audit is for the team to offer the warden, superintendent, sheriff, or other manager unbiased recommendations for improving security or other operations of the institution. It is also a way for the commissioner or director to gain an awareness of the managerial and leadership abilities of the warden and her or his subordinates.

Once the audit is completed, the individual responsible for conducting the audit should submit a written report to the warden, chief probation officer, jail administrator, or sheriff, calling his or her attention to issues that need to be corrected. There are two kinds of issues to be addressed: directed changes that are necessary to comply with procedure, court order, or law; and recommendations that apply to issues that will make the organization more professional or comfortable or enhance employee satisfaction. To illustrate the difference figure 13.4 shows a few issues pointed out by an audit team during an audit of a penitentiary during the 1980s.

Audits are an important tool for organizational control. However, most correctional organizations do not use them because they are small jails or probation agencies with just a few employees who fail to see the importance of an audit when the sheriff or chief is in daily contact with everyone. One suggestion is for the chief probation officer or jail administrator to designate an employee to be responsible for internal audits. Or two to five organizations or counties could form a coalition and take turns auditing each other's operation. However, many judges, sheriffs, and chief probation officers may be hesitant to pursue this sensible course for a variety of reasons, such as the fear that deficiencies will be used against them or that the media will make unfounded negative claims if the results of the audits are leaked. None of the fears are truly valid, of course, and only serve to perpetuate unsound and even unsafe correctional practice.

Fundamentals of Service Management and Control

Service management and control refers to activities necessary to create a service. Those activities include personnel management, purchasing, warehousing, transportation, security, programs, and the like. Not all of these activities will be discussed here as they vary from jurisdiction to jurisdiction. We will discuss new technology and designs as they relate to the managerial subsystem and budget.

Remote Surveillance

Technological innovations have brought many improvements to the field of corrections. Strategically placed closed-circuit TV cameras increase the range of corrections officers' surveillance. Cameras allow officers in the control center to inspect persons attempting to enter restricted areas and to maintain surveillance of corridors, housing units, and to monitor suicidal inmates. Many new jails and prisons have placed microphones in strategic places in order to overhear conversations with the goal of assuring the safety of staff and inmates. Finally, individual locaters tuned to a "panic button" on a radio or body alarm allow control officers to immediately locate an officer in trouble without speaking to him or her on the radio.

Probation and parole agencies have been greatly helped by home detention equipment. There are two kinds of home detention devices. Both require the offender to wear a nonremovable ankle or wrist bracelet tied to a computer box that is plugged into a telephone jack. The first allows the offender to move about freely within a specified distance from the telephone jack: for example, 150 feet. If he or she moves outside of that boundary, a signal is sent to a central location, where the date and time of the infraction are noted on a computer printout. At that time or the next morning, depending on agency policy and procedure, a probation or parole officer will investigate the matter.

The second type of device is individualized in that it allows the offender to leave his or her home for a specified period: for example, to go to work. The probation or parole officer will have programmed the computer to call the offender at random times between her or his return from work and departure the next morning. An electronic voice controls the reporting procedure. The voice may say something like the following: "This is the Acme County Probation Department calling. You have ten seconds to insert your bracelet into the control box." The offender then must place his or her octagon-shaped wrist monitor into a similarly shaped hole in the control box, causing the two computer chips to mate and send a signal to the computer, signifying the operation is completed. "Thank you," says the voice.

If the offender is absent or for some other reason is unable to complete the procedure, the computer will return the call a specified number of times. All transactions are noted on a printout for the probation or parole officer to review and take action if necessary. In addition, all conversations are recorded in order for the officer to make a determination in regard to slurred speech or anything else that may be pertinent.

While remote surveillance technology is a boon to practitioners, it must be kept in mind that it can never be a substitute for hands-on supervision. People respond to people. A camera or computer never makes judgments. It is the individual probation officer, parole officer, or corrections officer who affects safety, security, and the life of the offender.

Facility Design

Managers should understand how facility layout influences management and realize that there are many layout designs. The layout and philosophy behind the Pennsylvania and Auburn Systems have already been discussed in chapter 2. Security has always been the primary concern of the prison, and approaches to design have reflected that concern. There are many categories of prison and jail design, and within each of these categories there is a good deal of variation.

Paul Tappan[14] offers a good summary of the evolution of early prison designs. The rectangular cell house is based upon the design of the Papal Prison of Saint Michael, opened in 1704 in Rome. This pattern was followed by the designers of the New York prisons at Auburn and Sing Sing, who allowed for considerably larger and longer corridors. The Pennsylvania system was copied from the workhouse at Ghent, Belgium, and the Panopticon plan of Jeremy Bentham was followed in the construction of the Illinois State Penitentiary at Stateville. The last of the Panopticon-design cell houses at Stateville was destroyed in the 1980s, but we can see its influence in some contemporary prison designs, such as the Illinois Shawnee Correctional Facility. The Panoptican design features a circular system with cells constructed around the circumference of the cell house.

Self-Enclosed Design

Many prisons are designed so that an exercise yard is enclosed by cell houses. One wall of the cell house comprises the exterior wall of the prison. Towers may then be strategically placed on the roof of the structures.

Telephone Pole Design

The telephone pole design features one long corridor with cell houses and other buildings extending outward along the corridor. The de-sign was first used in the construction of the prison at Fresnes, France, which opened in 1898. Today it is not uncommon to find the telephone pole design combined with separate rectangular buildings for industry, administration, and other support activities.

Until the last ten to fifteen years architects have failed to recognize the specialized nature of prisons and jails. Even today it is not uncommon to come across a new jail that is nothing more than a concrete box with doors. Such poorly designed facilities are unsafe for employees and inmates as well as demeaning to the spirit.

While a "good" design does not assure safety and sound programs, it goes a long way toward these goals. "Direct-supervision" jails appear to have had a profound effect on both prison and jail design. Anyone who has worked in prisons can assert that they have always worked in a direct-supervision situation. However, jails usually follow the linear or remote supervision design pattern, and it was (or is) a great challenge for many jailers to become accustomed to hands-on supervision. Two concepts have combined to reshape the design of U.S. prisons and jails. The first is the introduction of Functional Unit Management by the U.S. Bureau of Prisons with the Kennedy Youth Center at Morgantown, West Virginia. The second is the influence of Unit Management.

Once the U.S. Bureau of Prisons opened the Metropolitan Correctional Center in Chicago in 1974, architects and prison administrators began to note the value of soft architecture and soft furnishings in promoting a sense of ownership and harmony.[15] Nearly every state now has at least one new prison and several jails that are designed with the users in mind, illustrating the influence of the direct-supervision jail. Many prisons appear to be more like campuses than prisons, and the "cell houses" hardly do justice to the name.

FIGURE 13.5
Three Types of Jail Design

Linear Intermittent Surveillance

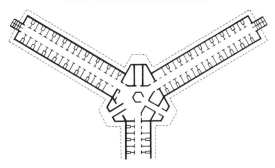

Podular Direct Supervision

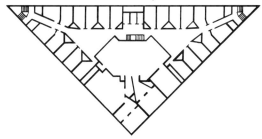

Podular Remote Surveillance

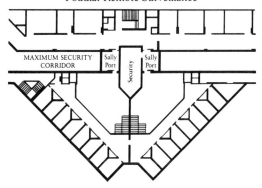

Source: W. Ray Nelson, Michael O'Tool, Barbara Krauth, and Coralie G. Whitman. *New Generation Jails: Corrections Information Series.* (Boulder: National Institute of Corrections, 1983).

Design and Control

What does design have to do with management? Quite a lot. Zupan[16] offers a good case for direct-supervision jails and reports that fear on the part of inmates and staff is reduced and that perceived orderliness is improved. Houston,[17] et al., also report improved perceptions of orderliness but find that social climate, as measured by the Correctional Institution Environment Scale, has little to do with the physical attractiveness of the facility. Clearly, something else must be at work. Early jails and prisons were characterized by many unsupervised areas, harsh architecture, and poorly trained staff. Today we are witnessing a new generation of prison and jail employees who are more committed and much better trained than their predecessors. Architecture is also improving. New approaches to prison and jail design stress safety and comfort without sacrificing cost-effectiveness. The National Institute of Correction's Jail Center,[18] in a publication aimed at jurisdictions contemplating building new jails, offers eight principles that are applicable to new generation jails and prisons.

- *Effective Control.* Jails and prisons are controlled environments where it is important to assure the safety and security of employees and inmates. Without total control and easily surveillable areas, service is faulty.
- *Effective Supervision.* The new generation institution allows staff to be proactive rather than reactive. It is important that staff be able to look out for each other and for the inmates. Effective leadership on the part of staff fosters effective supervision techniques.
- *Need for Competent Staff.* The well-managed correctional institution requires effective, competent staff who are unafraid of responsibility and leadership.
- *Safety of Staff and Inmates.* Kauffman[19]

and many others have documented the response of staff and inmates to an unsafe environment. If the manager is able to provide an environment where both inmates and staff are free from fear, everyone is a winner.

- *Manageable and Cost-Effective Operations.* New generation jails and prisons are at least more affordable than the old ones. New generation jails and prisons are characterized by: reduced construction costs, a wider range of architectural options, and reduced vandalism. Further, they anticipate fundamentals such as the inmates' need to communicate with others and they foster good sanitation and orderliness.
- *Effective Communication.* Communication between staff members, between staff and inmates, and between staff, inmates, and the administration is fostered by new generation jails and prisons.
- *Classification and Orientation.* An effective classification system is the bedrock upon which sound inmate management rests. Without it, chaos is likely to result, with injury to inmates and staff a strong possibility. New generation jails and prisons allow the proper classification of inmates and the housing of compatible types.

Budgets

Budgets are not only a tool for allocating resources, a mirror of organizational priorities, and a reflection of overall policy; they are also a tool for control. The organizational budget is a plan for allocating funds. As a control tool, it enables the manager to use receipts and records of expenditures to show that the organization is moving toward the accomplishment of stated objectives. If it is not, the manager is able to implement strategies aimed at bringing

expenditures into line with his or her philosophy.

The Management Information System (MIS)

Correctional organizations use four types of resources to accomplish their objectives: money, people, time, and information. McCleery[20] documents the importance of information and information control in a prison. He points out that "the pattern of communications in a social system may be considered a functional equivalent of power and a necessary supplement to force in the maintenance of a stable system of authority."[21] In today's world a corrections manager's inability to effectively organize and use information to enhance service, security, and the financial health of the organization may terminate his or her career.

Management information systems are computer based. The systems are used to store and sort the usual information relating to budget, personnel, inmate classification, and related items. They are also invaluable for storing other kinds of valuable information, such as vital facts about co-defendants who need to be separated and about inmates who have threatened to kill other inmates. Such cases must be tracked and kept separate. Other information relating to violence, escapes, and transfers are also helpful to the corrections manager.

MIS Defined

The corrections enterprise is big business and getting bigger every year. It is important that resources be used effectively and responsibly. Simply speaking, a management information system (MIS) is defined as "a network established within an organization to provide managers with information that will assist them in

FIGURE 13.6
Establishing an MIS

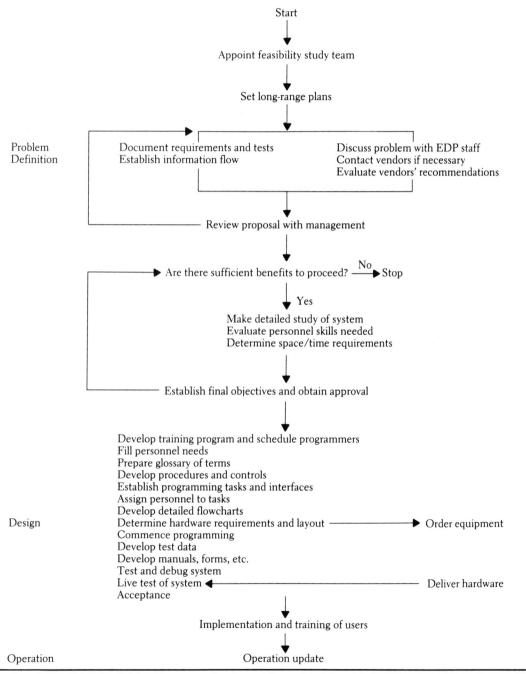

Source: Samuel Certo, *Principles of Modern Management: Functions and Systems,* 3d ed. Copyright © 1986 by Allyn and Bacon, Reprinted by permission.

decision making."[22] The Management Information System Committee of the Financial Executives Institute provides a more detailed definition of MIS:

> MIS is a system designed to provide selected decision-oriented information needed by management to plan, control, and evaluate the activities of the [organization] corporation. It is designed within a framework that emphasizes profit planning, performance planning, and control at all levels. It contemplates the ultimate integration of required business information subsystems, both financial and non-financial, within the company (organization).[23]

While Holms had private enterprise in mind when he conceived his definition, it is still valid for the public sector—substitute *service* for *profit, organization* for *corporation* or *company* and the definition remains apt. The important point to remember is that an MIS is a tool to help the manager understand and use the overwhelming amount of information that is available today. Wheeler provides us with a good definition of information: "the variables that are measured and aggregated to understand some aspect of the performance of the agency."[24] This definition encompasses variables such as "number of open cases per probation officer" and "number of inmates assigned to institutional case managers." Wheeler points out that today's manager often does not use this kind of information.

Twelve Steps to Developing an MIS

The workload of institutional and community programs personnel has increased greatly in recent years. Most agencies have an MIS in place, but some do not, and a few have made their systems available only to the central office.

The following twelve steps call our attention to the intricacies of developing an MIS:[25]

- *Developing a Mission Statement.* The importance of an organizational mission statement was discussed in an earlier chapter. Without it, the organization may be ineffectively organized.
- *Information and Agency Functions.* The organization's functions must be clarified in order to identify information required to support them. We can divide the functions into management support functions and service delivery functions. The manager must determine which functions are performed by the organization and which are not and which the MIS should support.
- *Work Flow and Information Systems.* Client service delivery functions need to be supported by the MIS in order for the manager to effectively perform his or her job. Before beginning, the manager and his or her subordinates need to thoroughly analyze the work flows, service functions, and management structure. Once the activities have been identified, a flow chart should be developed to illustrate the work flow.
- *Set Information Priorities to Support Decisions.* Users within the organization need to confer and identify the information needed for each activity and organizational component. For each activity, the following points must be considered: information needed for each step, the source of the information, where the information is recorded, and how the information generated by the activity will be used in the next activity in the work flow sequence.
- *System Resources and Constraints.* It is important that managers identify resources available for developing an MIS. It is also important to identify constraints. Questions to ask include: "Are personnel available who can design and program an MIS?"

"What is the operational deadline, and can we meet it?" "Is there enough money to do a good job?" "Can we adequately justify the cost?"

- *Choosing a System Development Group.* Basically, the manager has three options: do it within the organization (Is there already someone on the payroll with the expertise?), hire an expert (retain an outside consultant on contract), or transfer a system (find an already-operating system in another agency and replicate it for your own). This step includes hiring a company to maintain and troubleshoot the system.

- *Developing a Detailed Workplan.* The manager should require a workplan that includes tasks and activities as well as allotted times and dates. This should include GANTT and PERT charts to keep the project on time and within budget.

- *Completing the System Design.* After the hardware system has been selected, a detailed system design must be completed to include database design; a flowchart of the system; and identification, flowcharts, and specifications for each program.

- *Installing the System.* Install the hardware, write the programs (or load another agency's programs into the system), test the programs, make a test run of data to weigh the system's user-friendliness, design and conduct training programs for users, and develop and implement quality control procedures for the data.

- *Using the Information to Make Decisions.* The information the system generates is of no value if no one looks at it. Make sure the correct data are being collected, avoid misusing information, and use comparative data to help the manager understand the data.

- *Refine the System.* Be prepared to chop some reports, add others, and refine yet others. Do not be afraid to alter the system as the organization changes.

Unfriendly Systems

There are several pitfalls to having a management information system in the organization. Almost anyone could make a list of these, and all the lists would include a few of the following:

1. Too much information—we are able to use only so much information.
2. Incomprehensible printouts—If managers cannot understand the information on the printouts, they will go into the trash unused.
3. Useless reports—This is related to the first pitfall. We are often hesitant to delete reports.
4. Failure to update the system to keep abreast of court or legislative requirements.
5. Poor security—Inmate traffic should not prevent the placing of a terminal in any work area. Proper security includes assigned keys to turn the terminal on and off, procedures prohibiting inmates or clients from going near the terminal, and proper staff training in using the terminal.

Summary

The control function maintains organizational activity within the limits necessary to achieve organizational objectives. Related activities include establishing policy, budgeting, leading and managing groups, and planning. There are three important types of control: precontrol, concurrent control, and feedback control. Precontrol is control measures taken before the task is undertaken, such as standards that must be met. Concurrent control refers to control undertaken while the work is being performed, such as inventory control. Feedback control refers to control measures taken after the work is completed. The audit is an important feedback control tool.

The design of facilities is an important part of controlling activities of staff and inmates or clients. An important contribution to institutional control has been made through Unit Management and architecture. The management of information is also of critical importance. A management information system (MIS) is important to understanding and controlling the overwhelming amounts of information the correctional manager has to deal with.

In spite of the advances being made in the social sciences and in technology, managers often still believe that control is inherent in their position and that merely writing a memo, or worse, ignoring an issue will make it go away. The good manager knows that effective control begins long before he or she arrives at the office in the morning.

Reviewing the Case

Mr. Bingham knows that if the organization is to successfully supervise probationers, serve the needs of the court, and protect the public, the chief probation officer must have effective control measures in place. Knowing the organiza-tional culture is important, as is drawing competent subordinates into the process.

It is just as important, however, to correctly time organizational change and to explain the need for change. Only these will permit control mechanisms to be accepted as necessary rather than intrusive. Such control mechanisms may include performance evaluation, periodic staff meetings, and meeting organizational standards. Mr. Bingham points out that the organization that strives for excellence can only do so through teamwork and effective quality control.

For Further Study

James G. Houston, Don C. Gibbons, and Joseph F. Jones, "Physical Environment and Jail Social Climate," *Crime and Deliquency*, 34:4 (October 1988), pp. 449–66.
Amatai Etzioni. *A Comparative Analysis of Complex Organizations* (New York: The Free Press, 1975).

Key Terms

Control
Panoptican Design
Telephone Pole
    Design

Precontrol
Management
    Information
    System

Decision Making

CHAPTER 14

Case Study: Four Sites Weighed for New Prison

In 1989 the governor of Delaware was searching for a site for a new prison.[1] Spurring the search was a looming court-approved deadline for a decision on rebuilding the state's women's prison, along with chronic crowding in men's prisons.

In November 1988 Corrections Commissioner Robert J. Watson recommended building a $57 million, 600-bed prison in the Wilmington area to help solve the crowding problem. He said 200 of the beds may be needed for female inmates if the state opts to close the Women's Correctional Institution near Claymont.

By January 1989 the potential site list had been narrowed to four possibilities:

- The former Budd Metal Company, Inc., steel plant on U.S. 13A (South Herald Street) just south of the Wilmington line near South Bridge, Eden Park Gardens, and Hamilton Park.
- A former F. A. Potts Coal Company tract at the Port of Wilmington, once considered for purchase by the city to expand the port. The purchase was scuttled when suspicions surfaced that the property was contaminated.
- Property near Gander Hill Prison on East 12th Street.
- A Department of Transportation tract on Terminal Avenue east of I-495.

The finance secretary added that the administration intended to work closely with civic leaders and communities near the site that is eventually chosen in order to limit the project's effect on neighborhoods. The site selected would then be considered for local zoning review.

The finance secretary headed a committee of state, county, and city officials that collected information on possible locations for several weeks. The group reviewed both state and private properties throughout New Castle County north of the Chesapeake and Delaware Canal.

The secretary said the committee purposely avoided public discussion of potential sites in order to avoid creating what he described as needless worry in nearby communities. Details of the effort were kept under wraps.

Meanwhile, a state legislator said that the state should exclude the city's northeast section from consideration. The representative, calling for a meeting with Governor Castle, said the area was already home to the badly overcrowded Gander Hill Prison, which housed approximately 700 inmates, and to the 180-bed Plummer House Work Release Center. Gander Hill is designed to hold 360 inmates.

"We also consider it an insult when they say they want to make it more convenient for the residents of the area to visit members of their family," remarked the legislator. "We don't feel this is the only area of the state that has crime."

Prison officials have said they favor development of a prison north of the Chesapeake and Delaware Canal. They cited the rising cost of transporting detainees and inmates to and from court in New Castle County and the burden on families hoping to maintain contact with inmates.

"The committee believe they have a persuasive argument, given the location of Gander Hill and Plummer House Work Release Center, and we have taken that into consideration when we looked at the sites that were presented to us," the finance secretary said.

In a court-approved agreement on improving prison conditions state-wide, the administration agreed to settle on plans for a new 200-bed prison for women by January 31. The agreement called for the state to develop a new prison at the present site, the former Woods-Haven Kruse School for Girls, if the state fails to choose another spot by the deadline.

Introduction

There are few fields where the decision-making skills of managers and front-line personnel are so critical as in corrections.

The public must rely on the corrections bureaucracy to promote rationality in the organization, and the effective corrections manager must rely on rational, comprehensive decision making that specifies objectives and the most satisfactory means to achieve them. Some practitioners state that this approach is not always compatible with today's conditions and that the corrections manager must be capable of making decisions quickly, often in the heat of conflict. While this is true, most decisions are made in offices or committee meeting rooms. The task is difficult, but as Klofas, et al., point out:

> Improvement in decision making means rational decisions. But that goal must be considered within the content of the limits of rationality in the decision-making process. Organizations, individual decision makers, and information itself constrain decision making and assure that a purely rational model of decisions is not possible under the conditions of ambiguity that exist in criminal justice.[2]

Indeed, ambiguity and the U.S. corrections system seem to be synonymous. The pressures of overcrowding, AIDS, gangs, increasing numbers of long-term inmates, and an avalanche of clients in our probation and parole systems appear to render rational decision making most difficult. In addition, pressure from the courts, the legislature, special interest groups, and the media have created a climate capable of giving severe heartburn to the most seasoned decision maker.

Decision Defined

A decision is a judgment. It is a choice between two or more alternatives.[3] It is rarely a choice between right and wrong, but as Drucker points out, "it is at best a choice between 'almost right' and 'probably wrong'—but much more often a choice between two courses of action neither of which is probably more nearly right than the other."[4]

Corrections managers make decisions every day. Some of the decisions are significant and alter the course of the organization. Most are relatively insignificant, but necessary. A 1988 article in the *New York Times*[5] illustrates the types of decisions and the working climate of corrections managers.

The Connecticut Department of Corrections was playing a time-consuming game of musical beds because of overcrowding, so most of the state's correctional institutions were a half-step behind in meeting daily needs for beds. For example, the Connecticut State Penitentiary at Somers experienced such overcrowding that inmates were often transferred during the night to free up beds for new arrivals. In spite of all their best efforts, the staff often had to put mattresses on the floor of dayrooms just to keep up. The population pressure created a need to make decisions like the following on a daily basis:

- who to transfer and who to keep;
- because of high staff turnover, who to hire;
- because of budget constraints, which repair and maintenance jobs to begin and which to postpone; and
- which programs and budget requests to approve; what new facilities to build and where to site them.

Many of Connecticut's problems have been ameliorated somewhat through programs and an aggressive construction plan,[6] but overcrowding continues to be a major problem, as it is in most states. Small wonder that corrections managers develop strong decision-making abilities.

Decision Making in General

Johnson[7] identifies four models for decision making: the rational decision-making model, the organizational process model, the governmental politics model, and the garbage can model.

Rational Decision Making

Rational decision making requires first that the goals be clearly specified, next that all evidence and alternatives be considered, and finally that the best alternative be selected. Simon[8] and others point out that this model is an ideal that decision makers should adhere to as closely as possible.

There are several deliberate steps in this process. First, one identifies the goals to be achieved by the selected alternative. They should be ranked in order of priority. Second, alternative means of reaching each goal should be clearly defined. Third, the costs, risks, and consequences for each alternative should be listed, as well as the probability of whether the chosen alternative will achieve the goal. Fourth, alternatives should be compared to determine the relative costs of achieving each goal. Fifth, the optimum alternative should be chosen on the basis of cost and its likelihood of achieving the goal(s). Sixth, the chosen alternative should be implemented.

This approach's applicability to corrections is questionable. A great deal depends on the accuracy of information and the context of the decision. The rational decision-making model is contrasted with the **incremental model of decision making.** This less formal procedure "is a means of proceeding when the goals are not precise, the evidence and alternatives incomplete, and when political controversy inevitably shapes the final decisions."[9] Lindblom (introduced in chapter 2) discusses the incremental method and points out that it is "impossible to take everything important into consideration unless 'important' is so narrowly defined that analysis is in fact quite limited."[10] The incremental model stresses a short time horizon and is a means of attaining consensus among a group of people who do not agree on the goals or the means of achieving them. Thus, the incremental method stresses small victories and incremental steps in decision making rather than grand, sweeping decisions that immediately alter the course of an organization.

The Organizational Process Model

The **organizational process model** is a variation of the incremental model. In this model choices are less the product of rational thought than the output of a large organization behaving in an accustomed manner. Organizations have an established job to do, and given normal circumstances, certain decisions are made in the same manner day after day. For example, prison employees are responsible for the safety of the community. Therefore, each inmate must be assigned a close, medium, or minimum custody level. The decision about custody level may have originally been a rational selection, but sticking to that decision need not take much thought. The institution's aim is to minimize the time and effort necessary to make the decision as well as the tendency for staff members to bargain among themselves.

The Governmental Politics Model

The **governmental politics model** of decision making views decision making as the product of bargaining among the participants. It focuses on "the perceptions, motivations, positions, power, and maneuvers of the players."[11] In a sense, governmental politics decision making is a struggle for governance as much as it is a decision-making model. Competing actors have their own ideas of the right decision and compete to assert their views over others.

The Garbage Can Model

The **garbage can model**[12] is the opposite of the rational decision-making model.

> Choices emerge from a highly diverse network of decision makers that could be called "organized anarchy." Its members are many and changing. Its processes are not well grasped even by its regular participants, and they do not hold agreed-upon or consistent preferences. It lacks all of the qualities needed to sustain the rational process. . . . The "garbage can" itself does not really contain garbage but rather a collection of ideas about problems and solutions from which participants can draw depending on their interests and opportunities.[13]

Current problems with overcrowding illustrate the garbage can model. There are many views of what the highest priority should be: building more prisons, home detention, offering incentives for the counties to keep some of the felons, intensive probation, boot camps, and so on. Each is a goal and a means to other goals, including decreasing overcrowding in our prisons. The various levels of government pick ideas out of the garbage can, which leads to conflicting decisions.

Correctional Decisions

There are two kinds of decisions in corrections: inmate or client decisions, usually called case management decisions, and organizational or agency decisions. As in most other organizations, the position one holds determines the type of

FIGURE 14.1
Organizational and Case Management Decisions

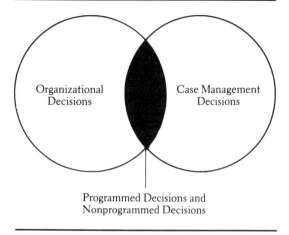

Organizational Decisions

Case Management Decisions

Programmed Decisions and
Nonprogrammed Decisions

decisions one makes on a regular basis. Thus, case managers and probation/parole officers make case management decisions that directly affect the community and its safety. Supervisors, department heads, and executives make decisions more directly related to policy and planning.

It is sometimes difficult to separate case management decisions from organizational decisions. For example, how does one categorize the psychologist's decision to recommend that an inmate she or he has determined is dangerous should be transferred to a more secure facility? Or the warden's decision to terminate the honor housing unit? Clearly, these decisions affect inmates and the organization. Figure 14.1 illustrates the overlap in case management and organizational decisions. Further, some of these decisions are programmed, that is, they are routine, repetitive decisions; and others are nonprogrammed, that is, they are novel, one-time occurrences.

Case Management Decisions

Case management decisions are those decisions that are made relative to custody or levels of supervision, programs, housing assignments, and the like. Case management decisions are based upon a classification system whose most important goal is to maintain institutional security. Apao[14] points out that in prisons traditional approaches to classification rely heavily on the clinical judgment and experience of corrections staff. Typically, the newly arrived inmate undergoes a battery of educational, medical, and psychological tests. He or she is interviewed, watched, and kept apart from the general population until a complete case summary or classification packet is completed. Often this is completed in a diagnostic and reception center where the inmate is kept until the classification process is completed. At that time he or she is transferred to an appropriate institution.

Obviously, most of the classification work is an attempt to predict future behavior. Decisions are made relative to the following questions:

- Will the inmate attempt to escape?
- Will the inmate exhibit episodes of violent behavior?
- Will the inmate be involved in misconduct in the institution?

Thus, predictive validity is important. Apao asserts, however, that predictive validity is difficult to achieve and that few, if any, instruments are of value in predicting an inmate's behavior while in prison. In his study of the National Institute of Corrections' (NIC) Custody Classification System he concluded that the accuracy of the model's predictions remains to be determined.

Specifically, he found that:

- Only five of the nineteen classification items were positively related to misconduct. The other fourteen were either negatively correlated or uncorrelated with misconduct.

- More of the needs assessment variables were significantly related to misconduct than were the custody classification variables.
- Correlations between total risk scores and misconduct indicate that attempts to discriminate between high- and low-risk inmates are useless.[15]

Predictive validity is important in that staff must be assured that what they observe is a reasonable indication of future conduct. The absence of reliability in case management decisions leads to arbitrary and capricious decisions, which in turn lead to sagging inmate morale, litigation, and even inmate disturbances. It should also be pointed out that overcrowding may completely invalidate classification procedures.

Thus, case management decision making is an imperfect science. The attempt to objectify the classification process is an illustration of the rational decision-making model. It is also an illustration of the organizational process model, in which the institution attempts to minimize time and effort in making decisions relative to such things as custody, housing assignments, and programs.

Figure 14.2 illustrates a matrix used by the U.S. Bureau of Prisons to establish the security level of an inmate. The team periodically reviews each inmate's security level to keep abreast of changes in sentence status, disciplinary reports, and so on. Traditionally these decisions were made intuitively, with judgments based upon prior record, instant offense, and institutional conduct. Since the 1970s, a more objective approach to case management decision making has been implemented.

The American Correctional Association points out that twenty-three states use some form of risk assessment when considering an inmate for parole.[16] The United States Parole Commission has been using parole guidelines

FIGURE 14.2
Security Matrix—U.S. Bureau of Prisons Custody Classification Form

A. **Identifying Data**	1. Institution	2. Unit	3. Date	
4. Name			5. Register Number	

6. Sentence Limitations	A—None B—Misdemeanants	C—NARA D—YCA	E—Study F—Parole or Mandatory Release Viol. Hearing	

7. Management Variables	A—None B—Judicial Recommendation C—Age D—Release Residence E—Population Management F—Racial Balance (Discont.) G—CIMS	H—Voluntary Surrender (Discont.) I—Med/Psych Treatment J—Custody K—Detainer L—Discipline M—Grandfather N—Program Participation	O—Security P—Sent. Limit Q—Sliding Scale R—Work Cadre S—PSF Waived T—Other	

8. Public Safety Factors	A—None B—Security Thrt. Group C—Grtst. Sever. Offense	D—Firearms E—High Drug (Discont.) F—Sex Offenders	G—Thrt Govt. Official H—Deportable Alien I—Sent. Length J—Des. Assmt. (Discont.)	

B. Base Scoring //

1. Type of Detainer	0 = None	1 = Lowest/Low Moderate	3 = Moderate	5 = High	7 = Greatest	

2. Severity of Current Offense	0—Lowest 1—Low Moderate	3—Moderate 5—High	7—Greatest	

3. Projected Length of Incarceration	0 = 0–12 mos.	1 = 13–59 mos.	3 = 60–83 mos.	5 = 84 + mos.	3A_____	

4. Type of Prior Commitments	0 = None	1 = Minor	3 = Serious	

5. History of Escapes or Attempts 6. History of Violence		None	>15 Yrs.	10-Yrs.	5–10 Yrs.	<5 Yrs.	
	Minor	0	1	1	2	3	
	Serious	0	4	5	6	7	

7. Precommitment Status	0 = Not Applicable	(–3) = Own Recognizance	(–6) = Voluntary Surrender	

8. Base Score	

C. Custody Scoring ///

1. Percentage of Time Served	3 = 0–25%	4 = 26–75%	5 = 76–90%	6 = 91 + %	

2. Involvement with Drugs/Alcohol	2 = Within Past 5 Years	3 = More Than 5 Years Ago	4 = Never	

3. Mental/Psychological Stability	2 = Unfavorable	4 = No Referral or Favorable	

4. Type & Number of Most Serious Incident Report	0 = Any Greatest (100) in Past 10 Yrs. 1 = More Than 1 High (200) in Past 2 Yrs. 2A = Only 1 High (200) in Past 2 Yrs. 2B = More Than 1 Moderate (300) in Last Yr.	3A = Only 1 Moderate (300) in Past Year 3B = More Than 1 Low Mod. (400) in Past Yr. 4 = Only 1 Low Mod. (400) in Last Year 5 = None	

5. Frequency of Disciplinary Reports in Past Yr.	0 = 6 +	1 = 2 Thru 5	2 = 1	3 = None	

6. Responsibility Demonstrated	0 = Poor	2 = Average	4 = Good	

7. Family/Community Ties	3 = None or Minimal	4 = Average or Good	

8. Custody Total	

9. Custody Variance — Custody Total (Section C, Item 8)

BASE SCORE	10	11	12	13	14	15	16	17	18	19	20	21	22	23	24	25	26	27	28	29	30
0–6 Pts.	+10	+9	+8	+7	+6	+5	+4	+3	+2	+1	0	0	0	–1	–2	–3	–4	–5	–6	–7	–8
7–9 Pts.	+10	+9	+8	+7	+6	+5	+4	+3	+2	+1	0	0	0	0	–1	–2	–3	–4	–5	–6	–7
10–13 Pts.	+10	+9	+8	+7	+6	+5	+4	+3	+2	+1	0	0	0	0	0	–1	–2	–3	–4	–5	–6
14–22 Pts.	+10	+9	+8	+7	+6	+5	+4	+3	+2	+1	0	0	0	0	0	0	0	–1	–2	–3	–4
23–36 Pts.	+10	+9	+8	+7	+6	+5	+4	+3	+2	+1	0	0	0	0	0	0	0	0	–1	–2	–3

10. Security Total—Add or Subtract Custody Variance (Above) to Base Score (Section B, Item 8)	
11. Security Level	

FIGURE 14.2 *(Continued)*
Security Matrix—U.S. Bureau of Prisons Custody Classification Form

Custody Classification—Page 2	

12. Custody Change Consideration
    A. If custody variance score (Section C, Item 9) is in the plus range, consider a custody increase
    B. If custody variance score (Section C, Item 9) is in the minus range, consider a custody decrease
    C. If custody variance score (Section C, Item 9) is zero, the present custody should continue.	

Section D: Institution Action	
1. Type of Review: (Exception or Regular)	
2. Current Custody: (Maximum, In, Out, Community)	
3. New Custody: (Maximum, In, Out, Community)	
4. Action: (Approve, Disapprove)	
5. Date of Next Review	
6. Chairperson's Name and Signature	
7. For Exception Review Name (Warden or Designee) and Signature	
8. Summary of Final Action: Security Level Custody	

Source: Courtesy of U.S. Bureau of Prisons.

since the mid-1970s. The guidelines, called Salient Factor Scores, are historical (that is, they rely upon the past history of the individual) and attempt to predict future behavior.[17] Bartollas and Conrad discuss judges' use of sentencing guidelines. While many members of the judiciary object to their use, many others appreciate their value.

The use of a matrix by parole boards and judges is part of an overall attempt to objectify difficult decisions. Things are no different for the institutional case manager, counselor, or probation officer. Difficult decisions must be made, and the task is made easier by use of a matrix. As pointed out earlier in the chapter, the U.S. Bureau of Prisons and several other departments of corrections use a computer-generated matrix to determine security levels of inmates.

Organizational Decisions

The difference between case management decisions and organizational decisions lies in the kind of job one has in the organization and the manager's level in the organization. As a rule, the higher-up the manager, the greater discretion she or he is able to exercise. The higher one goes in the managerial hierarchy, the more frequently broad, complex problems "that defy routine or detailed solutions are encountered. Decision criteria are vague, and solutions to decision problems are ordinarily given in terms of policy guidelines."[18]

FIGURE 14.3
Salient Factors and Their Scores

U.S. Department of Justice	Preliminary Assessment/Parole-Reparole
United States Parole Commission	Guideline Worksheet

Institution _____

Name: _____ Reg. No. _____ Hearing Date: _____

Reasons: (*Circle and complete each applicable reason*)

1. Your (*offense*) (*parole violation*) behavior has been rated as Category _____ severity because
_____
_____
_____

Your salient factor score (SFS-81) is _____ (*See below*). You have been in (*federal*) (*state*) (*state and federal*) confinement as a result of your behavior for a total of _____ months. Guidelines established by the Commission indicate a range of _____ months to be served for cases with a good institutional adjustment and program achievement.

2. Also, you (*failed to appear*) (*escaped or attempted to escape*) (*from*) (*secure*) (*non-secure*) (*custody*) (*with voluntary return in 6 days or less*) which requires (*0–6*) (*6–12*) (*8–16*) months to be added to your original guideline range.

3. In addition, you have committed rescission behavior classified as administrative. Guidelines established by the Commission indicate a range of (*up to 8 months per drug-related infraction*) (*and*) (*up to 2 months for non-drug related infractions*). You have committed (_____ *drug-related infraction(s)*) (*and*) (_____ *non-drug related infraction(s)*).

4. Your aggregate guideline range is _____ months to be served.

SALIENT FACTORS

A. PRIOR CONVICTIONS/ADJUDICATIONS (ADULT OR JUVENILE) . . . . ☐
   None = 3; One = 2; Two or three = 1; Four or more = 0

B. PRIOR COMMITMENT(S) OF MORE THAN THIRTY DAYS (ADULT OR JUVENILE) . . . . ☐
   None = 2; One or two = 1; Three or more = 0

C. AGE AT CURRENT OFFENSE/PRIOR COMMITMENTS . . . . ☐
   Age at commencement of current offense;
   26 years of age or more = 2*; 20–25 years of age = 1*; 19 years of age or less = 0
   *EXCEPTION: If five or more prior commitments of more than thirty days
   (adult or juvenile), place an 'x' here——and score this Item = 0

D. RECENT COMMITMENT FREE PERIOD (THREE YEARS) . . . . ☐
   No prior commitment of more than thirty days (adult or juvenile) or
   released to the community from last such commitment at least three
   years prior to the commencement of the current offense = 1; Otherwise = 0

E. PROBATION/PAROLE/CONFINEMENT/ESCAPE STATUS VIOLATOR THIS TIME . . . . ☐
   Neither on probation, parole, confinement, or escape status at the time
   of the current offense; nor committed as a probation, parole, confinement,
   or escape status violator this time = 1; Otherwise = 0

F. HEROIN/OPIATE DEPENDENCE . . . . ☐
   No history of heroin/opiate dependence = 1; Otherwise = 0

TOTAL SCORE . . . . ☐

On the basis of available documents concerning your case, the Commission has prepared a preliminary guideline assessment for your review prior to your in-person hearing. The final guideline determination in your case will be made after your in-person hearing. At the time of your hearing, you may present to the examiner panel documentary information concerning the evaluation of your case, which you believe may affect your guidelines.

5. After review of all relevant factors and information presented,
   (a) A decision outside the guidelines at this consideration is not found warranted.

(*continued next page*)

FIGURE 14.3 (*Continued*)
Salient Factors and Their Scores

(b) A decision (*above*) (*below*) the guidelines appears warranted because:
 ☐ Your offense behavior involved the following (*aggravating*) (*mitigating*) factors;
 ☐ You are a (*poorer*) (*better*) risk than indicated by your salient factor score in that:
 ☐ You are a more serious risk than indicated by your salient factor score in that:
 ☐ You have a record of (*institutional misconduct*) (*superior institutional program achievement*), specifically:
 ☐ A decision above the guidelines is mandated in that you have a minimum sentence which exceeds the guideline range.
 ☐ The following (*exceptional*) (*circumstances*) are present:

_____

_____

_____

_____

_____

_____

Note: When using more than one reason in 5(b), number each and draw a line from the colon to each applicable continuation.

6. Other _____

_____

_____

7. The above decision includes a _____ month credit for superior program achievement; specifically:

_____

_____

8. A decision more than 48 months above the minimum guideline range is warranted because _____

_____

_____

Note: For Category Eight, no upper limits are specified due to the extreme variability of the cases within this category. For decisions exceeding the lower limit of the applicable guideline category BY MORE THAN 48 MONTHS, the pertinent aggravating case factors considered are to be specified in the reasons given (*e.g., that a homicide was premeditated or committed during the course of another felony; or that extreme cruelty or brutality was demonstrated*).

9. As required by law, you have also been scheduled for a statutory interim hearing (*during* _____ (*during the docket immediately preceding completion of the minimum term*).

Revocation hearing checklist (*TYPIST DO NOT TYPE*)   Examiner's Initials:
                    _____ (Primary)
                    _____ (Secondary)

 ☐ Has received notice of hearing
 ☐ Has completed Forms CJA-22 and I-16(F-2)
 ☐ Advised of right to Counsel (*retained or court-appointed*)
 ☐ Advised of right to have voluntary witnesses
 ☐ Has had sufficient time to prepare case and/or confer with attorney
 ☐ Advised of right to cross-examine adverse witnesses (*mention only if adverse witnesses are present*)
 ☐ Advised of informal, non-adversary nature of hearing
 ☐ Advised will receive recommendation today and final decision in 21 days, except in emergencies
 ☐ Advised of right of appeal
 ☐ Has received a copy of Form H-20 (*warrant application*), including supplements
 ☐ Advised of right to present explanation of charges, after admitting or denying same

Source: Courtesy of U.S. Parole Commission.

While the case manager or probation officer is primarily concerned with case management decisions, correctional managers are concerned with nonprogrammed decisions relating to policy, budget, and personnel. Further, the type of organizational structure has a great deal to do with who participates in what decisions.[19]

Who Makes Decisions?

There are many different kinds of decisions to be made in a correctional organization, ranging from what supplies and equipment should be purchased to whom should be recommended for discharge from probation or for parole. Other decisions involve policy, budget, and personnel. The unifying goals of such diverse decisions are safety to the community, service, and management of organizational resources. With such variety in types of decisions, there must be some rationale for who makes what decision.

One approach to decision making is based upon two factors: (1) the scope of the decision and (2) the level of management. The **scope of the decision** refers to how much of the management subsystem is involved in the decision, and the **level of management** refers to line, mid-level, or executive management.

At the line level, the case manager and the team, which usually includes other staff such as psychologists, officers, counselors, or the probation officer, decide who is to be recommended for parole or discharged from probation. The mid-level manager, such as the unit manager, mechanical services manager, or supervisor in a large probation department, will determine whom to recommend for promotion and whether to purchase a piece of equipment or machinery (if budgeted). The executive will decide on programs and policy. In most of these decisions, the manager can ask for group input

and solicit the advice of others. This is the point at which the style of leadership and type of organization enter into the process (see chapters 10, 11, and 13). Figure 14.4 illustrates the levels of management and the responsibility for making decisions. Note that it corresponds roughly to figure 11.5, which shows that the subordinate-centered leader allows more input from subordinates.

Types of Decisions

Decisions are of two types: **programmed** and **nonprogrammed**. A programmed decision is routine, and usually the organization has developed ways to make it. For example, when an inmate requests a lower security rating, a routine procedure allows the matter to be considered. A nonprogrammed decision is unstructured, novel, and often one-time. For example, building a new jail involves a nonprogrammed decision. Other nonprogrammed decisions include whether to start a new drug treatment program or alter visiting hours in a penitentiary.

The Decision-Making Process

It is impossible to divorce the planning process from the decision-making process. Planning is the **premise**. Once we are certain of our goals, the next step is to develop alternatives. There are always alternatives to every situation that need to be discussed. Perhaps it is this process that sets Japanese business organizations apart from their U.S. counterparts. Americans tend to focus on the answer; the Japanese stress definition of the question. In Japanese organizations no one is forced to take sides during the debate; thus, defeat for one side or the other is ruled out. Consensus is obtained, but at the expense of time. Westerners find this

FIGURE 14.4
Managerial Responsibility and Decision Making

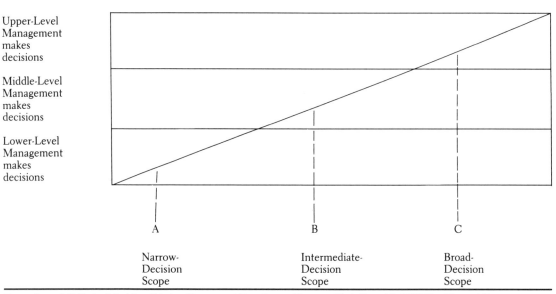

Source: Samuel C. Certo, *Principles of Modern Management: Functions and Systems,* 3d ed. Copyright © 1986 by Allyn and Bacon.

frustrating. David Halberstam in *The Reckoning* points out that during the early 1970s the Japanese had to be "dragged kicking and screaming into the American automobile market."[20] One suspects that this reluctance signified not so much a fear of defeat, as he noted, but the Japanese approach to decision making. However, once the goal was clarified and the question defined, it did not take long for the Japanese to corner a large share of the U.S. automobile market, thus illustrating the value of planning, discussions, and thoughtful decision making.

There are four identifiable steps in rational decision making: (1) premising (planning), (2) identifying alternatives, (3) evaluating alternatives in light of the goal, and (4) choosing an alternative (making a decision).[21] Planning has already been discussed in detail.

Identifying Alternatives

Once the goal is identified, the decision maker must identify alternatives. If no alternatives have been identified, then perhaps the manager has not thought hard enough or has surrounded him- or herself with "yes men." Alfred P. Sloan, famed CEO and chairman of the board of General Motors from 1937 to 1956, is reported to have said at a committee meeting, "Gentlemen, I take it we are all in complete agreement on the decision here." Everyone present nodded agreement. "Then," continued Mr. Sloan, "I propose we postpone further disussion of this matter until our next meeting to give ourselves time to develop disagreement and perhaps gain some understanding of what the decision is all about."[22] One of Sloan's strengths was his refusal to arrive at a conclusion and then cast about for facts and/or supporters to back it up.

There are three reasons why dissent is necessary.[23]

- It safeguards the decision maker from becoming a prisoner of the organization. Everyone wants something from the manager, and the only way to avoid preconceived notions and pressure from special interests is to encourage thoughtful and well-documented disagreement.
- Disagreements alone can provide alternatives to a decision. For example, a sheriff once had to deal with overcrowding in an old, decrepit jail. His goal, of course, was to provide a measure of safety to the taxpayer at a reasonable cost. The alternatives were to push for a large, new jail or to rehabilitate the old jail and to expand the use of other sanctions, including a work-release center where inmates could work and pay at least a portion of the costs of housing them. The sheriff initiated a heated debate over the two alternatives that lasted several weeks. Eventually he obtained a measure of consensus on the decision to rehabilitate the old jail and open a work-release center. The decision saved the county several millions of dollars and has worked out to everyone's satisfaction.
- Disagreement is necessary to stimulate the imagination. Bureaucracies are known for their stifling of imagination and creativity. If we are to find creative solutions, we need to step outside of traditional ways of looking at problems and solutions and find or develop new paradigms.[24]

Evaluation of Alternatives

A manager must accept "**limited rationality**"; that is, the limitations of information, time, and certainty. He or she must recognize that one is not always able to choose the best of all alternatives. Often one must settle for the best alternative possible under the circumstances. Simon calls this *satisficing*.[25] For example, a chief probation officer wants to create a new position for a probation officer who will supervise and counsel clients with a history of drug abuse or addiction. Since it is a small, rural county, county council will not approve the new position. However, after some negotiation, the council does set aside a lesser amount of money for limited counseling for clients. *Satisficing*: a reality all too familiar to corrections managers.

In chapter 6 the QSPM is discussed as a way to assess policy alternatives. The QSPM is merely a more elaborate process of one that we often carry out in our daily lives. This is rational decision making in simplified form. We break the process into three steps: (1) we list the alternatives; (2) we assign a level of probability for success to each alternative; and (3) we select the alternative that represents the best chance for achieving the stated goal.

Tools for Specifying Alternatives

There are several methods to help the manager evaluate alternatives. Two of these methods are scenario writing and simulation.

Scenario Writing

Scenarios are descriptions of future conditions and events.[26] When we make a decision, we are attempting to shape the future. However, the future is not only unknown, it is also subject to external events and conditions. Scenario writing is an attempt to predict the future based upon known quantities. That is, we try to make the incomprehensible comprehensible.

Since our knowledge of the future is imperfect, we attempt to improve our understanding through the **Modeling Technique;** that is, a method of showing causal relationship between two events.

$$Y \longrightarrow Z$$

Simply stated, a change in Y leads to a change in Z.

Hirschhorn[27] offers a typology of scenarios. Two are offered below:

- *State Scenarios*—These are broken into end state and process scenarios. A **state scenario** is based upon an imagined condition in the future; a **process scenario** specifies a chain of events that leads up to a particular future state.
- *Predictive/Planning Scenarios*—These scenarios are used primarily for planning. Emphasis is on accuracy and validity. The decision maker can also use the scenario to stimulate further discussion and to provoke unexpected ideas.

Simulation

Computers are indispensable to simulation. The technique is frequently performed when there are a large number of variables, making exploration of each variable impracticable. The decision maker or analyst must have a good grasp of the factors involved and how they interact.

> Like scenario writing, the process of constructing a simulation reveals the interrelationships among variables, some of which are presumably under the analyst's control. The effect of changing some of these variables can be predicted by changing the computer program accordingly. Assuming that the model is an accurate representation of the way in which factors produce outcomes, the policy consequences of various administrative actions can be predicted with the simulation. The technique is thus particularly valuable when actual experiments on target populations are impractical, unethical, or too slow to be of practical benefit.[28]

Choosing an Alternative

Many managers rely heavily on intuition and other subjective means[29] to make decisions. However, two of the more popular objective means of decision making are probability theory and decision trees.

Probability Theory

It is very difficult to quantify variables, and some managers rebel at attempts to quantify relationships.[30] We use statistics to describe a sample population, and we say that, for example, probationers in our court are on average 22.4 years of age or that they possess 11.6 years of formal education.

On the other hand, "probability is the 'reverse' of statistics: in probability we use the population information to infer the probable nature of the sample."[31] Probability is important in decision making. For example, do you allow an inmate to participate in a community program to help clean state parks when he has absconded from probation and parole and attempted an escape from a medium-security institution? Your answer should be an emphatic "No!" If the man has demonstrated that he has been unwilling in the past to stay home while on probation or parole and has attempted an escape, we say that it is improbable that he will refrain from further attempts just a few months after the latest episode.

In corrections management we face two types of situations relative to decision making: **deterministic** situations and **stochastic** situations. The former are situations in which the environment approaches certainty; that is, before the decision is made all relationships relevant to the decision problem are known precisely as well as the values of all relevant variables. In this instance we are often able to make the best possible decision. The latter are situations in which the environment is uncertain. In other words, relationships relevant to the decision problem and values of relevant variables are unknown. Thus, in a stochastic situation we do not know whether we have made the right decision until after the decision has been implemented.[32]

For example, if we flip a two-headed coin, we can say with certainty that if we call heads, we will be correct 100 percent of the time. In other words, out of ten tosses of the coin we will get ten heads. On the other hand, using a conventional coin we have a 50 percent chance of getting heads on any given coin toss. Thus, we say that in all probability we have a 50–50 chance of getting heads. No matter how many times we toss the coin we still have a probability of 50–50 coming up heads.

The same process, albeit much more sophisticated, is used to examine many variables for many cases in developing the actuarial tables called sentencing guidelines used by judges and parole guidelines used by boards of parole. Thus, we can see that there is a certain power of quantitative techniques in managerial decision making.

Most often money is used as the quantifier when the manager is concerned about costs and services. In this period of greater demand for services and shrinking budgets, many policymakers' and analysts' decisions are driven by financial considerations. The **expected outcome** for an alternative is the **cost** (C) incurred by the taxpayer divided by any **offsetting income** (I). Expressed:

$$EO = \frac{C}{I}$$

Thus, the decision maker will implement the outcome that has the least cost to the taxpayer and the greatest probability of a return on the investment.

For example, the assistant commissioner for community services has been allotted $250,000 for start up of one work-release center. Two cities need the center equally, as determined by numbers of parolees returning to the city annually. One way of making the decision can be based on the number of jobs available to parolees, who are then able to reimburse the state a portion of income for room and board. City A, for example, has suffered severe economic hardship for a decade. Industries have moved, and welfare roles are the highest in the state. City B, on the other hand, is rebounding. Jobs in manufacturing and service are available, and the commissioner and parole board are willing to tolerate inmate transfers and transfer of supervision of inmates from City A to City B. Consequently, in considering the formula $EO = \frac{C}{I}$ the assistant commissioner concludes that opening a work-release center in City B is the best decision because it will allow the Department of Corrections to recover a portion of day-to-day operating costs through room-and-board charges to the residents.

Decision Trees

Most important decisions facing the corrections manager will not be made right away. Rather, the manager will take the time to gather information, develop alternatives, and evaluate the alternatives. One tool available to managers is the *decision tree*. A **decision tree** is "a graphical model that displays the sequence of decisions and the events that comprise a sequential decision situation."[33] The value of the decision tree is that it (1) enables the manager to construct a model to identify inadequacies in her or his mental model, (2) helps the manager determine whether additional information is needed, and (3) serves as an organized external memory and helps the manager communicate with subordinates.[34]

FIGURE 14.5
The Decision Tree (Branches)

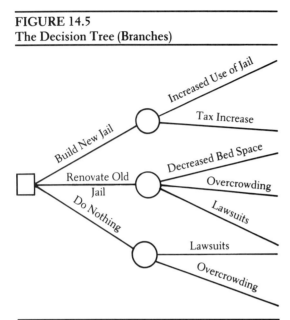

FIGURE 14.6
The Decision Tree (Leaves)

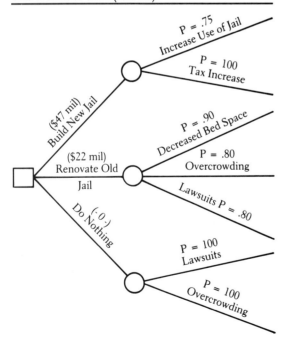

Constructing a Tree—the Branches
Begin at the left and work to the right:

- Lay out the alternatives like branches. In figure 14.5 the decision maker laid out as branches the alternatives of building a new jail, renovating the old jail, and doing nothing. The square from which the fork originates is called a *choice fork*.
- Choosing an alternative leads to one or more outcomes. This is represented by the manager's drawing of a circle at the end of each alternative branch. The circles represents outcome forks. The manager may then draw branches corresponding to various positive or negative outcomes of the alternatives.

Constructing a Tree—the Leaves

- For each alternative, indicate the costs of implementation. Some costs can be calculated, such as costs of building a new jail or renovating the old jail. Other costs associated with outcomes can only be estimated.
- For each outcome, indicate the probability of its occurrence.
- If applicable, indicate the gross payoff (in dollars) at the end of the outcome branch.

Constructing a Tree—Pruning
Once the information has been gathered and the tree constructed, it may be necessary to aggregate the information and construct a new tree. To do this:

- Compute the net expectation at each outcome fork in terms of probability. In our example, we conclude that the only feasible alternatives are to either build a new jail or renovate the old one.
- Estimate the expected probability for each outcome.
- If applicable, estimate the dollar payoff each alternative provides.

Summary

A decision is a judgment, a choice between alternatives. Every day corrections managers make critical decisions that affect the safety and well-being of the community. In corrections there are two types of decisions: case management decisions and organizational decisions.

FIGURE 14.7
The Decision Tree (Pruning)

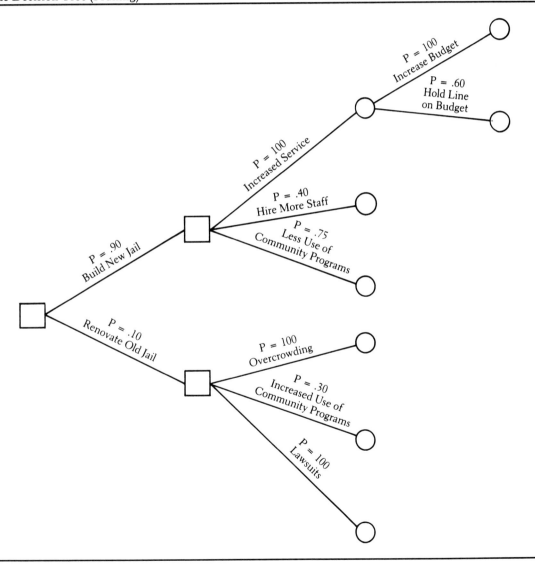

What decisions one makes depends upon the position one holds in the hierarchy. The higher up the manager is in the organization, the more likely it is that he or she will be concerned primarily with organizational decisions.

Decisions are of two types: programmed and nonprogrammed. Programmed decisions are those that are routine and for which the organization has a procedure that allows all similar decisions to be handled in the same way. Nonprogrammed decisions are unstructured, novel, and often one-time.

Two tools available to help the decision maker are scenario writing and simulation. Both tools attempt to make the incomprehensible comprehensible. Finally, probability theory and decision trees help the manager choose an alternative. It is important to remember that decisions are made at all levels in corrections and that all are important to the safety of the community.

Reviewing the Case

The Department of Corrections had a difficult decision to make. Overcrowding had forced the decision to build a new institution in order to accommodate the increasing numbers of inmates. Following that decision a site needed to be selected, and presumably following that

decision an architect and a design were selected.

Difficult choices indeed, but if the commissioner of corrections ordered subordinates to give him the best alternatives, they knew that they had several tools at their disposal. Probability theory would have allowed them to quantify alternatives, and a computer simulation could have allowed them to consider all variables for each site and provide information about a prison's impact on each probable site.

The decision to build is an example of a nonprogrammed decision arrived at after much work. After the institution opens and the inmates arrive, staff will be involved in case management decisions, many of which will be programmed decisions.

For Further Study

Richard D. Bingham and Marcus E. Ethridge, eds., *Reaching Decisions in Public Policy and Administration* (New York: Longman, 1982).

John Michalasky, "ESP in Decision Making," *Management Review* (April 1975), pp. 32–37.

Key Terms

Decision	Programmed Decisions
Case Management Decisions	Limited Rationality
	Decision Tree

TOPICS OF SPECIAL INTEREST

PART VI

The field of corrections is riddled with problems, such as health issues, an aging population, overcrowding, and ethical questions. The three chapters in this section touch on nearly all pressing problems that the corrections manager must deal with today.

Chapter 15 points out that Unit Management is both a management approach and a service delivery system. Corrections executives need to view Unit Management as a way to address staff and inmate problems. Since quality of service is uppermost on the minds of elected officials and executives, the final part of the chapter deals with Total Quality Management and the role Unit Management can play in assuring the quality of security and programs.

A major issue in the field of corrections today is overcrowding. Some entrepreneurs and elected officials have pushed privatization as an answer to that problem. Does privatization offer a solution to the problem of overcrowding? What are some of the ethical problems with privatization? Do private corporations do as good a job as public agencies? These and other questions are probed in chapter 16.

The final chapter looks at ethics and the corrections employee. A critical review of ethics and the field of corrections is presented, followed by a suggested standard for ethical decision making. Finally, the social responsibility of correctional organizations is looked at in an effort to arrive at a model.

Unit Management in a Correctional Institution

Case Study: Lockdown at Prison Heightens Tensions

Pendleton, Ind.—An unprecedented lockdown at the Indiana Reformatory here has turned the prison into a "hornets' nest," buzzing with rumors and leaving residents depressed and frustrated, friends of inmates say.[1]

Although no date has been set for lifting the restrictions, prison officials say they are trying to address the situation with a proposal to isolate the most dangerous inmates. The plan, expected in the form of a task force report, could be in place within months at the maximum-security prison.

"The changes will be significant," said Superintendent Jack Duckworth.

The 1,650 inmates have been restricted to their cells since November 2. Normally, they would spend at least seven hours a day out of their cells at an education class or a prison industry. Warden Duckworth stated that the new guidelines would affect inmates known by correction staffers as "predators," who prey upon weaker inmates through extortion and sexual abuse.

"We are endeavoring to put together a place and program for those individuals so they can be incarcerated and still not be a threat," said Duckworth, who estimated that 15 percent of the offenders are considered "predatory."

CHAPTER 15

The guidelines would "separate them from the general population so the majority of the institution can go ahead and operate and follow positive pursuits instead of being in fear," Duckworth said. The task force developing the guidelines also has been reviewing the operation of the entire prison during what is believed to be the longest lockdown ever at the sixty-nine-year-old institution.

Timetable May Be Set

Correction officials will not say when the lockdown will end. This week the warden will give Correction Commissioner James E. Aiken a proposed timetable for resuming normal operations at the prison. In the meantime, interviews with family members who have seen inmates since visits resumed last month suggest tensions are increasing.

"It is like a hornets' nest. If you bottle it up and shake it up, the madder the hornets are going to get.... That is the tone of the letters we are getting," said Richard A. Waples, legal director for the Indiana Civil Liberties Union.

Margaret J. Bogard, a registered nurse at a local hospital who corresponds with several inmates, said the extended lockdown appears to be affecting the inmates' physical and mental health.

"These guys look like death warmed over," she said after a recent visit. "I'm a psychiatric nurse, and they [prison staffers] are doing a perfect job, like the Nazis did on the Jews. They want them weak so they won't do anything when they get out."

Telephone privileges were severed, and inmates are limited to just a few showers per month. While correction officers swept the institution for weapons and other contraband, inmates received cold sack lunches in their cells. Currently, each inmate receives one hot meal per week.

"The person I visited is getting depressed, and angry, and extremely frustrated," said an Indianapolis woman who has been visiting the inmate for more than a decade.

"Over the weeks it has developed into bitterness and a lot of anger. He was just so upset [during a recent visit] that I just sat and listened," she said, asking that her name be withheld.

Dozens of Rumors

The length of the lockdown has prompted rumors to swirl through the sprawling complex on the outskirts of Pendleton.

Some were relayed to *The Indianapolis Star* by friends and relatives of reformatory inmates. All the rumors were denied by the Indiana Department of Correction. They include:

- A theory that the lockdown took place so officers could search the complex for missing documents that would show prison officials have misspent or stolen $50,000.
- Allegations that the lockdown is designed to provoke a riot that would draw attention away from official mismanagement of the maximum-security facility.
- A report that correction officers presented Duckworth with a petition asking for the lockdown to end. (Union officials also denied this.)
- Allegations that many of the weapons displayed to the news media last month were recovered in earlier searches.

Breaking a long-term official silence on the specific reason for the lockdown, Glenn Lawrence, a Department of Correction spokesman, said it was prompted by two factors:

- The first was a demonstration in the prison exercise yard. The silent protest by a handshaking circle of 150 inmates was a show of support for inmates who had engaged in a thirty-seven-day hunger strike to protest conditions at Westville Correctional Center. Institutional officials generally dislike organized displays of unity among inmates.
- The second factor involved reports of possible threats against staff at the prison, Lawrence said. "We received some information that there were names of our people, not necessarily officers, but also administrators who were targeted for retaliation. We also learned of some plans to disrupt the operation of the institution," said Lawrence. "We heard everything from filing grievances to hostage taking and even further," he said, but declined to elaborate.

Lockdown Needed?

Despite the security claims made by the department, family members and friends of the inmates doubt the continuing lockdown is needed. The shakedowns [search for weapons] occurred during December, and some families wonder what the point of the current lockdown is at this late date. "Was it the demonstration in the exercise yard? Did they get so upset or frightened that they overreacted?" wonders an Indianapolis woman who visits an inmate. She also asked that her name be withheld.

Civil Liberties Union legal director Waples is also increasingly skeptical of the department's security concerns.

"They have had enough time to search that institution from top to bottom five times," he said.

"We have jawboned with the DOC, as has the Legal Services Organization, to get them to either shorten the lockdown or unlock the institution. They keep saying it is going to end real soon," said Waples.

Since the lockdown began, requests for legal aid from reformatory inmates have tripled, and the Civil Liberties Union may file a lawsuit to try to bring an end to the lockdown.

"One of the most onerous aspects of the lockdown is that some of the inmates have been denied the opportunity to engage in educational activities," Waples said.

Lawrence agreed that some of the inmates who are taking courses offered by Ball State University at the prison might have to take incompletes.

"Programs and jobs go on the back burner, and security becomes paramount," Lawrence said.

When asked if the continuing lockdown was being conducted so Warden Duckworth and his staff could regain control over a prison that friends or relatives of inmates say is actually being run by the inmates, Lawrence responded "We feel the environment of the institution, which has been tenuous at best over the past many years, will be more secure." In spite of the promise of future security, the lockdown continues to grate.

"This is one of the longest, and I am afraid it has taken its biggest toll on the person I go visit," said an inmate's friend.

Introduction

The management of prisons and jails is a difficult task. Traditionally, many institutions and their parent agencies have relied on the pyramidal type of organizational structure, with most decisions and policy moving top to bottom. During the 1970s the U.S. Bureau of Prisons pioneered Unit Management and revolutionalized the way many corrections executives view correctional management.

Unit Management springs from notions about decentralization. Adherents point to two central arguments in favor of decentralization:

- Certain matters may be handled better at the local level and should remain there.
- Administrative officials at the center may act in an arbitrary and capricious manner.[2]

The decision by the U.S. Bureau of Prisons to adopt Unit Management reflected a general trend in the 1970s to decentralize. Many companies in the private sector as well as public agencies learned that their structure was too rigid to quickly adapt to market conditions or public need. In government there began a move toward decentralization and the adoption of work teams. Many probation and parole agencies adopted the team approach with successful results.

The Bureau of Prisons had been a traditional pyramidal agency with the director at the top and layers of the organization spreading out beneath him. Policy and budgetary decisions were sent out in a top-down approach that often failed to take account of input from lower levels.

By 1970 the U.S. Bureau of Prisons had two needs.[3] One was to reduce tension and violence in many institutions and to protect weaker inmates who were vulnerable to more predatory inmates. The second was to deal with substance abusers. The Narcotic Addict Rehabilitation Act (NARA) units were already proving to be successful, and the BOP recognized the need for programs to deliver services to those inmates who had histories of substance abuse but did not qualify for a NARA unit. Unit Management was an idea whose time had come. It was time for a paradigm shift, and the U.S. Bureau of Prisons was the instrument that provided the shift. Roy Gerard, Robert B. Levinson, and then-director of the U.S. Bureau of Prisons Norman Carlson[4] embarked upon a journey that has revolutionized prison management.

Unit Management Defined

There may be as many definitions of Unit Management as there are agencies and institutions that have implemented the concept. For example, Webster[5] acknowledges the importance of direct supervision in Unit Management and points out that the average unit houses between 100 and 200 inmates. However, Webster fails to adequately define the concept. Similarly, Pierson notes that the Missouri Department of Corrections houses between 150 and 300 inmates in each unit and that each unit has its own staff but points out that the correctional officers' hierarchy is traditional.[6] Both Webster and Pierson speak of the unit as an autonomous entity with its own staff and location. These definitions of a unit, however, are largely in terms of the number of inmates the units accommodate.

According to the U.S. Bureau of Prisons[7] a unit is a small, self-contained, inmate living and staff office area that operates semiautonomously within the larger institution. The essential components of a unit are:

- A small number of inmates (50–120) who are permanently assigned together.
- A multidisciplinary staff (unit manager, case manager[s], correctional counselor[s], full- or part-time psychologist, clerk-typist, and correctional officers whose offices are located within or adjacent to the inmate housing unit and are permanently assigned to work with the inmates of that unit).
- A unit manager who has administrative authority and supervisory responsibility for the unit staff.
- A unit staff that has administrative authority for all within-unit aspects of inmate living and programming.
- Inmates who are assigned to a unit because of age, prior record, specific behavior typologies, need for a specific type of correctional program such as drug abuse counseling, or random assignment.
- Unit staff who are scheduled by the unit manager to work in the unit evenings and

weekends, on a rotating basis, in addition to the unit correctional officer.

The Scope of Unit Management

Because there have been no surveys it is difficult to state exactly how many systems have implemented Unit Management. However, table 15.1 lists states that are believed to have implemented this method.[8]

Classification and the History of Unit Management

To understand the purpose of Unit Management it is important to understand the classification process in correctional institutions. Classification is defined as "a method by which diagnosis, treatment planning, and the execu-

tion of the treatment program are coordinated in the individual case."[9] As a concept, classification grew rather slowly, first with the segregation of the sexes and of children from adults. Slowly institutions began to add educational and spiritual programs, along with vocational training. During the reformatory period (1870–1900), efforts to rehabilitate youth by providing them with education and counseling of a sort began to take hold. Many states had relatively well-refined classification systems by the 1930s, when the U.S. Bureau of Prisons instituted classification as a central intake procedure.

Keve notes that as the Bureau of Prisons grew, it "introduced classification as a major prisoner management tool."[10] Until the 1930s the Bureau of Prisons utilized only rudimentary classification procedures, but by then new institutions had been constructed so that prisoners of varying age groups could be sent to different institutions, with female prisoners going to

TABLE 15.1
Unit Management in the United States

State	Date Begun	Facilities: Number and Percent in Unit Management		Size Range (average) Ideal	Staffing Pattern	Staff/Inmate Ratio
Connecticut	—	—	—	— —	—	—
Georgia	—	—	—	— —	—	—
Iowa	—	—	—	— —	—	—
Michigan	1973	24/24/	100%	120-450/175/200	3	1:58
Missouri*	—	—	—	— —	—	—
Nebraska	1979	6/6	100%	82-130/100/100	7	1:14
New Hampshire	1986	1/1	100%	25/200/150/175	4.5	1:33
New York City (June)	—	—	—	— —	—	—
North Carolina	1982	2/11	18%	93/120/110/100	4	1:28
Ohio	1986	13/17	75%	150/400/250/300	6	1:42
Oklahoma	1986	13/13	100%	120/180/150/150	6	1:25
South Carolina	1982	4/10	40%	126/312/150/150	5	1:30
Tennessee**	1988	0/14	—	—160—	6	1:27
Virginia	1985	1/10	10%	72/100/72—	3	1:24
Bureau of Prisons	1965***	47/47	100%	150/400/250/200	6	1:42

Source: Correspondence with the National Institute of Corrections.
*Obtained from other sources.
**The NIC provided the information with no explanation as to how Tennessee could claim to have units but show no institutions involved.
***The 1965 date reflects the BOP's first experiments with the forerunner of unit management at the National Training School.

Alderson, West Virginia. By the 1950s the Bureau of Prisons classified prisoners by means of a classification committee composed of the associate warden(s), captain, psychologist, superintendent of education, chaplain, superintendent of industries, and chief of classification and parole. It isn't hard to imagine an inmate's demeanor before the committee. Whatever the committee suggested, the inmate was bound to answer, "Yessir."

Treatment Team

During the early to mid-1960s, the concept of the treatment team began to take shape. The early treatment team was a group of staff (case manager, liaison officer, and teacher) who were responsible for classification, periodic program review, and all other case management matters. Today the treatment team is composed of unit manager (chair), a correctional counselor, a teacher, and a mental health worker, if available. In larger units a case manager will chair the team. Based upon earlier research by Glaser,[11] which found that psychologists, case managers, and teachers have less impact on inmates than previously assumed, a new position was created. In the beginning a senior officer specialist was assigned to work with the case manager to handle much inmate contact. Later the position of correctional counselor at a GS-9 nonsupervisory rank was created. Candidates for the new correctional counselor position were chosen from the ranks of senior officer specialists who were believed to possess good communication skills. Once selected, they underwent additional training in counseling and interviewing.

Assigned to a treatment team chaired by a case manager, the correctional counselor was responsible for day-to-day contact with the inmate, such as preparing the visiting list, acting

as a liaison with the inmate's detail supervisor, and so on. The new system worked, and as it turned out, the correctional counselor got the more exciting jobs while the case manager completed the more mundane and tedious paperwork.

Unit Management

Unit Management and the treatment team appeared to be made for each other. However, Unit Management as a concept in the Bureau of Prisons had an even earlier beginning[12] at the National Training School for Boys (NTS) in Washington, D.C., where inmates on one caseload were moved into one housing unit and an interdisciplinary staff worked with them to implement a counseling and recreational program. As a result of the success of this effort, the entire institution was reorganized according to this model.

In 1963 the Federal Youth Center at Englewood, Colorado, established a "unit system" featuring unit officers and a separate case manager for each unit. But it wasn't until the Kennedy Youth Center at Morgantown, West Virginia, opened in 1969 that Unit Management got off the ground as a means of organizing an institution.

The experience at the Kennedy Youth Center (discussed in the introductory essay to chapter 6), which had been preceded by the Narcotic Addict Rehabilitation Act (NARA) units and then by the various drug abuse programs established by the Bureau of Prisons in the 1970s, more or less proved that the idea of Unit Management would work. Ultimately it worked in a variety of settings, such as penitentiaries and the less-secure Federal Correctional Institutions (FCIs). The treatment teams replaced the old classification committee, and whereas previously a program was imposed on the inmate, the inmate came to be viewed as a member of the team and is now allowed input.

Advantages of Unit Management

The advantages of Unit Management are many. It allows for staff to take as much responsibility as they wish. It makes achievements visible, enabling the unit manager to recognize subordinates' good work. That recognition often leads to advancement. Further, the work itself is considered more satisfying. Shared decision making and participation in the policy process are also advantages. In short, staff feel that they are involved in the total workings of the institution.

The multidisciplinary nature of Unit Management improves communication between staff and inmates and allows for discussion while making both classification decisions and organizational decisions. Several other advantages are also noted:[13]

- Unit Management divides the large number of inmates into small, well-defined, and manageable groups whose members develop a common identity and close association with each other and their unit staff.
- It increases the frequency of contacts between staff and inmates and the intensity of their relationships, resulting in:

  1. better communication and understanding between individuals;
  2. more individualized classification and program planning;
  3. more valuable program reviews and program adjustments;
  4. better observation of inmates, enabling early detection of problems before they reach critical proportions;
  5. development of common goals that encourage positive unit cohesiveness; and
  6. generally, a more positive living and working environment for inmates and staff.

- Decisions are made by the unit staff who are closely associated with the inmates, which increases the quality and swiftness of decision making.
- Program flexibility is increased because special areas of emphasis can be developed to meet the needs of the inmates in each unit, and programs in a unit may be changed without affecting the total institution.

Disadvantages of Unit Management

At least three disadvantages of Unit Management must be pointed out. They may account for the refusal of some jurisdictions to adopt this method.

- Unit Management is costly. Budgeted costs of an institution that has adopted Unit Management are higher than they are for a traditional pyramidal-shaped organization. For example, a cell house containing 200 inmates can be supervised by 5.2 correctional officers on three shifts, twenty-four-hours per day for 365 days a year. The salary cost at $25,000 per year per officer will be approximately $130,000 per year, not including employers' contribution to Social Security and other costs.

  For a 200-inmate unit using Gerard's staffing formula, the cost is much higher. One unit manager, two case managers, four nondegreed counselors, and one secretary would amount to approximately $206,000. However, the $76,000 additional cost for Unit Management is artificially inflated, because there are already secretaries in the institution; nondegreed counselors are already on the work force (and even if these must be replaced because of promotion, it is initially at a lower salary); case managers are already on staff (but some additional positions need to be created). The position of unit manager is new. Thus, we see that to an extent Unit Management is more costly. On the other hand, many jurisdictions have found that the extra costs are made up in savings on overtime, repairs to damage from vandalism and disturbances, and even litigation.

- It takes time and resources to implement Unit Management. It is not an idea that comes about through wishful thinking; executive staff must spend time planning and developing it. Funds must be allocated, needed positions identified, opponents won over, staff training and education conducted, and often physical plant renovation completed.

- Unit Management threatens the established hierarchical order. Many executives and supervisors do not want their position or authority challenged or changed and see Unit Management as a threat to their position. In many ways it is a threat. Power is redistributed, information flows to the unit manager, and security and case management decisions are made by unit staff members. Executives and supervisors need to be able to see the advantages without worrying about their role. Such a view requires commitment to the organization and a strong sense of personal security.

Unit Management as a Service-Delivery Vehicle

Flexibility is a key advantage of Unit Management. In the early days of Unit Management, the units were specialized to deal with substance abuse and difficult-to-manage inmates. For example, the Narcotic Addict Rehabilitation Act of 1966 delegated to the U.S. Bureau of Prisons the responsibility of offering treatment to certain eligible felons who had committed their offense in order to support a serious heroin habit.

In 1968 the first NARA unit was established at the Federal Correctional Institution in Dan-

bury, Connecticut. Shortly afterwards other units were established at the FCIs at Terminal Island, California, and in Milan, Michigan. In the early 1970s two others were opened in Fort Worth, Texas, and Lexington, Kentucky. Additionally, a number of drug abuse programs were established in a number of FCIs and penitentiaries, followed by an alcoholism unit at FCI Fort Worth and the S.T.A.R.T. unit at the U.S. Penitentiary at Marion, Illinois, for the most intractable inmates. Many of the programs followed the therapeutic community approach, but others adopted a different method of treatment.

As a rule, inmates meet with a unit correctional counselor within twenty-four hours of their arrival to compose a preliminary visiting list and discuss various concerns or fears. After preliminary medical, psychological, and educational testing is completed, the inmate is moved into his or her unit. Within a short time (usually one to two weeks), the inmate meets with the treatment team to develop a program that attempts to meet the inmate's education, counseling, and work needs. Other concerns are also addressed, such as custody and institutional work assignment. Periodically the inmate is brought before the team for review of program and custody classification. The process may vary somewhat by institution, but it has remained basically the same for at least fifteen years.

In the best circumstances the inmate benefits from the programs and the prompt attention; at least he or she learns that staff is approachable and that certain ones will really listen to him or her. While there may not be many specialized treatment units left, the treatment team continues to be the cornerstone of classification.

Unit Management allows the staff to follow the inmate closely and to see him or her daily. It enables staff and inmates to interact on a more equal level as individuals and human beings. This proactive approach has, in many instances, brought unruly and mutinous institutions under control.

Unit Management as Effective Management

In chapter 10 Likert's[14] system-four organization is described as having three characteristics: supportive relationships, group decision making, and group methods of supervision and high performance goals. Unit management is able to deliver on all three dimensions. Staff are able to make decisions autonomously. They want to feel worthwhile, and they value making a contribution to the greater good.

Supportive relationships. The elements of danger and authority[15] cause staff to look to each other for support on the job, and working in proximity to one another brings mutual interests to light. Some unit managers are very good at nurturing those relationships through staff meetings and other formal unit meetings. Additionally, social relationships often develop, and it is not unusual for staff and their families to congregate at one another's homes for holidays and special occasions. Unit management is also an excellent vehicle for resolving conflict among staff and for bringing group pressure to bear on the occasional staff member who may not be carrying a full share of the workload. Such an occurrence is rare. Most likely staff willingly share the extra work when one of their number is ill or on vacation.

Group decision making and group methods of supervision. As relatively small, autonomous entities units are excellent vehicles for shared decision making. As pointed out in chapter 14, case management decisions are made daily by the unit team, and some organizational decisions are made by unit staff. In very few instances should case management decisions be made unilaterally. All staff should contribute to deliberations on everything from inmate requests for a custody change or a furlough to

parole eligibility and forfeiture of privileges. Other decisions, such as program changes, require the input of all staff as well. The typical unit staff will include individuals with many years of service to relative newcomers, and often the unit staff member with the most years of service will be the unit officer. He or she needs to be listened to and heeded, because often the intuitive insight of the veteran will prove to be accurate.

The unit staff is capable of functioning as a self-directed team. It is almost as if the unit manager is there for the sake of accountability only. Given the wide array of specialties in a typical unit, there is usually no problem getting the job done.

High performance goals. Quality circles have been described as a tool for improving service delivery and for involving staff in improving quality of service. Unit staff comprise a preexisting work group that naturally focuses on problems and quality of service in the unit. All the unit manager has to do is listen. The power of unit staff to accomplish tasks within the unit is so great that with leadership, they automatically establish high performance goals and relentlessly pursue those goals.

Herzberg and Unit Management

Frederick Herzberg identified five factors that are strong determinants of job satisfaction: achievement, recognition, the work itself, responsibility, and advancement. Five other factors stand out as determinants of job dissatisfaction: policy and administration, supervision, salary, interpersonal relations, and working conditions. Herzberg calls the former group **satisfiers** and the latter group **dissatisfiers.**

Assuming that environmental conditions are reasonably good, can outstanding performance be generated? Yes! Unit Management provides the vehicle for generating outstanding performance, and the person to generate it is a

Theory Y manager. Under **Corrections Z** (see Chapter 10), forging a team that pulls together and has a commitment to each other and to the organization motivates employees to excellence. The unit manager is in a position to recognize achievement, design jobs, assign tasks and responsibilities, and, within agency regulations, assure advancement as a reward for outstanding performance. Coincidentally, the dissatisfiers are blunted by the unit manager acting proactively by including staff on discussions of policy, by following the principles of the Theory Y manager (see chapters 2 and 9), and by doing what he or she can do to improve working conditions.

The Impact of Unit Management

The impact of Unit Management on institutions has been spectacular in some instances and more subtle in others. Staff are included in the decision making and planning process. Inmates have close interaction with staff and oftentimes participate in Unit Management processes. Generally, in those institutions that have implemented Unit Management, it has been found that few areas are unaffected by its use.

Efficiency and Cost-Effectiveness

In one of the earliest efforts to determine the impact of Unit Management, Rowe, et al.,[16] found that inmate assaults on other inmates in intermediate adult U.S. Bureau of Prisons institutions decreased after implementation of Unit Management. Assault rates appeared to increase in institutions with Unit Management housing the younger, more violent offender. The authors surmised that assaults are more likely to be reported or observed in functional units because there is better surveillance and better inmate-staff rapport. Prior to implementation of Unit Management, there were significantly more inmate as-

saults on staff at young adult institutions than at intermediate-term adult institutions during the four-year study period. In young adult institutions, where inmate assaults are more frequent, the implementation of Unit Management, whether adjusted for density or not, was shown to cause a small but real decrease in the rate of inmate assaults on staff. A small positive relationship was found between the rate of inmate assaults on staff and the implementation of Unit Management in intermediate-term adult institutions.

Another indication of institutional tension is overtime pay, not only during disturbances but also during more tranquil periods. Overtime pay and abuse of sick days can also be used as an indicator of staff morale. Rowe and his colleagues also found that young adult institutions showed a significant reduction in overtime pay after Unit Management was implemented. In the intermediate adult institutions, when the relationship of Unit Management to overtime pay was adjusted for the impact of density, the relationship was reduced to near zero. Overall, overtime pay decreased from $11.55 per 100 inmate man days before Unit Management to $2.21 per 100 inmate man days after bureau-wide implementation of Unit Management.

Further research was conducted by the U.S. Bureau of Prisons[17] using Rudolf Moos's *Correctional Institutions Environmental Scale (CIES)*. The CIES was administered to staff and inmates at the Federal Correctional Institution in Milan, Michigan, both before and after implementation of Unit Management. The number of staff who felt they were involved in decision making rose from 31 percent to 42 percent. The number of staff who perceived increased order rose from 48 percent to 65 percent. The number of those who believed they were serving as role models for inmates rose from 23 percent to 37 percent, while 68 percent believed there was active involvement with the outside community, compared with 55 percent previously.

The number of inmates reporting increased

staff contact rose from 40 percent to 67 percent. Forty-five percent believed that staff contact was important, contrasted with just 26 percent who previously believed it important. Before Unit Management was implemented, 18 percent of the inmates believed that counseling programs were of value, and after Unit Management was implemented that figure rose to 34 percent. Inmates also believed that living conditions improved and that they were getting help in preparation for future employment. In addition, during the same period the escape rate while on furlough decreased from 2.3 percent to 1.7 percent. Interestingly, during the same period the furlough policy was liberalized.

Robson[18] reports that the change to Unit Management has been found to be more efficient and cost-effective. Pierson[19] reports that Missouri implemented Unit Management with success. There have been modifications in the concept to allow for budget constraints; for example, units house from 150 to 300 inmates instead of the 50 to 100 advocated by Levinson and Gerard.[20] Five benefits from Unit Management are noted by the Missouri Department of Corrections:

- Closer interaction with inmates has improved security.
- The custody-treatment rivalry has been lessened, if not eliminated.
- New career ladders were created, providing promotion opportunities for both custody and noncustody personnel.
- Unit Management has provided the time for top management to engage in long-range planning.
- Unit Management prompted the department to begin using an internal classification system.

The Ohio Study

The most recent evaluation of Unit Management was completed by the Ohio Department of Cor-

rections during 1991. Central office staff conducted interviews and on-site reviews at twenty of the department's twenty-two institutions. With few exceptions, the report concludes:

> We have found it [Unit Management] to be both an effective and efficient means of addressing the concerns of managing an expanding inmate population while remaining sensitive to community expectations and the responsibilities we share with our legal system. Since the transition to Unit Management, we have observed a marked improvement in the overall operation of our institutions.[21]

The report found improvement in a variety of areas. Among other improvements, the authors reached conclusions about security, safety, and administrative efficiency.

Security
- Escapes dropped significantly from 3.04 per 1,000 inmates (1981) to .25 per 1,000 (1991).
- Inmates are held more responsible for behavior and program involvement.
- Unit Management has provided a means for the early detection of potential problems.
- Noncustody staff became more knowledgeable of security policies and procedures.

Safety
- Inmate assaults on staff dropped from 396 (in 1986) to 153 (in 1990).
- The number of reported inmate on inmate assaults increased. (In the past many, if not most, such assaults went undetected.)

Administrative Efficiency
- The multidisciplinary team approach has improved the delivery of correctional services.

- Inmate needs and concerns are addressed more quickly.
- Line staff are more aware of management's expectations and department policy. Lines of communication have become more clear.
- Differences in custody and treatment issues have been reduced or rendered nonexistent.
- The team approach has resulted in unit staff being exposed to all facets of institutional operations, thus broadening their overall experience and knowledge.
- With unit staff managing day-to-day operations, executives are now able to devote more time to strategic planning and are more visible and accessible to staff.

Ohio was not the first jurisdiction to adopt Unit Management, but it is an excellent example of the commitment needed from executive staff if Unit Management is to succeed. Obviously, initial interest is in the area of inmate management, but as the U.S. Bureau of Prisons and the Ohio Department of Corrections found, the relevance of Unit Management to involving staff in job design, rewarding performance and creativity, and decision making ("everything") is just as important as good inmate management.

Unit Management and Its Implementation

Certainly any decision to implement Unit Management will be the result of policy decisions made by the commissioner of corrections and his or her top executives. There may be variations on the theme of Unit Management, and each institution and its mission must be considered before a policy organization is established to begin the implementation process.

Ten Commandments of Unit Management

Roy Gerard,[22] one of the originators of Unit Management, recognizes the various needs of institutions and the influence of budgetary restrictions. In answer to the question of how flexible the concept of Unit Management is, he offers the following guidelines:

- The concept of Unit Management must be understood by and have the support of top-level administration.
- There must be three sets of written guidelines: a policy statement issued by the central office, an institution procedures manual, and a plan for each unit.
- There must be a table of organization that has unit managers at a "department head" level, giving them responsibility for staff and inmates assigned to their unit; this table has them and the head of security report to the same supervisor.
- The unit's population size should be based on its mission: General Unit—150 to 250 inmates; Special Unit—75 to 125 inmates.
- Inmates and unit staff should be permanently assigned to the unit; correctional officers should be stationed for a minimum of nine months.
- Staffing should consist of:

	General Unit	Special Unit
Unit Manager	1	1
Case Manager	2	2
Correctional Counselor	2	2
Secretary	1	1
Mental Health	$1/2$	1

Part-time education, recreation, and volunteer staff.
Twenty-four-hour coverage by correctional officers.

- In addition to correctional officer coverage,

unit staff should provide twelve-hour supervision Monday through Friday and eight-hour supervision on each weekend day.

■ Staff offices should be located on the unit or as near to it as possible.

■ Unit personnel should receive initial and ongoing formal training concerning their roles and responsibilities.

■ Unit Management audits conducted by knowledgeable central or regional office staff should occur on a regularly scheduled basis at least once a year.

The implementation of Unit Management requires a great deal of planning and effort. Staff at all levels must be drawn into the process and made to feel ownership. Research should attempt to determine numbers of general units and special units (mental health, drug/alcohol treatment) needed in the future. Finally, an implementation organization (see chapter 6) should be established to initiate, coordinate, and monitor implementation efforts.

A Model Unit Management Program

The establishment of unit programs are a policy matter left up to the warden, assistant wardens, and the respective unit managers (in consultation with staff). Some units will offer only required services relative to case management needs and minimal individual counseling. It is likely that these types of units will be found in institutions for older, more sophisticated inmates. However, for the younger inmate and for inmates with specialized needs such as substance abuse, a program can be devised that attends to the needs of the inmate.

A successful unit program is based upon a unit plan. It is important that all staff participate in developing a unit plan. This is much like a master plan that defines "unit missions and goals, describes programs, [defines] responsibilities, prescribes how the unit will evaluate its operation."[23] Once staff have developed a program and determined what activities will be offered, they can go to work. One approach is to divide the day into equal segments from 8:00 A.M. to 9:00 P.M. Assuming adequate space for group counseling and executive approval of the program, the inmates can be required to fill each segment of the day constructively. The following sample program illustrates the number of options available to unit staff:

8:00–10:00 A.M.	Work (industries)
10:00–12:00 NOON	Work (industries)
12:00–1:00 P.M.	Lunch (cell time)
1:00–3:00 P.M.	School (GED)
3:00–4:30 P.M.	Group Counseling
4:30–6:00 P.M.	Count, Cell Time, Supper
6:00–7:30 P.M.	Group Counseling
7:30–9:00 P.M.	Self-Help Group (tutoring, P.E.T., etc.)

Any schedule is arrived at in consultation with the inmate at the time of classification and allows the unit staff to maintain close watch over the activities of the inmate. In addition, as one segment of the program is completed, (e.g., GED), another activity can be inserted into the vacant time slot.

Some critics may point out that programs and security do not go well together and that as a consequence, programs are given short shrift in favor of security. The problem is not that programs and security are incompatible but rather that programs are imposed on the security framework. The beauty of Unit Management is that security is part of the approach, and programs and security are viewed from the same side of the fence. In the above plan, unit staff are a full partner in security efforts by demanding accountability from the inmate as to his or her conduct for eleven hours out of the day.

Unit Management and Total Quality Management (TQM)

Today's managers and executives are hearing a lot about **Total Quality Management (TQM)**. In this approach management assumes the responsibility for assuring quality. *Business Week* notes, "Managing for quality means nothing less than a sweeping overhaul in corporate culture, a radical shift in management philosophy, and a permanent commitment at all levels of the organization to seek continuous improvement."[24] The Department of Defense defines TQM as a continuous quality-improvement process that demands top management's leadership and continuous involvement in the process.[25] These somewhat vague definitions can be stated more clearly: leadership must inspire the organization to tolerate zero defects. A major obstacle to implementing TQM is that it requires the complete support of top management.

There may be as many views of TQM as there are people who claim to use it. For corrections, the implications are many, and Unit Management is the vehicle for its implementation (see chapters 9–11).

The father of TQM is W. Edwards Deming, a university professor and management consultant who originally made a name for himself as a statistician who recognized that the "powers of prediction, or—more precisely—the lack thereof causes statisticians and companies to run into problems. . . . [Deming] points out that the business of applying statistical theorums to real world problems often produces inaccurate results."[26] The key, he points out, is to draw everyone into the search for quality. Deming is probably most famous for his Fourteen Points,[27] which have come to be viewed as a guide to building constant awareness, reducing variation, and nurturing constant change and improvement in an organization.

TQM rests on the idea that processes are flawed, not the people who work in the organization.[28] As a result, implementation of TQM demands hard thinking about the following questions:

- What is quality?
- Why should we be concerned about improving quality?
- What is Total Quality Management?
- What is the purpose of Total Quality Management?
- What activities are involved in implementing Total Quality Management?[29]

Since Unit Management is based upon the team approach, the following keys are major contributors to TQM in a correctional setting:

- Training is provided to all management team leaders and team members.
- Teams solve problems and are included in implementing solutions.
- Teamwork is encouraged and modeled.
- Recognition is provided.
- Teams work on problems from their area or areas of expertise.
- Management is responsive to teams and challenges them to higher levels.[30]

The importance of Unit Management to TQM is that everyone feels a part of a team. Decisions are based on fact, individuals are given recognition, the multidisciplinary nature of the teams allows diversity of opinions and expertise to be brought to bear on issues, and the team challenges everyone to ever higher levels of performance.

Summary

Unit Management is both a management approach and a service-delivery vehicle. It grew out of the U.S. Bureau of Prisons' need to re-

Deming's 14 Points	1. Create constancy of purpose toward improvement of product and service, with the aim of becoming competitive and staying in business and providing jobs. 2. Adopt the new philosophy. We are in a new economic age. Western managers must awaken to the challenge, must learn their responsibilities and take on leadership for change. 3. Cease dependence on inspection to achieve quality. Eliminate the need for inspection on a mass basis by building quality into the product in the first place. 4. End the practice of awarding business on the basis of price tag. Instead, minimize total cost. Move toward a single supplier for any one item, in a long-term relationship of loyalty and trust. 5. Improve constantly and forever the system of production and service to improve quality and productivity and thus to constantly decrease costs. 6. Institute training on the job. 7. Institute leadership (see Point 11). The aim of leadership should be to help people and machines and gadgets do a better job. Leadership of management is in need of overhaul, as is leadership of production workers. 8. Drive out fear so that everyone may work effectively for the company. 9. Break down barriers between departments. People in research, design, sales, and production must work as a team, to foresee problems of production and use that may be encountered with the product or service. 10. Eliminate slogans, exhortations, and targets for the work force. Ask for zero defects and new levels of productivity. 11. a. Eliminate work standards (quotas) on the factory floor. Substitute leadership. b. Eliminate management by objective. Eliminate management by numbers, numerical goals. Substitute leadership. 12. a. Remove barriers that rob the hourly worker of his or her right to pride of work. The responsibility of supervisors must be changed from sheer numbers to quality. b. Remove barriers that rob people in management and engineering of their right to pride of work. This means, among other things, abolishment of the annual or merit rating and of management by objective and management by number. 13. Institute a vigorous program of education and self-improvement. 14. Put everybody in the company to work to accomplish the transformation. The transformation is everybody's job.

duce tension in its institutions, to protect weaker inmates, and to provide a vehicle to deliver substance abuse programs. Early units, such as the NARA units and the Drug Abuse Program units, proved that the concept would work and provided the impetus to expand Unit Management throughout the Bureau of Prisons.

Today, fourteen states, besides the BOP, claim to use Unit Management, and the concept appears to be growing internationally as well. The success of Unit Management can be attributed to staff's ability to relate to inmates better, staff's being more satisfied with their jobs, and increased program flexibility. Unit Management is responsible for bringing many tough, hard-to-manage institutions under control. A model unit program is offered to illustrate the opportunities for inmate programming and staff involvement in a functional unit. Finally, Total Quality Management is introduced, and light is shed on its natural link to Unit Management.

Reviewing the Case

The Indiana Reformatory has a history of disturbances, lockdowns, and racial tension. The lockdown that occurred in the spring of 1992 was not unusual for the institution. While it is important to consider other solutions to the prison's problems, the best solution might be the implementation of Unit Management as a means of bringing a difficult-to-manage institution under control.

If the administration is serious about separating the more predatory inmates from the weaker ones, they could develop a number of functional units and devise a classification system that would place certain inmates in particular units. They would need to house the weaker inmates in one or two units and the predatory inmates in one or two units. All other inmates could then be assigned in some manner to still other units.

An important element would be the approval of adequate positions to properly staff the units. Once that was accomplished and the units were opened, the proactive stance of staff would do a great deal to head off future conflict. Another important factor would be the positive impact on staff. They would be included in many processes from which they now feel excluded. Security would also be enhanced. With additional staff in the unit for twelve hours per day, inmates would be discouraged from creating problems.

For Further Study

Hans Toch, "Functional Unit Management: An Unsung Achievement," *Federal Prisons Journal*, 2:4 (Winter 1992), pp. 15–19.
Andrea Gabor, *The Man Who Discovered Quality*. (New York: Random House, 1990).

Key Terms

Unit
Treatment Team
Supportive
  Relationships

Classification
Total Quality
  Management
  (TQM)

Privatization

CHAPTER 16

Case Study: Prison Privatization Downplayed by Allen

Augusta—Only three days after Governor John R. McKernan proposed hiring private contractors to take over at least part of the Maine Youth Center, Corrections Commissioner Donald L. Allen appeared Saturday to back away from the idea.[1] Allen, testifying before the legislature's Appropriation Committee, said the McKernan administration will study "privatizing" the South Portland juvenile facility before deciding if the private sector could offer the same services for less.

"We're not going to pursue" the idea unless that study shows the state would save money without jeopardizing programs, he said. Later in the interview he pointed out that the "feasibility analysis" will take several months to complete.

Allen's reassessment came during the Appropriations Committee's second day of hearings on McKernan's plan to cut spending, including more than $50 million in state aid to schools and municipalities, to cover a projected $121.5 million budget shortfall.

Saturday's session at the Augusta Civic Center, which attracted hundreds of state employees protesting threatened layoffs, focused on proposed cuts and emergency spending increases in corrections, mental health, and human services.

After the hearings conclude Tuesday with a review of cuts in school aid and other areas, the bipartisan committee will try to reach unanimous agreement on a budget-balancing bill. The governor hopes to call a special session of the legislature to act on that bill before Thanksgiving.

The Department of Corrections stands to lose no money under McKernan's plan and the Department of Mental Health and Mental Retardation stands to gain $3.2 million in supplemental appropriations. Both agencies are at the center of McKernan's controversial push to "privatize" key institutional services, starting this year in some cases.

McKernan announced last week that he wanted to "contract with private organizations" for key mental health and correctional programs "in order to guarantee quality care at a reduced cost." The affected institutions include the Maine Youth Center, state mental hospitals in Augusta and Bangor, the Pineland Center for the retarded, and smaller mental health facilities.

Allen's testimony Saturday led to more criticism that McKernan has not provided a clear explanation of which prison and mental health services he would contract out, how he would do it, and when he would implement the changes.

"Are we or are we not privatizing your entire department?" Representative Donnell P. Carroll, D-Gray, a member of the Appropriations Committee, asked Mental Health Commissioner Robert Glover Saturday. The committee hopes to get a precise answer to that question later this week.

Willis Lyford, McKernan's press secretary, said last week that the governor planned to contract out "some functions" at the Maine Youth Center this year. Yet Allen's remarks Saturday appeared to contradict that statement and McKernan's stated determination to contract prison services for juveniles.

Similarly, the governor wants to save more than $300,000 this fiscal year by hiring contractors to care for mentally ill senior citizens now housed at state mental hospitals in Augusta and Bangor. Yet Mental Health Commissioner Robert Glover said last week that no decision has been made on whether to contract long-term care for other patients.

That vagueness, coupled with small projected savings this fiscal year, prompted Senator Joseph C. Brannigan, D-Portland, co-chairman of the Appropriations Committee, to suggest Saturday that the legislature postpone action on "privatizing" institutions if it is nothing more than a "nebulous" scheme.

Such criticism intensified when state employees and advocates for inmates and the mentally ill told the committee that the proposals might endanger people now under state care to obtain savings that one union official described as "undocumented, unfounded, and unsubstantiated." Critics also charged that the administration has not explained how the changes would work and did not fully research the issue before proposing contracted services.

McKernan's proposed cuts in welfare benefits to help trim more than $5 million from the Department of Human Services budget came under attack Saturday from advocates who said the state should lift sales-tax exemptions and other tax breaks to raise revenue.

McKernan and legislative leaders have pledged that taxes are off the table this time around following recent increases in income, sales, gasoline, and meals taxes to cope with an earlier budget mess, but some rank-and-file Democratic lawmakers hope to blunt spending cuts by lifting tax breaks.

"The people at [the Augusta Mental Health Institute] are more important that some fat cat's tax exemptions," Darryl Scholz, a mental health worker at AHMI, told the committee.

Introduction

Few topics in the field of corrections stimulate as much discussion today as the topic of privatization. Privatization is defined as the movement of private corporations into areas of public service. Proponents argue that contracting with private corporations for correctional services will result in substantial savings to the taxpayer and allow government to quickly respond to need. Opponents argue that privatization will undermine governmental control of the correctional process and that inmates in private institutions will suffer at the expense of operators seeking to maximize profits.

While there are good arguments on both sides, it appears that privatization of corrections is now a fact of life. How and when did the movement begin? Who are the major players? And what are the legal, economic, and ethical issues involved? Besides exploring these questions, this chapter will provide some answers for those thinking about contracting for correctional services and discuss governmental shortcomings in the contracting process.

The Beginnings of the Privatization Movement

Christopher Hibbert[2] calls our attention to the earliest private prisons in thirteenth-century England, where the jailer earned his pay by providing essentials such as food as well as some amenities such as gin and the services of a prostitute. It was also the practice of the time for the family of the prisoner to provide him or her with the necessities or money to purchase them. The colonists brought the English concepts of the jail and its fee system with them to the New World.

After the colonies gained independence from England, entrepreneurs were able to utilize convict labor for a variety of purposes. For example, in 1825 the state of Kentucky leased the state prison to an individual for "not less than $1,000 per year." The prison quickly showed a net profit.[3] In other states inmates worked in prison factories, turning out everything from boots to barrels, thus earning a profit for the businessmen involved as well as for the state. In 1885 thirteen states had contracts for prisoners to work on private agricultural endeavors,[4] and in 1894 Tennessee received $100,000 for leasing its entire prison population to the Tennessee Iron and Coal Railroad.

There was a reaction to using convict labor to manufacture goods sold on the open market. By 1900 some states had already passed laws prohibiting the sale of prison-made goods on the open market.[5] In 1929 the U.S. Congress passed the Howes-Cooper Act, which banned the interstate shipment of prison-made goods.[6] By 1940 every state had passed legislation prohibiting the sale of prison-manufactured goods on the open market. As a consequence, private involvement in prisons became a thing of the past.

As the United States entered the 1980s, the need for more prison beds and to hold costs down caused many jurisdictions to explore alternatives to constructing and staffing prisons and jails. Bish and Ostrom[7] point out that serious attention should be given to contractual and intergovernmental relationships. They outline a two-tier approach to government that allows federal, state, and large local governments to provide some services and smaller, more responsive governmental units to provide other services. This is called the public-choice approach to gov-

ernment. It allows for competition and innovation in meeting public need. One innovation pursued by government is contracting for correctional services by nonprofit and profit organizations.

No one can exactly pinpoint when the private corrections enterprise was reborn. Certainly the privatization of other public services in such areas as trash collection, public transportation, security, and even fire protection laid the groundwork for individuals and corporations to pioneer private corrections.

The new private corrections entrepreneurs appeared in community corrections. Two of the earlier programs were run by Correctional Services Associates, Inc. (CSA), and Canon and Company. Both organizations were just a few miles apart in South Central Los Angeles and Inglewood, California. CSA, founded by Don Hartly in 1976, entered private corrections as a drug treatment program for federal probationers and parolees. Hartley's experience as a probation officer had convinced him of the need for a responsible aftercare program that met a variety of needs for former addicts, including reliable detection of those suspected of using drugs. CSA contracts with federal probation and U.S. pretrial services in the Southern California area to provide counseling, urinalysis, psychological evaluation, narcotic evaluation, and signs/ symptoms (commonly called a skin check).

From 1977 to 1980 Canon and Company operated a halfway house for pre-releasees and held contracts with the U.S. Bureau of Prisons and the state of California. The company opened a second halfway house in Las Vegas, Nevada, in 1978 and a third facility in West Covina, California.[8]

Through the late 1970s the idea of privatization spread through the efforts of Canon and Company, Behavioral Systems Southwest, and Eclectic Communications. These three companies were organized according to California state law as private, for-profit corporations. As such they may have laid the groundwork for what was to follow.

Thomas and Logan[9] offer a good summary of the historical development of private corrections. They point to Thomas W. Beasley and Doctor R. Crants as the "fathers" of private corrections. In 1983 Beasley and Crants formed the Corrections Corporation of America (CCA), with headquarters in Nashville, Tennessee. Their ample working capital allowed them to boldly pursue whatever possibilities arose. At the same time, they were able to persuade a number of highly qualified corrections managers to move from public corrections to private corrections. Perhaps most important, according to Thomas and Logan, Beasley's "flamboyant, charismatic presentation of himself and CCA"[10] benefited the corporation greatly.

Shortly after CCA entered the field, opposition to the privatization of corrections began to be heard from the National Prison Project of the ACLU; the National Sheriffs Association; the American Bar Association; and the American Federation of State, County, and Municipal Employees (AFSME). By and large, that opposition continues today. But in spite of opposition, private corrections has continued to grow. In the period from 1983 to 1986 CCA obtained contracts to operate local jails in Bay County, Florida; Hamilton County, Tennessee; and Santa Fe County, New Mexico; as well as federal facilities in the Texas cities of Houston and Laredo (1984).

When CCA's success became apparent, others began to enter the field. Eclectic Communications, which had previously operated only a halfway house in Santa Barbara, received a contract from the California Department of Corrections to operate a parole violation facility. Pricor, Inc., contracted to manage a jail in Tuscaloosa, Alabama, in 1986, and the U.S. Corrections Corporation contracted to operate a facility for Kentucky in 1986.

By the end of the 1980s, privatization was a "legal and contracting reality in Alabama, California, Florida, Kentucky, Louisiana, New Mexico, Tennessee, and Texas."[11] In addition, private corrections contractors operated facilities for the U.S. Bureau of Prisons, the Immigration and Naturalization Service, and the U.S. Marshal's Service in Colorado, New York, and Washington.[12] Several states have recently approved enabling legislation for contracting with private corrections companies. Rarely has an industry grown so quickly in the face of such opposition.

Private Corrections Today

The push by government to reduce costs in the face of declining tax revenues and the cutting of federal assistance to the states have resulted in many changes in the way government does business. Corrections is no exception. A main problem for government is that the prison population rose 138.8 percent between 1980 and 1990. The jail population rose approximately 55.1 percent.[13] Many jurisdictions have responded to this increased need for correctional services by contracting with private corporations such as CCA to build and/or manage facilities for convicted offenders.

Today there are fourteen private companies offering institutional corrections services, providing a total of 13,348 beds with another 5,436 planned for the upcoming year.[14]

Figure 16.1 shows a census summary of each of the companies. Table 16.1 shows the type, size, and contracting agency for private corrections facilities. There are twenty-three minimum-custody facilities, two medium-custody facilities, twenty minimum/medium-custody facilities, ten minimum/medium/maximum-custody facilities, and one minimum/maximum-custody facility.

A recent survey by Huskey and Lurigio[15] reveals that there are a number of private companies that operate intermediate sanctions and services for offenders. They report that respondents

FIGURE 16.1
Private Corrections Facility Census Summary

Management Firm	Number of Facilities Under Management	Rated Capacity of In-Operation Facilities	Present Population of Facilities	New Facilities to Open During Upcoming Year	Planned Expansion for Upcoming Year
Concepts, Inc.	2	1,900	750	1	450
Correctional Management Affiliates	2	589	300	0	0
Corrections Corporation of America	14	4,798	4,449	2	1,712
Dismas House Charities	1	100	95	0	0
Eclectic Communicatons, Inc.	3	490	472	0	620
Eden Detention Center, Inc.	1	565	450	0	0
Esmor, Inc.	1	103	98	1	470
Gary White & Associates	1	240	260	0	0
Management and Training Corp.	1	400	400	0	0
Mid-Tex Corrections, Inc.	2	736	705	0	0
Pricor, Inc.	3	854	824	0	0
U.S. Corrections Corp.	3	1,350	1,350	0	0
Volunteers of America	2	117	85	0	0
Wackenhut Corrections Corp.	8	3,234	3,110	3	2,184
Total	44	15,476	13,348	7	5,436

Source: Charles W. Thomas and Suzanna L. Foard, Private Corrections Project Center for Studies in Criminology and Law, University of Florida—Gainesville (November 1991). Permission granted

serve those arrested for drug possession, nonviolent/property offenses, drug sales and manufacture, DUI, and personal/violent offenses. They conclude that (1) privately operated community programs serve a significant number and range of offenders; (2) the agencies appear to be responsive to correctional concerns; (3) the private agencies save the public considerable money through wages earned, restitution, and taxes paid; and (4) offenders have a low re-arrest rate, suggesting that they are a minimal threat to the public.

Issues in Correctional Privatization

While private corrections is not a new idea, it has been recently reborn. At present, private corrections is fraught with legal, political, and administrative issues that need to be addressed. Opinions in all three areas are continuing to evolve. Following is a discussion of some of these issues.

Legal Issues

Is it legal for the government to contract with a for-profit corporation for correctional services? "Although some would disagree, the answer appears to be an emphatic 'Yes!' States may contract out the responsibilities of running entire institutions or certain selected prison services unless it is specifically prohibited by state law."[16] Federal law clearly states that prisoners may be confined in a facility maintained by the federal government or "otherwise." "Otherwise" has been interpreted to include not-for-profit and for-profit organizations. Many states have moved to enact legislation to permit private contractors to operate within their boundaries. Most recently, Virginia, West Virginia, and Wyoming passed enabling legislation, and Nebraska, North Carolina, and Pennsylvania are actively considering such legislation.[17] Many other states have enacted legislation opposing

FIGURE 16.2
States that Prohibit Private Corrections

State	
Alabama	North Carolina*
Connecticut	Oregon
Delaware	Pennsylvania*
Iowa	Rhode Island
Maine	South Dakota
Maryland	Vermont

*States that are considering legislation to approve privatization.

privatization.[18] Figure 16.2 lists the states prohibiting private corrections at the present time.

Protection of Inmate Rights

Opponents of privatization have argued that in the event of civil rights violations inmates lodged in private facilities may not have full access to redress guaranteed under 42 U.S.C. Section 1983, which states:

> Every person who under color of any statute, ordinance, regulation, custom, or usage, of any State or Territory or the District of Columbia, subjects, or causes to be subjected, any citizen of the United States or other person within the jurisdiction thereof to the deprivation of any rights, privileges, or immunities secured by the Constitution and laws, shall be liable to the party injured in an action at law, suit in equity, or other proper proceeding for redress.

Thomas[19] points out that government in the form of prisons and jails has not been an overly zealous guardian of prisoners' rights and calls our attention to the fact that private corrections thus far have failed to be the bogeyman opponents had expected. In fact, few if any lawsuits under Section 1983 have been filed against private practitioners, since 1980 when private corrections began its real growth.

On the other hand, in all probability the

TABLE 16.1
Private Facilities

State	Facility	Location	Contracting Agency	Capacity	Security Level	Private Contractor	Date Opened
Alabama	Tuscaloosa	Tuscaloosa	Tuscaloosa Co.	144	Minimum	Pricor, Inc. Metropolitan Detention Fac.	June 1986
California	Baker R-T-C Facility	Baker	California DOC	250	Minimum	Eclectic Communications, Inc.	Aug. 1987
California	Mesa Verde R-T-C Facility	Bakersfield	California DOC	340	Minimum	Gary White & Associates	Apr. 1989
California	Eagle Mt. R-T-C Facility	Desert Center	California DOC	400	Minimum	Management & Training, Inc.	Sept. 1988
California	Hidden Valley Ranch	La Honda	California DOC	120	Minimum	Eclectic Communications Inc.	Jan. 1986
California	Leo Chessley Center	Live Oak	California DOC	220	Minimum	Eclectic Communications Inc.	Aug. 1988
California	McFarland R-T-C Facility	McFarland	California DOC	200	Min/Med	Wackenhut Corrections Corp.	Jan. 1989
Colorado	Aurora INS Processing Center	Aurora	INS	167	Min/Med	Wackenhut Corrections Corp.	May 1987
Florida	Hernando Co. Detention Facility	Brooksville	Hernando Co. and USMS	252	Min/Med/Max	Corrections Corp. of America	Oct. 1988
Florida	Monroe County Correctional System	Key West	Monroe Co.	200	Min/Med/Max	Wackenhut Corrections Corp.	Feb. 1990
Florida	Monroe County Correctional System	Marathon	Monroe Co.	60	Min/Med/Max	Wackenhut Corrections Corp.	Dec. 1990
Florida	Monroe County Correctional System	Plantation	Monroe Co.	60	Min/Med/Max	Wackenhut Corrections Corp.	Feb. 1990
Florida	Bay County Jail	Panama City	Bay County	204	Min/Med/Max	Corrections Corp. of America	Oct. 1985
Florida	Bay County Jail & Annex	Panama City	Bay County	257	Min/Med	Corrections Corp. of America	Apr. 1986
Kansas	Leavenworth Correctional Facility	Leavenworth	U.S. Marshal's Service	440	Med/Max	Corrections Corp. of America	Jan. 1992
Kentucky	Dismas House of Portland	Louisville	Jefferson Co.	225	Minimum	Dismas House Charities, Inc.	Jan. 1987
Kentucky	Dierson Correctional Center	Louisville	Kentucky DOC	80	Minimum	Dismas House Charities, Inc.	Aug. 1990
Kentucky	Lee Adjustment Center	Beattyville	Kentucky DOC	500	Minimum	U.S. Corrections Corp.	Aug. 1990

State	Facility	City	Contracting Agency	Capacity	Security	Company	Date
Kentucky	River City Correctional Center	Louisville	Jefferson Co.	350	Minimum	U.S. Corrections Corp.	Jan. 1990
Kentucky	Dismas House of Owensboro	Owensboro	Kentucky DOC	100	Minimum	Dismas House Charities	June 1990
Kentucky	Marion Adjustment Center	St. Mary's	Kentucky DOC	500	Minimum	U.S. Corrections Corp.	Jan. 1986
Louisiana	Allen Parrish Correctional Facility	Allen	Louisiana DOC	600	Medium	Wackenhut Corrections Corp.	Dec. 1990
Louisiana	Winn Parrish Correctional Facility	Winnfield	Louisiana DOC	610	Medium	Corrections Corp. of America	March 1990
New Mexico	Estancia Regional Correctional	Estancia	U.S. Marshals Service	256	Minimum	Corrections Corp. of America	Dec. 1990
New Mexico	NM Women's Correctional Facility	Grants	New Mexico DOC	200	Min/Med/Max	Corrections Corp. of America	June 1989
New Mexico	Santa Fe County	Santa Fe	Santa Fe County Fed. BOP, USMS	201	Min/Med/Max	Corrections Corp. of America	Aug. 1986
New York	New York INS Processing Center	Queens	Immigration and Naturalization Service	100	Min/Med	Wackenhut Corrections Corp.	Oct. 1989
Tennessee	Silverdale Unit #1, Men's	Chattanooga	Hamilton County	320	Min/Med/Max	Corrections Corp. of America	Oct. 1984
Tennessee	Silverdale Unit #2, Co. Women's	Chattanooga	Hamilton County	117	Min/Med/Max	Corrections Corp. of America	Oct. 1984
Tennessee	Mason Regional Correctional Facility	Mason	U.S. Marshal's Service	256	Min/Med	Corrections Corp. of America	Oct. 1990
Tennessee	Metro Davidson Co. Correctional Facility	Nashville	County and State	872	Min/Med	Corrections Corp. of America	March 1992
Texas	Angelina County Detention Fac.	Diboll	Angelina County	500	Min/Med	Pricor, Inc.	Feb. 1991
Texas	Big Spring Correctional Center	Big Spring	City of Big Spring	350	Minimum	Mid-Tex Corrections, Inc.	Aug. 1989
Texas	Bridgeport Pre-Release Center	Bridgeport	Texas DOC	500	Min/Med	Wackenhut Corrections Corp.	Aug. 1989
Texas	Cleveland Pre-Release Center	Cleveland	Texas DOC	500	Minimum	Corrections Corp. of America	Sept. 1989
Texas	Houston Processing Center	Houston	Immigration and Naturalization Service Texas Board of Prisons	350	Min/Med	Corrections Corp. of America	Apr. 1984
Texas	Eden Detention Center	Eden	City of Eden	324	Min/Med	Eden Det. Center, Inc.	Oct. 1985

(continued next page)

TABLE 16.1 (Continued)
Private Facilities

State	Facility	Location	Contracting Agency	Capacity	Security Level	Private Contractor	Date Opened
Texas (closed)	Houston Reintegration	Houston	Texas Board of Pardons and Paroles	223	Minimum	Pricor, Inc.	June 1987
Texas	Kyle Pre-Release Center	Kyle	Texas DOC	500	Min/Med	Wackenhut Corrections Corp.	June 1989
Texas	Laredo Processing Center	Laredo	U.S. Dept. of Justice	208	Minimum	Corrections Corp. of America	March 1985
Texas	LaSalle County Detention Fac.	Cotulla	LaSalle County	500	Min/Med	Pricor, Inc.	Nov. 1990
Texas	Limestone County Detention Fac.	Limestone County	Limestone County	500	Min/Med	Detention Systems, Inc.	Jan. 1991
Texas	Lockhart Facility	Lockhart	City of Lockhart	500	Minimum	Wackenhut Corrections Corp.	Fall 1991
Texas	Mineral Wells Pre-Parole	Mineral Wells	Texas Board of Pardons and Paroles	500	Minimum	Concepts Inc.	N/A
Texas	Newton County	Newton County	unknown	440	Min/Med/Max	Tx Detention Mgmt, Inc.	Spring 1991
Texas	Reeves County Law Enforcement	Pecos	Federal BOP, U.S. Marshals Service	532	Minimum	Corrections Corp. of America	Sept. 1988
Texas	Starr County Detention Fac.	Rio Grande City	Starr County	776	Min/Max	Pricor, Inc.	Feb. 1992
Texas	Pecos County Detention Fac.	Ft. Stockton	Pecos County	500	Min/Med	Pricor, Inc.	Dec. 1990
Texas	Central Texas Parole Violator Facility	San Antonio	Texas Board of Pardons and Parole, USMS	619	Min/Med	Wackenhut Corrections Corp.	Jan. 1989
Texas	San Saba County Detention Fac.	San Saba	San Saba County	500	Min/Med	Pricor, Inc.	March 1991
Texas	Sweetwater Pre-Parole Center	Sweetwater	Texas Board of Pardons and Parole				
Texas	Swisher County Detention Fac.	Tulia	No Single Agency	210	Minimum	Pricor, Inc.	July 1989
				500	Min/Med	Pricor, Inc.	Jan. 1991
Texas	Falls County Detention Fac.	Marlin	No Single Agency	500	Min/Med	Pricor, Inc.	Feb. 1991
Texas	Venus Pre-Release Center	Venus	Texas DOC	500	Minimum	Corrections Corp. of America	Aug. 1989
Texas (closed)	Zavala Detention Ctr.	Zavala County	Zavala County	226	Min/Med	Detention Systems, Inc.	Feb. 1989
Washington	Esmore	Seattle	Immigration and Naturalization	90	Minimum	Esmor, Inc.	June 1989

Source: Linda Hanson, "The Privatization of Corrections Movement: A Decade of Change," *Journal of Contemporary Criminal Justice*, 7:1 (1991), pp. 1–28. Permission granted

states will not be able to shield contractors or the state from civil liability if prisoners' rights are abridged. Thus, agency exposure may be reduced by requiring the contractor to post a bond, and the state in return would specify that the contractor would be indemnified against any award of damages and costs.[20]

Deadly Force

Opponents of privatization point out that private facilities have a vested interest in preventing the bad publicity that would arise from escapes and riots but that they lack authority to use ultimate force in preventing such occurrences, thereby putting the safety of the community in jeopardy. Hackett, et al., are of the opinion that "private prison employees would likely be able to use reasonable and appropriate restraint in the absence of any other specific statutory or case law guidance."[21]

Mayer[22] points out that any employee of a private contractor already possesses the same limited power to arrest and right to use force as any private citizen. Most jurisdictions have laws regarding arrests and use of force by ordinary citizens, and Mayer asserts that those same rights apply to private prison officers who use force to prevent a felony in the form of riot, escape, or assault.

On the other hand, a recent Supreme Court decision, *Tennessee v. Garner*,[23] holds that "the Fourth Amendment sets more stringent limits on police use of deadly force than do many state statutes with roots in the common law"[24] and effectively invalidates many state statutes based on common law. Mayer then raises a good point:

> Since the right of a police officer to use deadly force is generally more extensive than the right of a private citizen, it seems clear that a private corporation guard's use of deadly force to prevent an escape would be restricted at least as

much as the Garner standard and possibly more restricted. For disturbances other than escape, unless the guard was acting in self-defense or in defense of another person, deadly force would probably be excessive, making the guard liable under criminal law and the guard, contractor, and possibly the state, liable under civil law.[25]

The remedy, of course, is for the state to extend statutory authorization to private sector employees to use legitimate force in preventing escapes or commission of other felonies that endanger the public or other inmates or staff. On the other hand, perhaps the issue will not have to be addressed head on. For at least 100 years reformers and academicians have been preaching the gospel according to compassion and humanitarian treatment. Private facilities are managed by intelligent, capable people who recognize that profits depend on a steady flow of "customers" and that regular use of force, intimidation, and brutality in general will result in cancellation of contracts. Clearly, private contractors will be motivated to offer services that conform to the canons of sound correctional management that we have preached for so long. In this instance, at least, the profit motive may well enhance quality of service rather than depreciate it.

Use of Inmate Labor by Private Industry

The construction and operation of private facilities by private companies are only part of the question. Another part is "What do you do with the inmates when they are confined?" State and federal institutions employ a large number of inmates in prison industry. How does the private contractor deal with issues relating to exploitation of inmate labor?

One way is to establish an industry that is part of the state prison industry to manufacture or repair goods or provide a service according to established custom and law. Some states, such as Florida, have taken the lead in involving the private sector in prison industries.[26] In 1981 the Florida legislature approved legislation creating the Prison Rehabilitative Industries and Diversified Enterprises, Inc. (PRIDE), a non-profit corporation established to manufacture goods to be sold exclusively to state and local governments. However, PRIDE is forbidden to compete with the private sector. Much like Federal Prison Industries, begun by Eleanor Roosevelt with donations from wealthy friends, PRIDE was created with seed money from various Florida businesses. It serves a great need within Florida prisons.

States like the following have allowed private entrepreneurs to establish shops within the prison walls and to generate a profit while paying prisoners the prevailing wage.[27]

Arizona. Best Western has installed a reservation system at a women's prerelease center, and Wahlers, a manufacturer of furniture and room dividers, has contracted for the labor of twelve inmates.

Iowa. A salvage yard has contracted for inmates to demolish and sort old motors; elsewhere inmates sort and repackage out-of-season greeting cards.

Kansas. Zephyr Products, Inc., employs inmates from the state's sign shop to make printline products.

Minnesota. Control Data Corporation began a computer component assembly line at Stillwater State Prison in 1981.

Mississippi. Koolmist, an air conditioning corporation, employs twenty inmates to manufacture condensing units under DOC supervision.

Nevada. The General Household Items Company employs fifteen inmates to make brooms, and a frozen food plant employs twenty inmates at the same facility.

Utah. A graphic arts company employs twenty-six inmates, and a sewing operation employs thirty inmates.

It is likely that private industry has made further inroads since the above survey was made, and perhaps the exact number of inmates employed by private industry is not known. What is known is that private corrections facilities can successfully employ inmates. However, private contractors must keep an eye on legislation and special interest groups who may attempt to stop the employment of inmates in prison. In addition, any attempt to pay less than minimum wage would be asking for trouble.

Inmate Discipline

In order to maintain discipline within any facility, the administration must establish a system that follows due process requirements and promotes institutional tranquility. The private contractor need only follow the policies and procedures on inmate discipline that have been formulated by the contracting agency.[28] In regard to the notion that private contractors have a vested interest in keeping the populations of their institutions at a high level, notification of infractions requiring forfeiture or withholding of earned good time should be forwarded to a DOC official. To afford maximum protection to the contractor, the state should specifically authorize it to handle disciplinary cases and to require staff to complete necessary training in disciplinary policy and procedures.

Contracting

Most states and local jurisdictions require that proposals be solicited and contracts awarded on the basis of merit and cost considerations. Naturally, this process sometimes goes awry.

At times a Request for Proposal (RFP) is "wired"; that is, written with a specific contractor in mind. Since in the past some contractors have gone to considerable trouble to wire a contract, it may be advisable for interested applicants to determine whether this has happened previously before going to the trouble of submitting a proposal. This is a sore point not only in private corrections but also in other areas of government service, and some may take offense at the indictment. But attempts to wire a contract have led to a good deal of skullduggery, particularly in the earlier history of private corrections.

In private contracts, the amount to be spent on the contract will vary. Obviously, the amount will be determined by a number of variables, including salaries and benefits; capital costs; equipment; and operations, including food, utilities, and so on. It is a complicated process. This brings us to why private corrections is a profitable enterprise. To simplify the issue, it costs the same amount of money to guard one inmate as it does to guard twenty-five inmates. Naturally, twenty-five inmates will consume more food and water than one inmate, but salaries and utilities, for example, remain relatively constant. These economies of scale make the endeavor attractive, and because once the break-even point for a certain number of inmates is reached, a large part of the additional reimbursement is profit. It is not unusual for smaller community programs to operate at a profit margin of 50 percent or more.

For example, a small work release center contracting with a state department of corrections has a contract for $30 per day per inmate. That is, the facility will generate roughly $657,000 per year with expenses totalling roughly $460,000 per year. Thus, forty-two or forty-three inmates constitute the break-even point for expenses, less food costs, for example, for eighteen inmates. Thus, the enterprise earns roughly $200,000 in pretax profits.

There are two ways agencies can contract for services: a straight per diem cost per inmate and a variable contract. The per diem method is the most popular as it allows the contractor to maximize profits. The second accounts for the economies of scale and attempts to limit the amount of profit. The National Institute of Justice (NIJ)[29] found only one example of variable prices when the contract for running the Bay County Jail (Florida) was awarded to Corrections Corporation of America. The contract stipulated three price levels, depending on the average number of prisoners per month: $29.81 per day for up to 310 prisoners, $20.74 for 311 to 329 prisoners per month, and $7.50 for each additional prisoner above 330.

These examples demonstrate that private corrections is a profitable enterprise. However, it requires a sound financial base, experienced correctional managers, a willingness on the part of government to innovate, and enabling legislation.[30] Gone are the times when a project could be funded on a shoestring.

Monitoring of Contracts

If one area can be identified as the most frequent cause of corruption or bad press in regard to private corrections, it is faulty or nonexistent monitoring on the part of government agencies. To simply throw money at a contractor with instructions to "go to it" is to invite trouble.

The contracting agency should clearly spell out how and when the contractor will be monitored and evaluated and then abide strictly by the guidelines. The NIJ[31] recommends two processes:

- Yearly reviews/audits/inspections by special teams of government personnel; and
- monitoring through periodic reporting or onsite observers or agency employees who visit the facility daily, weekly, or monthly.

FIGURE 16.3
Issues in Facility Management Contracting

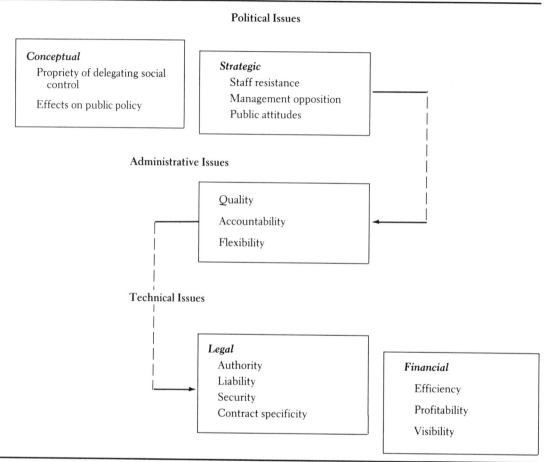

Source: Joan Mullen, "Corrections and the Private Sector," *Research in Brief* (National Institute of Justice: U.S. Department of Justice, May 1985), p. 5.

Contracting for private corrections is a sometimes lengthy and tricky process in which the administrator must be aware of a number of variables. Figure 16.3 shows the issues in contracting. The important point to remember is that if the contracting agency fairly and legitimately awards the contract and then closely monitors the activities of the contractor, the results will admirably serve the needs of the public.

Quality of Service

The issue of whether or not private correctional facilities adequately perform the work they are hired to do seems to be the bottom line in an era of escalating inmate populations and declining revenues. Oddly, relatively few studies have been conducted on the ability of private corrections firms to deliver services. Thomas and Logan[32] neatly summarize what we know about the quality-of-service issue and conclude that without question private correctional facilities perform at least as well as public institutions and on many variables outperform their public counterparts.

One study looked at Silverdale, the Hamilton County (Chattanooga, Tennessee) Penal Farm, and concluded that "the private prison was more highly rated by inmates on its physical improvements, upkeep, and cleanliness; staff competence and character; work assignments; chaplain and counselor services; requests and grievances; correspondence and telephone; and outside contacts."[33]

Another study sponsored by the National Institute of Justice and conducted by the Urban Institute compares private and public institutions. A roughly matched sample, including two minimum-security adult institutions in Kentucky and two secure juvenile treatment facilities in Massachusetts, were investigated. Data reveal that the private facilities hold a small advantage. Staff and inmates both rate the private facilities more favorably, and the evaluators found staff at the private facilities to be more enthusiastic, more involved with their work, and more interested in working with inmates.[34]

A third study conducted by Logan included a private New Mexico facility for women, the state operation of that facility one year before, and a federal prison for women. Logan found that "the private prison outperformed its state and federal counterparts on all dimensions except care (where the state scored slightly higher) and justice (where the federal prison matched the private)."[35]

Other comments by Sheriff James A. Gondles, Jr., executive director of the American Correctional Association,[36] point to the high level of service delivered by private corrections. Thus, it appears that profit and public service are not mutually exclusive concepts.

A Glimpse of the Future?

The quality of service provided by private corrections organizations appears to be at least as good as that provided by public sector organizations. Will there be more and more private companies entering the market or will one company, or a few, dominate the private corrections scene? This is a difficult question to answer. Several companies appear to have the financial strength to endure for some time, but one company stands out as being dominant in the field of private corrections.

Corrections Corporation of America (CCA) is a Delaware corporation with headquarters in Nashville, Tennessee. It was founded in 1983 by Thomas W. Beasley and Doctor R. Crants to develop and manage prisons and other types of correctional facilities such as detention centers and juvenile facilities. From that beginning, CCA now owns and/or operates twenty-one facilities with a total capacity of 7,066 beds.[37]

Beasley and Crants have not worked alone. Both men, who graduated from West Point in 1966, one subsequently earning an MBA and the other a law degree, persuaded a number of other capable people to serve on the board of directors. They include Sam W. Bartholomew, Jr., also a 1966 graduate of West Point with a degree in law; two former commissioners of corrections; one warden; a former U.S. senator; a former Kentucky deputy general counsel; and others who bring to the corporation a wide array of experience in business and public service.

In October of 1986 Corrections Corporation of America held an initial public offering of stock in order to raise funds for expansion. This was a first, as all other private corrections companies are closely held corporations. The stock sold quickly over the counter, and as of March 31, 1992, there were approximately 1,880 shareholders of record located in forty-nine states, the District of Columbia, Australia, Can-

Privatization is Not a Panacea

Private Jails Fail To Fill Cells, Counties' Coffers

Five of Six Facilities Built by Company Sit Empty;
Bondholders Seek State Bailout

AUSTIN—In the small towns of Tulia and Marlin, San Saba, and Fort Stockton, jails meant jobs. Houston-based N-Group Securities convinced officials in six counties that they could sell bonds to construct the jails. If you build the jails, the inmates will come, went the pitch.

They would come from places with bulging prison populations, places willing to spend money to relocate their inmates. Even the state of Texas, forced to release inmates early to make room for new felons, could use a little breathing room, the counties figured.

The jails were completed during the summer of 1991, but the inmates didn't come. Today, five of the six jails built by N-Group sit empty. Bondholders and others connected with the jails are counting on the state to bail them out, hoping taxpayers will buy the facilities as drug treatment centers at cut-rate prices. But state officials feel that these small cities, desperate for an economic infusion, might be too little and too inconvenient for the Texas prison system.

Only the jail in Angeline County, in East Texas, is in operation, housing inmates from the overcrowded Harris County system. In Pecos, San Saba, La-Salle, Swisher, and Falls counties, the jails are empty.

"The rest of the counties have invested their good names and invested a lot of time and effort in the projects and have not received any of the benefits to date," said Richard Porter, a Dallas attorney representing bondholders.

Officials say state and federal laws severely limit the number of inmates available to private jails. Also, other counties have been reluctant to pay for inmates to stay in private jails. In addition, Mr. Porter said, the counties "are tied up in what looks to be a very messy proposition in trying to unravel these transactions."

In October in Pecos, a grand jury indicted N-Group officers Michael and Patrick Graham on a rarely used antitrust statute. The indictment accuses them of failing to competitively bid contracts for the construction of the jails.

The attorney for the brothers could not be reached for comment. The Grahams have said they are innocent of any wrongdoing. A trial date has not been scheduled.

Mr. Porter said that in the next few weeks, the bondholders—including several large institutional investors—will make a proposal to the Texas Criminal Justice Board.

Although the county financial organizations issued $12 million in bonds for each of the six jails, there is little hope of getting a buyer to pay that price, Mr. Porter said.

"I'm not at liberty to say what we feel would be a fair resolution," Mr. Porter said. "We would just hope to be treated fairly. [The bondholders] don't believe they are entitled to any windfalls, and then neither is the state of Texas."

Voters in November authorized the state to use bonds to build drug treatment facilities for 12,000 inmates. Bondholders say the jails meet the state's needs. Selden Hale, an Amarillo lawyer who is chairman of the criminal justice board, said last week that he would prefer not to buy the jails.

"We could build a little bit better, more efficient units for quite a bit less money than what they did," he said.

Mr. Hale also said there is no money budgeted by the state to staff the jails, so having them immediately available is unnecessary.

He also cited insufficient medical facilities and the lack of trained counselors in the small cities.

"You could put one of these 500-bed treatment facilities in a place like Fort Worth . . . and there's probably already people there that we can hire within two weeks after we open it up," he said. "How are you going to get a drug treatment counselor to move to a place like Tulia?"

Mr. Hale said he has toured the jails built by N-Group three times and found ventilation and security problems.

"There's just a whole lot of things wrong with them," Mr. Hale said.

He acknowledged there has been intense lobbying to get the state to bail out the bondholders and the counties, which could suffer drops in their bond ratings. But Mr. Hale said he prefers not to buy the jails. He likened it to a Texas car company building a bad automobile.

"Nobody would expect the highway patrol to buy 100 bad cars just because these guys couldn't sell them," he said. "And I don't see why the board of criminal justice should be expected to buy a bunch of bad jails."

Eventually, the state is expected to build about twenty-four drug treatment centers. Cities throughout the state have been asked to submit proposals for the centers by January 15. The cities are required to donate the land and utility hook-ups for the facilities.

Mr. Hale said that regardless of the offers by the bondholders, he would wait to see how they compare to the cities' proposals.

"If their price got real low, then we'd probably have to buy it, but I just hope we can avoid it," he said.

Mr. Porter said that Department of Criminal Justice officials have toured the jails and have said the jails could meet state needs. He said he understands the reluctance of the state to deal with jails that have been the subject of grand jury investigations.

"That's something we've tried hard to overcome," Mr. Porter said. "There's no doubt that there's an appearance of wrongdoing on the part of the Grahams and possibly others.

"But like I have said, we have indications that these facilities are well constructed and can be used for the purposes for which they are designed."

Mr. Porter also said proceeds from the bond sales are sufficient to pay back interest on the bonds until August 1992. After that, the jails face default.

"A fair price is all the bondholders have been seeking from the state," he said.

Source: Christy Hoppe, *Dallas Morning News,* December 31, 1991.

ada, Germany, Great Britain, and Taiwan.[38] The issue raised approximately $16,471,084[39] for operating capital and to fund new facilities under contract. No dividends have been paid and none are anticipated in the future, as all profits are kept by the company for working capital. Two million shares of stock were sold at $9 per share, and as of March 1994 the value of each share had increased to 13¼. *Investors Daily* rates CCA as an average investment but awards it a B-rating for future growth potential, with an A as the highest possible rating.

The growth of CCA has been just short of spectacular. Obviously, sound management principles, planning, and a thorough knowledge of the political process have aided its growth. With 1991 revenues of $67,883,076[40] CCA is a force to be reckoned with, and indications are that the company will continue to be a dominant force in the field of corrections for some time to come. Is CCA a glimpse of the future? Yes and no. Not all states will allow private corrections, not all private corrections companies will decide to go public, and not all private corrections companies will be able to employ as many top-level executives who can use their reputation and influence to help their organization. On the other hand, private providers who hope to succeed must take note of CCA's planning, aggressiveness, and ability to respond to the needs of the various jurisdictions.

A Public-Private Partnership

There is an alternative to public or private provision of correctional services. Cox and Osterhoff[41] suggest developing a partnership between the public and private sectors. They argue that it is in the best interests of both the public and private sectors to form cooperative relationships to solve the complex problems of state and local governments. By doing so the two sectors can pursue their own organizational goals and at the same time contribute to the greater good.

Cox and Osterhoff view the public-private partnership as a continuum with strictly public-sector responsibilities at one end and strictly private-sector responsibilities at the other.

> At the end of the continuum where private sector involvement is more acceptable are jail services and programs, including medical and mental health care, food service, and alcohol and drug treatment programs. At the end of the continuum where public control is more acceptable are jail (and prison) management, operation, and facility ownership. Toward the center of the continuum are community-based correctional facilities and programs, jail industries, and selected special-purpose facilities and programs that can be operated jointly by the public and private sectors.[42]

Mullen, et al.[43] suggests that such a partnership has distinct advantages:

- It allows rapid mobilization, experimentation, decentralization, specialization, and regionalization.
- It allows for experimentation with innovative programs and new service-delivery methods without making permanent commitments to programs until an evaluation has been completed.
- The decentralization of correctional facilities and services allows greater geographic and program diversity.
- It allows correctional institution and program specialization.

Clearly, privatization will not go away. In debating whether to allow privatization, policy makers ought to consider pursuing a two-tier approach to corrections. Cox and Osterhoff's continuum allows that choice. The needs of the public, clients, and prisoners are best served by acknowledging that some programs and needs are best met by the public sector and others by the private sector.

Summary

Prison and jail populations rose precipitously during the 1980s. The increased demand for correctional services proved to be burdensome, and many jurisdictions cast about for alternatives. The contracting of services to private providers was one solution.

Beginning in the late 1970s, private entrepreneurs began to offer services in community programs, institutional management, food service, medical care, and the like. The entry of the private sector into corrections has caused a good deal of controversy about such issues as the legality of private corrections, protection of inmate rights, use of deadly force, inmate labor, inmate discipline, contracting, and monitoring of contracts.

Quality of service has been a major concern. The general finding of the few studies that have been conducted is that private facilities give at least as good service as public facilities. The number of private service providers has grown from just a handful to fourteen companies in the area of institutional management alone. Whether that number will continue to grow remains to be seen. However, one company has assumed a dominance that will be difficult to overcome. With 7,066 beds, Corrections Corporation of America (CCA) is the largest private corrections company. Its 1991 revenues were $67,883,076.

It is much too early to state whether contracting for correctional services is the wave of the future. However, it is not likely to go away. Therefore, in order to best serve the needs of the public and inmates/clients, government must assure integrity in the contracting process as well as effective and honest monitoring. Another possibility is to forge a public-private partnership in which the needs of the public and inmates/clients are met by a two-tier approach to service delivery.

Reviewing the Case

The privatization of corrections is an issue that is being considered all over the nation. There are those who hotly protest inroads by the private sector for a variety of reasons. Governor McKernan's problem was to make up a projected $121 million shortfall, and the privatization of one juvenile facility was viewed as a partial solution.

Critics of the proposal are afraid of program cutbacks and reduction in quality of service. One legislator even raised the question of whether the entire Department of Corrections was going to be privatized. Whatever one's views, the issue is controversial. The fears of state employees, taxpayers, and inmates or clients have been raised, and those fears must be carefully addressed before proceeding.

For Further Study

Roy Amara and Andrew J. Lipinski, *Business Planning for the Future: Scenarios and Strategies* (New York: Pergamon Press, 1983).

John Naisbitt, *Megatrends* (New York: Warner, 1984).

Paul Sedenstat, ed., *Privatizing Correctional Institutions* (New Brunswick, N.J.: Transaction Books, 1992).

Key Terms

Privatization	Legitimate Force
Section 1983	Public-Private Partnership

Ethics and Social Influence

CHAPTER 17

Case Study: MCI Drug Probe Finds Corruption, Smuggling Statewide; Fifteen Arrested

In August 1990 an investigation into drugs and money at Florida's Martin Correctional Institution eventually spread throughout the state, turning up evidence of widespread corruption of prison officers and leading to fifteen arrests.[1]

"Operation Crumbling Rock" began at MCI in May 1989 after officials discovered drugs and large amounts of money being sent to inmates through the mail.

"This is a historic case. That's why it has taken fifteen months to get this far," said Florida Department of Law Enforcement agent J. R. Miller, who headed the investigation.

MCI officials had asked state law enforcement and federal postal authorities to investigate. The investigation uncovered an organization of inmates who bribed corrections officers to serve as "mules" to smuggle in drugs and cash supplied by people on the outside. Five other corrections officers, who worked at four different prisons, were arrested during the investigation. Authorities also searched for, and questioned, many people outside the institution.

As of August 1990, Agent Miller stated, another sixty inmates, twenty-five corrections officers, and fifty civilians had been identified as suspects, but most of them had not yet been charged. They include inmates serving life sentences who were not arrested, he said.

"It would be unrealistic for the state to bear the cost of prosecution and travel required to bring those inmates to trial," he said.

"Hopefully, a lot of them will be disciplined administratively within the Department of Corrections."

Stacks of telephone, telegraph, and postal records revealed evidence of the transactions between officers, inmates, and their friends and relatives.

"The inmates knew who to go to. They knew which ones were the corrupt officers," stated Miller.

Court records show the network ran like a business—a lucrative business in which drugs often sold for three times their street value—with a phone number or post office box where inmates could place orders for drugs or cash. The inmate who handled the money kept a ledger of transactions. (Inmates are not allowed to handle money in large sums in prisons because it causes fights.)

The drugs were delivered to corrections officers by mail or by inmates' relatives visiting the prisons and then were smuggled into the compound by the officers. Records show that officers were paid between $200 and $300 per delivery.

FDLE agents, postal inspectors, and prison officials arrested two MCI officers after they showed up for work one morning at the prison north of Indiantown. Another officer and four former MCI officers later surrendered at the FDLE office in Fort Pierce.

Inmates were arrested at four prisons, a former inmate was arrested at his home in Seminole County, and two inmates' wives were taken into custody. The brother of a former inmate and his wife also were arrested near their home in Broward County. One inmate boasted about the number of corrections officers he had corrupted at several prisons since 1983.

Pedro Camejo, sentenced in 1981 to twenty-five years for second-degree murder in Dade County, was "one of the ringleaders and brokers for illegal drugs" in the prison system, Miller said.

MCI Superintendent David Farcas blamed greed and "attitudes that they can get away with it" for corrupt officers' actions.

"It hurts the criminal justice system when we have to arrest one of our own," he said. "It's a sad day when this occurs. It hurts."

Former MCI superintendent William Rouse, who requested the investigation in 1989, said he never thought it would lead to the arrest of corrections officers. In his twenty-seven years with the prison system, he said, he never had heard of an investigation of this magnitude.

Officers James Tolbert and Louis Richardson, Jr., both of whom had worked at MCI for more than four years, were greeted at the prison by authorities who charged them with using drugs at an MCI officer's home in Fort Pierce. Neither was charged with supplying contraband to inmates inside the prison.

"I don't even know what it's all about," Tolbert said as agents led him from the prison's administrative offices and put him in a car heading for the Martin County Jail. Both men, graduates of Fort Pierce Westwood High School, subsequently resigned from their jobs.

A third MCI officer was arrested at the FDLE office in Fort Pierce after agents left a note on the front door of his Fort Pierce apartment asking him to report to their office. The officer had been employed at MCI since 1986 and resigned after being charged with bribery, introducing marijuana and money into the prison, as well as possessing cocaine and marijuana at home.

Former MCI officer Bryan Brusseau of Tequesta, whom agents called "one of the primary mules for the inmates," also surrendered at the FDLE office. Brusseau, who graduated from South Fork High School in 1984 and coached at MCI, was charged with racketeering and possession with intent to distribute cocaine and marijuana in the prison. He was released from the Martin County Jail after posting a $10,000 bond.

He confessed to supplying drugs and money to at least fifteen inmates between August 1987 and August 1989, Miller said. Brusseau also allegedly acted as a collection agent for one inmate who owed $1,000 to another for a drug debt, records show.

Two other former MCI officers, Kenneth Gipson and Anthony Jackson, also surrendered to agents in Fort Pierce. Gipson was charged with delivering money to an inmate at the prison in January 1989, and Jackson was accused of taking money from inmates' relatives in February and keeping it.

Farcas said he doesn't know what the prison system can do to prevent corruption among officers, but said he hopes to begin drug testing of prison employees.

"I wish there was a magic method of hiring people to assure these things would not occur, [but] law enforcement does have bad officers—it happens."

Introduction[2]

Workers in corrections are repeatedly tempted to cut corners or to participate in acts deemed unethical or illegal. For example, the case manager or prison counselor who recommends a furlough or early release for an inmate who is always at her beck and call is treading on a slippery slope indeed. Other temptations are not so debatable, such as the food services manager who accepts free trips or other favors for purchasing goods from a particular vendor. Other acts are more flagrantly illegal, such as bringing drugs into the institution for money or participating in the beating of a "deserving" inmate.

Probation and parole officers are not exempt, either. There is a strong temptation to overlook certain violations on the part of some clients for questionable reasons. When such an incident occurs, it is justified as discretionary decision making. The above examples illustrate that people who work in corrections are human. If someone is to be assigned the blame for such occurrences other than the perpetrator, it must be politicians and administrators who have not provided the necessary tools to help staff make critical and ethical decisions.

Another reason administrators have fallen short is that they have developed what Jeffery A. Schwartz[3] calls a "fortress mentality," in which the administrator tries to "hide in plain sight." Further, many administrators act as if they were separate from the community and make no effort to help other community leaders improve the community at large. This chapter explores how to teach ethical decision making to staff and how agencies and organizations can be a positive social influence.

The Growth of Concern

The need to ensure ethical conduct by police has been recognized for at least the last 165 years. For example, in England, upon the passage of the Metropolitan Police Act of 1829, Sir Robert Peel issued a set of instructions that stated in part, "When in any division offenses are frequently committed there must be a reason to suspect that the police are not in that Division properly conducted."[4]

Neither has corrections been immune to charges of brutality and corruption. The Boston Prison Discipline Society[5] noted that "suitable punishments" can only be inflicted by men of good character. Since that time periodic media accounts of corruption and brutality have led to efforts to reform prisons and jails. Corruption in corrections often takes the form of corruption of authority, often with unfortunate results. For example, a prisoner named Joan Little was sexually assaulted by her jailer, resulting in his being stabbed to death.[6] Other examples include inmate victimization that occur with the knowledge, if not consent, of staff. Hawkins and Alpert[7] assert that correctional staff become involved in the sub-rosa economy of the institution partly because of low salaries and that alienation pushes staff to become involved in drug trafficking and other corrupt activities.

In an attempt to shed light on corruption in corrections, McCarthy[8] reviewed the files of the internal affairs unit of a department of corrections and found that corruption could be divided into five broad categories: theft, trafficking in contraband, embezzlement, misuse of authority, and a residual or miscellaneous category. A sixth category—brutality—should also be included. These six areas appear to be appropriate bases for a discussion of the misbehavior of corrections managers and employees.

A review of the literature on police and prison employee corruption and brutality seems to show that the police are far ahead of corrections in attempts to deal with the issue. This may be because police are a highly visible part of the criminal justice system, and transgressions are apt to come to light rather quickly, as in the case of Malice Green, a Detroit motorist who died as a result of a beating administered by on-duty police officers in 1992. Corrections is another story. Sheltered behind walls and traditionally protected by isolation, corrections has largely been left alone as long as there were no major disturbances to call the public's attention to the activities of the officials. Jeffery Schwartz[9] asserts that many corrections problems stem from officials' "fortress mentality," characterized by paranoia of the media and the belief that if one "holds onto negative information tightly enough, one will be able to hide in plain sight."

Casual conversation with laypersons would lead one to believe that the public feels that inmates deserve their lot. Few people seem to take notice of what goes on in prisons as long as they are quiet. Corruption is another matter. The taxpayer insists that those we hire to work in prisons or supervise probationers and parolees set an example for honesty and integrity. For both police and corrections workers, expectations of conduct are often unrealistically high, and when the occasional officer or staff member steps over the line, there is much head-shaking and hand-wringing.

Ethics and Criminal Justice Today

Considering the stresses associated with working in corrections, it is remarkable that most men and women go about their jobs faithfully, never becoming involved in corruption of any sort or beating an inmate unnecessarily. However, most corrections workers will confide to close associates that they have been tempted on occasion to cross over the thin line that separates ethical from unethical conduct. In anticipation of such temptations, and often because of them, corrections managers have attempted to devise programs that address the problem before the employee assumes his or her duties.

Sadly, these efforts are wide of the mark. First, while they effectively communicate the expectations of executives and elected officials, they do not provide a tool for the officer or staff member to use when attempting to resolve difficult ethical issues. Second, these efforts fail to account for the influence of peer culture. Sherman[10] points out that there are two ways to learn police ethics: on the job and in a setting removed from the streets. The second way is often through "war stories" told in the academy and by the recruit's field training officer. New employees in corrections also undergo the same moral instruction process as police officers, which includes a brief lecture on integrity or "ethics" at the academy, with the real instruction to follow during the new recruit's probationary period.[11]

A recent article[12] is illustrative of efforts to deal with the issue of ethics. It states that the challenge to executives and police officers "is to sustain the highest level of integrity when there is daily opportunity for integrity to break down."[13] Further, the article exhorts the reader to "install the highest standards of integrity on the part of the individual officer while simultaneously establishing an environment that makes it difficult for officers to sustain corrupt activities."[14]

Equating ethics and integrity, the authors assert that maintaining departmental integrity involves three processes:

1. a thorough background investigation of all applicants to ensure the screening out of unwanted values;
2. a reinforcement of integrity by ensuring that officers have a greater understanding of its importance in policing; and
3. a reduction in the opportunity for human failure by the creation of an anticorruption environment.[15]

These are lofty aims that are better left to the personnel department and to supervisors. One is compelled to ask, "How well do these aims apply to the individual case manager, the probation officer, or for that matter the officer working a cell house or yard patrol?" The only conclusion is, "Not very well." Practitioners have fooled themselves by substituting declarations of intent for substance. We have harangued our recruits and employees and failed to provide the analytic tools necessary for the task. In the meantime, it has been business as usual on the streets or in the cell house, with older officers and employees handling the moral instruction and indoctrinating new employees into a culture that stresses solidarity and silence.

In a recent, and excellent, article critical of our handling of the issue, Davis[16] asks, "Do Cops Really Need a Code of Ethics?" He answers his own question with a resounding "Yes!" The problem, he points out, is that current codes of ethics are poorly written and contradictory and of such lofty aspirations that few police officers are able to live up to them. As a consequence, the recruit gives little thought to them once she or he leaves the academy. As Davis points out, "Codes that seem to come from above generally do not touch the world below."[17] It is important that corrections employees be able to view each situation and temptation in light of a framework that will provide real guidance. Rule-Utilitarianism offers a framework that is a valuable guide to conduct.

Rule-Utilitarianism: A Standard for Evaluating Actions

It is difficult to construct a standard for the moral evaluation of actions for at least three reasons. First, morality is only one of many rational standards for the evaluation of actions. Other standards include self-interest, altruism, and various economic standards. For this reason

a moral evaluation of an action may be incompatible with other standards of evaluation. This leads to a second difficulty in moral reasoning: a standard for the moral evaluation of actions can only serve as a guide to persons who want to act morally. Some persons are simply not interested in acting morally. A third problem arises from ambiguity of moral language. Moral reasoning is prone to equivocation.

There are many standards for evaluating actions. Early in Dickens's A *Christmas Carol*, Scrooge is asked to contribute to a fund for the poor. He refuses, explaining that his taxes help pay for prisons and workhouses. When informed that many would prefer death to living in these places, Scrooge responds that this would be good because it would decrease the surplus population. We must ask, "Why are we inclined to condemn his judgment?"

Clearly, we do not want to claim that his judgment is irrational. If we apply Scrooge's purely economic standard, we might argue that death is a cost-effective solution to the problem of the poor. We are horrified by Scrooge's judgment because moral considerations seem to play no role in it. But whatever we may think of Scrooge as a person, we cannot say that his judgment is irrational. A theory of normative ethics does not imply that morality is the only rational motivation for actions. As John Stuart Mill notes:

> It is the business of ethics to tell us what are our duties, or by what test we may know them; but no system of ethics requires that the sole motive of all we do shall be a feeling of duty; on the contrary, ninety-nine hundredths of all our actions are done from other motives and rightly so done, if the rule of duty does not condemn them.[18]

Thus, even if an action is morally wrong there may be good reasons to do it.

People often expect too much from a nor-

FIGURE 17.1
ACA Code of Ethics

PREAMBLE

The American Correctional Association expects of its members unfailing honesty, respect for the dignity and individuality of human beings and a commitment to professional and compassionate service. To this end, we subscribe to the following principles.

Members will respect and protect the civil and legal rights of all individuals.

Members will treat every professional situation with concern for the person's welfare and with no intent of personal gain.

Relationships with colleagues will be such that they promote mutual respect within the profession and improve the quality of service.

Public criticisms of colleagues or their agencies will be made only when warranted, verifiable and constructive in purpose.

Members will respect the importance of all disciplines within the criminal justice system and work to improve cooperation with each segment.

Subject to the individual's right to privacy, members will honor the public's right to know and will share information with the public to the extent permitted by law.

Members will respect and protect the right of the public to be safeguarded from criminal activity.

Members will not use their positions to secure personal privileges or advantages.

Members will not, while acting in an official capacity, allow personal interest to impair objectivity in the performance of duty.

No member will enter into any activity or agreement, formal or informal, which presents a conflict of interest or is inconsistent with the conscientious performance of his or her duties.

No member will accept any gift, service or favor that is or appears to be improper or implies an obligation inconsistent with the free and objective exercise of his or her professional duties.

In any public statement, members will clearly distinguish between personal views and those statements or positions made on behalf of an agency or the Association.

Each member will report to the appropriate authority any corrupt or unethical behavior where there is sufficient cause to initiate a review.

Members will not discriminate against any individual because of race, gender, creed, national origin, religious affiliation, age or any other type of prohibited discrimination.

Members will preserve the integrity of private information; they will neither seek data on individuals beyond that needed to perform their responsibilities, nor reveal nonpublic data unless expressly authorized to do so.

Any member who is responsible for agency personnel actions will make all appointments, promotions or dismissals in accordance with established civil service rules, applicable contract agreements and individual merit, and not in the furtherance of partisan interests.

ADOPTED AUGUST 1975 AT THE 105th CONGRESS OF CORRECTION
REVISED AUGUST 1990 AT THE 120th CONGRESS OF CORRECTION

mative ethical framework, which is intended only as a rational guide for the ethical evaluation of actions. It should not be rejected simply because some will choose not to be guided by its proscriptions. Some may be unaware of the duties proscribed and others may be unable to correctly apply its principles. In the words of Mill: "There is no difficulty in proving any moral standard whatever to work ill if we suppose universal idiocy to be conjoined with it."[19] In addition to these considerations, we should keep in mind that some might simply ignore the ethical implications of their actions. A normative ethical framework can only serve those who want to act morally.

A final difficulty in moral reasoning arises from the ambiguity of moral language. Since moral language is often ambiguous, it is important that we avoid equivocation. Consider, for example, the term *right*, which has at least three distinct meanings in moral reasoning.[20]

We often use the term *right* to express a positive moral evaluation of an action. One might say that Traci, a client, was right to keep her promise to meet with her probation officer this afternoon. With this statement, one is expressing moral approval of her action. If we want to make a negative evaluation of an action, we speak of it as being wrong.

There is a second sense of *right* often found in moral reasoning. People often use the phrase *right to* as a synonym for permission. I might say that Jim has the right to speak out on the current budget imbalance that will bring about a cutback in corrections funding. It is clear that I am not expressing a positive moral evaluation of his remarks because I can consistently hold that Jim has the right to speak out even if I find his views morally repugnant. I am simply asserting that Jim is permitted to express his view on this matter; he is under no obligation to do so.

We understand a third sense of *right* when we talk about persons having rights. For exam-

ple, it is assumed that by virtue of being a person, a prisoner possesses as a right that which protects him or her from brutality. When we say this we are not making a positive evaluation about brutality, nor are we simply asserting that it is permissible for a prisoner not to be brutalized. If this were the case, then it would follow that it is also permissible to brutalize a prisoner. We are asserting that a prisoner has something that implies moral obligation on the part of others. What is this obligation? It depends upon whether it is a negative or a positive right.[21]

A **negative right** implies an obligation to refrain from acting in certain ways. It is called a noninterference right. For example, if the prisoner's nonbrutality right is a negative right, then it implies only that a corrections practitioner is obliged to refrain from actions that pose a threat of brutality to the prisoner. It does not, however, imply that the practitioner has an obligation to take positive action to prevent others from brutalizing the prisoner.

A **positive right** implies an obligation to act positively. This is often referred to as an entitlement right. It seems plausible to assert that a prisoner's right not to be brutalized implies more than simply a corrections worker's obligation not to act. Most would argue that a corrections professional has an obligation to take positive steps to prevent any act of brutality against a prisoner.

In this chapter we shall not be concerned with what rights persons possess nor with whether those rights are positive or negative. Our framework will provide a standard for making those judgments. We stress only that in moral reasoning, as in other types of reasoning, unclear language can lead to confusion. If one is not careful, one can arrive at some rather unusual judgments.

We are proposing a framework for a theory of normative ethics for corrections practitioners. **A normative moral framework can best be understood as a device for producing**

justified specific moral judgments. It is an attempt to provide the criteria that will enable a person to evaluate actions morally and determine whether an action is permissible, obligatory, or forbidden.

There are a number of distinct approaches to normative ethics. Kant[22] and others have argued that the rightness or wrongness of an action is a function of the person's motive or intention for acting. Kant posits that an action is morally good only if the person's motive is to act morally. Those who adopt this duty-based approach, the deontologists, maintain that the consequences do not determine the moral value of an action. What is important is the person's reason for acting. A morally good action is simply an action that is motivated by the intention to do one's duty.

This approach can be contrasted with a consequentialist or teleological approach. Consequentialists maintain that the rightness or wrongness of an action is exclusively a function of its consequences. In this view an action's rightness or wrongness has nothing to do with the person's motive for acting. An action is morally good only if it produces good consequences, and it is morally good even if the person who performs it is acting from a nonmoral motivation. In John Stuart Mill's view: "He who saves a fellow creature from drowning does what is morally right, whether his motive be duty, or the hope of being paid for his trouble."[23] Thus, in this view, it is possible for a person to act morally even if he or she is not being motivated by the desire to act morally. Although Mill insists that the motivation for an action is irrelevant in determining an action's moral worth, it would be a mistake to assume that a person's motivation for action plays no role in Mill's theory.

Mill distinguishes between the moral evaluations of persons and of actions. In his view, a person's motivation for acting is only important for the moral evaluation of persons. A morally good person is a person who is motivated by the desire to produce good consequences. We can distinguish between a morally good person and a morally good action. A morally good action is any action that produces good consequences. In Mill's view it is possible for a morally good person to perform a morally bad action and for a morally bad person to perform a morally good action.

In proposing a framework of normative ethics for the corrections practitioner, it was necessary to first decide on an approach. In the end, consequentialism was adopted. The reason is simple: our primary concern is to provide a clear framework that will give the corrections practitioner the tools to act morally, whether the practitioner is motivated by duty or some other consideration. There are many kinds of consequentialist normative ethical theories; the one adopted for this framework is utilitarianism. **Utilitarianism can be understood as the view that acting morally consists, in some sense, of maximizing the greatest good for the greatest number.** Before proceeding we need to answer the question: What is the good that we are to maximize?

We have decided to adopt Mill's Greatest Happiness Principle as our standard of good. Mill endorses this principle as the standard for the moral evaluation of actions. Mill states: "Actions are right in proportion as they tend to promote happiness, wrong as they tend to produce the reverse of happiness."[24] It is important to note that the scope of happiness should not be limited to the self. Happiness is to be maximized "to the greatest extent possible, secured to all mankind; and to them only, but so far as the nature of things admits to the whole sentient creation."[25]

We must now ask: What is the best way to apply this principle? Some argue that the best way to produce the greatest good is on a case-by-case basis. This view, often called act-utilitarianism, maintains that a right action is simply the action that is most likely to produce the greatest good for the greatest number, given the particular circumstances at hand. Since the time of Jeremy Bentham, act-utilitarianism has been subjected to a number of objections. These objections often rely on counter-examples based on unusual circumstances that seem to imply that actions such as killing and torturing are sometimes morally obligatory. Others reject act-utilitarianism because it requires persons to perform complicated, expected, utility calculations whenever a moral judgment must be made. Problems like these have led some to reject act-utilitarianism in favor of rule-utilitarianism.

Rule-utilitarians argue that the Greatest Happiness Principle should be applied to types of actions rather than to individual actions. In this view, the Greatest Happiness Principle is to be used to derive a set of moral rules. These rules are justified by an appeal to the greatest good for the greatest number. For a rule-utilitarian, acting morally consists of acting according to moral rules.

The reason for choosing rule-utilitarianism as the framework for a theory of normative ethics for the corrections practitioner is twofold. First, the utilitarian approach seems well suited to the task because public policy lends itself to utilitarian justifications. Second, rule-utilitarianism is rather simple and does not require the corrections practitioner to perform complicated, expected, utility calculations. For the corrections professional, acting morally is simply a matter of following rules.

Utilitarianism has had a profound effect on social institutions. In a democratic society we often evaluate social institutions in terms of the greatest good for the greatest number. If it can be shown that a particular social institution works against the greater good, it is taken as a justification for changing or abolishing it. Thus, utilitarianism is well suited to the task of providing a moral framework for police and correction officers.

The framework proposed here is fairly easy to apply. We must attempt to provide a set of direct rules that, if acted upon by corrections employees, are likely to promote the greatest happiness for the greatest number. It is not our intention to provide a complete set of rules. However, it is not difficult to see that any rule will be compatible with our common moral assumptions.

It should come as no surprise that the Greatest Happiness Principle can be used to formulate rules prohibiting theft, trafficking in contraband, embezzlement, misuse of authority, and brutality. These types of actions do not promote the greatest good for the greatest number, and they are thus morally prohibited. Thus, the advantage of a rule-utilitarian framework is that it enables us to provide a coherent justification for the rules. We do not have to appeal to unclear notions such as integrity, a sense of duty, or respect for the job or the organization. Rather than relying on indoctrination, we can provide the corrections professional with a clear set of moral rules. Most important, these rules are derived from a clear, utilitarian principle. The above acts are prohibited because they are not the type of actions that will maximize the greatest happiness for the greatest number.

One question arises whenever a rule based on a normative moral framework is proposed: What do we do in situations where the rules conflict? In such cases we are faced with a moral dilemma. Suppose, for example, a general obligation to refrain from brutality conflicts with a general obligation to protect the innocent. The rule-utilitarian would say that since the rules find their justification in an appeal to the Greatest Happiness Principle, it seems reasonable that the corrections practitioner ought to obey the rule that is most likely to produce the greatest happiness, given the situation. It is important to note, however, that the corrections officer, case manager, or probation officer is required to perform expected happiness calculations only in cases where the rules conflict. Acting morally is otherwise simply a matter of following rules.

Is this enough? Some might argue that our framework will not solve an important problem. What are we to say to the corrections practitioner who does not believe that he or she is constrained by moral considerations? Should we be satisfied with a framework that will guide only the corrections professional who wants to act morally? We cannot arrive at answers to these questions by an appeal to our framework. A normative ethical framework is a rational guide for the moral evaluation of actions. It cannot be expected to answer all moral questions. This point can be understood by considering two distinct moral questions.

What is the morally correct thing to do? This is a question of normative ethics. When a person asks this question he or she is seeking advice on how to make a correct moral judgment. This is the sort of question our framework is intended to answer. The corrections professional is obliged to act according to the set of direct moral rules that derives from some form of the Greatest Happiness Principle. If the corrections practitioner wishes to act morally, then he or she need only follow the rules.

There are, however, other moral questions that cannot be answered on the normative level. Why should one adopt a rule-utilitarian framework? This is not a normative issue. We are not being asked to morally evaluate an action. This is a question about our choice of a normative framework. It is a metaethical issue, and it cannot be resolved by an appeal to the standards of the normative framework. A person who asks this question will not be convinced by an appeal to the Greatest Happiness Principle. This person is asking why the principle is relevant in moral matters. Any response that involves an appeal to the Greatest Happiness Principle would be correctly rejected as circular. A normative framework cannot be self-justified.

This does not mean that the question has no answer, only that we must look beyond our framework. We have already suggested at least one possible answer. Utilitarianism seems well suited to issues of public policy. That is to say, the appeal to utilitarian considerations seems consistent with our assumptions about public institutions. In many cases their very existence is justified by utilitarian considerations. There is, however, something else that can be said.

We have already mentioned the case of Malice Green. It seems clear that the unnecessary beating of an unarmed man is not the type of action that is justified by an appeal to the Greatest Happiness Principle. Thus, on the normative level, the beating of Malice Green was wrong. What are we to say if the corrections practitioner is not moved by this appeal to a moral standard? We can suggest a response to this question that avoids circularity.

A flagrant misuse-of-power case has come to light from the Georgia Women's Prison at Hardiwick.[26] Fourteen former employees have been indicted on charges including rape and sodomy. Investigators claim that prison employees traded favors for sex as well as forced some inmates to have abortions. The attorney for the inmates claims that such behavior was an accepted part of the subculture and came to light only because women's rights have come to the fore both in prison and in the community at large. We can safely say that such an incident has decreased the public's trust in the Department of Corrections as well as the inmates' respect for the officers and thus is not in the best interests of the staff. To illustrate, one repercussion of the scandal might be to render the Department of Corrections less likely to obtain increased funding for programs and equipment. That is to say, the sexual abuse of women inmates was not only wrong from a utilitarian viewpoint, it was also contrary to the interests of the officers who participated in the abuse. Thus, adhering to a normative ethical framework is often in one's best interest, which serves as a strong reason to adopt it. Once again, according to the framework, it does not matter whether corrections practitioners are motivated by a concern for morality or by a concern for their own benefit. We want them to act morally.

It is interesting to note that similar points can be made regarding other types of corruption. Theft, trafficking in contraband, embezzlement, and misuse of authority are all types of actions that weaken public confidence and trust in the corrections enterprise. It can therefore be argued that these activities are contrary to the long-term interests of the corrections practitioner.

There is no assurance that acting according to the rules will always be in the best interests of the corrections professional. There may be specific cases where acting contrary to a rule will provide an immediate benefit. We wish to stress only that there may be a greater long-term benefit in obeying the rules.

It is important to note that the suggested framework provides guidance even in those cases where the morally correct action is contrary to the interests of the corrections professional. It enables the practitioner to see that this situation is not a true moral dilemma. It is not a result of two seemingly inconsistent moral obligations. It arises as a result of two distinct standards of rational evaluation. That is to say, the corrections professional must decide between a moral action and a self-interested action.

What are we to say to the corrections professional who asks: "Why should I be moral?" This is not a normative question. The person is not asking about the nature of his or her obligations. It is not a metaethical issue. The officer is not asking us about our choice of frameworks. A person who asks this question can agree with our framework and its justification. He or she is simply asking us why morality matters.

One cannot expect to base an answer to this question on any normative framework. A normative ethical framework is irrelevant to a person who sees no need to act morally. It can only tell Scrooge why he is morally obliged to help the poor at Christmas. If Scrooge is not moved by moral considerations, our personal reasons for acting morally will not convince him to behave similarly. If one does not buy into the need for morality, one will see no reason to follow the rules.

Advantages of a Rule-Utilitarian Framework

The primary advantage of a rule-utilitarian framework as a basis for a code of professional ethics for corrections officials is that it enables a person to think more clearly about ethics. It also leads to the solution of the problem cited by Davis. We agree that many codes of ethics are poorly written, inconsistent, and unnecessarily vague. The advantage of a rule-utilitarian framework is that it relies on one fundamental moral principle. All claims about morality must be justified by an appeal to the Greatest Happiness Principle. Using this standard, one can produce a clear set of consistent moral rules, so the corrections manager need not rely on lofty and impractical aspirations. Acting morally is simply a matter of following a set of direct moral rules.

We have noted that morality is only one of many standards for evaluating an action. The rules generated from the Greatest Happiness Principle clearly define the nature and extent of corrections practitioners' moral obligations. It enables them to distinguish moral obligations from other types of obligations.

Consider the obligation to keep silent about the wrongdoing of others. Is a corrections worker morally obliged to keep silent about the abuses of others? Our framework implies that he or she is not morally obliged to keep silent. Silence about corruption or brutality, for example, leads only to its continuation. Since corruption is the sort of activity that will lead to a decrease in happiness, it is morally prohibited. Keeping silent about corruption or brutality is **not** a moral obligation. Any attempt to justify it rests on a nonmoral standard of evaluation.

A second advantage of the framework is that it enables one to clarify moral language. We can replace unclear, vacuous notions such as "integrity" and "duty" with clear statements about obligation. All claims about obligations must be derived from the Greatest Happiness Principle. If a proposed rule fails to satisfy this principle, then there is no obligation. Consider again the earlier discussion about the term *right*.

If a person makes a positive, moral evaluation of an action, we are in a position to assert whether it is true or false. If someone says that a person is morally right to keep quiet about corruption, the corrections practitioner has a standard that enables her or him to evaluate this claim. With this standard he or she can arrive at a justified, moral judgment by determining what contributes to the Greatest Happiness.

If one claims to have a right, that is to say, is permitted, to beat a helpless prisoner, the corrections practitioner now has a standard to evaluate this claim. If it can be shown that this type of activity is contrary to the greatest good for the greatest number, then the right does not exist. The person is prohibited to do so, and the manager can provide a consistent set of reasons for why this is so.

This framework also enables us to think more clearly about rights. Does a prisoner have a nonbrutality right? Is it a negative right or a positive right? The above framework can resolve all these issues. Since rights generate obligations, we have a standard for resolving disputes. This is because all rights must be justified by the Greatest Happiness Principle. If one proposes a right that does not satisfy this principle, a mistake has been made. Persons have rights only insofar as they lead to the greatest good.

Our framework also provides a means for resolving moral dilemmas. A moral dilemma is simply a situation in which there is a conflict between rules. A moral dilemma can be resolved by a direct appeal to the Greatest Happiness Principle. If the rules provide contradictory judgments in a particular case, we are obliged to resolve the conflict on the basis of our estimation as to which of the rules is more likely to lead to the greatest good, given the situation.

This framework also provides a means for resolving moral questions when no rules seem to apply. Since our primary obligation is to promote the greatest good, the corrections practitioner in that situation must calculate the expected utility of the various options and select the one that is most likely to lead to happiness.

Tools for the Future

Ensuring ethical conduct of guards in early prisons and of modern day corrections practitioners has been a thorny problem for managers and executives. Law enforcement is far ahead of corrections in attempting to deal with the problem through training. However, contemporary efforts to give practitioners effective tools to help them make ethical decisions are lacking for two reasons: first, efforts fail to account for the influence of peer pressure, and second, efforts fall short on substance.

The elements of danger and authority serve to increase group solidarity, often at the expense of ethical conduct. Efforts to overcome group solidarity have not been successful. The suggested framework addresses this by noting that the corrections practitioner is not under a moral obligation to remain silent about corruption or brutality. It also can be argued that acting morally enhances a climate of trust that fosters public support and best serves the interests of the corrections practitioner.

The normative framework that has been discussed will provide those who work in corrections with the tools needed to clarify the difficult task of moral reasoning. Rule-utilitarianism is well suited to this task. It states in a clear way that all moral judgments must, in the end, be justified by an appeal to the Greatest Happiness Principle. It provides a clear set of moral rules that enable the corrections practitioner to derive moral judgments. Our justification for this is threefold. First, public policy is often justified by an appeal to utilitarian justifications. Second, rule-utilitarianism is a simple theory to apply. For the corrections professional, acting morally is mostly a matter of following rules. Third, it also provides a means for resolving moral dilemmas. Rule conflicts are resolved by an appeal to the greatest good.

This discussion has attempted to clarify what can and cannot be expected of any theory of normative ethics for those who work in corrections. A normative theory can only provide a rational guide for the moral evaluation of actions; it can only tell us what we are obliged to do. A normative theory also empowers staff with a means for clarifying the often-confusing nature of moral language. It cannot ensure that these moral judgments are compatible with other nonmoral standards of evaluation. The poor visibility and isolation of corrections workers demand that practitioners adhere to the highest standards of ethical conduct. If executives and trainers apply the suggested framework, they will have a useful tool for making justified ethical decisions.

Empowering the Corrections Employee

Swift, Houston, and Anderson[27] attempt to answer the question of how to meet the need for training in ethical decision making. Based upon a survey of officers in law enforcement, jails, and a medium-security prison, they tentatively conclude that utilitarianism is at least as im-

portant to ethical decision making as societal expectations and more important than religion or the Golden Rule. These researchers handed out 143 questionnaires to a sample of day- and evening-shift police officers, jail officers, and prison officers. Respondents returned 109 questionnaires, out of which 23 were rejected. Of the 86 respondents there were 77 males, 9 females, and one who did not respond to that question. Respondents' average age was 35.6 years. The respondents were overwhelmingly white (79), with 3 reporting to be of Hispanic heritage, 2 of African-American heritage, and 2 of Native American heritage.

The questionnaires presented a series of moral dilemmas and asked questions about how the respondents would resolve them. Based upon the data, we suggest the following training program in a one-day format. The program is not a panacea and does not make immoral employees moral, but it does answer some questions for concerned and motivated employees.

One-Day Training Program

A. Scope of the Problem
   1. How much corruption exists within the field of corrections
   2. Cost to taxpayers
B. Identifying the Problem
   1. Brutality
   2. Corruption
   3. Theft
   4. Trafficking in contraband
   5. Embezzlement
   6. Misuse of authority
C. What to Do about It
   1. How we usually resolve moral dilemmas
      a. inconsistency
      b. situational factors
   2. The ways people often look at ethics
      a. religion

b. societal expectations
c. golden Rule
d. utilitarianism
D. Rule-Utilitarianism
1. What it is
2. How is it useful
3. How we can put it to work on the job
and in our everyday lives
E. Summary and Conclusions

Positive Social Influence and Social Responsibility of the Corrections Organization

Society presents corrections managers with enormous problems in the forms of high populations or caseloads, gangs, budget reductions, and many other difficult-to-solve issues. Beginning about World War II corrections philosophy began to be informed by the rehabilitation ideal. During the 1970s this philosophy began to be replaced by a "just deserts" philosophy. Today, when there are more men and women under correctional supervision than at any time in our history, critics assert that prisons are nothing more than human warehouses.

During the 1960s the public began to demand more accountability from businesses and public agencies in areas relating to the public good. Corrections organizations have been largely exempt from these demands because it was believed that they fulfilled a necessary social function. To be sure, social activists, academicians, and others took an interest in the inmates and clients caught up in the corrections system, but little attention has been paid to the corrections organization and its responsibilities to the community other than security or counseling.

Social Responsibility Defined

There have been a number of attempts to define social responsibility; however, those defini-tions are vague and somewhat incoherent. For example, Davis and Blomstrom define social responsibility as "the obligation of managers to take actions which protect and improve the welfare of society as a whole along with their own interests."[28] This definition is an excellent example of another difficulty in moral reasoning. It is incoherent because it rests on an inconsistent standard in that the interests of society are not always compatible with the interests of individuals.

For example, suppose a warden knows for a fact that a number of his employees have been brutalizing inmates. Suppose also that if this information were to come to light it would likely lead to his termination. If we were to adopt the Davis-Blomstrom definition of social responsibility, it might be argued that the warden has an obligation to report the brutality. This judgment rests upon the assumption that this type of activity is contrary to the welfare of society as a whole. It would also follow that he has an obligation not to report the brutality. This judgment rests upon the assumption that his termination is contrary to his own interests. The warden is obliged to report and not report the brutality. Thus, the Davis-Blomstrom definition is incoherent and must be rejected.

In our view, social responsibility cannot be distinguished from moral obligation. We have argued that all claims about obligation must be justified by an appeal to the greatest good for the greatest number. Thus, all obligations can be understood as social obligations. For this reason we need not posit a distinct definition of social responsibility for organizations.

It is also our contention that what Davis-Blomstrom refer to as social power[29] can be more clearly understood as the scope of social influence. Once again, in our view all claims about obligation must be justified by an appeal to the greatest good for the greatest number. A large penitentiary will have a greater social influence than a small work-release center simply because the actions of a large penitentiary directly and indirectly affect more people in the community. We are therefore proposing a model that outlines how organizations should adhere to the obligation to behave in a manner that maximizes the greatest good for the greatest number.

A Model for Responsible Social Influence

Proposition 1: Responsible social influence arises out of the general obligation to maximize the greatest good for the greatest number. We agree with Davis,[30] who argues that organizations such as business and public agencies possess varying influences in areas like minority employment and environmental pollution. This phenomenon is to be understood in terms of the scope of social influence. A large institution will have a greater influence on society simply because it affects the lives of more people. The greater the number of those affected, the greater the influence.

Proposition 2: Responsible social influence requires being open to input from the community. A willingness to disclose operations to the public is another essential element. An agency that is truly working for the greater good has nothing to fear from public scrutiny. If an agency is acting responsibly, there is no need for it to hide in plain sight.

Proposition 3: Responsible social influence requires a careful evaluation of social costs and benefits. Both short- and long-term consequences must be considered before any new service or activity is undertaken. For example, in most cases a comprehensive cost-benefit analysis should be carried out prior to decision making. Before a new correctional institution is constructed, a social and environmental impact statement is imperative. Sometimes it might be necessary to sacrifice a short-term gain for a long-term advantage.

Proposition 4: Responsible social influence requires a careful evaluation of real and hidden economic costs and benefits. Public interest demands disclosure of hidden costs. Those costs include loss of tax revenue, inflated welfare rolls, and hidden medical and/or education costs for the inmate. An agency's actions must be governed by the public's willingness to pay.

Proposition 5: Responsible social influence requires the full utilization of all institutional resources. For example, the skills and talents of inmates, clients, and staff must be used for the benefit of the community. An agency cannot achieve the greatest good if it ignores available resources that can benefit the community.

The preceding propositions are intended to guide the organization in its relationship with the community at large. These propositions also imply rules for the behavior of correctional organizations. In order to determine the extent of compliance to these rules a utility audit is proposed.[31] In our view, a utility audit is defined as the process of measuring an agency's compliance with the five propositions.

Summary

The corrections professional faces a difficult task. More than a few employees have carried contraband into the institution or have been seduced by an inmate or a client or by a friend of an inmate or a client. Such incidents usually have tragic consequences for the employee, and when that happens the image of the entire organization is tarnished. But ethical decisions are not limited to issues of drugs or sex. Corruption, abuse of authority, and brutality must also be considered as temptations to be dealt with.

FIGURE 17.2
Areas of Social Influence

Community Safety
Internal Safety:
  Counts
  Policies and Procedures
  Facility Design
  Audits
External Safety:
  Policies and Procedures
  Audits
  Adequate Classification

Employee Training and Education
Policy on Leaves of Absence:
  Full-Time Schooling
  Training Offered on Site
Dollars Spent on Training:
  Academy
  OJT
  Hours of Training Offered on Site
  Dollars Available for University and Off-Site Training
  Specialized Training
Plans for Future Training
Career Training and Counseling

Environmental Control
Measurable Pollution:
  Prison Industries
Violations of Government Standards
Resources Devoted to Pollution Control:
  Capital Expenditures
  Personnel Involved
  Programs to Keep Employees Alert

External Relations
Community Development
  Support of Minority and Community Enterprises
    Through:
    Purchasing
    Contracting

Organizational Philanthropy
Contribution to:
  Arts
  Education
  Poverty Programs
  Health
  Community Development
Hours of Work Donated
Programs for Permitting Employee/Inmate Involvement
    in Social Projects:
  On Work Time
  After Hours
  Use of Organizational Facilities and Equipment
  Human Resources Support:
    Number of People
    Work Hours

Minority and Women Employment and Advancement
Current Hiring Practices
Affirmative Action Program
Percent Minority and Women:
  Employment
  Advancement
  Compared with Other Governments and Businesses:
  Specialized Minority and Women Career Counseling
  Special Recruiting Efforts

Employee Relations Benefits and Satisfaction with
    Work
Wage Comparisons with Comparable Occupations:
  Retirement Plans
  Turnover and Retention by Position
  Maternity and Day Care
  Insurance and Health Programs
  Comparisons of Units on Promotions, Terminations,
    Hires Relative to
    Age
    Sex
    Race
    Education
  Performance Review System:
    Communication
    Counseling for Poor Performance
  General Working Environment

Employee Safety and Health
Work Environment Measures
  ACA Standards
  OSHA Requirements
Safety Performance
  Assaults
  Accident Severity—Work Hours Lost
Services Provided to Employees:
  Mental Health
  Alcohol/Substance Abuse
Employee Health Measures:
  Sick Days Used
  Wellness Programs

Source: Adapted from Samuel C. Certo, *Principles of Modern Management: Functions and Systems*, 3d ed.: Copyright © 1986 by Allyn and Bacon. Reprinted by permission.

Corrections executives and politicians have attempted to deal with the issue of ethics by hiring only the "right" people and then haranguing them about integrity. This chapter attempts to address ethics in the workplace by providing a framework to help the employee make tough ethical decisions. Utilitarianism is adopted as a framework and the Greatest Happiness Principle as the guide to applying utilitarianism. The advantages of utilitarianism are that it clarifies ambiguous language, it resolves dilemmas or conflict between rules, and it accounts for peer influence. A one-day training session is suggested as a way to acquire tools for ethical decision making.

Organizations as well as individuals are obligated to contribute to the greatest good. Five propositions are suggested that, if followed, will allow the organization to take a leadership role in the community in several areas. Finally, a social audit is suggested so that agency executives can assess the degree of compliance to some sort of positive social influence model.

Reviewing the Case

The MCI officers' involvement in smuggling drugs is a tragic example of the temptations confronted by corrections employees every day. Fortunately, most are able to make the correct decision and do not become involved. For others, the temptation is too much to resist, and the case study illustrates the results.

Moral reasoning is difficult. If Florida DOC officials had provided tools to help the officers reason morally, perhaps some of them would not have become involved. For those who chose to be immoral, no amount of training would have stopped or altered their behavior. However, if the officers had been introduced to rule-utilitarianism in an understandable form, they would have been able to justify the "right" decision. They would have been able to reason out the correct answer and to justify a decision that maximizes the greatest good for the greatest number. In other words, following the rules and acting in one's own self-interest will go a long way in keeping one out of trouble.

For Further Study

Raymond A. Bauer and Dan H. Fenn, Jr., "What Is a Corporate Social Audit?" *Harvard Business Review* (January-February 1973), pp. 37–48.

Bernard J. McCarthy, "Keeping an Eye on the Keeper: Prison Corruption and Its Control," in Michael C. Braswell, Belinda R. McCarthy, and Bernard J. McCarthy, eds., *Justice, Crime, and Ethics* (Cincinnati: Anderson, 1991).

Key Terms

Negative Right
Normative Moral Framework
Greatest Happiness Principle
Positive Right
Utility Audit
Consequentialist Approach
Social Influence

NOTES

Chapter 1

1. Condensed from Tharp, M. (1987, April 22). "Oregon's overcrowded prisons reflect a nationwide problem." *The Wall Street Journal*, Vol. 37:1, pp. 37–38.
2. Since the publication of this article, the California inmate population has topped 100,000.
3. Bureau of Justice Statistics, *Correctional Populations in the United States* (Washington, D.C.: Bureau of Justice Statistics, 1990 and 1991).
4. David Duffee, *Correctional Management* (Englewood Cliffs, N.J.: Prentice-Hall, 1980), p. 8.
5. Douglas Shannon, "Correctional Executives: Who's Leading the Way?" *Corrections Today*, (1990) 49:1, pp. 48, 94.
6. Bruce Wolford, "Wardens and Superintendents: A Diverse Group," *Corrections Compendium*, 1988, 13:1–7, in Champion, *Corrections in the United States*, 1990.
7. Dean J. Champion, *Corrections in the United States: A Contemporary Perspective* (Englewood Cliffs, N.J.: Prentice-Hall, 1990), pp. 312–16.
8. Champion, *Corrections in the United States*, p. 316.
9. Alan R. Coffey, *Correctional Administration* (Englewood Cliffs, N.J.: Prentice-Hall, 1975), in Duffee, *Correctional Management*, p. 8.
10. Richard McCleery, *Policy Change in Prison Management* (East Lansing: Michigan State University, 1957).
11. Jameson W. Doig, *Criminal Corrections: Ideals and Reality* (Lexington, Mass.: Lexington Books, 1983).
12. John DiIulio, *Governing Prisons* (New York: The Free Press, 1987).
13. Ibid., p. 256.
14. Duffee, *Correctional Management*.
15. William G. Archambeault and Betty J. Archambeault, *Correctional Supervisory Management* (Englewood Cliffs, N.J.: Prentice-Hall, 1982).
16. John Klofas, Stan Stojkovic, and David Kalinish, *Criminal Justice Organizations: Administration and Management* (Pacific Grove, Calif.: Brooks/Cole, 1990).
17. Paul Tappan, *Crime, Justice, and Correction* (New York: McGraw-Hill, 1960), pp. 593–619.
18. Ibid., p. 599.
19. Ibid., p. 604–606.
20. Ibid., p. 604–606.
21. John Irwin, *Prisons in Turmoil* (Boston: Little, Brown, 1980), pp. 26–27.
22. Donald R. Cressey, ed., *The Prison: Studies in Institutional Organization and Change* (New York: Holt, Rinehart and Winston, 1961).
23. Erving Goffman, "On the Characteristics of Total Institutions: The Inmate World," in Cressey, ed., ibid.
24. Gresham Sykes, "Men, Merchants, and Toughs," *Social Problems* 4 (October 1956), pp. 130–37.
25. Ibid., p. 137.
26. Goffman, "Characteristics."
27. Gresham Sykes and Sheldon L. Messinger, "The Inmate Social System," in *Theoretical Studies in Social Organization of the Prison*, by Richard A. Cloward, Donald R. Cressey, George H. Grosser, Richard McCleery, Lloyd E. Ohlin, Gresham M. Sykes, and Sheldon L. Messinger (New York: Social Science Research Council, 1960), pp. 130–44.
28. Gresham Sykes, *The Society of Captives* (Princeton: Princeton University Press, 1958).

29. Stanton Wheeler, "Socialization in Correctional Communities," *American Sociological Review* 26 (October 1961), pp. 697–712.

30. George Grosser, "External Setting and Internal Relations of the Prison," in *Theoretical Studies,* by Cloward, et al., pp. 130–44.

31. Donald R. Cressey and John Irwin, "Thieves, Convicts, and the Inmate Culture," *Social Problems* 10 (Fall 1962), p. 142.

32. Lucien X. Lombardo, *Guards Imprisoned* (New York: Elsevier North Holland, 1981).

33. Ibid., p. 55.

34. Richard McCleery, "Communication Patterns as Bases of Power," in *Theoretical Studies,* by Cloward, et al., pp. 39–77.

35. Donald R. Cressey, "Limitations on Organization of Treatment in the Modern Prison," in *Theoretical Studies,* by Cloward, et al., pp. 78–110.

36. James Jabobs, *Stateville: The Penitentiary in Mass Society* (Chicago: University of Chicago Press, 1977).

37. Kelsey Kauffman, *Prison Officers and Their World* (Cambridge: Harvard University Press, 1988).

38. David Dressler, *Practice and Theory of Probation and Parole* (New York: Columbia University Press, 1959), p. 6.

39. Ibid., pp. 13–14.

40. Bureau of Justice Statistics (Bulletin), "Probation and Parole 1990" (Washington, D.C.: Bureau of Justice Statistics, 1990).

41. Dean J. Champion, *Corrections in the United States: A Contemporary Perspective* (Englewood Cliffs, N.J.: Prentice-Hall, 1990).

42. Dressler, *Practice and Theory,* pp. 48–50.

43. Ibid., pp. 51–52.

44. Champion, *Corrections,* p. 247.

45. Bureau of Justice Statistics, "Probation and Parole," 1990.

46. DiIulio, *Governing Prisons,* p. 255.

Chapter 2

1. Condensed from Patricia Phelps Schupple and H. David Jenkins, "Maryland's Division of Corrections: Forming Partnerships for the Future," *Corrections Today,* December 1988, pp. 110–12.

2. Leonard D. White, *The Federalist* (New York: Macmillan, 1948).

3. Robert B. Denhardt, *Theories of Public Organization* (Monterey, Calif.: Brooks/Cole, 1984), p. 41.

4. Ibid., p. 43.

5. Woodrow Wilson, "The Study of Administration," *Political Science Quarterly* (June 1887), pp. 197–222.

6. Ibid., p. 198.

7. Ibid., p. 218.

8. Samuel C. Certo, *Principles of Modern Management: Functions and Systems,* 3d ed. (Dubuque: Wm. C. Brown, 1985), p. 27.

9. Fredrick W. Taylor, "Time Study, Piece Work and the First Class Man," in Harwood F. Merrill, ed., *Classics in Management* (New York: American Management Association, 1960), p. 69.

10. H. L. Gantt, "A Bonus System of Rewarding Labor," in Merrill, ed., *Classics in Management,* pp. 134–35.

11. Certo, *Principles of Modern Management,* p. 34.

12. Henri Fayol, "General Principles of Management," in D. S. Pugh, ed., *Organization Theory,* 2d ed. (New York: Penguin Books, 1984), pp. 135–56.

13. H. H. Gerth and C. Wright Mills, trans. and eds., *From Max Weber: Essays in Sociology* (New York: Oxford University Press, 1946).
    A. M. Henderson and Talcott Parsons (trans. and eds., *Max Weber: The Theory of Social and Economic Organization* (N.Y.: The Free Press, 1947).

14. George F. Wieland and Robert A. Ullrich, *Organizations: Behavior, Design, and Change* (Homewood, Ill.: Richard D. Irwin, 1976), p. 7.

15. Fred Luthans, *Organizational Behavior,* 4th ed. (New York: McGraw-Hill, 1985), pp. 528–29.

16. Henry C. Metcalf and L. Urwick, "Introduction to Mary Parker Follett," in *Dynamic Administration* (New York: Harper and Brothers, 1940), pp. 9–29.

17. Ibid., p. 9–29.

18. Mary Parker Follett, *The Creative Experience* (New York: Longmans, Green, 1924).

19. James D. Mooney, *The Principles of Organization* (New York: Harper and Brothers, 1947).

20. Ibid., p. 5.

21. Lyndall Urwick, *The Elements of Administration* (New York: Harper and Brothers, 1944).

22. Chester I. Barnard, *The Functions of the Executive* (Cambridge: Harvard University Press, 1938).

23. Elton Mayo, "Hawthorne and the Western Electric Company," in D. S. Pugh, ed., *Organizational Theory,* 2d ed. (New York: Penguin Books, 1984) pp. 279–92.

24. Fremont E. Kast and James E. Rosenzweig, *Organization and Management,* 3d ed. (New York: McGraw-Hill, 1979), p. 78.

25. Ibid., pp. 78–82.
26. Denhardt, *Theories of Public Organization*, p. 71.
27. Ibid., p. 72.
28. Ibid., p. 72.
29. Charles E. Lindblom, "The Science of Muddling Through," in Fred A. Kramer, ed., *Perspectives on Public Bureaucracy: A Reader on Organization* (Cambridge: Winthrop, 1973).
30. Douglas McGregor, "Theory X and Theory Y," in D. S. Pugh, ed., *Organization Theory*, 2d ed. (New York: Penguin Books, 1984), p. 327.
31. F. Herzberg, "The Motivation-Hygiene Theory," in D. S. Pugh, ed., *Organization Theory*, 2d ed. (New York: Penguin Books, 1984).
32. Ludwig von Bertalanffy, "The Theory of Open Systems in Physics and Biology," *Science* 13 (January 1950).
33. Kast and Rosenzweig, *Organization and Management*, p. 98.
34. L. Thomas Hopkins, *Integration: Its Meaning and Application* (New York: Appleton-Century-Crofts, 1937), pp. 36–49.
35. Kast and Rosenzweig, *Organization and Management*, pp. 108–15.
36. James G. Houston, "The Impact of Physical Environment on the Social Climate of Two Jails" (Ph.D. diss., Portland State University, 1987).

Chapter 3

1. Janet K. Mason, Executive Director, Halfway House of Northern Illinois.
2. Georgette Bennett, *Crimewarps: The Future of Crime in America* (Garden City, N.Y.: Anchor/Doubleday, 1987), p. xiv.
3. Thomas Bender, *Community and Social Change in America* (Baltimore: The Johns Hopkins University Press, 1978), pp. 3–4.
4. Don C. Gibbons, *Society, Crime, and Criminal Behavior*, 6th ed. (Englewood Cliffs, N.J.: Prentice-Hall, 1992), pp. 350–53.
5. Kathleen Maguire and Timothy J. Flanagan, *Sourcebook of Criminal Justice Statistics—1990* (Washington, D.C.: Bureau of Justice Statistics, 1991), p. 296.
6. David Duffee and Edmund F. McGarrell, *Community Corrections: A Community Field Approach* (Cincinnati: Anderson, 1990), p. 26.
7. Gideon Sjoberg, *The Preindustrial City* (New York: The Free Press, 1960).
8. Janet abu-Lughod, *Changing Cities* (New York: HarperCollins, 1991).
9. Norman J. C. Pounds, "The Urbanization of the Classical World," *Annals of the Association of American Geographers*, Vol. 59 (March 1969), pp. 135–57, in Janet abu-Lughod *Changing Cities*, ibid., p. 33.
10. abu-Lughod, *Changing Cities*, p. 35.
11. abu-Lughod, *Changing Cities*, p. 11.
12. abu-Lughod, *Changing Cities*, p. 53.
13. J. L. Hammond and Barbara Hammond, *The Town Laborer: The New Civilization 1760–1832* (Garden City, N.Y.: Doubleday Anchor, 1968), p. 34.
14. U.S. Bureau of Commerce, Bureau of the Census, *Census of Population: 1920–1980, Statistical Abstract of the United States* (Washington, D.C.: Government Printing Office, 1991), p. 7.
15. Ibid.
16. David J. Rothman, *Discovery of the Asylum* (Boston: Little, Brown, 1971), p. 82.
17. Ibid., pp. 82–83.
18. Louis Wirth, "Urbanism as a Way of Life," *American Journal of Sociology*, Vol. 44 (July 1938).
19. abu-Lughod, *Changing Cities*, p. 128.
20. Henry Maine, *Ancient Law*, 10th ed., cheap ed. (London: Murray, 1905).
21. Ferdinand Tönnies, *Community and Society*, in Bender, *Community and Social Change*, pp. 19–20.
22. Emile Durkheim, *The Division of Labor in Society*, George Simpson, trans. (New York: The Free Press, 1933).
23. Georg Simmel, "The Metropolis and Mental Life," in *The Sociology of Georg Simmel*, Kurt H. Wolff, ed. (New York: The Free Press, 1950).
24. Max Weber, *The Theory of Social and Economic Organization*, Talcott Parsons, trans. (New York: The Free Press, 1964).
25. Stephen P. Robbins, *Organization Theory: Structure, Design, and Applications*, 2d ed. (Englewood Cliffs, N.J.: Prentice-Hall, 1987), pp. 232–36.
26. William Graham Sumner, *Folkways* (New York: Mentor Books, 1960).
27. Robert Redfield, *Tepoztlan: A Mexican Village* (Chicago: University of Chicago Press, 1930).
_____, *The Folk Culture of the Yucatán* (Chicago: University of Chicago Press, 1941).
28. Oscar Lewis, *Life in a Mexican Village: Tepoztlán Restudied* (Urbana: University of Illinois Press, 1951).
29. Bender, *Community and Social Change*.
30. Claude S. Fisher, *The Urban Experience*. 2d ed. (San Diego: Harcourt Brace Jovanovich, 1984), pp. 163–66.

31. Bender, *Community and Social Change.*

32. Brian Berry, *The Human Consequences of Urbanization* (New York: St. Martin's Press, 1973).

33. Louis Wirth, "Urbanism as a Way of Life," *American Journal of Sociology*, 44 (1938), pp. 3–24.

34. John Irwin, *Scenes* (Beverly Hills: Sage, 1977).

35. Bender, *Community and Social Change.*

36. W. W. Pilcher, "The Portland Longshoremen: A Dispersed Urban Community" (New York: Holt, Rinehart and Winston, 1972).

37. Fisher, *The Urban Experience*, p. 127.

38. ABA, "Not in My Neighborhood," *American Bar Association Journal*, 70 (June 1984), pp. 27–29.

39. Ibid.

40. During the middle 1970s, the author and a colleague attempted to establish a halfway house in Torrence, California. Permission was applied for, and the subsequent Planning Commission meeting was a near melee in which hysterical neighborhood residents effectively voiced their opposition. Eighteen months later the author successfully established a halfway house in North Las Vegas, Nevada, but subsequent opposition by the press led to its closing six months later.

41. K. S. Abrams, et al., "The Socioeconomic Impacts of State Prison-Siting on the Local Community," Joint Center for Environmental and Urban Problems, Florida International University (May 1985), in George O. Rogers and Marshall Haimes, "Local Impact of a Low-Security Federal Correctional Institution," *Federal Probation* (September 1987), pp. 28–34.

42. James B. Jacobs, "The Politics of Corrections: Town/Prison Relations as a Determinant of Reform," *Social Service Review*, Vol. 50 (1976), pp. 623–31.

43. H. A. Tully, J. P. Winter, J. E. Wilson, T. J. Scanlon, "Correctional Institution Impact and Host Community Resistance," *Canadian Journal of Criminology*, Vol. 24 (April 1982), pp. 133–39.

44. Jerrald D. Krause, "The Effects of Prison Siting Practices on Community Status Arrangements: A Framework Applied to the Siting of California State Prisons," *Crime and Delinquency*, 38:1 (January 1992), pp. 27–55.

45. Rogers and Haimes, "Local Impact."

46. K. S. Abrams, et al., "Socioeconomic Impacts."

47. Ibid.

48. Jacobs, "The Politics of Corrections."

49. Tully, et al., "Correctional Institution Impact."

50. Rogers and Haimes, "Local Impact."

51. Jacobs, "The Politics of Corrections."

52. Ibid.

53. Tracy Rose, "Volunteers in Prison: The Community Link," *Corrections Today* (April 1988), pp. 216–18.

54. Reginald Wilkinson, "Urban Prisons Use Community Resources," *Corrections Today* (April 1989), pp. 26–30.

55. Herbert G. Callison, *Introduction to Community-based Corrections* (New York: McGraw-Hill, 1983), p. 165.

56. See Elmer Johnson, Work Release: Factors in Selection and Results. Research Grant RD-2427-G-67, Division of Research and Demonstration Grants, Social and Rehabilitation Service, Department of Health, Education, and Welfare (1968).
　　　　　 "Work Release: Conflicting Goals Within a Promising Innovation," *The Canadian Journal of Corrections*, Vol. 12, No. 1 (January 1970).
　　　　　, *The Staff Looks at Community-based Corrections: A Preliminary Survey of Attitudes in One State Program* (1972). Research Report of the Center for the Study of Crime Delinquency and Corrections, Southern Illinois University, Carbondale, Illinois.
　　　　　, *Progress Report on Work Release in the United States* (1972). A Research report of The Center for the Study of Crime, Delinquency, and Corrections, Southern Illinois University, Carbondale, Illinois.
Elmer Johnson and Kenneth E. Katch, "Two Factors in Development of Work Release: Size and Location of Prisons," in *Journal of Criminal Justice*, Vol. 1, No. 1 (1972), pp. 43–50.

57. Gordon P. Waldo, Theodore G. Chiricos, and Leonard E. Dobrin, "Community Contact and Inmate Attitudes: An Experimental Assessment of Work Release, *Criminology*, Vol. 11, No. 3 (November 1971), pp. 345–81.

58. Ibid., p. 369.

59. Gordon P. Waldo and Theodore G. Chiricos, "Work Release and Recidivism: An Empirical Evaluation of a Social Policy," *Evaluation Quarterly*, No. 1 (February 1977), pp. 87–105.

60. Edward Latessa and Harry E. Allen, "Halfway Houses and Parole: A National Assessment," *Journal of Criminal Justice*, Vol. 10, No. 2 (1982), pp. 152–63.

61. David F. Mrad, Robert Kabacoff, and Paul Duckro, "Validation of the Megargee Typology in a Halfway House Setting," *Criminal Justice and Behavior*, Vol. 10, No. 3 (September 1983), pp. 252–62.

62. David A. Dowell, Cecelia Klein, and Cheryl Krichmar, "Evaluation of a Halfway House for Women," *Journal of Criminology*, Vol. 13, No. 3 (1983), pp. 217–26.
63. Edward J. Latessa and Lawrence F. Travis III, "Halfway House or Probation: A Comparison of Alternative Dispositions," *Journal of Crime and Justice*, 14:1 (1991), pp. 53–75.
64. Wilkinson, "Urban Prisons."
65. Bruce Borcherdt, "Influx of Prisons Brings Job Boom to UP," *Detroit Free Press* (August 23, 1989).
66. David Beasley, "State Prisons Bringing Jobs to Depressed Rural Georgia," *Atlanta Journal* (May 21, 1989).
67. Kit Menecher, "Florence Pins Hopes on Prisons," *Denver Post* (April 14, 1991).
68. Jeanie Senior, "A Prisoner of Economics," *The Oregonian* (August 21, 1988).
69. Warden John Conte confirmed that Coalinga has indeed entered the prison business. The city receives a set fee over and above operating costs.

Chapter 4

1. By Greg Shipley, Public Information Officer, Maryland Department of Corrections.
2. Ben M. Crouch and James W. Marquart, *An Appeal to Justice: Litigated Reform of Texas Prisons* (Austin: University of Texas Press, 1989), p. 238.
3. Ronald Goldfarb, *Jails: The Ultimate Ghetto* (New York: Anchor Press/Doubleday, 1973).
4. Ibid., p. 349.
5. *Mapp v. Ohio*, 367 U.S. 643 (1961).
6. *Escobedo v. Illinois*, 378 U.S. 478 (1964).
7. *Miranda v. Arizona*, 384 U.S. 436 (1966).
8. *Monroe v. Pape*, 365 U.S. 167 (1961).
9. 83 S. Ct. 822 (1963).
10. 83 S. Ct. 745 (1963).
11. 83 S. Ct. 1068 (1963).
12. *Sanders v. United States*, 83 S. Ct. 1068 (1963).
13. *Cooper v. Pate*, 378 U.S. 546 (1964).
14. William G. Archambeault and Betty J. Archambeault, *Correctional Supervisory Management: Principles of Organization, Policy, and Law* (Englewood Cliffs, N.J., Prentice-Hall, 1982).
15. Ibid., p. 198.
16. Ibid., p. 198.
17. Goldfarb, *Jails*, p. 352.
18. *Sweeny v. Woodall*, 344 U.S. 86 (1952).
19. *Dye v. Johnson*, 338 U.S. 864 (1949).
20. *Sweeny v. Woodall*, 344 U.S. 86 (1952) at 92–93.
21. *Jordan v. Fitzharris*, 257 F. Supp. 674 (N.D. Cal., 1966).
22. Goldfarb, *Jails*, p. 354.
23. Goldfarb, *Jails*, p. 355.
24. *Sostre v. Rockefeller*, 312 F. Supp. 863 (S.D.N.Y., 1970) in Goldfarb, *Jails*, p. 356.
25. *Holt v. Sarver*, 300 F. Supp. 825 (E.D. Ark., 1969) in Goldfarb, *Jails*, p. 358.
26. *Bell v. Wolfish*, 441 U.S. 559, 99 S. Ct., 1984, 60 L. Ed. 2d 481 (1979).
27. *Long v. Parker*, 390 F. 2d 816, 820 (Ed Cir., 1968).
28. *Cooper v. Pate*, 378 U.S. 546 (1964).
29. *Cruz v. Beto*, 405 U.S. 319, 31 L. Ed. 2d 263 (1972).
30. *Sostre v. Otis* in Goldfarb, *Jails*, p. 373.
31. *Morales v. Turman*, 326 F. Supp. 677 (E.D. Texas, 1971); also see *Carothers v. Follette*, 314 F. Supp. 1014, 1021, 1025 (S.D. N.Y., 1970), and *Procunier v. Martinez*, et al., 416 U.S. 396, 94 S. Ct. 1800, 40 L. Ed. 2d 224 (1974). The Court held that censorship of inmate correspondence is not justified on the grounds that inmate social intercourse is somehow fundamentally different from that of free people. On the other hand, it is necessary to preserve the legitimate order of the institution, and as a consequence, inmates may not send or deliver plans concerning escape or information in regard to other criminal activity.
32. Goldfarb, *Jails*, p. 386.
33. *Sostre v. Rockefeller*, 312 F. Supp. 863 (S.D.N.Y., 1970).
34. *Morris v. Travisono*, 310 F. Supp. 857 (D.R.I., 1970).
35. *Wolf v. McDonnell*, 419 U.S. 539, 94 S. Ct. 2963, 41 L. Ed. 2d 935 (1974).
36. Crouch and Marquart, *Appeal*, pp. 124–28.
37. Ibid, pp. 236–38.
38. American Correctional Association, *Correctional Officer Resource Guide* (Washington, D.C.: St. Mary's Press, 1989), p. 124.
39. Ann Yuskanin, "PIO's Rate News Media in Recent Survey," *Corrections Today* (February 1989), p. 80.
40. Ibid., p. 124.
41. Robert W. Landon, "Relating to the News Media," *The Police Chief*, Vol. 54:3, March 1987, p. 7.
42. Arthur F. Nehrbass, "Promoting Effective Media Relations," *The Police Chief*, Vol. 56:1, January 1989, pp. 40–44.
43. Ibid., p. 42.
44. Ibid., p. 44.

45. Melvin Mencher, *Basic News Writing*, 3d ed. (Dubuque: Wm. C. Brown, 1989), p. 219.
46. M. L. Stein, *Getting and Writing the News: A Guide to Reporting* (New York: Longman, 1985), p. 46.

Chapter 5

1. Milton Rokeach, *The Nature of Human Values* (New York: The Free Press, 1973).
2. Jeanne M. Liedtka, "Value Congruence: The Interplay of Individual and Organizational Value Systems," *Journal of Business Ethics* (October 1989), pp. 805-15.
3. Fred R. David, *Fundamentals of Strategic Management* (Columbus: Merrill, 1986), p. 84.
4. Glenn Boseman and Arvind Phatak, *Strategic Management: Text and Cases*, 2d ed. (New York: John Wiley and Sons, 1989), pp. 51-52.
5. David, *Fundamentals*, pp. 84-97.
6. Richard M. Cyert and James G. March, *A Behavioral Theory of the Firm* (Englewood Cliffs, N.J.: Prentice-Hall, 1963), p. 26.
7. Fremont E. Kast and James E. Rosenzweig, *Organization and Management*, 3d ed. (New York: McGraw-Hill, 1979), pp. 153-65.
8. James G. Thompson and William J. McErven, "Organizational Goals and Environment: Goal Setting as an Interaction Process," *American Sociological Review* (February 1958), pp. 23-31.
9. Ibid., p. 27.
10. Charles Perrow, "The Analysis of Goals in Complex Organizations," *American Sociological Review*, Vol. 26 (1961), pp. 854-66.
11. Francis G. Scott, "Action Theory and Research in Social Organizations," *American Journal of Sociology*, Vol. 64 (January 1959), pp. 386-95.
12. John Klofas, Stan Stojkovic, and David Kalinish, *Criminal Justice Organizations: Administration and Management* (Pacific Grove, Calif.: Brooks/Cole, 1990), pp. 37-38.
13. Thomas J. Atchison and Winston W. Hill, *Management Today: Managing Work in Organizations* (New York: Harcourt Brace Jovanovich, 1978), p. 63.
14. Kast and Rosenzweig, *Organization*, p. 161.
15. Jay W. Lorsch and John J. Morse, *Organizations and Their Members: A Contingency Approach* (New York: Harper & Row, 1974), in Kast and Rosenzweig, ibid., p. 163.
16. Lyman W. Porter and Edward E. Lawler III, *Managerial Attitudes and Performance* (Homewood, Ill.: Richard D. Irwin and The Dorsey Press, 1968), in Kast and Rosenzweig, ibid., p. 163.
17. Kast and Rosenzweig, ibid., p. 163.
18. Ibid., pp. 163-64.
19. John T. Whitehead, *Burnout in Probation and Corrections* (New York: Praeger, 1989), pp. 19-21.
20. Robert K. Merton, *Social Theory and Social Structure*, 1968 enlarged edition (New York: The Free Press, 1968), pp. 186-214.
21. Kast and Rosenzweig, *Organization*, p. 165.
22. Samuel C. Certo, *Principles of Modern Management: Functions and Systems*, 3d ed. (Dubuque: Wm. C. Brown, 1985).
23. James W. Vander Zanden, *Social Psychology*, 3d ed. (New York: Random House, 1984), p. 318.
24. Kelsey Kauffman, *Prison Officers and Their World* (Cambridge: Harvard University Press, 1988), p. 167.
25. John Klofas and Hans Toch, "The Guard Subculture Myth," *Journal of Research in Crime and Delinquency*, Vol. 19 (July 1982), pp. 238-54.
26. Kauffman, *Prison Officers*, p. 85.
27. Ibid., pp. 86-114.
28. Amitai Etzioni, "Power, Goals, and Organizational Compliance Structures," in *The Sociology of Corrections*, Robert G. Leger and John R. Stratton (New York: John Wiley and Sons, 1977), p. 15.
29. Andrew Von Hirsch, *Doing Justice* (New York: Hill and Wang, 1976).
   David Fogel, "We Are the Living Proof . . ." *The Justice Model for Corrections* (Cincinnati: Anderson, 1975).
   James Q. Wilson and Richard J. Herrnstein, *Crime and Human Nature* (New York: Simon and Schuster, 1985).
30. Paul W. Tappan, *Crime, Justice, and Correction* (New York: McGraw-Hill, 1960), pp. 237-61.
31. Don C. Gibbons, *Society, Crime, and Criminal Behavior*, 6th ed., (Englewood Cliffs, N.J.: Prentice-Hall, 1992), p. 462.
32. Larry E. Sullivan, *The Prison Reform Movement: Forlorn Hope* (Boston: Twayne, 1990), pp. 25-43.
33. Lawrence F. Travis III, Martin D. Schwartz, and Todd R. Clear, *Corrections: An Issues Approach*, 2d ed. (Cincinnati: Anderson, 1983), p. 174.
34. Robert Martinson, "What Works? Questions and Answers about Prison Reform," *Public Interest*, 35 (Spring 1974), pp. 22-54.

35. Douglas Lipton, Robert Martinson, and Judith Wilks, *The Effectiveness of Correctional Treatment: A Survey of Treatment Evaluation Studies* (Springfield, Mass.: Praeger, 1975).
36. Patricia Van Voorhis, "Correctional Effectiveness: The High Cost of Ignoring Success," *Federal Probation* (March 1987), pp. 56–62.
37. Ibid.
38. Francis T. Cullen, "The Privatization of Treatment: Prison Reform in the 1980s," *Federal Probation*, pp. 8–16.
39. Ibid.
40. Ibid.

Chapter 6

1. By Robert B. Levinson, Ph.D., ACA, Special Projects Manager.
2. These are specially trained veteran correctional officers whose primary role became counseling a group of inmates in how to handle the daily problems encountered in institution living.
3. Robert E. Levinson and Roy E. Gerard, "Functional Units: A Different Correctional Approach," Federal Probation, XXXVII, #4 (1973), pp. 8–15.
4. To some degree, this has changed since 1979, following the introduction of the American Correctional Association's prison accreditation process (ACA, 1990).
5. Aaron Wildavsky, *Speaking Truth to Power: The Art and Craft of Policy Analysis* (Boston: Little, Brown, 1979), p. 62.
6. Heinz Eulau and Kenneth Prewitt, *Labyrinths of Democracy* (Indianapolis: Bobbs-Merrill, 1973) in Charles O. Jones, *An Introduction to the Study of Public Policy*, 2d ed. (North Scituate, Mass.: Duxbury Press, 1977), p. 5.
7. Samuel C. Certo, *Principles of Modern Management*, 3d ed. (Dubuque: Wm. C. Brown, 1985), p. 147.
8. Jeffrey L. Pressman and Aaron B. Wildavsky, *Implementation* (Berkeley: University of California Press, 1973), pp. xiii–xv.
9. Ibid., p. xv.
10. Certo, *Principles*, p. 147.
11. American Correctional Association, *Standards for Adult Correctional Institutions* (ACA Washington, D.C.: St. Mary's Press, 1990), p. vii.
12. Charles O. Jones, *An Introduction to the Study of Public Policy*, 3d ed. (Pacific Grove, Calif.: Brooks/Cole, 1984).
13. Ibid., pp. 49–50.

14. Ibid., p. 50.
15. Ibid., p. 50.
16. Ibid., p. 56.
17. Fred R. David, *Fundamentals of Strategic Management*, Columbus: Merrill, 1986. (Not all of David's tools are presented here as some of them may be impractical for the field of corrections.)
18. Ibid., p. 200.
19. Ibid., p. 202.
20. Adapted from David, ibid., p. 203.
21. Ibid., p. 205–14.
22. Ibid., p. 212.
23. Ibid., p. 223–26.
24. Fred R. David, "Evaluating Alternative Growth Strategies—An Analytical Approach," *Long Range Planning* (Spring 1986).
25. David, *Fundamentals*, pp. 223–24.
26. Jones, *Introduction*, p. 85.
27. Pressman and Wildavsky, *Implementation*, p. xv.
28. Randall B. Ripley and Grace A. Franklin, *Bureaucracy and Policy Implementation* (Georgetown: The Dorsey Press, 1982), p. 4.
29. Ibid., p. 9.
30. Daniel A. Mazmanian and Paul A. Sabatier, *Implementation and Public Policy* (Glenview, Ill.: Scott, Foresman, 1983).
31. Ibid., p. 37.
32. Ibid., p. 71–74.
33. Karen Sue Trisco and V. C. League, "Evaluation of Human-Service Programs," *The 1980 Handbook for Group Facilitators* (San Diego: University Associates, 1980), pp. 224–32.
34. Garry D. Brewer and Peter de Leon, *The Foundations of Policy Analysis* (Pacific Grove, Calif.: Brooks/Cole, 1983), p. 93.
35. Ben M. Crouch and James W. Marquart, *An Appeal to Justice: Litigated Reform of Texas Prisons* (Austin: University of Texas Press, 1989), p. 117.
36. Ibid., p. 123.
37. Ibid., pp. 151–84.

Chapter 7

1. John N. Conte, Warden, Claremont Custody Center, Coalinga, California.
2. Bureau of Justice Statistics, *Justice Expenditure and Employment, 1988*, U.S. Department of Justice (July 1990).
3. Douglas C. McDonald, "The Cost of Corrections: In Search of the Bottom Line," National Institute of Corrections, *Research in Corrections*, 2:1 (February 1989), p. 22.
4. Ibid.

5. Lee Iacocca, *Iacocca: An Autobiography* (New York: Bantam Books, 1984), pp. 38–45. Iacocca discusses the importance of creative "do'ers" being in charge of the organization. He points out that in the 1970s the "bean counters" nearly let the Ford Motor Company die because they delayed in making important market decisions.
6. Aaron Wildavsky, "Political Implications of Budgetary Reform," Albert C. Hyde and Jay M. Shafritz, eds., *Government Budgeting* (Oak Park, Ill.: Moore, 1978).
7. Ibid., p. 43.
8. Nicholas L. Henry, *Public Administration and Public Affairs*, 3d ed. (Englewood Cliffs, N.J.: Prentice-Hall, 1986), pp. 164–76.
9. Ibid., p. 166.
10. Ibid., p. 169.
11. Bertram M. Gross, "The New Systems Budgeting," Albert C. Hyde and Jay M. Shafritz, eds., *Government Budgeting: Theory, Process, Politics* (Oak Park, Ill.: Moore, 1978), pp. 142–69.
12. Ibid., p. 143.
13. Henry, *Public Administration*, p. 170.
14. Graeme M. Taylor, "Introduction to Zero-Based Budgeting," *Government Budgeting*, Albert C. Hyde and Jay M. Shafritz, eds. (Oak Park, Ill.: Moore, 1978).
15. Ibid., pp. 272–73.
16. Henry, *Public Administration*, p. 177.
17. David H. Rosenbloom, *Public Administration: Understanding Management, Politics, and Law in the Public Sector*, 2d ed. (New York: Random House, 1989), p. 267.
18. Ibid., p. 276.
19. Ibid., pp. 276–78.
20. Aaron Wildavsky and Arthur Hammond, "Comprehensive Versus Incremental Budgeting in the Department of Agriculture," in David H. Rosenbloom, ibid., p. 278.
21. Peter Drucker, "What Business Can Learn from Nonprofits," *Harvard Business Review* (July–August [4], 1989), pp. 88–93.

Chapter 8

1. Condensed from Jack Fisher, *San Jose Mercury News*, October 25, 1991.
2. Chris Argyris, *Management and Organizational Development* (New York: McGraw-Hill, 1971).
_____, *Intervention: Theory and Method* (Reading, Mass.: Addison-Wesley, 1970).
_____, *Interpersonal Competence and Organizational Effectiveness* (Homewood, Ill.: The Dorsey Press, 1962).
3. W. Warner Burke, *Organization Development and Practices* (Boston: Little, Brown, 1982), p. 9.
4. Donald F. Harvey and Donald R. Brown, *An Experiential Approach to Organization Development*, 2d ed. (Englewood Cliffs, N.J.: Prentice-Hall, 1982), p. 8.
5. Michael E. McGill, *Organization Development for Operating Managers* (New York: AMACOM, 1977), p. 3.
6. A. H. Maslow, *Motivation and Personality* (New York: Harper and Brothers, 1954).
7. Frederick Herzberg, "The Motivation-Hygiene Theory," *Work and the Nature of Man* (New York: World, 1966), pp. 71–91.
8. E. E. Lawler, *Motivation in Work Organizations* (Monterey: Brooks/Cole, 1973).
9. Victor Vroom, *Work and Motivation* (New York: Wiley, 1964).
10. B. F. Skinner, *Science and Human Behavior* (New York: Macmillan, 1953).
_____, *Beyond Freedom and Dignity* (New York: Knopf, 1971).
11. J. R. Hackman and G. R. Oldham, *Work Redesign* (Reading, Mass: Addison-Wesley, 1980).
12. Burke, *Organization*, p. 98.
13. M. R. Weisbord, "Organizational Diagnosis: Six Places to Look for Trouble with or Without a Theory," *Group and Organizational Studies* (1976), 1:430–47.
_____, *Organizational Diagnosis: A Workbook of Theory and Practice* (Reading, Mass.: Addison-Wesley, 1978).
14. Robert C. Preziosi, *The 1980 Annual Handbook for Group Facilitators* (San Diego: University Associates, 1980).
15. Burke, *Organization*, p. 173.
16. Udai Pareek, "Motivational Analysis of Organizations—Climate (MAO-C)," *The 1989 Annual: Developing Human Resources*, J. W. Pfeiffer and L. D. Goodstein, eds. (San Diego: University Associates, 1989), pp. 161–80.
17. R. Likert, *The Human Organization* (New York: McGraw-Hill, 1967).
18. G. Litwin and R. Stringer, *Motivation and Organizational Climate* (Cambridge: Harvard University Press, 1968).
19. Mark Alexander, "Organizational Norms," *The 1977 Annual Handbook for Group Facilitators* (San Diego, University Associates, 1977), pp. 123–25.

20. R. F. Allen and S. Pilnick, "Confronting the Shadow Organization: How to Detect and Defeat Negative Norms," *Organization Dynamics* (American Management Association, 1973), I (4) pp. 3–18.
21. For a more detailed explanation of the staff subculture, see Kelsey Kauffman, *Prison Officers and Their World* (Cambridge: Harvard University Press, 1988), pp. 85–117.
22. Alexander, "Organizational Norms," pp. 123–24.
23. Mark Alexander, "Organizational Norms Opinionnaire," *The 1978 Annual for Group Facilitators* (San Diego: University Associates, 1978), p. 81.
24. J. William Pfeiffer, Richard Heslin, and John E. Jones, *Instrumentation in Human Relations Training*, 2d ed. (San Diego: University Associates, 1976), pp. 11–17.
25. John Klofas, Stan Stojkovic, and David Kalinich, *Criminal Justice Organizations: Administration and Management* (Pacific Grove, Calif.: Brooks/Cole, 1990), p. 300.
26. Roger Harrison, "Choosing the Depth of Organizational Intervention," *Journal of Applied Behavioral Science* (1970), 6:181–202.
27. E. F. Huse, *Organization Development and Change*, rev. ed. (St. Paul: West, 1980).
28. Burke, *Organization Development*, pp. 230–57.
29. Ibid., p. 231.
30. Lucien X. Lombardo, *Guards Imprisoned* (New York: Elsevier/North Holland, 1981).
31. Thomas A. Harris, *I'm O.K.—You're O.K.* (New York: Avon, 1969).
32. William Glasser, *Reality Therapy: A New Approach to Psychiatry* (New York: Harper and Row, 1975).
33. Russell Grieger and John Boyd, *Rational Emotional Therapy: A Skills-Based Approach* (New York: Van Nostrand Reinhold, 1980).
34. John Klofas, Stan Stojkovic, and David Kalinich, *Criminal Justice Organizations: Administration and Management* (Pacific Grove, Calif.: Brooks/Cole, 1990), pp. 102–103.
35. J. R. Hackman, G. R. Oldham, R. Janson, and K. Purdy, "A New Strategy for Job Enrichment," *California Management Review* (Summer 1975), pp. 57–71.
36. J. R. Hackman, "Work Design," *Improving Life at Work*, J. R. Hackman and J. L. Suttle, eds. (Santa Monica: Goodyear, 1977), p. 136.
37. While the announcement made the newspapers around the state and region, Nic Howell, Public Information Officer for the Illinois Department of Corrections, revealed in a conversation with the author that the remaining fifty-eight positions were reinstated by the General Assembly. The fifty-eight employees, prior to the announcement, were offered positions in the DOC in other locations, some with reduced pay and a few with promotions. Because of ties to their home community, not all of the employees took the jobs.
38. R. Beckhard, *Organization and Development: Strategies and Models* (Cambridge, Mass.: Addison-Wesley, 1969).
39. R. Beckhard and R. T. Harris, *Organizational Transitions: Managing Complex Change* (Cambridge, Mass.: Addison-Wesley, 1977).
40. Ibid., chapter 8.
41. McGill, *Organizational Development*, p. 3.

Chapter 9

1. Condensed from Amy Wallace, *Atlanta Journal* April 22, 1988.
2. David McClelland, ed., *Studies in Motivation* (N.Y.: Appleton-Century-Crofts, 1955), in George F. Wieland and Robert A. Ullrich, *Organizations: Behavior, Design and Change* (Homewood, Ill.: Richard D. Irwin, 1976), p. 141.
3. Bernard Berelson and Gary A. Steines, *Human Behavior: An Inventory of Scientific Findings* (New York: Harcourt, Brace, and World, 1964), pp. 239–40.
4. Fred Luthans, *Organizational Behavior* (New York: McGraw-Hill, 1973), p. 392.
5. Abraham H. Maslow, *Motivation and Personality* (New York: Harper & Row, 1954).
6. Chris Argyris, *Personality and Work* (New York: Harper & Row, 1957).
7. Ibid., pp. 50–51.
8. Samuel C. Certo, *Principles of Management: Functions and Systems*, 3d ed. (Dubuque: Wm. C. Brown, 1985), p. 341.
9. Victor H. Vroom, *Work and Motivation* (New York: John Wiley and Sons, 1964).
10. Ibid., pp. 15–16.
11. F. Herzberg, B. Mausner, and B. B. Snyderman, *The Motivation to Work* (New York: John Wiley and Sons, 1959); Frederick Herzberg, "The Motivation-Hygiene Theory," *Work and the Nature of Man* (World, 1966), pp. 71–91.
12. Barry L. Reece and Rhonda Brandt, *Effective Human Relations in Organizations*, 3d ed. (Boston: Houghton Mifflin, 1987), p. 144.

13. Phillip G. Clampitt, *Communicating for Managerial Effectiveness* (Newbury Park, Calif.: Sage, 1991), pp. 1–23.
14. William G. Archambeault and Betty J. Archambeault, *Correctional Supervisory Management: Principles of Organization, Policy and Law* (Englewood Cliffs, N.J.: Prentice-Hall, 1982).
15. Gary L. Kreps, *Organizational Communication* (New York: Longman, 1986), p. 196.
16. Ibid., p. 197.
17. Ibid., p. 198.
18. Ibid., pp. 202–206.
19. For an excellent discussion of informal power in a prison, see Richard McCleery, "Communication Patterns as Bases of Systems of Authority and Power," *Theoretical Studies in Social Organization of the Prison* (Social Science Research Council, 1960).
20. K. Davis, "The Organization That's Not on the Chart," in *Readings in Interpersonal and Organizational Communication*, R. C. Huseman, C. M. Logue, and D. C. Freshley, eds., 2d ed. (Boston: Holbrook, 1973).
21. Kreps, *Organizational Communications*, p. 204.
22. Douglas McGregor, *The Human Side of Enterprise* (New York: McGraw-Hill, 1960).
23. Reece and Brandt, *Effective Human Relations*, p. 146.
24. John Irwin, *Prisons in Turmoil* (Boston: Little, Brown, 1980).
25. Ernest J. McCormick, *Job Analysis: Methods and Applications* (New York: AMACOM, 1979), pp. 272–305.
26. John Klofas, Stan Stojkovic, and David Kalinish, *Criminal Justice Organizations: Administration and Management* (Pacific Grove, Calif.: Brooks/Cole, 1990), pp. 114–18.
27. C. D. Doering, *A Report on the Development of Penological Treatment at Norfolk Prison Colony in Massachusetts* (New York: Bureau of Social Hygiene, 1940) in ibid., pp. 114–15.
28. Linda Zupan, *Jails: Reform and the New Generation Philosophy* (Cincinnati: Anderson, 1991). See also Linda Zupan and Ben A. Menke, "The New Generation Jail: An Overview," in Joel A. Thompson and G. Larry Mays, eds., *American Jails: Public Policy Issues* (Chicago: Nelson-Hall, 1991), pp. 180–94.
29. McCormick, *Job Analysis*, p. 227.
30. Phillip C. Grant, "Why Employee Motivation Has Declined in America," *Personnel Journal* (December 1982), pp. 905–909.
31. George S. Odiorne, "Human Resource Strategies for the 80's," *Training* (January 1985), pp. 47–51.
32. Douglas L. Fleuter, "Flextime—A Social Phenomenon," *Personnel Journal* (June 1975), pp. 318–19.
33. Zane K. Quible, "Quality Circles: A Well-Rounded Approach to Employee Involvement," *Management World* (September 1981), pp. 10–11, 38.
34. Murray R. Barrich and Ralph A. Alexander, "A Review of Quality Circle Efficacy and the Existence of Positive-Findings Bias," *Personnel Psychology*, 40 No. 3 (Autumn 1987), pp. 579–91.
35. Thomas Li-Ping Nang, Peggy Smith Tollison, and Harold D. Whiteside, "The Effect of Quality Circle Initiation on Motivation to Attend Quality Circle Meetings and on Task Performance," *Personnel Psychology*, 40 No. 4 (Winter 1987), pp. 799–814.
36. Quible, "Quality Circles," p. 38.

Chapter 10

1. Condensed from Michael K. Burns, *Baltimore Sun*, April 19, 1991.
2. Elton Mayo, "Hawthorne and the Western Electric Company," in D. S. Pugh, ed., *Organizational Theory*, 2d ed. (New York: Penguin, 1984), pp. 279–92.
3. Eric Sundstrom, *Work Places: The Psychology of the Physical Environment in Offices and Factories* (Cambridge: Cambridge University Press, 1986), p. 316.
4. Seth Allcorn, "Understanding Groups at Work," *Personnel*, Vol. 66 (August 1989), pp. 28–36.
5. Floyd H. Allport, "The J-Curve Hypothesis of Conforming Behavior," *Journal of Social Psychology*, Vol. 5 (1934), pp. 141–83.
6. Rensis Likert, *The Human Organization: Its Management and Value* (New York: Harper & Row, 1967).
7. George F. Wieland and Robert A. Ullrich, *Organizations: Behavior, Design and Change* (Homewood, Ill.: Richard D. Irwin, 1976), p. 60.
8. Ibid., p. 61.
9. William G. Ouchi, *Theory Z* (Reading, Mass.: Addison-Wesley Publishing Company, 1981).
10. Ibid., p. 17.
11. Ibid., p. 26.
12. Tom Peters, *Thriving on Chaos: Handbook for a Management Revolution* (New York: Harper & Row, 1987), pp. 343–65.

13. Ibid., pp. 346–48.
14. John J. DiIulio, Jr., *Governing Prisons* (New York: The Free Press, 1987), pp. 123–24.
15. Ibid., p. 124.
16. Ibid., p. 137.
17. J. Forbes Farmer, "A Study in Regaining Control of a Violent State Prison," in Stan Stojkovic, John Klofas, and David Kalinish, *The Administration and Management of Criminal Justice Organizations: A Book of Readings* (Prospect Heights, Ill.: Waveland, 1990), pp. 476–86.
18. Ibid., p. 486.
19. Marvin E. Shaw, *Group Dynamics: The Psychology of Small Group Behavior*, 3d ed. (New York: McGraw-Hill, 1981), p. 8.
20. James L. Gibson, John M. Ivancevich, and James H. Donnelly, Jr., *Organizations: Behavior, Structure, Processes*, 3d ed. (Dallas: Business Publications, 1979), pp. 136–37.
21. Shaw, *Group Dynamics.*
22. Gibson, Ivancevich, and Donnelly, *Organizations*, p. 138.
23. "Committees: Their Role in Management Today," *Management Review*, 46 (October 1957), pp. 4–10.
24. Allcorn, "Understanding Groups."
25. Gibson, Ivancevich, and Donnelly, *Organizations*, pp. 139–41.
26. Abraham H. Maslow, *Motivation and Personality* (New York: Harper & Row, 1954).
27. Kelsey Kauffman, *Prison Officers and Their World* (Cambridge: Harvard University Press, 1988), pp. 234–39.
28. Samuel C. Certo, *Principles of Modern Management: Functions and Systems*, 3d ed. (Dubuque: Wm. C. Brown, 1985).
29. J. L. Moreno, *Who Shall Survive?* (New York: Beacon House, 1953).
30. Robert F. Bales and Stephen P. Cohen, *SYMLOG: A System for the Multiple Level Observation of Groups* (New York: The Free Press, 1979).
31. Ibid., p. 3.
32. Ibid., p. 4.
33. John Irwin, *Prisons in Turmoil* (Boston: Little, Brown, 1980), pp. 182–206.
34. Leo Carroll, *Hacks, Blacks and Cons* (Lexington, Mass.: Lexington Books, 1974).
35. Irwin, *Prisons in Turmoil.* pp.192–206.
36. Lucien X. Lombardo, *Guards Imprisoned* (New York: Elsevier North Holland, 1981).
37. DiIulio, *Governing Prisons*, pp. 159–64.
38. Ibid., p. 255.

Chapter 11

1. Condensed from Patty Shillington, *Miami Herald*, February 11, 1991.
2. John J. DiIulio, Jr., *No Escape: The Future of American Corrections* (Scranton, Pa.: HarperCollins, 1991), pp. 39–59.
3. Hans Toch, a review of John J. DiIulio, Jr., *No Escape: The Future of American Corrections, Society*, 26 (Mar-Apr 1989), pp. 86–88.
4. Ben M. Crouch and James W. Marquart, *An Appeal to Justice: Litigated Reform of Texas Prisons* (Austin: University of Texas Press, 1989).
5. James Jacobs, *Stateville: The Penitentiary in Mass Society* (Chicago: University of Chicago Press, 1977).
6. Bernard Bass, *Stogdill's Handbook of Leadership* (New York: The Free Press, 1981).
7. John P. Kotter, *The Leadership Factor* (New York: The Free Press, 1988), p. 16.
8. Harold Koontz, Cyril O'Donnell, and Heinz Weihrich, *Essentials of Management*, 4th ed. (New York: McGraw-Hill, 1986), p. 397.
9. James MacGregor Burns, *Leadership* (New York: Harper Torchbooks, 1978).
10. Ibid., p. 4.
11. Ibid., p. 4.
12. Ralph M. Stogdill, "Personal Factors Associated with Leadership: A Survey of the Literature," *Journal of Psychology*, Vol. 25 (January 1948), pp. 35–64.
13. Samuel C. Certo, *Principles of Modern Management: Functions and Systems*, 3d ed. (Dubuque: Wm. C. Brown, 1985), p. 319.
14. Fred A. Fiedler, *A Theory of Leadership Effectiveness* (New York: McGraw-Hill, 1967).
15. Robert J. House, "A Path-Goal Theory of Leader Effectiveness," *Administrative Science Quarterly*, 16:3 (September 1971), pp. 321–38 in W. Clay Hamner and Dennis W. Organ, *Organizational Behavior: An Applied Psychological Approach* (Dallas: Business Publications, 1978), p. 391.
16. Ibid., p. 391.
17. Harold Koontz, Cyril O'Donnell, and Heinz Weihrich, *Essentials of Management*, 4th ed. (New York: McGraw-Hill, 1986), p. 413.
18. Ibid., p. 414.
19. Roger M. Stogdill and Alvin E. Coons, eds., "Leader Behavior: Its Description and Measurement," Research Monograph No. 88 (Columbus: Ohio State University Bureau of Business Research, 1957).

20. Paul Hersey and Kenneth H. Blanchard, *Management of Organization Behavior* (Englewood Cliffs, N.J.: Prentice-Hall, 1977).

21. Chris Argyris, *Integrating the Individual and the Organization* (New York: John Wiley and Sons, 1964).

22. Robert R. Blake and Jane S. Mouton, *The New Managerial Grid* (Houston: Gulf, 1978).

23. Ibid., p. 9.

24. Ibid., p. 119.

25. Robert Tannenbaum and Warren H. Schmidt, "How to Choose a Leadership Pattern," *Harvard Business Review* (March/April 1957), pp. 95–101.

26. Harold Koontz, Cyril O'Donnell, and Heinz Weihrich, *Essentials of Management*, 4th ed. (New York: McGraw-Hill, 1986), p. 13.

27. Herbert G. Hicks and C. Ray Gullett, *The Management of Organizations*, 3d ed. (New York: McGraw-Hill, 1976), p. 188.

28. Warren H. Bennis, *Why Leaders Can't Lead: The Unconscious Conspiracy Continues* (San Francisco: Jossey-Bass, 1989).

29. James Jacobs, *Stateville: The Penitentiary in Mass Society* (Chicago: University of Chicago Press, 1977).

30. Chris Lee, "Followership: The Essence of Leadership," *Training Magazine* (January 1991).

31. James M. Kouzes and Barry Z. Posner, "Eye of the Follower," *Administrative Radiology* (April 1986), pp. 55–56, 58, 63–64.
_____ *The Leadership Challenge: How to Get Extraordinary Things Done in Organizations* (San Francisco: Jossey-Bass, 1987).
_____ *Leadership Practices Inventory* (San Diego: University Associates, 1988).
An excellent summary of the above appears in James M. Kouzes and Barry Z. Posner, "Leadership Is in the Eye of the Follower," *The 1989 Annual: Developing Human Resources* (San Diego: University Associates, 1989), pp. 233–39.

32. Ibid.

33. Bennis, *Why Leaders Can't Lead*, pp. 114–15.

Chapter 12

1. Babe Crockett, Chief, Office of Strategic Planning, U.S. Bureau of Prisons.

2. Samuel Certo, *Principles of Management*, 3d ed. (Dubuque: Wm. C. Brown, 1985), p. 79.

3. James H. Donnelly, Jr., James L. Gibson, and John M. Ivancevich, *Fundamentals of Management* (Dallas: Business Publications, 1971), p. 57.

4. James Jacobs, *Stateville: The Penitentiary in Mass Society* (Chicago: University of Chicago Press, 1977).

5. Burt Nanus, "A General Model for a Criminal Justice Planning Process," *Journal of Criminal Justice*, Vol. 2:4 (Winter 1974), pp. 345–56.

6. James G. Houston, "Crisis Management for Corrections," paper presented to the Midwest Criminal Justice Association (Chicago, October 1990).

7. James G. Houston, previously unpublished research undertaken for inclusion in chapter 12. Much appreciation to Dennis Anderson, Southern Illinois University, Center for the Study of Crime, Delinquency and Corrections for his support and encouragement.

8. Stephen P. Robbins, *Organization Theory: Structure, Design, and Application*, 2d ed. (Englewood Cliffs, N.J.: Prentice-Hall, 1987), pp. 31–32.

9. Charles K. Warriner, "The Problem of Organizational Purpose," *Sociological Quarterly* 6 (Spring 1965), p. 140.

10. Certo, *Principles of Management*, p. 60.

11. Fremont Kast and James E. Rosenzweig, *Organization and Management: A System and Contingency Approach*, 3d ed. (New York: McGraw-Hill, 1979), p. 168.

12. Paul J. Stonich, "Formal Planning Pitfalls and How to Avoid Them," *Management Review* 64 (Part 1: June 1975), pp. 4–11 (Part 2: July 1975), pp. 29–35.

13. Some of these objectives are adapted from Certo, *Principles of Management*, pp. 81–82.

14. Don C. Gibbons, Joseph L. Thimm, Florence Yospe, and Gerald F. Blake, Jr., *Criminal Justice Planning* (Englewood Cliffs, N.J.: Prentice-Hall, 1977).

15. Nanus, "A General Model," p. 346.

16. Ibid., p. 352.

17. Certo, *Principles of Management*, p. 134.

18. Fred R. David, *Fundamentals of Strategic Management* (Columbus: Merrill, 1986), p. 4.

19. Gibbons, Thimm, Yospe, and Blake, *Criminal Justice Planning*, pp. 85–88.

20. Certo, *Principles of Management*, pp. 126–27.

21. Lee G. Boleman and Terrence E. Deal, *Modern Approaches to Understanding and Managing Organizations* (San Francisco: Jossey-Bass, 1984), pp. 31–32.

22. Harold Koontz and Cyril O'Donnell, *Principles of Organization and Management*, 3d ed. (New York: McGraw-Hill, 1984), p. 216.

23. Book of Exodus, 18:22.
24. Henry H. Albers, *Principles of Organization and Management*, 2d ed. (New York: John Wiley and Sons, 1965), pp. 85–87.
25. See James C. Worthy, "Organizational Structure and Employee Morale," *American Sociological Review* (April 1950), pp. 169–79.
W. W. Suojanen, "The Span of Control: Fact or Fable," *Advanced Management* 20 (November 1955), pp. 5–13.
26. James H. Healey, "Coordination and Control of Executive Functions," *Personnel* 33 (September 1956), pp. 106–117.
27. L. F. Urwick, *Scientific Principles and Organization*, Institute of Management Series, No. 19 (New York: American Management Association, 1938), p. 8.
28. American Correctional Association, *Standards for Adult Correctional Institutions*, 2d ed. (Washington, D.C.: American Correctional Association, 1981), p. 3.

Chapter 13

1. Robert L. Bingham, Chief of Court Services, 19th Judicial Circuit, Lake County, Illinois.
2. Harold Koontz, Cyril O'Donnell, and Heinz Weihrich, *Essentials of Management*, 4th ed. (New York: McGraw-Hill, 1986), p. 447.
3. Peter F. Drucker, *Management: Tasks, Responsibilities, Practices* (New York: Harper & Row, 1974), p. 494.
4. Max Weber, *The Theory of Social and Economic Organization*, Talcott Parsons, trans. (New York: The Free Press, 1964).
5. Amatai Etzioni, *A Comparative Analysis of Complex Organizations* (New York: The Free Press, 1975), pp. 3–100.
6. Ibid., p. 3.
7. Ibid., p. 31.
8. Ibid., p. 40.
9. Koontz, O'Donnell, Weihrich, *Essentials of Management*, p. 448.
10. Ibid., pp. 450–542.
11. Samuel Certo, *Principles of Modern Management: Functions and Systems*, 3d ed. (Dubuque: Wm. C. Brown, 1985), p. 406.
12. Fremont E. Kast and James E. Rosenzweig, *Organization and Management: A Systems and Contingency Approach*, 3d ed. (New York: McGraw-Hill, 1979), p. 456.
13. Certo, *Principles of Modern Management*, pp. 408–409.

14. Paul Tappan, *Crime, Justice, and Correction* (New York: McGraw-Hill, 1960), pp. 632–36.
15. Richard Wener and N. Clark, "Innovative Correctional Environments," *Environment and Behavior*, 12:4 (December 1980), pp. 478–93.
16. Linda L. Zupan, *Jails: Reform and the New Generation Philosophy* (Cincinnati: Anderson, 1991).
17. James G. Houston, Don C. Gibbons, and Joseph F. Jones, "Physical Environment and Jail Social Climate," *Crime and Delinquency*, Vol. 34:4 (Oct. 1988), pp. 449–66.
18. W. Ray Nelson, Michael O'Tool, Barbara Krauth, and Coralie G. Whitmer, *New Generation Jails: Corrections Information Series* (Boulder: National Institute of Corrections, 1983), pp. 7–18.
19. Kelsey Kauffman, *Prison Officers and Their World* (Cambridge: Harvard University Press, 1988).
20. Richard McCleery, "Communication Patterns as Bases of Power," in *Theoretical Studies in Social Organization of the Prison* by Richard A. Cloward, Donald R. Cressey, George H. Grosser, Richard McCleery, Lloyd E. Ohlin, Gresham M. Sykes, and Sheldon L. Messinger (New York: Social Science Research Council, 1960).
21. Ibid.
22. Certo, *Principles of Management*, p. 462.
23. Robert W. Holms, "Twelve Areas to Investigate for a Better MIS," *Financial Executive* (July 1970), pp. 24–31.
24. Charles E. Wheeler, *The Fourth Resource: Information and Management in Probation* (Washington, D.C.: Center for the Advancement of Human Service Practice, 1983).
25. Ibid.

Chapter 14

1. Condensed from Jeffrey Montgomery, *Wilmington Evening Journal*, January 11, 1989.
2. John Klofas, Stan Stojkovic, and David Kalinich, *Criminal Justice Organizations: Administration and Management* (Pacific Grove, Calif.: Brooks/Cole, 1990), p. 247.
3. Samuel Certo, *Principles of Management: Functions and Systems*, 3d ed. (Dubuque: Wm. C. Brown, 1985), p. 101.
4. Peter Drucker, *Management: Tasks, Responsibilities, Practices* (New York: Harper & Row, 1973), p. 470.
5. *New York Times* (Monday, March 21, 1988), p. 11.

6. Conversations with Rose Jones, executive assistant to the commissioner of corrections, indicate that Connecticut is doing all it can, considering budget limitations. Problems continue, but construction of new dormatories and the implementation of several programs have helped somewhat.

7. William C. Johnson, *Public Administration: Policy, Politics, and Practice* (Guilford, Conn.: The Dushkin Publishing Group, 1992), pp. 319–23.

8. Herbert A. Simon, *Administrative Behavior*, 3d ed. (New York: The Free Press, 1976).

9. Johnson, *Public Administration*, p. 320.

10. Charles E. Lindblom, "The Science of Muddling Through," *Public Administration Review*, 19 (1959), pp. 79–88.

11. Graham T. Allison, "Essence of Decision: Explaining the Cuban Missile Crisis" (Boston: Little, Brown, 1971), p. 6, in Johnson, *Public Administration*, p. 323.

12. Michael D. Cohen, James G. March, and Johan P. Olson, "A Garbage Can Model of Organization," *Administrative Science Quarterly*, 17 (March 1972), pp. 1–25, in Johnson, *Public Administration*, p. 323.

13. Ibid.

14. William K. Apao, *Improving Prison Classification Procedures: Application of an Interaction Model*, National Institute of Corrections Grant 84-IJ-CX-4027.

15. Ibid.

16. William R. Smith, Edward E. Rhine, and Ronald W. Jackson, "Parole Practices in the United States," *Corrections Today* (October 1989), pp. 22, 24, 26, 28.

17. Clemens Bartollas and John P. Conrad, *Introduction to Corrections*, 2d ed. (New York: HarperCollins, pp. 152–54.

18. Theo Haimann, William G. Scott, and Patrick E. Connor, *Managing the Modern Organization*, 3d ed. (Boston: Houghton Mifflin, 1978), p. 513.

19. Ibid., p. 514.

20. David Halberstam, *The Reckoning* (New York: William Morrow, 1986), pp. 286–300.

21. Harold Koontz, Cyril O'Donnell, and Heinz Weirich, *Essentials of Management* (New York: McGraw-Hill, 1986), pp. 136–40.

22. Drucker, *Management*, p. 472.

23. Ibid., p. 473.

24. Joel A. Barker, *Discovering the Future: The Business of Paradigms* (St. Paul: ILI Press, 1989).

25. Herbert A. Simon, *Administrative Behavior*, 3d ed. (New York: The Free Press, 1976), pp. 123–53.

26. J. Gershuny, "The Choice of Scenarios," in *Reaching Decisions in Public Policy and Administration*, Richard D. Bingham and Marcus E. Ethridge, eds. (New York: Longman, 1982), pp. 77–89.

27. Larry Hirschhorn, "Scenario Writing: A Developmental Approach," in Bingham and Ethridge, *Reaching Decisions*, ibid., pp. 89–106.

28. Bingham and Ethridge, ibid., p. 75.

29. John Michalasky, "ESP in Decision Making," *Management Review* (April 1975), pp. 32–37.

30. Fremont E. Kast and James E. Rosenzweig, *Organization and Management: A Systems and Contingency Approach*, 3d ed. (New York: McGraw-Hill, 1979), pp. 374–75.

31. James T. McClane and P. George Benson, *Statistics for Business and Economics*, 3d ed. (San Francisco: Dellen, 1985), p. 116.

32. Albert J. Simone, *Probability: An Introduction with Applications* (Boston: Allyn and Bacon, 1967), pp. 1–38.

33. George P. Huber, *Managerial Decision Making* (Glenview, Ill.: Scott, Foresman, 1980), p. 118.

34. Ibid., pp. 121–32.

Chapter 15

1. Condensed from David J. Remondini, *Indianapolis Star*, January 12, 1992.

2. Leonard D. White, "The Meaning of Principles in Public Administration," in *The Frontiers of Public Administration*, by John M. Gaus, Leonard B. White, and Marshall E. Demock, eds. (Chicago: University of Chicago Press, 1936), pp. 13–25.

3. Hans Toch, "Functional Unit Management: An Unsung Achievement," *Federal Prisons Journal*, 2:4 (Winter 1992), pp. 15–19.

4. Roy E. Gerard, "The Ten Commandments of Unit Management," *Corrections Today* (April 1991), pp. 32, 34, 36.

5. James H. Webster, "Designing Facilities for Effective Unit Mangement," *Corrections Today* (April 1991), pp. 38, 40, 42.

6. Timothy A. Pierson, "One State's Success with Unit Management," *Corrections Today* (April 1991), pp. 24, 26, 28, 30.

7. U.S. Bureau of Prisons, *Unit Management Manual* (Washington, D.C.: U.S.B.O.P., 1977), p. 6.

8. As far-reaching and revolutionary as the concept of Unit Management is, the author had no idea

how many states and institutions have implemented the concept. A call to the National Institute of Corrections revealed that no one else does either. I am grateful to Patricia Scholes for her work in putting together from available information most of the information that appears in figure 15.1. However, considering the popularity of Unit Management, this information should be viewed with skepticism because some jurisdictions may be using something that they call Unit Management but that does not conform to Gerard, et al.'s, definition.

9. Paul W. Keve, *Prisons and the American Conscience: A History of U.S. Federal Corrections* (Carbondale, Ill.: Southern Illinois University Press, 1991), p. 160.

10. Frank Loveland, "Classification in the Prison System," in Paul Tappan, *Crime, Justice, and Correction* (New York: McGraw-Hill, 1960), pp. 622–23.

11. Daniel Glaser, *The Effectiveness of a Prison and Parole System*, (Indianapolis: Bobbs-Merrill, 1964).

12. U.S. Bureau of Prisons, *Unit Management Manual*.

13. U.S. Bureau of Prisons, *Preliminary Evaluation of the Functional Unit Approach to Correctional Management*, unpublished report by the U.S. Bureau of Prisons (September 1975).

14. Rensis Likert, *The Human Organization: Its Management and Value* (New York: Harper & Row, 1967).

15. Jerome Skolnick, *Justice Without Trial: Law Enforcement in Democratic Society* (New York: John Wiley and Sons, 1966). Skolnick discusses the elements of authority and danger relative to the role of the police officer, but his notions of solidarity among police officers also has merit in a discussion of staff solidarity vis-à-vis inmates. The potential danger and the inherent authority of staff members create a press to look to each other for mutual support. See also Kelsey Kauffman, *Prison Officers and Their World* (Cambridge: Harvard University Press, 1988) and Lucien X. Lombardo, *Guards Imprisoned* (New York: Elsevier, 1981).

16. Ray Rowe, Euphesenia Foster, Karen Byerly, Norman Laird, and Jerry Prather, *The Impact of Functional Unit Management on Indicies of Inmate Incidents*, an unpublished research report by the U.S. Bureau of Prisons (1977).

17. U.S. Bureau of Prisons, *Position Paper on Functional Units*, an unpublished paper (no date).

18. Ron Robson, "Managing the Long Term Prisoner: A Report on an Australian Innovation in Unit Management," *The Howard Journal*, Vol. 28:3 (August 1989).

19. Timothy A. Pierson, "One State's Success with Unit Management," *Corrections Today* (April 1991), pp. 24, 26, 28, 30.

20. Robert B. Levinson and Roy E. Gerard, "Functional Units: A Different Correctional Approach," *Federal Probation*, Vol. 37:4 (1975), pp. 8–15.

21. Executive Summary, *A Report Prepared Pursuant to Amended Substitute House Bill 298* (Columbus: Ohio Department of Corrections, December 1991).

22. Roy E. Gerard, "The Ten Commandments of Unit Management," *Corrections Today* (April 1991), pp. 32, 34, 36.

23. U.S. Bureau of Prisons, *Unit Management Manual*, sec. 8072.

24. "The Push for Quality," *Business Week* (June 8, 1987), pp. 130–44.

25. Dorsey J. Talley, *Total Quality Management, Performance and Cost Measures: The Strategy for Economic Survival* (Milwaukee: ASQC Quality Press, 1991), p. 33.

26. Andrea Gabor, *The Man Who Discovered Quality* (New York: Random House, 1990), p. 35.

27. Ibid., pp. 17–30.

28. Mary R. Hamilton, Allan I. Mendelorvitz, and Richard L. Fogel, "TQM at GAO," *The GAO Journal* (Winter 1991/1992), pp. 39–47.

29. Steve Wall, seminar presented to the Iowa Corrections Association, Spring Conference (Davenport, May, 1992).

30. Ibid.

Chapter 16

1. Condensed from Paul Carrier, *Maine Sunday Telegram*, November 10, 1991.

2. Christopher Hibbert, *The Roots of Evil* (Boston: Little, Brown, 1963).

3. George G. Killinger and Paul F. Cromwell, Jr., *Penology: The Evolution of Corrections in America* (St. Paul: West, 1973).

4. Larry E. Sullivan, *The Prison Reform Movement: Forlorn Hope* (Boston: Twayne, 1990), p. 13.

5. Norman R. Cox, Jr., and William E. Osterhoff, "Managing the Crisis in Local Corrections: A Public-Private Partnership Approach," in Joel A. Thompson and G. Larry Mays, *American Jails: Public Policy Issues* (Chicago: Nelson-Hall, 1991).

6. Sullivan, *The Prison Reform Movement*, p. 39.
7. Robert L. Bish and Vincent Ostrom, *Understanding Urban Government: Metropolitan Reform Reconsidered* (Washington, D.C.: American Enterprise Institute for Public Policy Research, 1979).
8. Canon and Company, founded by the author, closed all facilities in 1980 after funding cutbacks by the Bureau of Prisons. By then others in a stronger position were able to pick up any slack created by the closing.
9. Charles W. Thomas and Charles H. Logan, "The Development, Present Status, and Future Potential of Correctional Privatization in America," in Paul Seidenstat, ed., *Privatizing Correctional Institutions* (New Brunswick, N.J.: Transaction Books, 1992).
10. Ibid.
11. Ibid.
12. Ibid.
13. Bureau of Justice Statistics, *Prisoners in 1990*, BJS Bulletin NCJ 129198 (Washington, D.C.: Office of Justice Programs, U.S. Department of Justice, May 1991).
14. Charles W. Thomas and Suzanna L. Foard, *Private Correctional Facility Census*, Private Corrections Project, Center for Studies in Criminology and Law, University of Florida, Gainesville (November 1991).
15. Bobbie Huskey and Arthur J. Lurigio, "An Examination of Privately Operated Intermediate Sanctions Within the U.S.," *Corrections Compendium*, 17:12 (December 1992), pp. 1–8.
16. Judith Hackett, Harry P. Hatry, Robert B. Levinson, Joan Allen, Keon Chi, and Edward D. Feigenbaum, *Issues in Contracting for the Private Operation of Prisons and Jails* (Washington, D.C.: National Institute of Justice, 1987), p. 11, Grant Number 85-IJ-CX-0068.
17. Thomas and Logan, "Correctional Privatization in America."
18. Linda Hanson, "The Privatization of Corrections Movement: A Decade of Change," *Journal of Contemporary Criminal Justice*, 7 (1) (1991), pp. 1–28.
19. Charles W. Thomas, "Prisoners' Rights and Correctional Privatization: A Legal and Ethical Analysis," *Business and Professional Ethics Journal*, 10:1 (1991), pp. 3–42.
20. Judith Hackett, Harry P. Hatry, Robert B. Levinson, Joan Allen, Keon Chi, and Edward D. Feigenbaum, "Contracting for the Operation of Prisons and Jails," *Research in Brief* (Washington, D.C.: National Institute of Justice, June 1987).
21. Hackett, et al., *Private Operation of Prisons and Jails*, p. 13.
22. Connie Mayer, "Legal Issues Surrounding Private Operation of Prisons," *Criminal Law Bulletin*, pp. 309–25.
23. *Tennessee v. Garner*, 105 S. Ct. 1694, 85L. Ed. 2d. 1 (1985), in Mayer, ibid.
24. Ibid., p. 318.
25. Ibid.
26. Joan Mullen, Kent John Chabotar, and Deborah M. Carrow, *The Privatization of Corrections* (Washington, D.C.: National Institute of Justice, February 1985), pp. 20–29.
27. Ibid.
28. Hackett, et al., *Private Operation of Prisons and Jails*, p. 14.
29. Ibid., p. 35.
30. Thomas and Logan, "Correctional Privatization in America."
31. Hackett, et al., *Private Operation of Prisons and Jails*, pp. 47–50.
32. Thomas and Logan, "Correctional Privatization in America."
33. Ibid.
34. Ibid.
35. Charles H. Logan, "Well Kept: Comparing Quality of Confinement in a Public and Private Prison" (1991), in Thomas and Logan, ibid.
36. Ibid.
37. Corrections Corporation of America, 1991 Annual Report, Doctor R. Crants, President and Chief Executive Officer.
38. Ibid., p. 34.
39. Prospectus, 2,000,000 Shares CCA Common Stock, Donaldson, Lufkin, and Jenrette Securities Corporation (October 1, 1986).
40. Corrections Corporation of America, 1991 Annual Report.
41. Norman R. Cox, Jr., and William E. Osterhoff, "Managing the Crisis in Local Corrections: A Public-Private Partnership Approach," in Thompson and Mays, *American Jails*.
42. Ibid., p. 236.
43. J. Mullen, *Corrections and the Private Sector*, National Institute of Justice Research in Brief (Washington, D.C.: Department of Justice, in Cox and Osterhoff "Managing the Crisis in Local Corrections" in Thompson and Mays, *American Jails*.

Chapter 17

1. Condensed from Pat Plarski and Scott Montgomery, *Palm Beach Post*, (Florida) August 25, 1990.

2. The foundation for this chapter is a paper presented by James G. Houston and Andrew M. Swift entitled "A Model for a Framework for a Professional Code of Criminal Justice Ethics," Academy of Criminal Justice Sciences, Pittsburgh, March 14, 1992. The author is indebted to Dr. Swift for his willingness to co-author this chapter.

3. Jeffery A. Schwartz, "Fortress Corrections," *Corrections Today* (August 1989), pp. 216, 221–22.

4. National Crime Prevention Institute, *Understanding Crime Prevention*, (Boston: Butterworths, 1986).

5. Boston Prison Discipline Society (1826–1854), Reprint of First 29th Annual Report (Montclaire, N.J.: Patterson-Smith, 1972).

6. Sheila Balkan, Ronald J. Burger, and Janet Schmidt, *Crime and Deviance in America* (Belmont, Calif.: Wadsworth, 1980).

7. Richard Hawkins and Geoffrey P. Alpert, *American Prison Systems: Punishment and Justice* (Englewood Cliffs, N.J.: Prentice-Hall, 1989), chapter 10.

8. Bernard J. McCarthy, "Keeping an Eye on the Keeper: Prison Corruption and Its Control," in Michael C. Braswell, Belinda R. McCarthy, and Bernard J. McCarthy, eds., *Justice, Crime and Ethics* (Cincinnati: Anderson, 1991), pp. 239–52.

9. Schwartz, "Fortress Corrections." p. 221.

10. Lawrence Sherman, "Learning Police Ethics," in Braswell, et al., eds., *Justice, Crime, and Ethics*, pp. 97–114.

11. See Lucien X. Lombardo, *Guards Imprisoned* for an interesting discussion on how a new officer at Auburn learned his job.

12. "Police Ethics," *The Police Chief* (January 1991), pp. 27–41.

13. Ibid.

14. Ibid.

15. Ibid.

16. Michael Davis, "Do Cops Really Need a Code of Ethics?" *Criminal Justice Ethics*, 10:2 (Summer/Fall 1991), pp. 14–28.

17. Ibid.

18. John Stuart Mill, "Utilitarianism," in *Utilitarianism and Other Writings* (New York: Median Books, 1971), p. 269.

19. Ibid., p. 275.

20. Bernard Rosen, *Ethics Companion* (Englewood Cliffs, N.J.: Prentice-Hall, 1990).

21. Isiah Berlin, Four Essays on Liberty (Oxford: Oxford University Press, 1969).

22. Immanuel Kant, *Groundwork for the Metaphysic of Morals*, A. J. Paton, trans. (New York: Harper & Row, 1964).

23. Mill, "Utilitarianism," p. 270.

24. Ibid., p. 257.

25. Ibid., p. 263.

26. Peter Applebome, "Jailers Charged with Sex Abuse of 119 Women," *The New York Times* (November 14, 1992).

27. Andrew M. Swift, James G. Houston, and Robin A. Anderson, *Cops, Hacks, and the Greater Good*. Paper presented to the Academy of Criminal Justice Sciences, Kansas City, March 18, 1993.

28. Keith Davis and Robert L. Blomstrom, *Business and Society: Environment and Responsibility*, 3d ed. (New York: McGraw-Hill, 1975), p. 6.

29. Ibid.

30. Keith Davis, "Five Propositions for Social Responsibility," *Business Horizons*, (June 1975), pp. 19–24.

31. Samuel C. Certo, *Principles of Modern Management: Functions and Systems*, 3d ed. (Dubuque: Wm. C. Brown, 1985), pp. 500–501.

Author Index

Subject Index

333